THE KEYBOARD SONATAS OF JOSEPH HAYDN

LÁSZLÓ SOMFAI

The Keyboard Sonatas of

Translated by the author in collaboration with CHARLOTTE GREENSPAN

Joseph Haydn

Instruments *and* Performance Practice, Genres *and* Styles

The University of Chicago Press *Chicago & London*

László Somfai is head of the Bartók Archives in Budapest and professor of musicology at the Franz Liszt Academy of Music. Charlotte Greenspan is an independent scholar.

The University of Chicago Press, Chicago 60637
The University of Chicago Press, Ltd., London

Printed in the United States of America
04 03 02 01 00 99 98 97 96 95   5 4 3 2 1

ISBN (cloth): 0-226-76814-7

Music typesetting by Sarolta Asztalos & Dénes Hárs, Budapest.

Originally published as *Joseph Haydn zongoraszonátái: Hangszerválasztás és előadói gyakorlat, műfaji tipológia és stíluselemzés,* © Somfai László 1979.

Publication of this work was made possible in part by a grant from the National Endowment for the Humanities, an independent federal agency.

Library of Congress Cataloging-in-Publication Data

Somfai, László.
[Joseph Haydn zongoraszonátái. English]
The keyboard sonatas of Joseph Haydn : instruments and performance practice, genres and styles / László Somfai ; translated by the author in collaboration with Charlotte Greenspan.
p. cm.
Translation of: Joseph Haydn zongoraszonátái.
Includes bibliographical references and indexes.
ISBN 0-226-76814-7
1. Haydn, Joseph, 1732–1809. Sonatas, piano. 2. Sonatas (Piano)—History and criticism. I. Greenspan, Charlotte Joyce, 1941– . II. Title. III. Title: Joseph Haydn zongoraszonátái.
ML410.H4S6713 1995
786.2′183′092—dc20   93-37627
CIP
MN

⊚ The paper used in this publication meets the minimum requirements of the American National Standard for Information Sciences—Permanence of Paper for Printed Library Materials, ANSI Z39.48-1984.

To the memory of Christa Landon (d. 1977)

Contents

PART II GENRES AND TYPES

PART III STRUCTURES AND STYLES

Preface

THIS BOOK WAS WRITTEN first and foremost for performers. Its original Hungarian form, published in Budapest in 1979, was motivated by my personal commitment to Haydn's music as well as by the somewhat quixotic belief that I could teach the musicians of a small nation to play Haydn well more easily than those who are exposed to a confusing mass of literature, scholarly and popular, old and new, written in many languages. The book was intended to be primarily a practical guide; at the same time it was meant to be a messenger of recent scholarly views, a polemical treatise regarding some questions of performance practice and ornamentation, an advocate for historical performance, and a criticism of stiff analytic methods. It was intended least of all to overwhelm the international community of Haydn scholars with newly discovered sources. I have never avoided source research. My scholarly career began as a music librarian at the National Széchényi Library in Budapest, which contains the largest collection of Haydn manuscripts in the world, and continued with complex source studies on Béla Bartók in the last three decades. My work on several aspects of Haydn's biography and music, the repertoire of Kapellmeister Haydn, Haydn iconography, the string quartet oeuvre, and related topics continuously involved source studies, and I have remained closely associated with Haydn research. In fact, for a while I had intended to write my unorthodox Haydn book about his string quartets; I was dissuaded only when I realized how small the hope was of successfully influencing the performing style of the small but exclusive guild of professional string quartet players. Furthermore, the definitive urtext of the quartets was still partly inaccessible.

In the early 1960s, thanks to my dear friend Christa Landon, I had the good fortune of watching from time to time the progress of the preparation of the *Wiener Urtext Ausgabe* of the Haydn piano sonatas. In those pioneering years—before musicological-editorial interpretations of Haydn's notational puzzles were tested by the experiments of historically informed performers—Christa Landon's fight for a musically intelligent urtext was almost unique. Although a second urtext, that of the *Joseph Haydn Werke* complete critical edition, soon became available, it was primarily the *Wiener Urtext* that inspired a tremendous interest in Haydn's sonatas for teachers and for performers in the concert hall and recording studio. As an adviser of one of the "complete" recordings in 1972–74, namely, the Hungaraton boxes, I came to understand that talented young pianists with a typical conservatory background were, for the most part, unable to penetrate the notational surface of the urtext edition to reach the characteristic features of Haydn's sonatas, which are so different from one another and individual in genre and stylistic aspirations. It became obvious to me that a book on Haydn's keyboard sonatas was needed. Clearly, such a book could have a wide influence. Haydn's sonatas are taught not only to future concert pianists but also to string and wind players, singers and conductors, and amateurs, particularly as the Haydn sonata is often considered an apt study for pianists of moderate attainments, as a preparation for Mozart and Beethoven. For many music students, the problems of performing certain ornaments, the question of repetition, the understanding of elementary musical sentences and forms, first occur when they play an easy sonata by Haydn. I believe that an unorthodox guide can be beneficial, even one in which settled rules are disputed, working hypotheses are presented, new terminology is introduced, and the dividing line between pure scholarship and practicality is frequently obscured.

In Haydn's instrumental music, the two central genres, symphony and string quartet, comprehend most of his achievements in creating a new, Classical musical idiom; these genres clearly deserve extended studies. Compared to them, the solo keyboard sonata might be considered the most variegated genre that Haydn cultivated from his youth to his London years. It is probably the best medium to study how Haydn first scrutinized and then influenced the musical taste of different layers of keyboard players among the dilettantes of his time. Moreover, the sonatas may reflect fresh stylistic influences in a more direct, less inhibited way; Haydn wrote a few true "workshop"-style experimental sonatas—an unusual phenomenon in his busy and practical life work. The challenge for today's musician, student as well as professional, is to discover the individual opus style or the individuality of a single sonata in a set, an individuality that goes beyond the well-understood, broad stylistic concepts of Viennese Classical music and Haydn's *Personalstil* in general. The hope of reaching such an intimacy with Haydn's sonata oeuvre may well justify a book dedicated to this genre.

From a musicologist's point of view, a monograph limited to Haydn's solo keyboard sonatas may be less justifiable. The early clavier divertimento and the later sonata proper coevolved, first with pieces with or without accompanying string instruments, sometimes ad libitum, and later with the "accompanied sonata"—the piano trio in Haydn's case. The changing interests of musicians, the appearance of new instruments, and new modes in *Hausmusik* all played a role in this evolution. Perhaps for the earliest keyboard divertimentos, in which the presence of Haydn's individual style and skill is weak and the authorship in some cases uncertain, a simplified study is more justifiable. The mature piano trio, however, was one of Haydn's central genres. From 1785 on, in fact, the accompanied sonata was Haydn's dominant keyboard genre. The trios are frequently referred to in this book, as are individual solo pieces, but they are not systematically treated. The twenty-nine piano trios proper belong to a relatively sophisticated and difficult chamber-music repertoire with characteristic problems of balance when played on modern instruments. Thus, they will always play a less crucial role in piano studies than the sonatas.

On the other hand, I hope that this book will be of use not only to pianists and teachers but also to violinists, singers, conductors, and chamber musicians as well. There is no single general introduction to performance problems in Haydn's works that has relevant answers for the most burning questions for the player today. In contrast to a few recent publications, I advocate a complex investigation of performance practice problems, one that is very much guided by an awareness of chronology and genre and that is constantly considering the musical notation—shorthand or elaborated, local or international, written for professionals or dilettantes—in the context of contemporary conventions.

As for the organization of the content of this book, the reader must understand that, in the case of Haydn's sonatas, the study of the intended instrument, the proper reading of the notation, and other aspects of performance must precede the investigation of style. Another irregularity of this book is that there are no detailed analytic descriptions of complete sonatas or full movements. Instead, types, genre trends, opus styles, routine procedures, and corrected versions of a pattern are the subject of study. It is my firm belief that a selection of note-by-note structural analyses is not needed in a handbook such as this. There are enough music-theory periodicals and books for publishing master analyses. Besides, I believe that such studies are most profitable in an oral presentation, the more so when the musician individually unfolds the secrets of a great work. The analytic approaches that I have used here are intended to lead the reader and performer from one piece to other related ones, from the stylistic surface of one movement to the understanding of the originalities of a single work in the context of the always self-improving but pragmatic styles of Haydn's piano sonatas.

* * *

The greater part of a book such as this is compilation; credit for the results of individual investigations and the personal interpretations of the authors is mainly hidden in footnotes. I cannot enumerate all those specialists in Haydn scholarship, musicologists or performers, who, through their studies of performance practice, critical editions, and stylistic analyses, have afforded me the benefit of their specialized knowledge. Their work will be referred to, but my friends and colleagues will recognize the profit of our exchange of views in the text anyway. Two of them in particular had already been mentioned when I wrote the Hungarian text in 1977–78: Christa Landon, who died in 1977, with whom I spent a great many hours discussing sources, interpretations, lectures, and ideas and to whom both editions are dedicated; and Malcolm Bilson, whose performances of Haydn on the fortepiano, from the time I first heard them in 1975, dramatically changed my recognition of Haydn's keyboard music. Particular thanks are due to my wife, Dorrit Révész, who not only urged me to focus on writing a new book and supported me in the process but also, as an expert editor of musicological works, helped realize the 1979 version (*Joseph Haydn zongoraszonátái,* published by Zeneműkiadó in Budapest).

The first stimulus for an English edition came from Edward Lowinsky, in March 1979, when he heard me lecturing at the University of Chicago on aspects of the still unpublished book. My dear old friend Jan LaRue of New York University and new friends at Cornell University, James Webster at the head, urged the translation of my "unintelligible" book. The preparations began in 1984. In addition to incorporating recent literature—principally the proceedings of the 1975 Haydn conference in Washington, D.C. (published in 1981 as *Haydn Studies*), critical opinions and dates in A. Peter Brown's *Joseph Haydn's Keyboard Music* (1986), and references to Sandra P. Rosenblum's *Performance Practices in Classic Piano Music* (1988), which I came to know only after the translation of this book had been completed—extensive revision, based on my own changed views, seemed to be needed only on a few questions of ornaments. The reader will recognize that my discussion of the sonata form precedes conceptually the one suggested by James Webster in his entry in *The New Grove Dictionary of Music and Musicians* (1980). His important analytical book *Haydn's "Farewell" Symphony and the Classical Style* (1991), as well as Elaine R. Sisman's *Haydn and the Classical Variation* (1993), and Katalin Komlós's *Fortepianos and Their Music* (1995), came too late to be reflected in my book. Furthermore, I did not want to comment on the rather embarrassing recent story of discovering lost Haydn sonatas (falsifications), although I had access to the copy of the supposed source. In 1985, a grant from the National Endowment for the Humanities provided funding for the translation. Erzsébet Mészáros (pt. I) and Kata Kövendi (pt. III) were my associates in setting up a rough translation, which then was turned into proper American English musicological prose by Charlotte Greenspan of Ithaca, New York. Grateful thanks are due to them for their labor, and to all of those at the University of Chicago Press who assisted me in the final editorial work. I would particularly like to thank Malcolm Bilson, who for years inspired, provoked, and helped me to the highest degree and who, amid his artistic engagements, had time to help shape the final version of the English book. Furthermore, James Webster, who read the text at several phases of the translation/transformation, was most helpful not only in chiseling the style and the presentation but also in sharing his critical views about this somewhat unorthodox book with me.

The Hungarian version of this book included a discography. It listed the complete recordings, four altogether at that time, and a selection of other recordings of Haydn's solo keyboard sonatas played on modern pianos as well as on period instruments. Since then, the list has grown considerably longer and now includes many performances on old instruments. In my opinion, the reader of this book should certainly listen to the pioneering performances of yesterday and today. Recordings of the sonatas such as those by Malcolm Bilson, in which artistic experimentation and scholarly experimentation go hand in hand, or those by Paul Badura-Skoda, which present the original sound of a Schantz fortepiano, have a great deal to offer the listener. Unfortunately, owing to rapid changes in the recording industry, many excellent performances recorded in the 1970s are no longer available, although old records are sometimes reissued on compact disc. We also find these days recordings in which enthusiasm for playing earlier instruments is not matched by zeal for learning the style of the time. Therefore, only a critically selected and annotated discography would be acceptable, and this would have its impractical aspects, not the least of which being that such a discography would quickly become outdated.

Finally, I must say a few words about the numbering of the Haydn sonatas in this book. I use the Christa Landon numbers of the *Wiener Urtext,* generally known among pianists and piano teachers—probably even more in Europe than in America—which give a far superior representation of the chronology than the Hoboken numbers. Moreover, in my opinion, the *Wiener Urtext* is still the best edition for practical purposes. A thematic locator at the very end of this book gives a concordance of the *WUE* numbers and the Hoboken numbers.

Abbreviations

BACH, *VERSUCH;* BACH, *ESSAY*

Bach, Carl Philipp Emanuel. *Versuch über die wahre Art, das Clavier zu spielen.* Pt. 1, Berlin, 1753; 3d rev. ed., Leipzig, 1787. Pt. 2, Berlin, 1762; rev. ed. Leipzig, 1797.

Essay on the True Art of Playing Keyboard Instruments. Translated by William J. Mitchell. New York: Norton, 1949.

BROWN, *KEYBOARD*

Brown, A. Peter. *Joseph Haydn's Keyboard Music: Sources and Style.* Bloomington: Indiana University Press, 1986.

DIES

Dies, Albert Christoph. *Biographische Nachrichten von Joseph Haydn.* Vienna, 1810. Translated in *Haydn: Two Contemporary Portraits* by Vernon Gotwals. Madison: University of Wisconsin Press, 1968.

EK

The *EK* (*Entwurfkatalog*) is a thematic catalog of Haydn's works from about 1765 on (with only the indication of title in some instances), mostly in Haydn's own hand. It, as well as the *HV,* was printed in Jens Peter Larsen's *Drei Haydn-Kataloge in Faksimile* (see Larsen, *3HC*).

FEDER, "PROBLEME"

Feder, Georg. "Probleme einer Neuordnung der Klaviersonaten Haydns." In *Festschrift Friedrich Blume zum 70. Geburtstag,* 92–103. Kassel: Bärenreiter, 1963.

GRIESINGER

Griesinger, Georg August. *Biographische Notizen über Joseph Haydn.* Leipzig, 1810. Translated in *Haydn: Two Contemporary Portraits* by Vernon Gotwals. Madison: University of Wisconsin Press, 1968.

HAYDN BERICHT

Badura-Skoda, Eva, ed. *Joseph Haydn: Bericht über den Internationalen Joseph Haydn Kongress, Wien 1982* = Proceedings of the International Joseph Haydn Congress. Munich: Henle, 1986.

HAYDN, *BRIEFE;* HAYDN, *CCLN*

Bartha, Dénes, ed. *Joseph Haydn: Gesammelte Briefe und Aufzeichnungen.* Kassel: Bärenreiter, 1965.

Landon, H. C. Robbins, ed. *The Collected Correspondence and London Notebooks of Joseph Haydn.* London: Barrie & Rockliff, 1959.

HAYDN STUDIES

Larsen, Jens Peter, Howard Serwer, and James Webster, eds. *Haydn Studies: Proceedings of the International Haydn Conference, Washington, D.C., 1975.* New York: Norton, 1981.

HOBOKEN, HOB.

Hoboken, Anthony van. *Joseph Haydn: Thematisch-bibliographisches Werkverzeichnis.* 3 vols. Mainz: Schott's Söhne, 1957–78.

HOLLIS, *INSTRUMENTS*

Hollis, Helen Rice. *The Musical Instruments of Joseph Haydn: An Introduction.* Washington, D.C.: Smithsonian Institution Press, 1977.

HV

The *HV* (*Haydn-Verzeichnis*) is a thematic catalog of Haydn's works completed in 1805, copied by Johann Elssler. It, as well as the *EK*, was printed in Jens Peter Larsen's *Drei Haydn-Kataloge in Faksimile* (see Larsen, *3HC*).

JHW

Joseph Haydn Werke. Cologne: Joseph Haydn Institut, 1958–.

KRITISCHE ANMERKUNGEN

Landon, Christa. *Joseph Haydn: Sämtliche Klaviersonaten: Kritische Anmerkungen.* Vienna: Wiener Urtext Edition, 1982.

LANDON, *HCW*

Landon, H. C. Robbins. *Haydn: Chronicle and Works.* 5 vols. Bloomington: Indiana University Press, 1976–80.

LARSEN, *3HC*

Larsen, Jens Peter. *Three Haydn Catalogues.* 2d facs. ed. New York: Pendragon, 1979.

LÖHLEIN, *CLAVIER-SCHULE*

Löhlein, Georg Simon. *Clavier-Schule, oder kurze und gründliche Anweisung zur Melodie und Harmonie.* Leipzig and Züllichau, 1765; 2d enlarged ed., 1773.

MOZART, *VIOLINSCHULE;* MOZART, *TREATISE*

Mozart, Leopold. *Versuch einer gründlichen Violinschule.* Augsburg, 1756; 3d enlarged ed., 1787.

A Treatise on the Fundamental Principles of Violin Playing. Translated by Editha Knocker, with a preface by Alfred Einstein. London: Oxford University Press, 1948.

NEW GROVE HAYDN, "WORK-LIST"

The New Grove Haydn. Work-List by Georg Feder. Composer Biography series. New York: Norton, 1983.

NEWMAN, *SONATA*

Newman, William S. *The Sonata in the Classic Era.* Rev. ed. Chapel Hill: University of North Carolina Press, 1972.

QUANTZ, *VERSUCH;* QUANTZ, *PLAYING*

Quantz, Johann Joachim. *Versuch einer Anweisung die Flöte traversiere zu spielen.* Breslau, 1752.

On Playing the Flute. Translated with notes by Edward R. Reilly. New York: Free Press, 1966.

ROSENBLUM, *PERFORMANCE PRACTICES*

Rosenblum, Sandra P. *Performance Practices in Classic Piano Music: Their Principles and Applications.* Bloomington: Indiana University Press, 1988.

TÜRK, *KLAVIERSCHULE;* TÜRK, *SCHOOL*

Türk, Daniel Gottlob. *Klavierschule.* Leipzig and Halle, 1789.

School of Clavier Playing. Translated with notes by Raymond H. Haggh. Lincoln: University of Nebraska Press, 1982.

WALTER, "KLAVIERE"

Walter, Horst. "Haydns Klaviere." *Haydn-Studien* 2, no. 4 (1970): 256–88.

WUA, WUE

Wiener Urtext Ausgabe: Haydn: Sämtliche Klaviersonaten. Edited by Christa Landon. Vienna: Universal Edition. Vol. 1, 1966; vols. 2–3, 1964. (4 vols. in later reprints.)

Wiener Urtext Edition: Joseph Haydn: Sämtliche Klaviersonaten. Edited by Christa Landon. Vols. 1a, 1b, 2, 3. Vienna: Wiener Urtext Edition, 1973.

See also *Kritische Anmerkungen.*

Throughout this book, Haydn's sonatas are identified by Christa Landon's numbers in the *Wiener Urtext* and by key; a thematic locator is provided for use by the reader to find the equivalent Hoboken numbers. Unless otherwise noted, the musical examples of the piano sonatas by Haydn are quoted according to the *WUE* texts, without the editorial fingering, however. Examples from the books of C. P. E. Bach, Löhlein, and Türk follow the original C-clef notation.

The sonatas will be referred to in a shortened way, e.g., "19 e" = *WUE* Sonata no. 19 in E Minor; "31 A♭ I" = the first movement of *WUE* Sonata no. 31 in A♭ Major; "58 C I, 7–8" = measures 7–8 of the first movement of *WUE* Sonata no. 58 in C Major.

In this book, the Hoboken numbers will be used for the XV: piano trios and the XVII: piano pieces. The XVI: piano sonatas are referred to by the *WUE* (ChL) numbers (see above) and the III: string quartets by opus number and key.

Pitch notation is as follows:

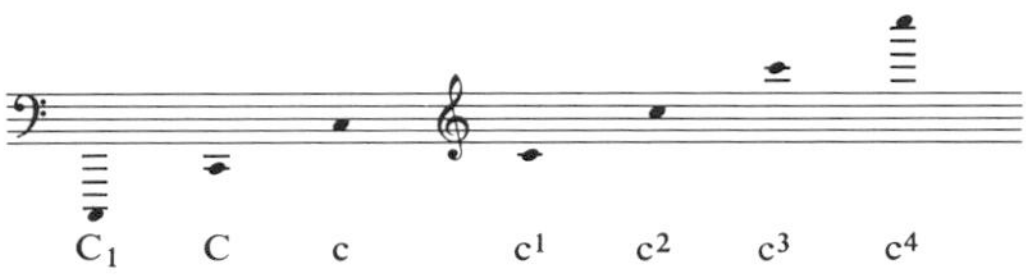

The special abbreviations for style analysis used in part III are explained in table 18, p. 228.

PART I

INSTRUMENTS, PERFORMANCE PRACTICE, *and* STYLE

One

Keyboard Instruments *in* Haydn's Time

1. *General Survey*

THE PERIOD OF APPROXIMATELY four decades (ca. 1755–96) during which Haydn composed keyboard works was the era of the coexistence of the harpsichord, the clavichord, and the fortepiano. The actual state of technical development of these instruments varied from country to country and from city to city; the choice of a given instrument in a particular time and place depended greatly on the desires of the individual composer or purchaser. Which instrument proved most suitable at a given time must have been determined by the occasion, the size of the room, and the genre and the scoring of the work in question.

Actually, none of these instruments was better or more highly developed than its companions in any absolute sense. Carl Philipp Emanuel Bach was not alone in declaring that, if expressive music was to be performed in a space the size of a small room, the clavichord was the most perfect instrument of the three.[1] It was considered the most suitable for learning purposes since it provided the greatest possibility for mastering subtlety in performance. And many composers, among them Haydn, used this discreet instrument when composing. The large, wing-shaped harpsichord had the biggest volume, however, and for a time the most even action. Its principal drawbacks were that the sound died away relatively quickly and that the instrument could not produce flexible dynamics. Although several harpsichords had already been fitted with the organ-like

1. Apart from C. P. E. Bach's *Versuch,* Türk's *Klavierschule* was also titled "clavichord tutor" as late as 1789.

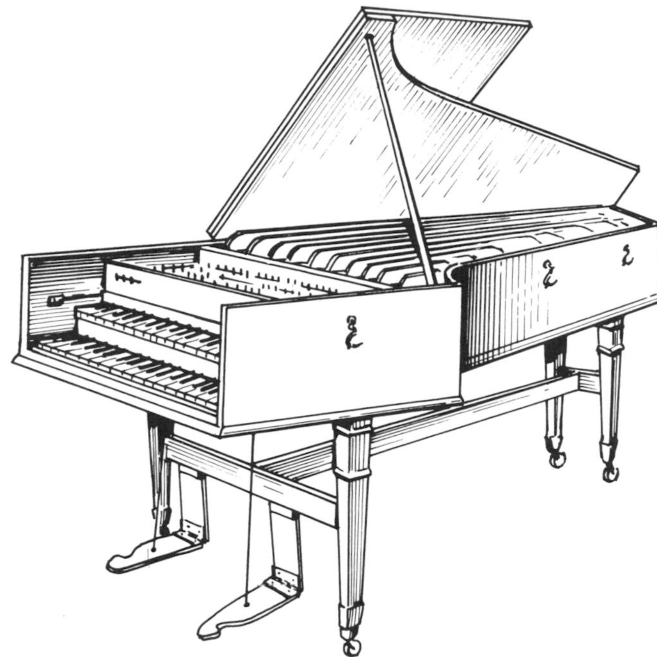

FIGURE 1 Harpsichord made by Shudi & Broadwood in London in 1775, then transported to Vienna. It has two keyboards, both with a compass of C_1–f^3. 2 × 8 feet, 1 × 4 feet, "lute," etc., with six hand stops and two pedals. The cover of the "Venetian swell" mechanism, producing crescendo and diminuendo, is open.

"Venetian swell" stops (see fig. 1), in imitation of crescendos and diminuendos,[2] they were unable, of course, to produce graduated loud and soft effects. With the exception of the *Bebung* effect available on the clavichord, the fortepiano was the most flexible in terms of shading. Nonetheless, its action proved fairly unsatisfactory for a considerable time,[3] and it produced less sound than a large harpsichord. In fact, many fortepianos were also equipped with registration stops and were quite similar in sound to a harpsichord.[4]

In this period, so amazingly abundant in experimentation, combination in-

2. The Venetian swell depicted in fig. 1 was installed regularly on larger harpsichords by Shudi & Broadwood in London as early as 1766.

3. As a solo instrument, Schubart preferred the fortepiano to the harpsichord as early as 1774 (*Deutsche Chronik* [Augsburg, 1774], 232): "The fortepiano exceeds the harpsichords by 20 percent, and since its transformation by Stein by even 100 percent." Frederick the Great, who had been very fond of the fortepiano in his youth, returned to the harpsichord in his old age, perhaps because of his acquaintance with the recent novelties of the English harpsichords. (In 1773, he had a Shudi harpsichord sent to the Empress Maria Theresa as a present.)

4. This accounts for the fact that C. P. E. Bach could write a double concerto (W 47 = H 479) in which the two instruments are set against each other in the traditional sense and also explains why

struments were manufactured—double-manual fortepiano-harpsichords, grand and vertical pianos, harpsichords transformed into fortepianos, pedal pianos,[5] and many other curiosities. The instruments emerging from various workshops differed immensely, with regard not only to perfection of the action but even to fundamental sound. A fortepiano of one instrument maker might be much more similar in sound to a harpsichord of that same maker than to a fortepiano of a maker in another city experimenting with a different action. Indeed, quite different developments were taking place with regard to square pianos (smaller instruments suited for the home and music-making middle-class families) and the more expensive wing-shaped concert instruments found in salons, large halls, and theaters; the latter were in any case more durable when properly cared for.

But, before looking for information in contemporary documents, it may be helpful to elucidate the meaning of certain terms, chiefly words in the original language with which Haydn would have been familiar and in documents from Austro-German territories in which he is mentioned.

CLAVIER, KLAVIER

This term had three different meanings. (1) It denoted "keyboard" instruments in general; the *Clavierist* was the player of keyboard instruments. (2) It referred, in a simplified and already somewhat obsolete usage, to the obvious keyboard instrument within a given context.[6] (3) As a term in current use it applied to the clavichord (in the writings of C. P. E. Bach and Türk[7] etc.); the diminutive term, *Clavierl,* was a name occasionally given to the small portable clavichord.

FLÜGEL

The *Flügel* (wing) was a wing-shaped instrument. When not modified, this German word was used unambiguously up to about 1800[8] for the long instrument

---

the inscription "for fortepiano or harpsichord" on title pages was, in general, not merely a business trick.

5. Thus, e.g., Mozart played a "free improvisation" at one of his concerts in the Burgtheater in 1785 on a combination instrument called *Grosses Forte piano Pedal.*

6. In his letter to Frau von Genzinger dated 27 June 1790, Haydn applied the words alternately—meaning fortepiano in both cases. Such usage is necessarily simplified in translation into foreign languages: "It is a pity that Your Grace doesn't own a Schanz fortepiano, . . . I know I ought to have composed this Sonata in accordance with the capabilities of your piano [*die Arth Ihres Claviers*]" (Haydn, *Briefe,* 242). In an autograph bill dated 28 April 1769 from Eisenstadt (Landon, *HCW,* 2:445), Haydn listed the price of raven quill used for repairing the *Clavier,* obviously meaning harpsichord ("4 flügl Raaben Kiel zur Zurichtung deren Claviern").

7. With the spelling *Clavicord* in Bach, *Klavichord* in Türk.

8. *Flügel* was also employed in connection with the grand fortepiano after it had displaced the harpsichord. When Haydn received a new piano from Érard of Paris in 1801 (fig. 5 below), Griesinger described it in a letter to Breitkopf & Härtel in Leipzig as "ein schöner Flügel nach englischer Art" (see Walter, "Klaviere," 279).

(today we would call it a *grand* in English) with a harpsichord action.[9] Its German dialect forms in contemporary documents are *Fligel* and *Flich* (in the instrument-repair accounts among the Esterházy documents). Frequent Italian and Italianate forms include *Clavi cembalo, Cembalo, Clavicymbal,* and *Klavicymbel* (particularly in manuscripts). On title pages of music in French, the harpsichord is called *Clavecin,* even in Vienna. Haydn editions in England naturally bear the inscription *harpsichord* (but *Fortepiano Flügel* meant grand fortepiano).[10]

TAFELKLAVIER

Tafelklavier (square piano) was a contemporary German expression used exclusively in reference to the oblong small fortepiano from the 1780s.

FORTEPIANO

In the second half of the eighteenth century, this was the name of the piano with hammer action; contemporary spellings include *Forte piano* (C. P. E. Bach, *Versuch*), *fortepiano* (Türk, *Klavierschule*), *Pianoforte* (Quantz, *Versuch*), etc. Haydn mostly used the form *Forte-piano.* On the title pages of contemporary printed editions of Haydn's sonatas and trios, the variants *Piano forte, Piano-forte,*[11] *Pianoforte,*[12] *Forte piano, Forte-piano,* and occasionally *Forté-piano*[13] will appear, with essentially equal frequency and chronological distribution between London, Paris, Berlin, and Vienna. (In recent German literature, the terms *Hammerklavier* and *Hammerflügel* are often used, whereas, in English, *fortepiano* became the common term.)

2. *Vienna*

Although Haydn spent most of his time in Eisenstadt and Eszterháza, he was well aware of the musical activities and musical life of the Austrian imperial capital. Thus, it is worth summarizing the information available regarding the instruments used in Vienna at the time and Haydn's own experiences with them.

9. The oblong-shaped small virginal and the trapezoidal spinet no longer figure in connection with Haydn's activities, certainly not as possible instrumental ideals, although there were spinets at Eszterháza (see n. 24 below).

10. In a letter of 12 March 1785, Leopold Mozart called the Walter instrument on which his son played at his Viennese concert a *Fortepiano Flügel* (Wilhelm A. Bauer and Otto Erich Deutsch, eds., *Mozart: Briefe und Aufzeichnungen* [Kassel: Bärenreiter, 1962], 3:379). The same instrument was referred to in a newspaper announcement as a *Fortepiano-Konzert.*

11. Thus, e.g., *Piano-forte* on the title pages of the editions of Haydn's works by Artaria of Vienna in 1786, 1790, 1798, etc.; *Forte piano* in 1780, 1788, etc.; *Forte-piano* in 1788 (Fantasy in C Major); etc.

12. On the title page of the 1783 first edition of Haydn's Sonatas 54–56 by the German Bossler of Speyer on the Rhine.

13. On title pages of the French publisher Sieber.

The first informant to draw on is Charles Burney, the English musicologist and composer.[14] In order to collect material for *A General History of Music* (published in four volumes between 1776 and 1789), Burney toured the musical centers of Europe, reaching Vienna in the late summer of 1772. There, he met with almost all the prominent musicians of the time, except Haydn, who was detained by his summer duties in Eszterháza. Burney portrayed the vivid musical life of Vienna in marvelously detailed and objective descriptions.[15] He came to know the celebrated masters of the time (Hasse, Gluck, Wagenseil, and, of course, the librettist Metastasio, who on more than one occasion entertained Burney in his home); he described the state of orchestras, theaters, and church music; he gave an account of street music—including the duet of *Falset soprano* and *Contralto* singers[16]—of salons, of libraries, and of the frightfully expensive workshops for copying music (music publishing was then still extremely rare in Vienna).

The information regarding keyboard instruments, drawn from Burney's chronicle of Vienna, reveals that he came across harpsichords almost exclusively. It was this instrument that Gluck[17] and Hasse used to play accompaniments. Wagenseil played solo pieces on the harpsichord and, with a young female pupil, duets on two harpsichords;[18] another of his students, a young count, performed "some very difficult harpsichord lessons."[19] Gasman (Gassmann) played harpsichord for his own opera; the admirable composer Mademoiselle Marianne Martinetz (Martinez) as well as the charming Countess Thun performed on the

14. For the 1750s and 1760s there is only indirect evidence available. For example, the keyboard music of Viennese composers such as Georg Christoph Wagenseil and Joseph Anton Steffan was published by Agostino Bernardi with the indication for *Cimbalo, Clavicembalo, Cembalo,* i.e., for harpsichord. According to Haydn's reminiscences in old age, he used to practice on a shabby *Clavier* (clavichord) or *Clavierl* (small portable clavichord) at the outset of his career. In his autobiography of 1776, he also writes of learning to play the *Clavier,* which might mean *keyboard* in the broader sense of the word since Haydn is known to have played the organ right from the beginning. In Vienna, no fortepiano was made before 1780. Recent studies by Eva Badura-Skoda point out that up to the mid-eighteenth century, both within and outside Italy, the new keyboard instrument with hammer action was still called *cembalo, cembalo di martellati, cembalo straordinario,* etc. (see, e.g., her "Domenico Scarlatti und das Hammerklavier"). With regard to Haydn's own terminology and his inscriptions on his autographs, I do not find this argument convincing since he knew C. P. E. Bach's book and was familiar with the word *Forte piano.*

15. Charles Burney, *The Present State of Music in Germany, the Netherlands, and United Provinces,* 2 vols. (London, 1773); see the chapter on Vienna, 1:202–367.

16. "At night two of the poor scholars of this city sung, in the court of the inn where I lodged, duets in *falset, soprano,* and *contralto,* very well in tune, and with feeling and taste. . . . They were taught music at the Jesuits' college" (ibid., 221).

17. "He began, upon a very bad harpsichord, by accompanying his niece" (ibid., 258).

18. "He had a harpsichord wheeled to him and he played me several *capriccios*"; "he had with him a little girl, his scholar, . . . with whom he played duets upon two harpsichords" (ibid., 325, 336–37).

19. Ibid., 337.

harpsichord also.[20] The only time Burney heard someone play the clavichord was when he visited the young and poor Vanhal in his home outside the walls of the city. Vanhal, who evidently possessed no better keyboard instrument yet, played sonatas on his little clavichord.[21]

The only information in Burney concerning the fortepiano is connected with a Mr. L'Augier, who "had himself been a good harpsichord player." "In Spain he was intimately acquainted with Domenico Scarlatti, who, at seventy-three, composed for him a great number of harpsichord lessons which he now possesses." Burney attended his concerts on several occasions: "Mr. L'Augier's concert . . . was begun by the child of eight or nine years old, whom he had mentioned to me before, and who played two difficult lessons of Scarlatti, with three or four by M. Becke, upon a small, and not good Piano forte. . . . I enquired . . . upon what instrument she usually practised at home, and was answered, 'on the Clavichord.' This accounts for her expression, and convinces me, that children should learn upon that, or a Piano Forte, very early . . . otherwise, after long practice on a monotonous harpsichord, however useful for strengthening the hand, the case is hopeless."[22] Burney's views seem to be in full agreement with the opinion of his time.

There is no reason to presume that fortepianos played a considerable role in Vienna before the late 1770s, given the competition of the cheaper clavichords, much in demand as an instrument for practicing and studying purposes, and the various harpsichords of Italian and probably German make, generally used as solo instruments and in ensemble playing in public performances.[23] In this respect, Vienna was more conservative than many European cities. It was only on the title pages of the editions prepared by Anton Huberty, who left Paris for Vienna to try his hand at music engraving and printing there between 1777 and 1781, that the purchaser of music caught sight of the fashionable inscription much in vogue to the west of Austria at that time: *pour le Clavecin ou Forte piano.*

As far as the musical household of the Esterházy family is concerned, the bills surviving from before 1781 relate mostly to the repair of the prince's *Cembalo,* the *Instrument oder cembalum,* the *Fürstl. Chor. Flich,* the *Fliegeln,* and

20. On Gassmann and Martinez, see ibid., 337 and 341, respectively. Of Thun, Burney wrote, "Her taste is admirable, and her execution light, neat, and feminine"; "she plays the harpsichord with that grace, ease, and delicacy, which nothing but female fingers can arrive at" (pp. 292, 216).

21. "We soon came to a right understanding; and finding he played the harpsichord, I got him to sit down to a little clavichord, and play me six lessons which he had just made for that instrument" (ibid., 352).

22. Ibid., 253, 247, 278–79.

23. Eva Badura-Skoda, however, engaged in research on the earlier appearance of the fortepiano in Vienna, dates to 1763 a payment "to Johann Baptist Schmidt for performing a concerto on the 'Fortipiano' in the Burgtheater" (*Haydn Studies,* 199).

the second *Flügel* installed at Eszterháza.[24] In 1781, a contract for repairing musical instruments was concluded with Anton Walter of Vienna, who, apart from repairing organs and harpsichords, was also already making fortepianos. Walter may have introduced the new instrument into the household of Haydn's master, although evidence on the possible date is lacking;[25] no fortepiano from the estate of the Esterházys has come down to us.

The year 1777 marks the advent of a new epoch in Viennese musical life. Johann Andreas Stein, the Augsburg builder of musical instruments who made the most decisive improvements in the fortepiano on the Continent, paid a visit to Vienna at that time. (In Augsburg, in the autumn of that same year, Stein fully won over Wolfgang Amadeus Mozart to this new instrument.)[26] At the imperial court, the harpsichord must still have been in fashion since Stein, together with his daughter Nannette, presented a *vis-à-vis Flügel* there.[27] However, Countess Thun, who was the subject of Burney's admiration, placed an order for a fortepiano with Stein.[28] Thus, the way for the fortepiano was cleared.

The first person to make excellent fortepianos in the imperial capital was Anton Walter, who settled in Vienna in 1780. His perhaps misleading title of

24. A relatively early bill, originating from 1764, is for the repair of the *fürstlichen klavikordi* at Eisenstadt, but sporadic data about smaller harpsichords (spinets) also exist. In 1767, a Pressburg (Bratislava) instrument maker made out a bill for having repaired *2 Sbinnetr* (two spinets), while, in 1781, a Viennese craftsman acknowledged the money received for repairing three *Spinetl* (Landon, *HCW,* 1:396, 2:136). This implies that, in addition to large, *Flügel*-shaped harpsichords, there must have been smaller keyboard instruments at Eszterháza.

25. According to his bill dated 3 March 1781, Walter had been repairing *Clavier* and *Flügel* instruments at Eszterháza for twelve days (Landon, *HCW,* 2:445). It was Haydn who supervised and certified his having performed the job. H. C. Robbins Landon's explanation of the word *Clavier* as unambiguously meaning fortepiano (ibid., 89) is a misunderstanding of the term; the instrument in question had to be a clavichord. The earliest reliable information on fortepianos at Eszterháza dates from 1796, when Walter tuned two of the prince's *Pianoforte.* The recollection of G. F. von R. (Rotenstein), published in *Sammlung kurzer Reisebeschreibungen* in 1783 (see Landon, *HCW,* 2:343), also deserves mention. He states that, on the second day of the visit of Empress Maria Theresa to Eszterháza in 1773, a concert was given in which a musician played on the *Piano-Forte* (*liess sich ein Musikus auf einem Piano-Forte hören*). Landon suspects the instrument to have been a small English square piano, a *Tafelklavier,* and does not exclude the possibility that the *Musikus* was none other than Haydn. However, news published ten years after the event, in a decade when the fortepiano was already much in vogue, may not be reliable. Landon's assumption requires further evidence to support it.

26. Leopold Mozart had only a clavichord and a harpsichord in his home; his son had been giving concerts on the harpsichord for some time. In the family portrait painted by Della Croce, Mozart is seen sitting at the harpsichord with his sister. Mozart sided with the fortepiano once and for all after he acquired a thorough knowledge of Stein's instruments in Augsburg in the autumn of 1777. (See his enthusiastic letter of 17 October 1777 [in Bauer and Deutsch, eds., *Mozart: Briefe und Aufzeichnungen,* 2:68–69].)

27. A fortepiano and harpsichord built together (cf. Schwarz, "Die Rolle des Cembalos in Österreich nach 1760").

28. Burney, *Present State,* 251. This may have been the instrument on which Mozart played in a contest with Clementi in the presence of Emperor Joseph II in 1781.

organ and instrument maker (*Orgel und Instrument Macher*) was due to his coming into possession of a license through his marriage to the widow of an organ builder. Within ten or fifteen years, several more instrument makers appeared on the scene. Apart from Jakesch, Nickl, and others, most notable were the Schan(t)z brothers, who were of Bohemian origin. Wenzel Schanz, active in Vienna from 1780 until his death in 1790, will be discussed in connection with Haydn's correspondence. After the death of Johann Andreas Stein in 1792, his children inherited his Augsburg firm. In 1794, Nannette, having married the composer Johann Andreas Streicher, decided together with her brothers to move their shop to Vienna. At this point, nothing stood in the way of calling Stein's German fortepiano action "Viennese action."

Another rich source of information, comparable to Burney's *Present State,* dates from 1796, the golden age of the fortepiano in Vienna. Johann Ferdinand Ritter von Schönfeld, author of the *Jahrbuch . . . 1796,* not only gave a description of the products of the major fortepiano makers of Vienna but also provided a vivid overall picture of the general use of *Klavier* instruments. At that time, the *Flügel* was practically restricted to accompanying singing and to giving the tempo in orchestras (especially opera orchestras). It was no longer used for solo playing in concerts, and the only people to cling to it persistently were the representatives of the old taste. According to Schönfeld, the following view was formed of the *Fortepiano:* "This instrument lets the heart speak, allows the soul to give vent to and communicate emotions; it makes painting, the spread of light and shadow, possible; it demands that you hear whether a pianist plays with feeling or mechanically [*ob ein Klavierspieler Empfindung oder Mechanismus hat*]. Earlier, one used to speak of *striking the keyboard;* now it is called *playing the fortepiano.*" Regarding the *Klavikord,* "This small instrument, so excellent by virtue of the flexibility of its sound, seems to be doomed to oblivion because of the Fortepiano. . . . It can only be found now among a few composers who, in the silence of the night, bring forth on it the products of their spirit."[29]

By 1796, the excellent fortepianos of Vienna were much in demand, although, according to the evidence of the *Jahrbuch . . . 1796,* they were far from cheap. The following table gives an idea of the prices of the instruments of various makers:[30]

29. Johann Ferdinand Ritter von Schönfeld, *Jahrbuch der Tonkunst von Wien und Prag: Faksimile-Nachdruck der Ausgabe 1796.* Mit Nachwort und Register von Otto Biba (Munich and Salzburg: Katzbichler, 1976), 184, 185.

30. A useful table giving equivalencies of currencies found in the various Haydn documents was published by Gotwals in *Haydn: Two Contemporary Portraits,* 213:

1 (gold) ducat (#) = 4 florins (gulden) (f) and 10–30 kreutzers
1 florin = 20 groschen
1 groschen = 3 kreutzers
1 Viennese ducat = 9–10 English shillings
2 Viennese ducats = 1 pound to 1 guinea

One fortepiano by Walter	50–120 ducats
One fortepiano by Joh. Schanz	40–100 ducats[31]
One square piano by Joh. Schanz	25 ducats
One fortepiano by Streicher	66 ducats

The *Jahrbuch . . . 1796* characterized Walter's instruments as having a full, clear-ringing sound with a powerful bass. Some of them, it states, may perhaps give a somewhat hollow sound at the beginning, but, when properly played in, the treble register is particularly effective. Should intensive use cause a metallic sound, this may be eliminated by covering the hammers with fresh leather. The main objection to these instruments is that either the bass or the treble is excessively predominant.

Johann Schanz, who, owing to the death of his brother, had been working alone for five years by 1796, produced a lighter yet equally clear fortepiano (fig. 2) that had a much pleasanter sound and a light action. Its keys had a shal-

---

To give an idea of the prices in general and how the cost of an instrument related to Haydn's earnings, some contemporary data are listed below. (Inflation was negligible in the 1780s.)

(*a*) The Viennese buyer paid the publishing house Artaria for printed music (in florins):

1 piano piece (e.g., the Variations in F Minor)	f 1
6 sonatas for piano (nos. 48–52 and 33)	f 3.30
1 longer sonata (no. 62 in E♭)	f 1.30
1 piano trio	f 1.30
6 quartets, i.e., parts (op. 33, 1782)	f 4
6 longer quartets, parts (op. 50, 1787)	f 4.30
3 late quartets, parts (op. 76, 1799)	f 3
1 symphony, i.e., 10 parts (no. 80, 1785)	f 2
3 symphonies, 13 parts (nos. 82–84, 1787)	f 5

(*b*) The average payment Haydn received from his publishers (in ducats):

1 piano sonata (e.g., 58 C, Breitkopf)	10 #
6 sonatas (Artaria)	60 #
6 piano trios	80 #
6 string quartets	100 #

(on the six sonatas and the six string quartets, see Bartha, *Briefe,* 199, 192).

(*c*) According to the contract renewed in 1780, Haydn's annual salary in cash (in addition to various payments in kind) for his work as conductor for the Esterházy's musical establishment amounted to f 782.30 (approx. 180 #). The total of his savings up to 1790 (according to Griesinger) was f 2,000 (approx. 462 #). The income of his benefit concert given in London on 4 May 1795 equaled (according to his diary) f 4,000 (approx. 924 #). The total value of his estate was about f 60,000.

31. It is a matter of conjecture (Walter, "Klaviere," 275; Hollis, *Instruments,* 14) what kind of a fortepiano by Wenzel Schanz Haydn could have bought for thirty-one ducats (cf. his letter to Artaria on 22 October 1788 [Haydn, *Briefe,* 195]). The amount is too much for a square piano but too little for a *Flügel*-shaped fortepiano. It is most likely that the instrument maker offered the famous composer a reduced price. That Haydn became an ardent partisan of Schanz's instruments may perhaps be partly attributed to this purchase. Evidence of his advocacy can be found in his persuasive and well-known arguments in his letters to Madame Genzinger (see n. 33 below). Before his death in 1809, Haydn sold this instrument, which he had obtained for thirty-one ducats, to an enthusiastic music lover for two hundred ducats. In my opinion, it must have been a fortepiano grand by Schanz.

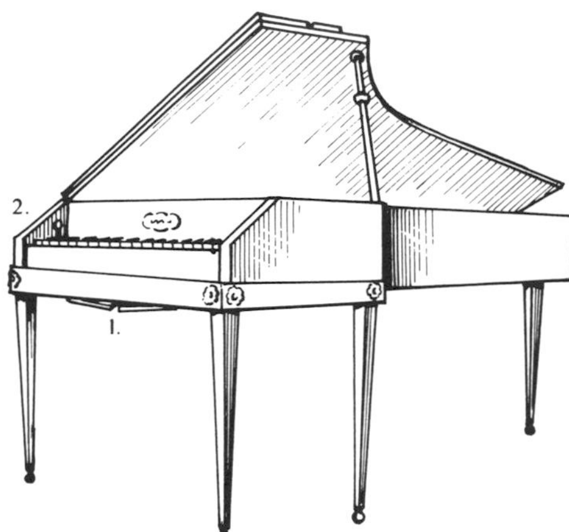

FIGURE 2 Fortepiano made by Johann Schanz (or Schantz) (ca. 1795). It probably resembles the instrument made by his brother, Wenzel Schanz, praised by Haydn. (1) Two knee levers to raise the bass and treble dampers. (2) Hand stop of the *Pianozug*.

lower dip and were also narrower. Schanz's fortepianos "are actually imitations, on a level with copies, of the fortepiano of the Augsburg artist Stein. . . . This master also makes many small fortepianos of English format that are easy to play and produce a fairly strong sound" (fig. 3).[32] We may leave to the Beethoven scholars a description of Madame Streicher's excellent fortepianos, as this instrument appeared on the scene after Haydn had ceased composing works for the piano.

Haydn expressed his opinion of the fortepianos of various makers in a letter he wrote to Madame Genzinger on 4 July 1790. Twice before he had urged her to buy a fortepiano of Wenzel Schanz's make;[33] he had owned such an instrument since 1788:

> It is quite true that my friend Herr Walther is very celebrated, and that every year I receive the greatest civility from that gentleman, but between ourselves, and speaking frankly, sometimes there is not more than one instrument in ten which you could really describe as good, and apart from that they are very expensive. I know Herr von Nikl's fortepiano: it's excellent, but too heavy for Your Grace's hand, and one can't play everything on it

32. Schönfeld, *Jahrbuch . . . 1796,* 89.

33. In letters dated 20 and 27 June 1790, Haydn had already urged his friend to buy a fortepiano made by Schanz. The wording of the letter dated 4 July leads us to believe that, in a letter that is now lost, Madame Genzinger must have asked Haydn for his evaluation of the other fashionable Vienna-made instruments (for the letters cited here, see Haydn, *Briefe,* 240–43). (The letters written by Madame Genzinger to Haydn are lost; we know the contents of only those few for which her drafts have survived.)

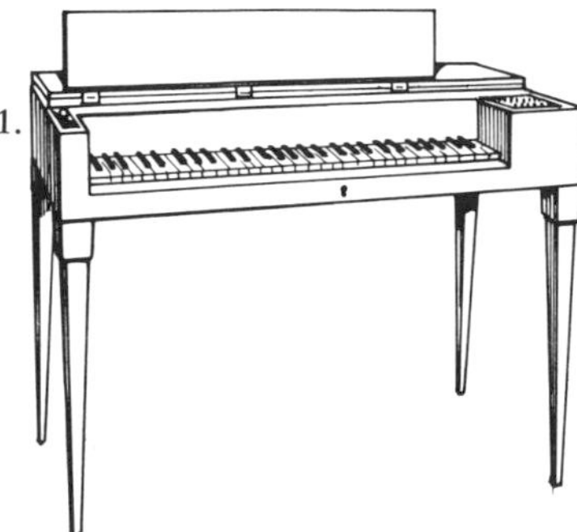

FIGURE 3 *Tafelklavier* (small square fortepiano) by Johann Schanz, without knee levers. (1) *Fortezug* hand stop.

> with the necessary delicacy. Therefore I should like Your Grace to try one made by Herr Schanz; his fortepianos are particularly light in touch and the mechanism very agreeable.[34] A good fortepiano is absolutely necessary for Your Grace, and my Sonata [59 E♭] will gain double its effect by it.[35]

It might seem that twenty years, by and large, sufficed for Vienna to have left behind the conservative taste that Burney described and to have established itself as an up-to-date center of keyboard playing where the fortepiano enjoyed absolute predominance. But was this really the case? There is no denying that by 1780 there were already several fortepianists famous for their achievements in Vienna. (One example is the Auenbrugger sisters,[36] who came to figure on the title page of the sonatas Haydn published that same year, nos. 48–52 and 33, often referred to as the *Auenbrugger* sonatas.) In their public concerts, Mozart and Kozeluch, the two great keyboard artists of Vienna of the 1780s, played the fortepiano.

Nevertheless, it was a considerable time before the old, valuable harpsichords began to disappear from the homes and salons of the music-making, music-loving, and music-consuming Viennese. This must have been the case since the firm Artaria—and they were far from unique in this—sold sonatas, solo movements, and trios "for harpsichord or fortepiano." This was done with

34. Haydn's own wording is "Seine piano forte haben eine ganz besondere Leichtigkeit, und ein angenehmes Tractament."

35. Haydn, *CCLN,* 107.

36. In the alphabetic index of the *Jahrbuch . . . 1796,* one of the sisters is described as follows: "Zois, Freyinn, née von Auenbrucker was once one of the first performers on the fortepiano, which instrument she played not only with skill but with taste as well. She has not been heard in academies for several years. Her melody is one of the most attractive ones you can hear. With her pleasant tone she combines a great number of embellishments that are not only graceful but also full of emotions" (p. 68).

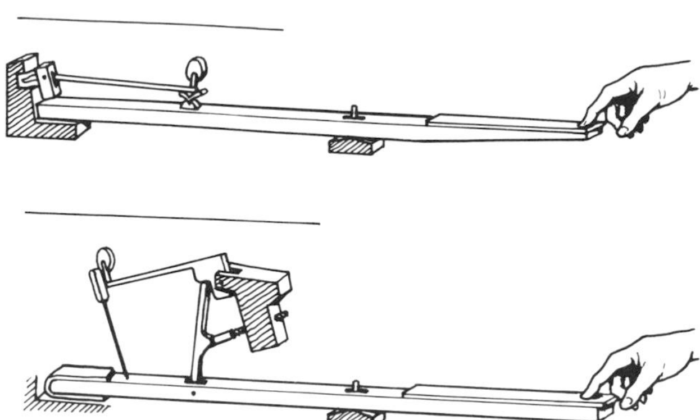

Simplified sketches of the *Prell-Mechanik* (Stein, Augsburg, 1773) above, and the *Stoss-Mechanik* (Broadwood, London, 1795) below.

Haydn's knowledge even as late as the beginning of the nineteenth century. Many of his pieces, now written unambiguously for the fortepiano, were printed with this instrumental designation in hopes of improving sales, such as the Fantasy in C Major (Hob. XVII:4) in 1789; the Sonata in E♭, no. 59 (the *Genzinger*), in 1791; the Sonata in E♭, no. 62 (the *London*), in 1798; and the Variations in F Minor (XVII:6) in 1799.

3. *London*

Haydn's visits to London between 1791 and 1795 brought him suddenly to the hub of fortepiano making. Significant new inventions appeared and were patented almost each year there, the result of the assiduous activity of several firms of instrument makers such as Longman and Broderip, who built solid instruments, the boldly experimental William Stodart, and, most important, John Broadwood. They built many variants, at different levels of technical development, of the mechanism known as *Stoss-Mechanik*.[37] On instruments incorporating the mechanism known as *Prell-Mechanik*, developed by Stein, each hammer was attached directly to the key and faced the player. On London instruments, however, the hammers faced away from the player; when the key was

37. Of the immense literature on early piano making, the book by Rosamond E. M. Harding, *The Piano-Forte*, is still the standard reference. For a survey of recent studies, see *The New Grove Piano*, (London, 1988), chap. 1, secs. 3 (by Philip R. Belt and Maribel Meisel) and 4 (by Derek Adlam and William J. Conner).

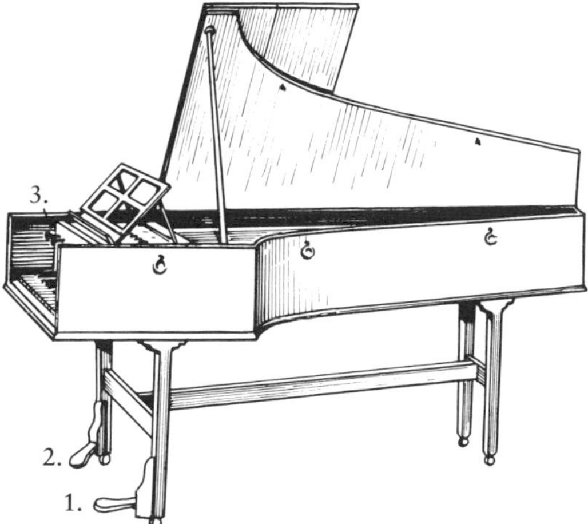

FIGURE 4 Fortepiano made by John Broadwood & Son in London in 1794. Haydn may have known this type in London. (1) Pedal to raise the damper. (2) Pedal operating *due corde* when pressed halfway down and *una corda* when pressed completely down. (3) Hand stops.

depressed, an intermediate mechanism pressed up on the tail of the hammer, impelling it toward the string. This mechanism, while harder to control, gave greater power. Broadwood also equalized the string tension throughout his grand pianos by dividing the bridge and having each of the hammers strike at a carefully determined point along the string's length. On triple-strung English instruments,[38] the entire action could be shifted so that the hammers would strike two strings or only one string (*due corde, una corda*) instead of all three. On the fortepianos by Broadwood, the operation of this shifting mechanism was already entrusted to the foot, that is, to a real pedal, by the time of Haydn's visits to London (fig. 4).

The registration possibilities of the fortepiano—inherited from the harpsichord and the organ and transferred to this instrument as an unmistakable sign of the taste of the age—and their contemporary German and English denominations will be briefly discussed here, solely to elucidate the most indispensable terms.

FORTEZUG/FORTE

The raising of the dampers (the right-hand pedal of the modern piano) was carried out either by a hand stop (e.g., on the square pianos) or by a knee lever

38. Stein's fortepiano, like many Viennese instruments of the 1780s, was double strung throughout the compass; the powerful upper register of a Walter fortepiano was a consequence of triple stringing of the upper octave and a half. (A good example is the ca. 1790 Walter in the Germanisches Nationalmuseum in Nuremberg.)

(*Kniepedal,* e.g., on the instruments built in Vienna during Haydn's time; see fig. 2) or, in London, from the time of J. Broadwood's patent of 1783, with a pedal proper (see fig. 4). The damper system was often divided into two halves, thus making it possible to damp the treble (from c^1 on) and bass registers independently, for example, allowing a fully vibrating sound of a left-hand chord while the right hand could enunciate a clear melody.

PIANOZUG/PIANO or MODERATOR
This meant one of two things. (*a*) Switching on the register brought a piece of cloth, felt, or leather between the string and the hammer, strongly coloring the tone.[39] (*b*) The dynamics and timbre of the sound were varied through a physical change of the stroke from the basic mode of operation. On the instruments built in Vienna, switching on the register brought the hammers closer to the strings. On the English fortepianos, the hammers were shifted to strike two strings, or even only one string.[40]

LAUTENZUG/LUTE
A piece of leather or felt lying across on the strings.

The less frequently found stops, or stops found more widely only after the mid-1790s, include:

HARFENZUG
A strip of wool or silk that damps the vibration of the strings (on German instruments).

HARP
A combination of the two kinds of *Pianozug,* that is, shifting mechanism plus a piece of leather (on English instruments).

FAGOTTZUG/BASSOON
A strip of paper or parchment placed on the lower register.

SCHWELLER/VENETIAN SWELL
A cover composed of slats, over the strings, that could be opened or closed much as modern Venetian blinds (for an example on a harpsichord, see fig. 1).

39. Its more powerful variant was the *Pianissimozug* applied from about the turn of the century.

40. Patents for the *una corda* shifting mechanism were obtained by Merlin in 1774 and by Walton in 1787 and on the first Continental instrument by Érard in 1794.

FIGURE 5 Fortepiano built by Érard Frères in Paris in 1801. It may be identical to the one the firm gave the aged Haydn as a present. The pedals: (1) "bassoon" to the lower strings; (2) damper; (3) *Moderator;* (4) *due corde;* (5) *una corda* knee lever.

JANITSCHARENMUSIK/DRUM
A mechanism, patented in 1797, that strikes the bottom of the sound board (thus imitating the sound of a drum) and that is often coupled with some kind of bell mechanism.

These registrations never occurred all together. The *forte* was present on even the small square pianos; around 1790 an average grand fortepiano would also contain some kind of *piano* as well (the English instruments would have an *una corda,* too) and frequently a *lute* stop. The maximum number of registrations that Haydn would have encountered on one instrument was the combination of four pedals plus one knee lever on a grand fortepiano built by Érard in 1801 (fig. 5), that is, only after he had finished writing works for keyboard. In music written or printed prior to circa 1795, no direct references to any particular use of registers can be found (for more details on this matter, see pp. 134–42).

To return to the impressions that Haydn might have had of the instruments in London, I imagine that these new possibilities must have struck his fancy. He tried out the magnificent, robust grand fortepianos with a range of five and a half octaves. He had occasion to listen to the virtuoso performances of Clementi, to the piano playing of Jan Ladislaus Dussek, who was famous for his pedaling, and to Johann Nepomuk Hummel, then touring as a child prodigy. He noted in his diary that the twelve- or thirteen-year-old John Field played the pianoforte excellently. Haydn took the dynamic range and action of the instruments he encountered in London into consideration when writing solo piano sonatas (nos. 60 in C, 62 in E♭, and perhaps even 61 in D) and trios[41] for Therese Jansen, fiancée of Gaetano Bartolozzi. (Haydn acted as best man at their wedding on 16 May 1795.) Moreover, the controversial *open Pedal* marking in the first movement of 60 C is of course related to the pedal on the London-built fortepianos. (For full particulars, see p. 139–40.) In only one movement (60 C III) did Haydn make use of the expanded range of the English keyboard. And the last group of Haydn's trios definitely bears the mark of the grandiosity of English pianofortes and the atmosphere of English concert life.

Nevertheless, Haydn's ideal of piano style did not undergo radical changes. The new impressions reached him too late for that, and his thinking was too pragmatic to exclude, out of hand, the Continental European and particularly the Viennese public from performing some of the significant groups of his works through excessively idiomatic writing.

It is not just a curiosity that in his public appearances in England Haydn himself played on both harpsichord and pianoforte. The relevant information on the two different orchestras employed and the various concerts given during his two visits to London is not completely reliable; at performances of his symphonies he might have directed from either the harpsichord or the pianoforte.[42] We do have definite information, however, that at the benefit concert of the singer La Mara, given on 1 July 1792, he played fortepiano, curiously enough, for Baroque music. He remarked in his diary in a mixture of German and English, "ich Accompagnierte ganz allein mit dem pianoforte ein sehr difficult English Aria von Purcell."[43]

4. *Haydn's Instruments*

Not a single keyboard instrument survives that could be claimed to have been the instrument at which or for which, in general or in particular, Haydn composed his sonatas.

Although the investigations into Haydn's instruments—those now lost or those later attributed to him—have not yet filled all the gaps, most of the ques-

41. See the remarks on the "London" texture of Haydn's piano works, p. 110.

42. The May issue of *Jackson's Oxford Journal* quotes him as saying, "I faithfully promised to play the Harpsichord at Mr. Hayward's Benefit Concert, the 18th." During the first series of Salomon's concerts, the announcement ended thus: "Mr. Haydn will be at the Harpsichord." The concerts of his second tour to London were already announced thus: "Dr Haydn will supply the Concerts with New Compositions, and direct the Execution of them at the pianoforte" (Landon, *HCW,* 3:80, 46, 232; cf. 214).

43. Haydn, *Briefe,* 491.

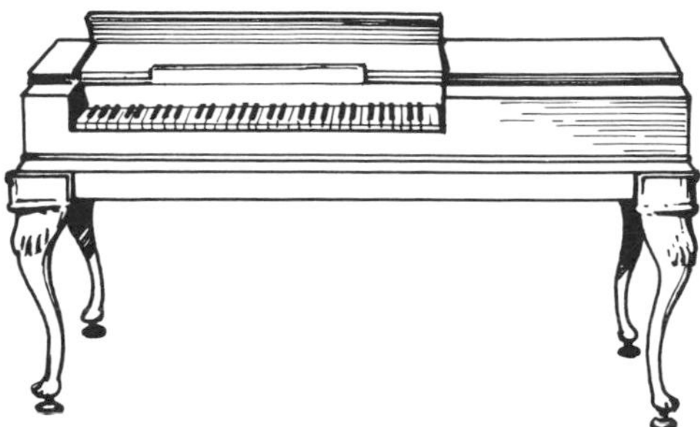

FIGURE 6 Clavichord made by Johann Bohak in Vienna in 1794. This was the instrument at which Haydn composed at Eisenstadt in his old age, after he had completed his piano sonata oeuvre. (Royal College of Music, London.)

tions are now considered settled by the frequently cited study by Horst Walter.[44] Only one authentic Haydn instrument has come down to us, a clavichord by Johann Bohak[45] (fig. 6), and this instrument has no relevance to Haydn's oeuvre for piano. On his return from London, starting in 1795 at the earliest, Haydn used this instrument for composing whenever he happened to be in Eisenstadt; he probably parted with it in 1803. *The Creation* is said to have been partly written at this clavichord, and that is conceivable.

What kind of instruments did Haydn possess? For the period prior to 1788 no reliable evidence exists. It is true that "the accident twice befell him of having his house in Eisenstadt burn down."[46] Haydn scholarship[47] suggests a relation between the fire in August 1768 and Haydn's use of a keyboard extending up to f^3 in his subsequent works—in distinction to the piano works, extending to d^3 only, in manuscripts dated earlier. Presumably, Haydn came into possession of a new, different instrument with a range of five octaves. From 1787 one utterly unreliable piece of information is available: the son of the engraver Bartolozzi went to see Haydn in his home at Eszterháza, where, according to his remarks, "an old spinett, or clavichord," was standing in his miserable single-room flat.[48] As is well known, Haydn had a four-room flat in the *Musikhaus;* thus, the description of misery is exaggerated. Moreover, no one who had any knowledge of keyboard instruments could confuse a rectangular clavichord with a trapezoidal spinet. Bartolozzi might, however, have seen a small clavichord in Haydn's home. At any rate, it is hardly conceivable that he would have failed to notice an enor-

44. See Walter, "Klaviere," and also his summary in "Haydn's Keyboard Instruments."

45. It was made by a Viennese *Klavier und Orgelmacher,* of Bohemian origin, in 1794 and has a range of five octaves (F_1–f^3). It is now kept in the Royal College of Music, London.

46. Griesinger; see Gotwals, *Haydn: Two Contemporary Portraits,* 17.

47. Feder, "Probleme."

48. His account of the visit appeared on 2 February 1787 in the *Gazetteer and New Daily Advertiser* in London.

mous, double-manual, expensive harpsichord by Shudi and Broadwood, had Haydn possessed one. The marvelous piece in the Kunsthistorisches Museum, Vienna, dating from 1775 (see fig. 1) had long been held to be an instrument given to Haydn as a gift by the London firm in 1775. But this legend has faded because in the extremely precise bookkeeping of the firm no mention of an instrument presented to Haydn can be found.

We now come to the most decisive evidence. In a letter of 26 October 1788, Haydn asked Artaria to make an advance payment on works to be written and pay the organ and instrument maker Wenzel Schanz thirty-one ducats because, "in order to compose your 3 pianoforte Sonatas [*Clavier Sonaten,* i.e., the piano trios Hob. XV:11–13] particularly well, I had to buy a new fortepiano [*Fortepiano*]."[49] This may have been the first new instrument Haydn owned and certainly his first fortepiano. It was this instrument that he kept praising so highly to Madame Genzinger.[50] He was fond of it up to the last year of his life; in old age he gave lessons on this instrument and was unwilling to let it be removed from his study until his doctor ordered it done, in 1803, to spare his hearing. Its loss is most regrettable, all the more so as no *Flügel*-shaped fortepiano by Wenzel Schanz has come to light to this day; only instruments by his brother are known.[51]

On his return from London Haydn was at last relatively well off. He had a house of his own in Gumpendorf, on the outskirts of Vienna, from 1797 onward. Visitors to the elderly composer report having seen four keyboard instruments. And, although his oeuvre for piano had been completed by that time, let us survey Haydn's instruments and follow up their fate.

1. Haydn transferred the grand fortepiano by Wenzel Schanz to one of his admirers for two hundred ducats shortly before his death in 1809. It is now lost.

2. A small *Klavier* (a square-shaped fortepiano or clavichord), whose volume his ears could still bear, was in Haydn's study between 1803 and 1806. It was removed from his study in 1806 and was lost sometime after his death. (It is not identical with the *Tafelklavier* by Johann Schanz that, according to tradition, had something to do with Haydn; see fig. 3.)

3. The grand fortepiano made by Longman and Broderip, bestowed on Haydn by his London publisher sometime in the 1790s, was the ornament of the music room; later it emerged in the possession of Abbé Stadler, then vanished.[52]

49. Haydn, *CCLN,* 79.

50. Edwin M. Ripin suggests that the "new" instrument mentioned in Haydn's letter may have replaced an earlier fortepiano in his possession (*Haydn Studies,* 306), but I doubt this.

51. The original fortepiano in the best state of repair I know of, one made by Johann Schanz ca. 1790, is in the possession of Paul Badura-Skoda. It was on this instrument that Badura-Skoda made his recordings of Mozart solo works in 1978 (*Pièces pour le Pianoforte,* Astrée AS 40) and his recordings of Haydn solo works in 1980–82.

52. Unless it is identical with the instrument that came into the collection of H. C. Robbins Landon, who asserts the possibility of its having been Haydn's piano. Its photo can be seen in Hollis, *Instruments,* 19; and H. C. R. Landon, *Haydn: A Documentary Study,* pl. 132. Another putative

4. The mahogany fortepiano with metal marquetry, which the firm of Érard gave Haydn as a present in 1801, was a truly decorative instrument and one of the most up to date of its time (similar to the one in fig. 5).[53] This precious piece of furniture in Haydn's music room was also lost after his death.

As a last source, one could study the keyboards shown in Haydn's portraits. Two authentic portraits must be taken into account here.[54] One is the undated oil painting by Ludwig Guttenbrunn, which survives in two versions, the second of which served as a basis for Schiavonetti's engraving of 1792.[55] It shows Haydn composing at a square piano on which even the two hand stops of the *Fortezug* can be recognized beside his left hand. The question arises whether the instrument depicted is a representation of one Haydn actually used. This is improbable, for the pose was one much in vogue in those days for a composer's portrait—an iconographical topos. It was made popular by a portrait of Paisiello by the famous Elisabeth Vigée-Lebrun,[56] in which the same kind of square piano and the identical shiny hand stops of the *Fortezug* can be seen. The young Guttenbrunn may have simply imitated the setting. The second picture is the oval gouache painting by Johann Zitterer[57] with the Andante of the *Drum Roll* Symphony on the music stand. The instrument depicted was perhaps meant to be a square piano, but the presentation of the instrument is so completely stylized[58] that, apart from Haydn's hand position, hardly anything deserves attention.

Haydn instrument, a *Joh. Jacob Konicke* [Könnicke] *Wien 1796* fortepiano of the Haydn-Museum, Vienna, is described in recent popular books as "a fortepiano used by Haydn in his last years" (R. Klein and E. Lessing, *Joseph Haydn* [Freiburg: Herder, 1981], pl. 37), but its authenticity is not documented at all.

53. See the photo in Hollis, *Instruments,* 20. According to Hollis, this is either the very instrument sent to Haydn or, what is more probable, an exact copy.

54. Thomas Hardy's portrait of Haydn (both his painting and his engraving) with a keyboard instrument in the background does not offer any clue as to the nature of the instrument (see László Somfai, *Joseph Haydn: His Life in Contemporary Pictures* [London and New York, 1969], pls. 247–48).

55. Ibid., pls. 228 and 229 and pl. A on p. 224, respectively.

56. Ibid., pl. 167, reproduced with an engraving by Vincent Alloja.

57. Ibid., pl. 293.

58. The black keys are depicted, not in groups of 3-2-3-2, but continuously.

Two

For What Kind *of* Instrument Did Haydn Compose?

THE DYNAMIC MARKS IN Haydn's solo and chamber keyboard music can be used to define two, or with subtle differentiation perhaps three, periods with respect to the proper instrument.[1] (1) Sonatas (ending with *WUE* 47) and the bulk of the other solo keyboard pieces (including the Capriccio in G Major, Hob. XVII:1, and the two sets of variations, in A and E♭, Hob. XVII:2, 3) written up to 1776, the early trios, and the so-called piano divertimentos (Hob. XIV) were written for *harpsichord.* (2) Sonatas that appeared between 1780 and 1788 (nos. 48–52 and 33, 53, 54–56) and the first group of his mature trios (XV:2, 5–10) were conceived in a *tentative fortepiano* idiom[2] (in which certain movements and at times even entire works completely lack fortepiano dynamics). (3) The keyboard music of the years 1788–96, that is, the five last sonatas (nos. 58–62), the Fantasy in C Major, the Variations in F Minor, and the majority of the trios (XV: 11–31), reflects a fully fledged, mature craftsmanship of *fortepiano* writing rooted in personal experience.[3]

1. The organ parts of his church music (among them the concertante part of the *Grosse Orgelmesse,* Hob. XXII:4) as well as the early Concerto in C Major (Hob. XVIII:1) have been left out of consideration here.

2. Even the well-known Concerto in D Major (Hob. XVIII:11), with a few ***fz*** signs in the solo sections of the slow movement, was printed by Artaria with the indication on the title page *per il clavicembalo o fortepiano* in 1784; the writing is more characteristic of harpsichord than of fortepiano.

3. According to Georg Feder's "Work-List," the sonatas that are definitely or possibly for the fortepiano are as follows (*WUE* nos.):

Harpsichord/fortepiano	48–52 + 33; 57
Harpsichord/(fortepiano)	34, 35, 53; 58
Fortepiano	54–56; 59; 60–62

All other works are said to be for harpsichord. In the case of no. 58, e.g., I do not agree with him.

This classification is certainly justifiable, but if used uncritically, it could lead to doctrinaire conceptions of performance. In order to be able to experiment with style and touch on the available modern instruments—or to be able to search for the historically authentic instrument among period instruments and their copies—we must form a clear notion of each relevant datum and examine whether it expresses a necessity or simply a possibility, whether it marks the only suitable instrument for an optimal performance or rather indicates a neutral situation with wider grounds for choice.

In the evaluation of the data, no precaution is too great. Authenticity itself can be imbued with so many meanings. For which instrument did the composer intend his work at the time of its genesis? Which instrument did he have in mind later, when sets of these works were published? To what extent did he concern himself, if at all, with performances on another instrument in another country or in the same country two decades later? Or should we ignore historical data on the grounds that Haydn's time was less preoccupied than ours with the choice of instruments? Should we cite only evidence in support of some present-day view of performance practice? Certainly not. Nonetheless, the authenticity of data from Haydn's time, referring to aspects of form as well as of content, may have absolute or relative standards and may be interpreted objectively or subjectively. One can objectively evaluate the reliability of the source itself. The designation of the instrument may survive (*a*) in Haydn's own hand; (*b*) in the hand of his own copyist; (*c*) in a print made under Haydn's supervision; or (*d*) in a secondary copy or pirated edition. On the other hand, it may be a matter of subjective judgment whether the designation of an instrument is, for example, (i) the result of a conscious decision and as such significant or (ii) a routine, conventionally written direction.

The first set of facts on which we may draw comprises the textual evidence supplied by the designation of the instrument (1) in the title of the work; (2) in the score, before the movements; (3) in Haydn's own work lists (*EK, HV*); and (4) in his correspondence and diaries and in recollections recorded by his biographers.

The authentic information through the 1770s (sources designated *a, b,* and *c* above) denotes harpsichord exclusively, albeit with different spellings (see table 1). The designation of instrument may have been only a recommendation—and partly an indication of what instrument was in fashion in a given city or country—by the time that the printing and distribution of large numbers of copies began. The *Esterházy* sonatas, nos. 36–41, written unequivocally for harpsichord, were printed as harpsichord works in Vienna, in Berlin (by Hummel), in Amsterdam (1777, *pour le clavecin*), and in London (by Birchall, 1783, *for the harpsichord*), whereas the title page of the Longman and Broderip edition (1781), also printed in London, bore the indication *forte piano or harpsichord.* In 1788, five of the so-called workshop sonatas, dating from around 1766–72,

TABLE 1 DESIGNATION OF INSTRUMENT

Haydn's Own Designation of Instrument	In His Manuscript, in the Title of the Work	In the *EK* Entry*
Clavicembalo Solo	13 G, 29 E♭	9 D, 14 C, (26 C, 27 A)
Cembalo Solo		13 G, 16 D, (21 d, 22 A, 24 B♭, 25 e), 28 D, 29 E♭, 31 A♭, XVII: 2, A Var.
Clavi Cembalo	33 c†	
Clavicembalo	44 F	
Cembalo‡	36–41 set§	(23 B), 30 D

* The works in parentheses are sonatas now lost and known only by their thematic incipits in the *EK*.

† A typical case of routine designation. The first version of the manuscript, dated 1771, already contains ***f-p-f-p*** series that cannot be executed on the harpsichord.

‡ The first page of the manuscript of 30 D bears neither a title nor a designation of instrument; 20 B♭ and 28 D survive as fragments of manuscripts with no title page whatsoever.

§ On the title page of the authentic Kurzböck edition of 1774, *Clavi-Cembalo* can be read; otherwise, *Cembalo* appears even on the copies of the *Anno 1776* set (nos. 42–47) made in a Viennese copyist's workshop.

were printed without Haydn's knowledge on the basis of stolen and smuggled copies; they appeared in Vienna (Artaria) with *clavicembalo o forte piano* on the title page in London (Longman & Broderip) with *piano forte or harpsichord.* In the view of publishers, and presumably of amateur musicians as well, these compositions, originally composed for harpsichord, could be performed acceptably on either instrument.

Before scrutinizing the information drawn from the musical notation, let us briefly survey the source data of the transitional period, starting around 1780, and of the period when Haydn was writing exclusively for fortepiano. Unfortunately, very few autographs survive from that period. Of the compositions for piano solo, the Sonata no. 59 in E♭, the *Genzinger,* bears the inscription *Sonata per il Forte-piano,* whereas no. 62 in E♭ has only *Sonata,* implying that, as with the manuscript of the Variations in F Minor, entitled *Sonata,* the instrument had become self-evident for Haydn by that time. In some cases, Haydn modified the original indication of instrument; *Cembalo* appears in the autograph manuscripts of the trios of the 1780s (Hob. XV: 5 in C, 7 in D, and 9 in A), but on the copies sent to the publisher Forster in London he writes *o forte piano* (XV: 3–5)[4]

4. Hob. XV: 3–4 are works by Pleyel; XV: 5 is by Haydn.

and *pour le clavecin ou piano forte* (XV:9). Still, routine designation of the instrument occurs as late as 1795 in the autograph manuscript of the Trio no. 31 in E♭ Minor (at the first movement *cembalo o p: f:* and at the second movement *cembalo*).

There is no autograph entry in the *EK* for these late works. There are, however, some important references in Haydn's letters. The set of sonatas nos. 48–52 and 33 (the *Auenbrugger* sonatas) as well as the sonatas nos. 58 in C and 59 in E♭ are mentioned as *Clavier Sonaten,* the Fantasy in C Major as *ein ganz neues capriccio für das fortepiano,* and the Variations in C Major similarly as *für das Forte piano.* Nevertheless, regarding the later editions printed with Haydn's knowledge, Artaria in Vienna persisted in indicating "for harpsichord or fortepiano" on the title page of works whose full value could be realized only when performed on the fortepiano (e.g., 59 E♭, 62 C, Fantasy in C). As a matter of fact, publishers in other cities were more reliable. The London first edition of Sonata no. 53 in E Minor bears an alternative designation with good reason.[5] On Bossler's first edition of the set of wedding-present sonatas, nos. 54–56, *pianoforte* was printed, while the Sonata no. 58 in C was printed by Breitkopf in 1789 in a potpourri volume entitled *Klavier-Sonaten.*[6]

To summarize, the designation *forte piano,* written in Haydn's own hand, first appeared in a trio in 1784 as an alternative to harpsichord. An exclusive inscription of or reference to *fortepiano* exists only from 1789 onward, that is, the year Haydn came into possession of an instrument made by Schanz. But we have no reason to doubt that (*a*) the title page of the *Auenbrugger* sonatas (1780) was printed as for *clavicembalo o forte piano* with Haydn's consent and that (*b*) the exclusive designation of instrument *pour le pianoforte* of the *Bossler* sonatas also reflected his intention. (No autograph manuscript of these sonatas survives.)

The second fund of information is drawn from the musical notation. This includes (1) the range and characteristics of the keyboard of the instrument necessary for performing the piece; (2) dynamic markings and accent signs; and (3) inferences from the notation and the texture.

Modern Haydn scholarship has thoroughly investigated the increasing compass of the various chronological groups of Haydn's music for keyboard instruments. In the course of this, significant insights have been gained that may be relied on in questions of dating. Georg Feder first noticed that Haydn did not go beyond d^3 in works written up to 1767 (this includes Sonatas 29 E♭ and 30 D).[7] In the sonatas composed after 1768, that is, after Haydn's house burned down

5. Although, in all manuscript sources, *harpsichord* is given.

6. In Leipzig, this could also mean clavichord; the 1792 edition by André is unambiguously inscribed *piano-forte.*

7. See Feder, "Probleme"; and also his remarks in *Haydn Studies,* 109.

on 2 August 1768 (31 A♭ etc. but also 20 B♭), the treble sometimes extends to f^3. Thereafter, almost all works by Haydn, excepting one single London movement (60 C III),[8] can be performed on a keyboard with a range of five octaves (F_1–f^3) typical of Continental instruments up to the end of the eighteenth century. A characteristic trait of Haydn's disciplined and practical thinking is that he did not struggle against the existing limits of his instruments (see fig. 7).[9]

The range of five octaves itself was, of course, not a determining factor in the choice of instrument since the keyboards of harpsichords and fortepianos, and even of the clavichord by Bohak, were much the same at that time. A few movements from the 1760s suggest a so-called short-octave arrangement of the lowest notes of the keyboard; these stem directly from harpsichord or organ building. The thorough investigations of Horst Walter[10] illuminate the variety of contemporary short-octave types in Haydn's geographic environment. Of the three best-known short-octave passages in Haydn's keyboard music—reproduced in example 1—those marked (i) may be played without arpeggiating the chord on a C short-octave keyboard[11] and that marked (ii) on a G short-octave keyboard. But, if both (i) and (ii) occur in the same piece, as in example 1*b*, they may be played without arpeggiation only on a rare instrument such as one finds occasionally in a museum as a curiosity.

Ex. 1. *a*, 19 e I, 11. *b*, Capriccio in G Major, mm. 25–26, 367–68.

Certain dynamic markings and accent signs help distinguish only two of the three instruments in question. Should the authentic notation contain *Bebung* (⁀… above one note), the piece could be executed only on the clavichord. This

8. It is typical that in this forward-looking movement—and only here—the sections that can no longer be performed on the average Continental instrument are provided with an 8va marking in a way that would allow them to be played *loco* if necessary (naturally, with octave transposition in the left hand). Note, however, that the typical five-octave keyboard was occasionally enlarged in Vienna in the mid-1790s too: e.g., a Johann Jacob Könnicke fortepiano (*Wien 1796*) in the Germanisches Nationalmuseum, Nuremberg, with a compass of F_1–a^3.

9. On the other hand, Haydn readily and cleverly made use of virtuoso high position effects for strings whenever there was a likelihood of a proper performance (cf. the first violin parts in his quartets, the solo cello part of the Concerto in D Major, the cello *obbligato* part of the Sinfonia concertante, etc.).

10. Walter, "Tasteninstrument," 239–42.

11. The diatonic key below F produces the pitch C, the divided chromatic key between F and G produces the pitches F♯ and D, and the divided chromatic key between G and A produces the pitches G♯ and E.

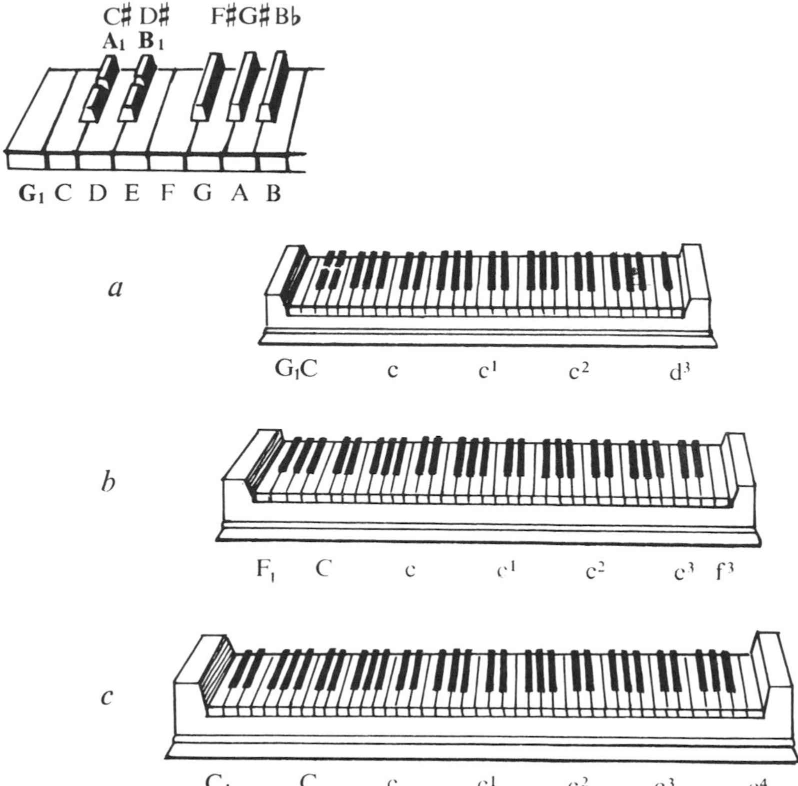

FIGURE 7 The increasing compass of the keyboard during the time Haydn was composing sonatas. *a,* G "short-octave" harpsichord keyboard, the instrument of the Capriccio in G Major, 1765. *b,* Five-octave harpsichord or fortepiano keyboard, the compass of Haydn's sonatas from 1768 onward. *c,* Six-octave fortepiano keyboard of London (60 C III: C–a^3; 60 C I–II, 61 D, and 62 E♭: F_1–f^3).

notation is completely absent from Haydn's keyboard music. If, however, the music includes crescendo or decrescendo signs, ***fz*** accents, note-by-note ***f-p-f-p*** series, or very rich and varied dynamic directions on the whole (and if the clavichord is not an ideal but rather an outdated instrument or one that has never been really significant in a given musical environment), only a performance on a fortepiano can fully realize the composer's directions.[12] (The dynamic markings of Haydn's sonatas—including occasional ***fz***, ***f***, and ***p*** signs in 31 A♭, 20 B♭, and 37 E—as well as the emergence of the distinctive fortepiano expression marks used from 1780 on, and particularly from 1788–89 on, are treated in a separate chapter.)

12. See my reasoning in connection with the Sonata in C Minor (pp. 131–32). See also Larsen's arguments on the possibility of a better performance on the clavichord of the second movement of the Sonata no. 30 in D (in *Haydn Studies,* 289).

The harpsichord has no distinguishing set of signs in Haydn; in effect, any writing that is not specifically fortepiano-like can be considered as meant for harpsichord. Moreover, no technical features or devices in his sonatas (such as crossing of parts etc.) require performance on a double-manual harpsichord. Consequently, in order to judge whether there are any idiomatic harpsichord-like elements written in Haydn's keyboard works before 1780, we must make use of the indirect hints in the notation. In fact, the many accents clearly appropriate for performance on harpsichord are scored by means of increasing the number of parts, using arpeggio effects, or using the extremes of the register. They will be examined in detail in connection with performing style (p. 129). For that matter, Haydn seems to have retained the "harpsichord accents," in a reflex-like manner, even in his mature writing for fortepiano, at least until his visit to London. His fortepiano music, up to the *Genzinger* Sonata, no. 59 in E♭ major, is imbued with the richly ornamented cantabile style of melodic writing that was meant to improve the singing capabilities of the fast-decaying sound of the harpsichord, a feature that Haydn incorporated into his fortepiano style in an extremely individual manner.

After extensive scrutiny of the information to be gained from the music, I have drawn the following conclusions.[13]

1. No abrupt, striking discrepancy of style exists between the works written for harpsichord (up to 1776) and those already conceived for fortepiano (1780 on). This is, first, because Haydn had already striven to attain a flexible expression, full of nuances, reminiscent of string playing and other kinds of chamber music (for which the harpsichord never proved sufficiently suitable)[14] and, second, because several of the idiomatic features of harpsichord writing can be detected in the fortepiano scores as well.

2. We may rather speak of an opus or a sonata being more strongly determined by one of these instruments. Thus, the set of the *Esterházy* sonatas, nos. 36–41, is more genuinely harpsichord music than the "workshop" sonatas of the previous years. There are works in "Schanz style" (58 C I, 59 E♭, Fantasy in C) and in "Broadwood style" (62 E♭, 60 C I and III, 61 D II), the difference of instrumental ideal between these occasionally being no less than the difference between a harpsichord and a fortepiano of Haydn's time.

13. Not even the relevant contributions to *Haydn Studies* by Ripin (p. 306) and Leslie Tung (pp. 323ff.), partly divergent in view, and A. Peter Brown's detailed discussion of "The Question of Keyboard Idiom" (*Keyboard,* 134–71) can shake my convictions about this.

14. As a result, from a historical point of view, there can be no objections to playing the sonatas written before 1776 on the fortepiano, which is still very harpsichord-like in its sound in many respects. Note that, as regards "historic performance" of Haydn on the harpsichord, at the moment (including Ton Koopman's recording of 42 G, 49 c♯, 53 e, and 59 E♭; Philips 9500 975) there are no real alternatives to the fortepiano interpretations of the standard sets by Malcolm Bilson and Paul Badura-Skoda.

Three

THE CHOICE *of* INSTRUMENTS *for* PRESENT-DAY PERFORMERS

A MUSICIAN ESTABLISHING OR RECONSIDERING his style of playing Haydn's music during the 1970s and 1980s was certainly in an extremely favorable situation—and this situation improves each year. For this is a period of serious, even passionate, experimentation. Changes are occurring more quickly than they did, say, when Wanda Landowska offered the performance of Bach's works on the harpsichord as an alternative to performance on the piano or when Alfred Deller, putting the countertenor voice in the limelight, launched the thoroughgoing revision of the vocal performance of early music.

The most decisive step in the new wave of Haydn interpretation was the appearance of several excellent urtext editions of Haydn's sonatas and other piano works in the 1960s. These offered a much-needed alternative to the earlier, overinterpreted performing editions. But crucial incentives came from other fields as well. Research into old instruments by instrument makers and performers systematically showed the many-sided relations between the style of a nation or an individual instrument-making workshop and the music composed in the corresponding place and time. The record market has also had an important impact since it has made available extraordinary new recordings, among them specialized renderings reflecting a keen knowledge of style and produced on authentic instruments in an acoustically accurate environment. These large undertakings have already produced and provided opportunities for a type of performing artist with musicological interests and training. Master courses and special classes at universities have sprung up in various countries. In the last decade, various artistic approaches to Haydn have materialized on a high professional level. The pioneering efforts of eminent artists (some of whom can be heard only at festivals or at concerts held in museums, some of whom are known only in university circles, but some of whom have made recordings) have effected a change in the needs and tastes of at least a certain segment of the audience. Today, many listeners notice the unique values of historically informed interpretations of Haydn's works, as opposed to conventional performances realized in the intersection of many artistic, technical, and practical business considerations.

In the midst of this undeniable change in Haydn interpretation, the choice of instrument is an important decision, but not the only one. The choice of historically and stylistically authentic instruments will not automatically yield a better rendering. On the other hand, a less suitable instrument will prevent one from acquiring certain musical experiences.[1] The question of instrument should not be a matter of concern only for the performers who are intent on specialization; music educators and performers giving concerts in traditional circumstances should not remain content with the "Steinway ideal." On the contrary, it is above all music educators who can take decisive steps in restoring the treasure of Haydn's sonata output, transferring it from its present stage of lower-level piano study to a higher and richer one. Within this framework, the study of how certain Haydn movements sound on a small or large grand piano, on an instrument with lighter or heavier action, on a harpsichord or a piano, on a small fortepiano made from a kit or built professionally, can be excellently used for forming a pupil's taste in a wider sense. And the student should become aware of the beautiful and transparent sounds that can be brought about by completely eliminating the damper pedal (or at least by restricting it to the rare cases where it is used in its original ornamental sense of blurring together certain harmonically static fields).

For most pianists, an ideal instrument will not always be available. But even when only modern pianos are available, there are several criteria for making a choice. Pianos with a more transparent bass register, those with a lighter action, or those that allow the player to form a melody with a natural touch and yet of discreet volume are all advantageous, not only for practicing, but also for performance.

We may touch on certain points concerning the performance of Haydn's keyboard music on the harpsichord. There is no denying the advantages to any pianist in having some experience and skills in playing the harpsichord (touch, phrasing, legato fingerings, fast ornaments, etc.). It must be noted, however, that—in spite of Landowska's endeavors—professional harpsichordists could still profit from enlarging their repertoire with many Haydn works. Among the early divertimento sonatas (up to *WUE* 19), there are already some mature harpsichord settings. Of the later sonatas, nos. 36–41, the *Esterházy* set, nos. 42–47,

1. Malcolm Bilson states, "Using old instruments doesn't guarantee a good interpretation. Some people who play old instruments haven't the slightest idea how to play the music, and others who have no idea about old instruments play marvelously. What old instruments do offer is a way to find out more than we used to know about Haydn's music" (in *Haydn Studies,* 267).

the *Anno 1776* set, and even certain of the *Auenbrugger* sonatas, nos. 48–52 (as well as the Capriccio in G Major and the variations including the set in E♭ major), are challenging pieces for the harpsichordist's repertoire; they are more harpsichord-like than the earlier "workshop" sonatas in experimental styles. The question remains as to what is the best type of harpsichord for the performance of Haydn's keyboard music. Haydn conceived and formulated his music with great imagination for a very modest one-manual Italian-type instrument.[2] The music itself demands the forceful exploitation of such an instrument.

The serious alternatives for the present-day performer are to play Haydn's music either on a modern or on a suitably selected historic instrument. Let us, for the moment, disregard practical difficulties such as having access to an original instrument or a copy and consider the advantages and disadvantages of the choice itself. Furthermore, let us temporarily simplify a complex question and speak of *fortepiano* throughout, being fully aware that certain works by Haydn could have a more authentic realization on an Italian harpsichord and that at least two types of fortepiano—the Viennese and the London—will have to be reckoned with later on. This hypothetical fortepiano of Haydn's time, which we will compare to the modern piano, could be, for example, an instrument made by Stein and imitated accurately by the Schanz brothers or a copy of the piano by Walter once owned by Mozart, that is, an instrument with a knee lever to raise the dampers and with an additional *Pianozug* register.

In the process of relearning the style of Haydn's piano music, the fortepiano will act as a primary source of instrumental and artistic experiences to be gained nowhere else. The capabilities lacking in a fortepiano, in comparison with a present-day piano, are not in fact needed for an authentic and fully satisfying rendering of Haydn's keyboard music played in a chamber-music-sized hall or a recording studio. It is superfluous, for example, to have strings that vibrate for a longer time because this music, by its very nature, is full of ornaments and is richly articulated with clear phrase endings as well as numerous rests. The modern damper-pedal action, easy to manipulate and rich in possibilities of shading and coloring, is likewise superfluous because this music is written with precise contours and only rarely admits pedaling, as an extraordinary ornamental effect. It is due to the remarkable balance of volume between the treble and the bass and the transparent low register of the fortepiano that one can finally discover, and play with powerful gestures, the cantabile and contrapuntal left-hand passages, *forte* staccatos, and *sforzando* phrase ends with full natural volume. In contrast to the highly sophisticated yet relatively sluggish action of the modern piano, the fortepiano is nimble, creating the illusion of a direct connection between the fin-

2. I doubt that large French and Flemish double-manual harpsichords are ideal for playing Haydn's sonatas.

gertip and the hammer set into motion. At the same time, the dampers function extremely effectively and stop the tone immediately after the release of the key, particularly on the Viennese instruments of Haydn's time. (The damping of the English pianos of the same period was much less effective.)

The sensitivity of the action of the fortepiano has a salutary effect in disciplining the touch and planning each note in terms of its musical purpose.[3] One can search for the specific articulations and accents of groups of two, three, four, six, and eight notes with the expectation that the instrument will responsively reproduce one's choices. The limitation of the dynamic encourages the use of other means of accentuation: phrasing, articulation, and agogics. This style of playing the fortepiano has much in common with playing a solo string instrument. This is what differentiates Haydn's piano music from his symphonies or even from the more muscular style of some of his quartets.

Work at the fortepiano aiming at a better understanding of the nature of Haydn's keyboard style, on the one hand, and the characteristics of the keyboard instruments of his time, on the other, is instructive even if we know in advance that the results of our experiments will have to be transferred, with additional serious artistic efforts, to the present-day piano. Pianists who have only limited access to a fortepiano, or who want to play Haydn's music in a program with a wide chronological range on concert tours where a different grand piano will be played each time, or who consider the volume of a good copy of a period instrument to be hazardously frail in a large concert hall, will have to approach the modern piano with an awareness of the musical experiences obtained from the fortepiano.

Playing on period instruments is already as real an alternative for performing Haydn's keyboard music as it is for J. S. Bach's. It is not unusual now for artists to perform Haydn's work on a modern grand piano in the concert hall but to turn to the fortepiano for recordings and radio or television broadcasts. Pioneering interpretations recorded under ideal circumstances (including excellent instruments and players with a thorough understanding of the instruments and the style of the music) will imprint themselves on the minds of listeners as a normative rendering of the work. Aberrations are still likely to occur. Some artists may be tempted to monopolize Haydn's sonatas exclusively for the historical instrument, while others will perhaps resentfully withdraw from playing Haydn's keyboard music altogether—and, in between, the mills of music schools and conservatories will grind out Haydn as teaching material in a variety of ways. This situation would be similar to that with the *Well-Tempered Clavier,* which is so fundamental to piano pedagogy that thousands of pupils in conservatories all

3. Fortepiano players will sooner or later acquire the tricks of adjusting and repairing the instrument, of covering the hammers with new leather, and of tuning and changing strings. By willingly accepting the merits and disadvantages of the instrument, while learning to control it, they will become masters and virtuosos of their fortepianos.

over the world practice it to learn piano playing in general and also higher elements of idiomatic piano playing, and yet in concerts and recordings it is heard almost exclusively on the harpsichord.

Haydn's keyboard music will survive interpretations on various instruments, embodying diametrically opposed conceptions, because it is better, richer, more interesting music than we yet know.

Four

An Introduction *to* Reading *the* Conventions *of the* Notation (Grace Notes, Ornaments)

THE PRESENT-DAY PERFORMER OF Haydn's sonatas is in the fortunate position of having at his disposal the *Wiener Urtext,* on the one hand, and the *Joseph Haydn Werke*, on the other, two editions with reliable texts; the former is one of the best "practical urtext" editions of our time and the latter a high-standard product of German scholarly editions.[1] Nevertheless, one should not automatically execute the performance suggestions and the recommendations in the footnotes of the *Wiener Urtext.* For our own education, and above all in order to distinguish between the obligatory features of the notation and those left to the performer's discretion, let us survey the most essential sources that serve as a guide to the conventions of the musical notation in Haydn's time and of Haydn's own keyboard music in particular.

Before embarking on this survey, we should, however, make clear that the major difficulty in interpreting the notation of *early music* (a term that today includes Viennese Classical music) is not understanding obsolete signs, but correctly comprehending those that continued into later notation. Musicians are

1. For less experienced performers of Haydn's works, and particularly for pianists playing exclusively on modern instruments, the performing edition *Haydn: 4 Keyboard Sonatas,* ed. Paul Badura-Skoda (Paris: Leduc, 1982), might seem quite serviceable (it contains 13 G, 31 A♭, 33 c, and 38 F). This handsome, two-colored (black-and-blue) edition goes into details in a remarkable way and contains innumerable pieces of good advice for reading and interpreting the notation. However, in my view, it has several questionable or even incorrect explanations of ornaments, as I will point out below. Thus, the pianist dealing seriously with Haydn is urged to use the urtext, reserving Badura-Skoda's performing edition for occasional consultation. A more recent performing edition based on the urtext and less prejudicial in its performance-practice advice is Howard Ferguson's *Haydn: Selected Keyboard Sonatas* (4 vols. [London: Associated Board of the Royal Schools of Music, 1985]), which contains twenty-three sonatas.

tempted to read these signs as if they were used in their later senses, regardless of the fact that many of the basic ones were originally meant to convey different meanings, some indeed quite different. This information may unfortunately be omitted during one's studies, nor is it sufficiently dealt with in any up-to-date books. Even in the relevant treatises of the period it is encountered only in the form of incidental references. This should not be surprising, for in the early instrumental and vocal tutors, the majority of the conventions for reading music that were universally understood in their own time did not have to be notated; only divergent signs, regarded by the author as the latest or as signs to be executed differently from one region to another, were notated.

One should not gloss over the fact that, while in most of the recent critical editions no effort is spared to establish an "urtext," not much is done in presenting in detail the conventions predominant in the notation of a given composer, not to mention discussing ambiguities in his writing. Much attention is lavished on deciding visual analogies and pseudoanalogies in a philologically correct way and on adding slurs etc. in brackets; however, suggestions are only occasionally made for the proper reading of dotted or triplet rhythms contrary to the written notation, and many basic issues, such as whether an "ordinary note" (*movimento ordinario*) lasts as long as written, are not touched on at all.

The proper understanding of the signs for ornaments and grace notes—of *embellishments,* to use the more comprehensive term—is only one aspect of reading an urtext edition correctly. Proper understanding must be followed by the more experimental, but indispensable, step of interpreting the conventions of the notation. Let us confine ourselves for the moment to the question of embellishments. I suggest that we follow the somewhat difficult path marked by C. P. E. Bach's terminology rather than a modern, systematically constructed survey (as recommended, e.g., in the *New Grove Dictionary of Music and Musicians*).

In the study of the notational conventions of Haydn's music, two types of basic sources emerge: contemporary theoretical writings and the illuminating inconsistencies in the composer's notation. We must rely on the relevant contemporary writings as theoretical sources, that is, on the explanations of musical orthography, embellishments, and the rules of composition that Haydn himself is likely to have known and with which he could reasonably have expected performers of his music to be acquainted. Disregarding books devoted to the realization of the continuo, a rigorous screening of the possible theoretical works reveals that there are very few. The most important is undoubtedly C. P. E. Bach's *Versuch über die wahre Art, das Clavier zu spielen* (Essay on the true art of playing keyboard instruments)[2] (pt. 1 appeared in 1753 and pt. 2 in 1762). Haydn ac-

2. This is the translation of the title used by William J. Mitchell in his edition of C. P. E. Bach's essay (see his note on p. 27). The very ambiguity of the word *Clavier* is completely appropriate to the *Versuch,* which is a keyboard *tutor* in the broadest sense of the word. However, Bach states at the outset that "the clavichord is needed for the study of good performance" (p. 38). Moreover, Bach's

quired this pivotal work of eighteenth-century music making early in his career—according to my hypothesis, presumably in 1762[3]—continued to study it, and held it in high esteem into his old age,[4] even if a copy of the *Versuch* was not to be found in his library after his death.

In addition to Bach's *Versuch,* three or four other well-known theoretical books should be consulted as essential secondary sources, however restricted their validity for our purposes may be (none of them was in Haydn's library, according to the inventory of the estate), since there are certain aspects of Haydn's notation in which he was not a follower of Bach. These works may supply us with information indispensable for understanding these aspects or assist us in expounding Bach's German terminology.

The *Versuch einer gründlichen Violinschule* (A treatise on the fundamental principles of violin playing) by Leopold Mozart (first printed in 1756 and reprinted in 1770 and 1787, the year of his death) was the most widely used, fun-

---

entire teaching on notation and embellishments is to be understood as meant for practicing the clavichord. Note that, while I quote from Mitchell's translation, Bach's C clef has been restored in the musical examples because the transcription into the G clef considerably alters the original notational picture in several instances. Furthermore, the errors in the musical examples of the English edition have been tacitly corrected, and original German terms have been added in brackets whenever it seemed reasonable to do so. It is difficult even for native speakers of German to construe the exact meaning of the terms in Bach's text; any translation is bound to entail a certain amount of distortion and misinterpretation. Anyone reading Bach's essay in the original should keep Peter Cohen's *Theorie und Praxis der Clavierästhetik Carl Philipp Emanuel Bachs* (Hamburger Beiträge der Musikwissenschaft, 13 [Hamburg: K. D. Wagner, 1974]) close at hand.

3. My hypothesis is founded on the apparent relation between a reproving, didactic remark in Bach's book and the decisive change that took place in Haydn's notation in 1762. Georg Feder had already pointed out ("Zur Datierung Haydnscher Werke") that, until sometime in 1762, Haydn notated only eighth-note appoggiaturas, even in places where a sixteenth note or a quarter note would have been needed. Variable appoggiaturas, expressing the rhythm of a given passage more precisely, first appeared in the arias of *Acide* in 1762. In connection with "variable appoggiaturas," Bach (*Essay,* pt. 1, chap. 2) states that writing these appoggiaturas in their real length had started only fairly recently: "Prior to this all were written as eighths" (p. 87). Note that the original German wording differs somewhat: "hat man seit nicht gar langer Zeit angefangen, diese Vorschläge nach ihrer wahren Geltung anzudeuten, anstatt dass man vor diese alle Vorschläge durch Acht-Theile zu bezeichnen pflegte" (not so long ago one started to indicate these appoggiaturas according to their real value instead of marking all appoggiaturas by eighths, as one did before). Similarly, two sentences later a remark—"bey unserm heutigen Geschmacke hingegen" (to our present taste, however)—is missing at the start of the sentence that reads, "Today, we could not do without the notation of their real value" (p. 87). This would presumably have impressed any young composer, including Haydn. Thus, it is fairly obvious that Haydn must have decided to differentiate the notation of appoggiaturas after reading Bach. (In a very detailed study about the question of C. P. E. Bach's influence, Brown [*Keyboard,* 219] came to similar conclusions.)

4. Dies recorded that Haydn had bought the writings of Bach in his youth, in a bookshop in Vienna: "In his opinion Bach's writings form the best, most basic and useful textbook ever published" (Dies, 95). On the issue of C. P. E. Bach's influence on Haydn, see also Bettina von Wackernagel, *Joseph Haydns frühe Klaviersonaten,* 62–101; A. Peter Brown, "Joseph Haydn and C. P. E. Bach"; and the statements by James Webster and Eugene Helm at the 1975 Haydn Congress in Washington (*Haydn Studies,* 338, 342 [Webster], 382–85 [Helm]).

damental treatise among musicians of the South German territories. Haydn, who was no less a violinist than a keyboard player, must have become acquainted, if only indirectly, with the basic information in the *Violinschule* in the course of writing the string parts of his early symphonies and quartets, probably before he became acquainted with C. P. E. Bach's writing. A feature of Haydn's notation that may presumably be attributed to the indirect influence of Leopold Mozart (and the Italian tradition in Vienna in general) is that he preferred writing out ornaments in small notes, which indicated the values more precisely and were easier for amateurs to read, than using conventional abbreviated symbols.

The *Versuch einer Anweisung die Flöte traversiere zu spielen* (On playing the flute), a famous flute tutor by Johann Joachim Quantz (1752), represents a somewhat more old-fashioned approach to ornaments and probably exerted very little influence on Haydn in this respect. Nevertheless, it proves a key work in other, general musical issues such as tempo.

The *Klavierschule,* which is actually a clavichord tutor, by Daniel Gottlob Türk (1789) appeared too late to be an external source of or inspiration for Haydn's notation. Its merit lies rather in illuminating the changes that the interpretation of C. P. E. Bach's theory underwent by the time Haydn's last sonatas appeared.[5]

The *Clavier-Schule, oder kurze und gründliche Anweisung zur Melodie und Harmonie* by Georg Simon Löhlein (1765; 2d enlarged ed., 1773) is, in comparison with the previous sources, only a tertiary source, one that was not known to Haydn at all.[6] The reason that it will nevertheless be cited occasionally is that it

5. Comparing Haydn's and W. A. Mozart's notation and ornamentation, I see the situation as outlined below:

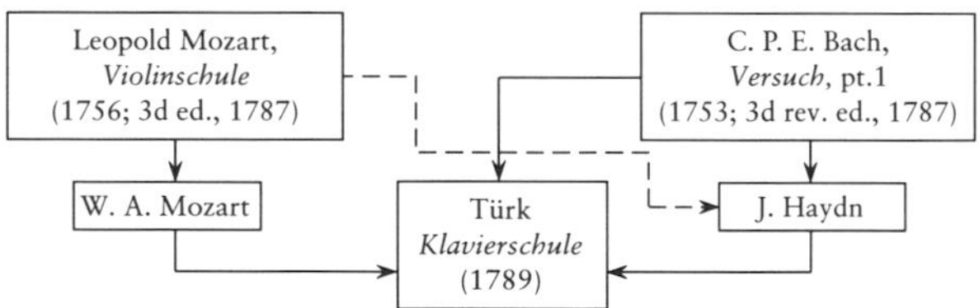

Mozart was an adherent of his father's teachings, without appearing to have been influenced by C. P. E. Bach. Haydn drew on Bach's book to improve his knowledge in the period following his formative years, during which he was largely self-taught with regard to notation. He must also have grown familiar with the simpler (string) notational tradition of Austrian musical practice, similar to and perhaps partly influenced by Leopold Mozart's teaching. As far as ornamentation is concerned, W. A. Mozart and Haydn do not seem to have learned from each other. Türk's book, while following Bach's principles, also reveals to a large extent how musicians of the time understood the notation of W. A. Mozart, Haydn, and their contemporaries.

6. In the later editions of Löhlein's work, knowledge of Haydn's sonatas is already apparent. This is borne out by the musical examples, cited anonymously and partly transposed, in the *Fünfte Auflage, umgearbeitet und vermehrt von Johann Georg Witthauer* (Leipzig and Züllichau, 1791).

reflects an approach to interpreting ornaments that is less substantial or elegant than Bach's but definitely practical, a circumstance that gives it value for understanding Haydn's notation.

Haydn's mechanical organ (*Flötenuhr*) pieces, realized by the Esterházy librarian, musician, and ingenious mechanic Joseph (Primitivus) Niemecz, were once thought to deliver authentic information about the contemporary understanding—although not necessarily Haydn's own reading—of the actual notes and rhythms of some typical ornaments and appoggiaturas. After the extremely careful transcriptions of the pieces of all three clocks became available,[7] it was obvious that Niemecz's realizations of the ornaments were neither unambiguous nor consistent. Thus, this is a significant source, but a relatively late (ca. 1792–93) and unreliable one. It will, however, be consulted on certain matters.

The second type of source is inconsistencies in the composer's notation, for example, when the same formula is written in the same movement at one time in small-note notation and at another in normal size notes or once with ornament signs and elsewhere with ornaments in small notes. The number of such examples is restricted because for these purposes only autograph manuscripts are reliable enough and only absolutely certain analogies may be taken into account. But these few sources allow us to resort to Haydn himself to resolve contradictions in certain disputed matters.

The pioneering work of Heinrich Schenker, *Ein Beitrag zur Ornamentik* (1904), no longer suffices for explaining Haydn's notation. Meant as a kind of introduction to the piano music of C. P. E. Bach, this book was also regarded as a key work on the ornamentation problems in Haydn, Mozart, and Beethoven by at least two generations. But Schenker burdened his fundamentally excellent work with so many arbitrary readings, and in the meantime our knowledge of Haydn's own notation has increased so much, that it appears more useful to go back to the primary sources of information rather than to continue arguing his points. Likewise, I cannot unreservedly recommend the work of Frederick Neumann, today's leading authority on ornamentation, in connection with Haydn. In his *Ornamentation in Baroque and Post-Baroque Music* (1978), and in his paper read at the Haydn Congress in Vienna in 1982, Neumann is so dead set against C. P. E. Bach and goes to such lengths to relieve us of false

Among the examples of the *unveränderlich-kurze* (short, invariable) appoggiaturas (p. 24), the beginning of two movements of the *Auenbrugger* sonatas (52 G II and 50 D I, respectively) can be found under the heading *Zu Anfange eines Stückes* (for the beginning of a piece):

7. Sonja Gerlach and George R. Hill, eds., *J. Haydn: Stücke für das Laufwerk*, vol. 21 of *JHW* (1984).

doctrines—without paying heed to the nature and chronological development of Haydn's notation—that I think we would arrive at new erroneous doctrines if we followed his ideas. Paul Badura-Skoda's concise study "Beiträge zu Haydns Ornamentik" has a similar anti-Bach trend in many ways; in some areas, such as the rendition of the trill and the short trill, it leads to unacceptable conclusions.

Sandra P. Rosenblum's *Performance Practices in Classic Piano Music* (1988), although not a Haydn study per se, is by far the best available guide concerning performance-practice problems in Haydn's keyboard sonatas, including ornaments. She does not have an anti-Bach prejudice but carefully scrutinizes all significant contemporary treatises, including their textual modifications and corrections in later editions, as well as the notation of the major keyboard composers of the era. One might question whether another study can be justified. Apart from the fact that the Hungarian edition of my book preceded Rosenblum's studies, a different approach, focusing on Haydn and based exclusively on the sources relevant to him, still seems to be useful.

In my opinion, Carl Philipp Emanuel Bach's book ought to be read by all pianists. In the following, excerpts from his most important statements will be cited that, I believe, hold good for Haydn's sonatas (and are not narrowly restricted to playing the clavichord or to special questions of composition). For pianists, the chapter on fingering is one of the most essential parts of Bach's book. Since in Haydn's piano sonatas fingerings by the composer himself occur only twice (29 E♭ III, 20: 3-2-1 right-hand repetition; 56 D I, 23: phrasing a triplet passage with a fingering 3-2-1), I will leave it to other authorities to deal with the subject of Bach's fingerings.[8]

Sections 1–9 of this chapter follow the order of the second part of volume 1

8. The fingering 3-2-1 of the repeated sixteenth notes in the Allegro di molto movement of the Sonata in E♭ Major goes beyond the advice given by Bach (pt. 1, chap. 1, par. 90: "Tones repeated at a moderate speed are played by a single finger, but alternating fingers are employed in fast repetitions. Only two fingers should be used at a time") since Haydn lets the repetitions be carried out with three fingers. The fingering for the Andante con espressione movement of the Sonata in D Major is particularly interesting: had Haydn not forestalled it with the given fingering, musicians of the time would have played the three-note figure starting ***fz*** with the same fingering repeated for each figure, with a change of position, in a kind of natural, *inégal* rhythm. This tiny practical solution of Haydn's notation has immense importance: it requires a rhythmically even motion, still modern in those days, that does not drag in spite of the ***fz*** accents:

(*a*, Haydn's fingering. *b*, Typical eighteenth-century fingering.)

of Bach's *Versuch*. I have supplemented Bach's discussion with examples taken from Haydn's sonatas, particularly instances that are not self-evident or clearly explained by Bach's book. Sections 10–12 are additions that I consider necessary; they cover further conventions of Haydn's notation.

1. *C. P. E. Bach on Embellishments* (Manieren) *in General*

§ 1. "They [embellishments] are, in fact, indispensable. . . . They connect and enliven tones and [if necessary] impart stress and accent; they make music pleasing and awaken our close attention. Expression is heightened by them [*sie helffen ihren Inhalt erklären*]; let a piece be sad, joyful, or otherwise, and they will lend a fitting assistance. Embellishments provide opportunities for fine performance as well as much of its subject matter. They improve mediocre compositions. Without them the best melody is empty and ineffective, the clearest content clouded."

§ 2. "In view of their many commendable services, it is unfortunate that there are also poor embellishments and that good ones are sometimes used too frequently and ineptly."[9]

§ 6. "Embellishments may be divided into two groups: in the first are those which are indicated by conventional signs or a few small notes; in the second are those which lack signs and consist of many [normal size] short notes." (Note that Bach specifies here that composers may actually notate embellishments in normal size notes and rhythm.)

§ 10. "We shall see presently that many passages allow for more than one kind of embellishment. In such cases, the art of variation may be used to advantage; introduce first a caressing ornament, then a brilliant one, or for a change, if the passage permits, play the notes directly as written but always in furtherance of the true affect and in accordance with the rules of good performance which will be treated later."

§ 13. "To understand many things more clearly, the performer must possess a knowledge of thorough bass. It is a matter of experience that those who are not well grounded in the study of harmony fumble in darkness when they use embellishments."

§ 19. "All ornaments stand in proportioned relationship to the length of the principal note, the tempo, and the affect of the piece. In those cases where a

9. The German original is more forceful: "So viel Nutzen die Manieren also stiften können, so gross ist auch der Schaden, wenn man theils schlechte Manieren wählet, theils die guten auf eine ungeschickte Art ausser ihrem bestimmten Orte und ausser gehörigen Anzahl anbringet" (As great as the advantages of embellishments may be, equally great is the harm done if, on the one hand, wrong embellishments are chosen or, on the other hand, good ones are employed awkwardly, outside their proper place, or too profusely).

variety of embellishments is used and the performer is not too restricted by the affect, note that the more tones contained in an ornament, the longer the principal note must be."[10]

§ 23. "All embellishments notated in small notes pertain to the following tone. Therefore, while the preceding tone is never shortened, the following tone loses as much of its length as the small notes take from it."

2. *Appoggiaturas*

§ 1. "Appoggiaturas are among the most essential embellishments. They enhance harmony as well as melody. They heighten the attractiveness of the latter by joining notes smoothly together and, in the case of notes which might prove disagreeable because of their length, by shortening them while filling the ear with sound. . . . Appoggiaturas modify chords which would be too simple without them."

§ 2. "Appoggiaturas are sometimes written in large notation and given a specified length in a bar. At other times they appear in small notation."

§ 4. "In execution some appoggiaturas vary in length; others are always rapid." (Note that this was Bach's way of distinguishing what is called the "long" appoggiatura [i.e., with determined length] from the "short" appoggiatura, in present-day usage.)

§ 5. "Because of their variability, such appoggiaturas have been notated of late in their real length (Fig. I). Prior to this all were written as eighths." (See ex. 2 for the relevant figures from Bach's book.)

§ 6. "We can readily see in the examples [of this figure] that at times appoggiaturas repeat the preceding note (a), at times they do not (b), and that the following note may lie a step above or below, or it may be separated from the ornament by a leap."

§ 7. "With regard to the execution we learn from this figure that appoggiaturas are louder than the following tone, including any additional embellishment, and that they are joined to it in the absence as well as the presence of a slur. . . . An undecorated, light tone which follows an appoggiatura is called the release [*Abzug*]."

§ 11. "In addition the examples of Fig. VI and their executions should be carefully studied."

10. Musical example from the third edition, 1787:

Ex. 2. Appoggiaturas from C. P. E. Bach's examples. Fig. I, Variable appoggiaturas (i.e., the so-called long appoggiaturas): 1), example by C. P. E. Bach; 2), the rhythm of the appoggiatura as described in Bach's text. Figs. VI–VII, Special cases of long appoggiaturas. Figs. VIII–IX, Invariable short appoggiaturas.

§ 12. "The examples under Fig. VII are [also] frequent occurrences." (Note that these types of appoggiaturas are certainly bewildering for present-day musicians, but they do occur in Haydn's music as well—with an even more careless notation of the rhythm of the appoggiatura.)

§ 13. "It is wholly natural that the unvariable short appoggiatura should appear most frequently before quick notes, Fig. VIII (a). It carries one, two, three, or more tails and is played so rapidly that the following note loses scarcely any of its length. It also appears before repeated (b) as well as unrepeated (c) long notes. Further, it is found in caesurae before a rapid note (d), and in syncopated (e), tied (f), and slurred passages (g). In all such cases, the character of the notes remains unchanged. Example (h) with an ascending appoggiatura is better when the ornament is played as an eighth. For the rest, the short appoggiatura remains short even when the examples are played slowly."

§ 14. "When the appoggiaturas fill in the interval of a third, they also are played quickly [they also are short]. However, in an Adagio their expression is more tender when [as in Fig. IX (a)] they are played as the first eighth of a triplet rather than as sixteenths. The accurate division of triplets can be learned from (b). For various reasons the resolving tone of a melody must often be quitted abruptly. . . . [The appoggiatura here] too must be played rapidly [very short] (c). . . . Appoggiaturas before triplets must also be played quickly so that the [triplet] rhythm remains clear (d) and distinguishable from that of (e). When the appoggiatura forms an octave with the bass it is played rapidly because of the emptiness of the interval (f). On the other hand, it is often prolonged when it forms a diminished octave (g)."

§ 20. "The decorating of appoggiaturas leads us to other embellishments which will be explained later. Because these are often written as small notes, it is better to write the appoggiatura in such cases as a large note with its length clearly notated."

§ 21. "However, appoggiaturas are often written in large notation as a means of indicating that neither they nor the following tones are to be decorated."[11]

These selected passages from C. P. E. Bach's essay provide a useful basis for distinguishing the typical appearances of the *short* and *long* appoggiaturas (as I will call them, for simplicity's sake) in Haydn's sonatas. I assume that the musician is using a modern urtext edition that, despite the undeniable risk of uniformity in certain areas, has already dispelled the confusion that resulted from the

11. The paragraph on *Nachschlag* in the chapter dealing with the appoggiatura is not cited here (see also Mitchell's note in *Essay*, 98). The phenomenon of passing appoggiaturas as an ornament, written in small notes (*Nachschlag* or, as described by Leopold Mozart, *durchgehender Vorschlag, Zwischenschlag*), does not play a significant role in Haydn's notation.

completely careless and inconsistent notation of the rhythm of the appoggiaturas in contemporary sources (at least the *Wiener Urtext* has). Anyone who has worked with Haydn's autograph manuscripts or with the otherwise reliable copies made by his copyists (not to speak of contemporary typeset or engraved editions) will know that a careful notation of appoggiatura rhythms in agreement with C. P. E. Bach's book was far from characteristic of Haydn. The secondary sources have further confused the state of his notation of appoggiaturas, through negligence or capriciousness.

Apart from some exceptional cases of a short appoggiatura preceding a long note (e.g., ♪𝅗𝅥, ♪𝅝), the urtext editions unify the notation of appoggiaturas by halving rhythmic values (e.g., ♩𝅗𝅥, ♪♩, 𝅘𝅥𝅯♪, 𝅘𝅥𝅰𝅘𝅥𝅯), although bolder urtext editors clearly mark the short appoggiatura (in the *WUE* with a ♪ sign).[12] Moreover, in the cadential formulas of minuets and other movements in triple time, the conventionally misleading Haydnesque notation of the appoggiatura in the proportion of 1:2 (e.g., in $\frac{3}{4}$, ♩𝅗𝅥. instead of 𝅗𝅥𝅗𝅥. = 𝅗𝅥♩) is followed and not regularly commented on in the editorial notes.

Most of the doubtful cases are in a gray area where executing a given formula with short or long appoggiaturas has an almost identical effect owing to rapid tempo or small rhythmic values. This is the only area with serious differences between Bach's explanations and Haydn's practice in his manuscripts. In Bach's fig. VIII (a) (see ex. 2), the ornament marked [NB] is a short appoggiatura according to Bach, but in Haydn's music it is unambiguously a long one. How can this be demonstrated? In addition to dozens of musical and motivic arguments and analogies, there exist, fortunately, some slips of the pen in the autograph manuscripts of some sonatas that shed light on the matter.

In case *a* of example 3, the passage in the recapitulation is carelessly notated in normal size notes, although, according to the eighteenth-century principle—to which Haydn adhered with an almost orthodox belief—unslurred, dissonant melodic notes occurring on an accented beat were supposed to be written in small notes. In this sense, the notation of case *c* is correct because the appoggiatura e^2 is a consonant tone of the chord. This accounts for the difference between the very first bar and the first bar after the repeat sign of the Minuet in E Major, case *d*. And it is in this sense that in the mixed notation of case *b* the notation with the appoggiatura is more correct. In general, it appears that Haydn understood ♪♩♫ to mean ♫♫ and 𝅘𝅥𝅯♩♬ to mean ♬♬.[13] Moreover, in relatively fast tempos, he would most likely write ♪♫ to mean ♫♪. When Haydn wanted to have a genu-

12. The eighth-note appoggiatura with a crossed flag used by the *WUE* editor is, of course, an indication of brevity only; when playing such a note, the value of the succeeding principal note must be shortened.

13. In the *Flötenuhr* realizations, however, there are unaccented short readings (i.e., appoggiaturas before the beat) too; see, e.g., no. II.2, mm. 15 and 19, of the 1793 clock and the undated clock.

inely short appoggiatura, as, for example, in a Moderato opening movement, he wrote it out in normal size notes (see ex. 4).

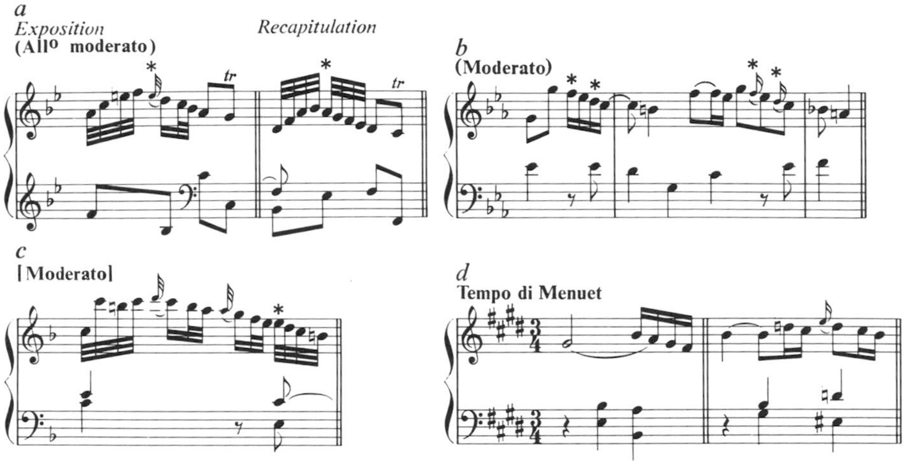

Ex. 3. *a*, 20 B I, 38 (exposition) and 116 (recapitulation). *b*, 29 E♭ I, 15. *c*, 38 F I, 42. *d*, 37 E III, 1, 9.

Ex. 4. 44 F I, 17–18.

For slow tempos, the situation may be different. The Adagio of the *London* C Major Sonata, no. 60, a less elaborate version of which had been published separately before the publication of the full sonata, throws an interesting light on the question of passages that are similar or thought to be analogous. Cases *a* and *b* of example 5 show the differences between the exposition and the recapitulation of the earlier version. The first is perhaps the conventional Adagio formula with written-out appoggiaturas (the supposed traditional notation is in brackets), while the latter is a rhythmically condensed (diminished) form. This is therefore a decorated variant belonging to the category of the varied reprise. The final version becomes a kind of revision in that *b* is notated in *c* and *d* with precisely given rhythm and articulation. Thus, the more stereotyped embellishment consisting of short appoggiaturas gave way to an exceptionally beautiful embellishment of long appoggiaturas.

Ex. 5. *a–b,* Adagio, early version of 60 C II, 7 (exposition), 40 (recapitulation). *c–d,* Final version of 60 C II, 7 (exposition), 40 (recapitulation).

Let us add two suggestions to the interpretation found in the *Wiener Urtext* that offers an explanation for innumerable special problems. However unusual the long-lasting dissonance between the right hand and the left and the long double appoggiatura may sound to our ears, it is most likely that a powerful effect of this sort—a stressed dissonance with a graceful resolution—was much favored in the eighteenth century. For that matter, the 2:1 resolution of the Sonata no. 20 in B♭ Major (ex. 6*a*) cannot be correctly executed any other way; the half-note/eighth-note suggestion for the secondary theme of the Sonata no. 33 in C Minor (ex. 6*b*) is reinforced by the special cases of C. P. E. Bach's fig. VI as well (see ex. 2). The appoggiatura here is not, after all, an old-fashioned device meant to be modestly concealed. Rather, it is a conscious ornament, an emphasized embellishment that contributes to making this new theme, establishing a new key, worthy of the magnificent opening theme and of other notable ideas of the exposition of the C Minor Sonata.

Ex. 6. *a,* 20 B♭ II, 15–16.

Ex. 6. cont. *b,* 33 c I, 15–17.

3. *Trills*

§ 1. "Trills enliven melodies and are therefore indispensable. In earlier times they were introduced chiefly after an appoggiatura, Fig. XXII (a) [ex. 7], or on the repetition of a tone (b). The first is called the enclosed trill [*angeschlossener Triller*]. Today they are used in both stepwise and leaping passages, immediately at the beginning of a movement, in succession, at cadences, and, in addition, on held tones (c), *fermate* (d), and caesurae without (e) as well as with (f) an introductory appoggiatura. Thus, this embellishment has become versatile with the passing of time [*Folglich ist diese Manier anjetzo viel willkührlicher als ehedem*]."

§ 3. "The accomplished keyboardist has four trills; the normal, ascending, descending, and half or short trill."

§ 4. "Each has its distinctive sign in keyboard pieces, although all may be indicated by either the abbreviation *tr* or a cross."

§ 5. "The normal trill has the sign of an ⁓, Fig. XXIII (a), which is extended when it appears over long notes (b). Its execution is illustrated in Example (c). Since it always begins on the tone above the principal note, it is superfluous to add a small note (d) unless this note stands for an appoggiatura."

§ 6. "At times two short notes from below are appended. These are called the suffix [*Nachschlag*], and they serve to make a more rapid [more lively] trill, Fig. XXIV (a). The suffix is often written out (b) as well as indicated through an addition to the symbol (c). However, since the long mordent has almost the same symbol, I think it better to retain the ⁓ and avoid confusion."

§ 7. "Trills are the most difficult embellishments, and not all performers are successful with them. They must be practiced industriously from the start. Above all, the finger strokes must be uniform and rapid. A rapid trill is always preferable to a slow one. In sad pieces the trill may be broadened slightly, but elsewhere its rapidity contributes much to a melody. With regard to the amount of pressure, the performer must be guided by the nature of the passage, be it forte or piano, in which the trill appears."

§ 8. "In practicing the trill, raise the fingers to an equal but not an excessive height. Trill slowly at first and then more rapidly but always evenly. The muscles must remain relaxed or the trill will bleat or grow ragged. Many try to force it. Never advance the speed of a trill beyond that pace at which it can be played evenly. . . . When the upper tone of a trill is given its final performance it is snapped; after the stroke the upper joint of the finger is sharply doubled and drawn off and away from the key as quickly as possible."

§ 16. "The unsuffixed trill is best used in descending successions, Fig. XXVIII (a), and principally over short notes (b). The suffix is omitted from successive trills (c) and from trills followed by one or more short notes which are capable of replacing it (d). . . . Further, the suffix is not employed over triplets (e)."

§ 18. "In very rapid tempos the effect of a trill can be achieved through the use of the appoggiatura, Fig. XXIX."

§ 22. "The descending trill with its symbol and execution appears in Fig. XXXIV."

§ 27. "The ascending trill with its symbol and execution appears in Fig. XLI. Aside from the keyboard . . . it is often notated in the manner of the asterisked example."

§ 30. "The half or short trill [*der halbe oder Prall-Triller*], which is distinguished from the others by its acuteness and brevity, is notated for the keyboard in the manner of Fig. XLV. . . . Despite the upper slur, which reaches from the beginning to the end of the example, all notes are played except the last *f*, which [the 2d ed. reads: 'except the second *g* and the last *f*, each of which'] is tied to its preceding tone by another slur which indicates that it must not be struck. The large slur merely specifies the attendant phrasing [*Schleiffung*]."[14]

§ 34. "The half or short trill appears only in a descending second regardless of whether the interval is formed by an appoggiatura or by large notes, as

14. In Türk's *Klavierschule*, the first note of the short trill is already slurred to the appoggiatura (p. 272 [p. 262 in Haggh's translation), whereby a corruption reminiscent of *Schneller* is recorded:

Türk stated that in different tutors *c* and *d* are suggested, but added: "When one considers . . . that this ornament is basically a shortened trill without termination, then the notation in *b* or * will be found more correct than in *c*, because the common trill begins with the auxiliary tone." For a trill above a shorter note in a descending passage, Löhlein recommended (in both the 1765 and the 1773 editions of his *Clavier-Schule*) a kind of three-note *Schneller* for executing the "Pralltriller oder Abzug":

Had the performing tradition undergone a profound change? Nothing of the sort. Rather, the problem is that it is not known which edition (the first, 1753, or the second, 1759) of Bach's *Versuch* Haydn owned. The two editions differ in the wording of this thirtieth paragraph, a fact that has been taken into consideration in the literature only since Neumann (*Ornamentation*, 369–70). According to the second edition, the notes must be struck "except the second g and the last f" (which are

depicted in Fig. XLVII. It is found over short notes (Example a) or over those made short by a preceding appoggiatura (b). In this latter respect, when it appears over a note extended by a *fermata,* the appoggiatura is held quite long and the trill is quickly snapped as the fingers withdraw from the keys (c)."

§ 35. "In addition to its employment at cadences and *fermate* it is found in descending passages of three or more tones, as in Fig. XLVIII. In this use it resembles the unsuffixed trill in a descending succession and, like it, appears in passages where long notes are followed by short ones (Fig. XLIX)."

§ 36. "With regard to the execution of this trill, it must be pointed out that it is almost insuperably difficult to play it lightly at the pianoforte. Because the snap [*Schneller*] requires pressure, its performance on this instrument increases the volume. Yet it is impossible to perform our trill without this characteristic element. Hence the performer is faced with a dilemma, worsened by the fact that the short trill either by itself or combined with the turn often follows an appoggiatura and therefore, according to the rules governing the execution of appoggiaturas, must be played softly. The problem arises in all snaps, but particularly here, where it assumes its most radical form. I doubt that the most intensive

---

tied). The modern edition of C. P. E. Bach's sonatas by Carl Krebs (*Die sechs Sammlungen von Sonaten, Freien Fantasien und Rondos für Kenner und Liebhaber* [urtext edition] [Leipzig: Breitkopf & Härtel, 1953]), prints Bach's example in the introductory notes on embellishments with the two g notes tied, in agreement with the second edition of Bach's *Versuch* (from 1759 on; see *a* below), and this is how the proper execution of the short trill has become general:

The first edition indicates legato execution, but with the first note of the short trill struck (see the arrow in *b* above).

The crucial point still unanswered in connection with Haydn is with which of the two editions he was familiar and what kind of short trill execution he had in mind. It is my firm belief that the short trills of the early sonatas (probably even up to the early 1770s) can be best understood along the lines of the printing error of the first edition and executed by striking the beginning of the embellishment repeatedly.

In connection with the first theme of the opening movement of the Sonata no. 33 in C Minor, where a three-note *Schneller* is usually played both in m. 4 and in m. 7, let me raise the point of the relation between ornamentation and articulation, which cannot be overstressed. Is the ~ played as if it were above an inside note of a legato group of notes? (See the dotted slurs in *a* and *c,* respectively, in the example below.) The three-note *Abzug* is natural, although the possibility of the more elegant delayed *Pralltriller* also emerges. But in the following example (33 c I: *a–b,* m. 7; *c–d,* m. 4), with relatively detailed articulation, Haydn does not demand legato here, as a result of which a *movimento ordinario* rhythmic performance becomes effective (see p. 115). That is, the note with the ~ begins after the separation (see *b* and *d* below); thus, a four-note short trill may be played. In my opinion, the latter better fits the instrument and the performing style of those days:

practice can lead to complete control of the volume of the short trill at the pianoforte."

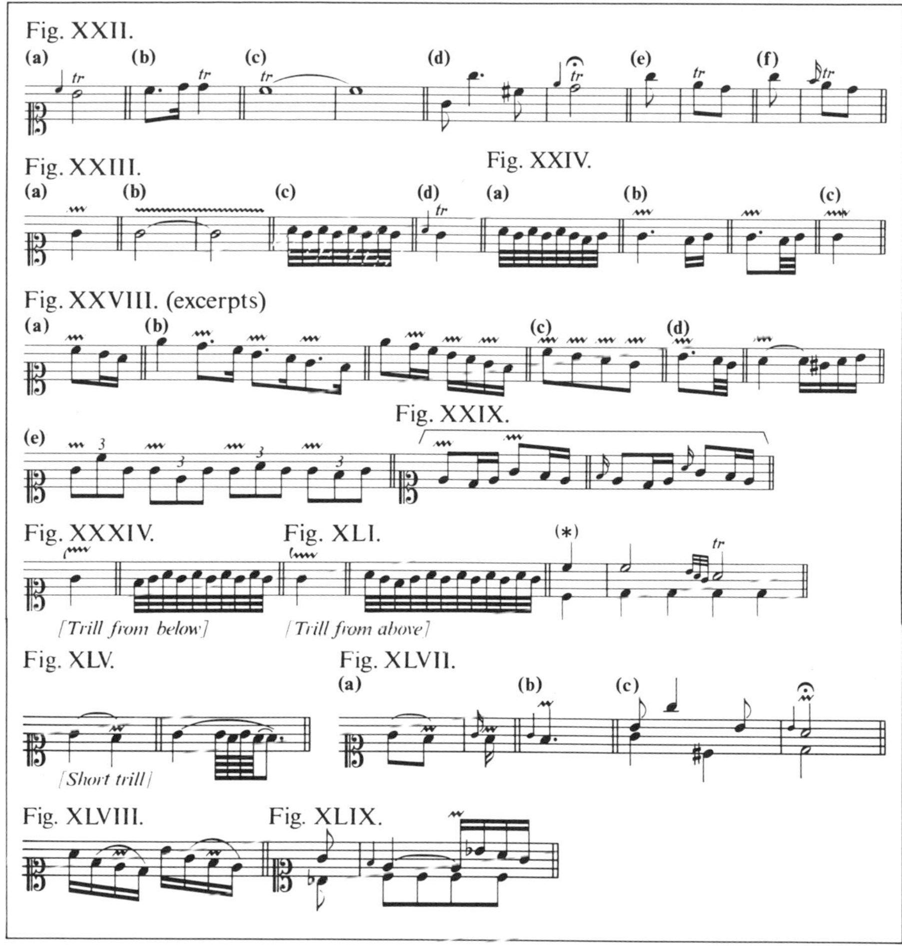

Ex. 7. Trills from C. P. E. Bach's examples.

Haydn's notation of trills (ex. 8) can generally be well interpreted by means of Bach's signs and explanations. As a rule, Haydn specifically indicated the less frequent kinds of trill, that is, those differing from the normal trill starting on the upper auxiliary note. To designate a trill starting on the lower auxiliary note he used both the trill found in Bach's Fig. XXXIV (in ex. 7; see ex. 8*a, e*) and the traditional notation in small notes (ex. 8*b*). In case *d* the d♯² beginning of the trill starts simultaneously with a♯¹ in the left hand precisely to avoid consecutive fifths (which accounts for the presence of this embellishment here). As a matter of fact, under normal conditions (i.e., in an unslurred passage, on a note after a rest, etc.), starting a longer trill with the principal note could be unambiguously expressed in the notation of the young Haydn's time only with the anticipation notated in normal size or small notes in front of the trill. Although the main-note trill seems to represent the "common" trill by the time of the *Flötenuhr* realizations of 1792–93, I find no serious evidence in Haydn's mature notation that he revised his upper-note trill concept on the basis of C. P. E. Bach's treatise and the tradition of Leopold Mozart.[15]

Ex. 8. *a*, 36 C I, 35. *b*, 33 c II, 10. *c*, 38 F I, 3. *d*, 37 E III, 6. *e*, 38 F II, 30. *f*, 60 C II, 17. *g*, 60 C I, 129. *h*, 52 G II, 59. *i*, 59 E♭ I, 33.

Haydn seems to have been as generous as his contemporaries in the matter of writing out the termination of the trill, either in normal-size notes or in small

15. A statistical analysis of all the trills in the *Flötenuhr* pieces would not give any definitive evidence. For one thing, the two clocks give different realizations of some of the same pieces. For example, in no. I.4, the 1792 clock gives an upper-note trill, the undated clock a main-note trill; in no. II.4, the 1793 clock gives an upper-note trill, the undated clock a main-note trill. Moreover, even in one version of a piece, the same trill motive may have different realizations; e.g., in no. II.4 of the undated clock, mm. 1ff. have trills starting on the upper note, and mm. 33ff. have trills starting on the main note.

notes; the performers of the day were fully aware of when it was necessary and when it was superfluous. If a performer had arbitrarily chosen an opposite solution and succeeded in executing it convincingly, it was all the more a credit to him. A trill without a suffix was preferred to one with a lazy or careless suffix, as C. P. E. Bach remarked (§ 21). Haydn's notation seldom leaves room for doubt. As a matter of special interest, we may note that a suffix sign not found in C. P. E. Bach also occurs (ex. 8*c*). The quarter-note long trill with suffix is written out in a reflex-like manner (♩. ♬), particularly in minuets (e.g., the theme of the Menuet of 40 E♭ and 44 F). In one of his late *London* sonatas, a strange, forward-leaping, springing appoggiatura (ex. 8*f*) takes the place of the suffix; it must naturally be played before the beat. In the mature works of Haydn, irregular, cadenza-like trills are not rare. One instance is the case when the left hand reaches over the right to trill and this trill chain does not get resolved to the neighboring note (60 C I, 129; 52 G II, 59).

Haydn's use of the symbol of a short trill (ex. 9) was not always in agreement with the teaching of Bach, who stated (in §§ 34–35 and in his examples in fig. XLV; see ex. 7 above) that the *Pralltriller* can occur only on a descending second and—as his examples show—on a weak beat; see, for example, the series of short trills in the first theme of 31 A♭ I. The short trills of the Presto of 46 E III fall right on the accented notes of the bar and are not slurred to the preceding notes (because it is staccato, a tone repetition). The short trills in the first theme of 50 D I (ex. 9*b*) are similarly crisp, harpsichord-like ornaments. These are indeed ordinary trills on short notes: a four note rendition (♬♬) is recommended.

Ex. 9. *a*, 46 E III, 1. *b*, 50 D I, 1. *c*, 36 C I, 2. *d*, 36 C I, 20. *e*, 36 C I, 31. *f*, 36 C II, 10. *g*, 36 C II, 14. *h*, 36 C II, 38. *i*, 36 C III, 33. (* Upper-note trills.)

Subjective interpretation of Haydn's approximate trill notation is, however, often unavoidable. Seven examples (ex. 9*c–i*) taken from one sonata, the 1773 *Esterházy* (36 C), for which we have the autograph as well as the authorized printed edition and which appears in the two modern urtext editions in slightly different versions, will show some typical problems. To distinguish between (1) four-note ordinary trills on short notes, (2) three-note true C. P. E. Bach short trills, and (3) *Abzug*-type three-note ornaments in the middle of a slurred group of notes, one has to know whether the trilled note is detached or slurred. The urtext editions are sometimes misleading because missing slurs are supplied only if there is a slur present in a similar passage. In example 9*d*, neither *WUE* nor *JHW* has a slur, but it is a cadential formula that would normally call for a slur. In *c* and *g*, *WUE* correctly adds a slur; notice the suggested rhythm of the second 𝆖 in *c*, a Haydnesque notation of a "grace-note-like" beginning. The *tr* and 𝆖 ornaments marked with an asterisk in these examples are upper-note trills; probably the second one in *f* is too. In *i*, the 𝆖 signs are not abbreviations for the preceding *Schnellers* but indicate sharp four-note trills.

Haydn's notation does not supply us with any information on the speed with which the trills are supposed to be executed. We do not know if he preferred accelerating free trills or evenly measured trills (the *Flötenuhr* realizations did not necessarily register the composer's habits). It is conceivable that some instances of his late, seemingly more accurate notation of the termination of trills—as, for example, in the *Genzinger* Sonata (59 E♭ I, 34)—were meant to denote an even trill (here thirty-second notes) in a cantabile allegro environment.

4. *The Turn (∾) and the Haydn Ornament (⁓)*

§ 1. "The turn is an easy embellishment which makes melodies both attractive and brilliant. Its symbol and execution are shown in Fig. L [ex. 10]. Leaps of an octave or other large intervals necessitate the use of four fingers in order to perform it."

§ 3. "The turn is employed in slow as well as fast movements, and over slurred as well as detached notes. . . . It does not appear to advantage over a very short note because the time demanded for the performance of its several tones may detract from the clarity of the melody."

§ 4. "The turn is sometimes found alone, sometimes in combination with the short trill, and also after one or two thirty-seconds in small notation which are placed before a large note and differ from the appoggiatura, as we shall see presently."

§ 5. "When the turn alone is used, its symbol may appear either directly over a note or after it, somewhat to the right."

§ 6. "In the first case it is employed, as illustrated in Fig. LI, in stepwise successions (a), leaps (b), caesurae (c)."

§ 18. "The lack of symbols [except for] the keyboard often leads to the setting of the trill's sign in places where this ornament is ill at ease. Sometimes the speed of a piece makes it impossible to execute. . . . The performer should play a turn here."

§ 21. "The turn by itself may appear between a note or appoggiatura and the following tone in three situations: first, when the note is fairly long, as in Fig. LXI, Example (a); second, over a tie (b); third, after a dotted note (c)."

§ 22. "The execution of all turns in example (a) [Fig. LXI] is shown in the last illustration of that group."

Ex. 10. Turn examples by C. P. E. Bach. Fig. L, The performance of a turn in different tempos. Fig. LI (excerpts), Turn above the note. Fig. LXI (excerpts): (a)–(b), Turn before a note; (c), Turn above the dot of a dotted formula. Fig. LXIII, "Trilled turn." Fig. LXX, "Snapped turn" (not to be mistaken for the case given under [NB]).

§ 24. "In the third case (Fig. LXI, Example c), the two tones acquire dots and the turn is placed between them as illustrated in the notated execution of Example 2."

§ 28. "The trilled turn [*prallender Doppelschlag*] (Fig. LXIII) occurs either with or without a preceding appoggiatura.[16] However, like the short trill it is used only in a descending second, the first note of which is drawn into the embellishment."

§ 34. "While the trilled turn may be introduced solely after a descending slurred second, it is precisely this situation alone which will not suffer a snapped turn [*geschnellter Doppelschlag*]."[17]

§ 36. "The snapped turn should not be confused with the simple turn after a note. . . . In order to differentiate the two more clearly their execution is illustrated in Fig. LXX."

The turn is the most frequent ornament in Haydn's mature style and probably the most problematic one as far as proper performance is concerned. Its notation changed and developed with Haydn but always had synonymous forms in his manuscripts, forms that were often misunderstood by his copyists and engravers or interpreted in a confusing way. Haydn himself was guilty of using a "master symbol" (~), which today we call the "Haydn ornament," for different ornaments, sometimes a four-note turn and sometimes a three-note mordent.

At this point, before proceeding with a detailed study of the facts and problems connected with Haydn's turns, a general chronological survey is needed. Table 2 shows how few symbols were used by Haydn in the early divertimento sonatas, how this catalog grew more and more sophisticated, and how the number of ornaments notated by diacritical marks (as opposed to small notes) diminished in the 1780s. Note that, in the table, (1) only solo keyboard sonatas were considered, indeed even here selecting from the earlier ones, and (2) the *JHW* text was used because generally it gives a "reproduction" rather than an "interpretation" of the ornament symbols found in the best sources. The classification of the main symbols and the subclasses is somewhat unorthodox. Because of Haydn's routine, it was necessary to differentiate between ⁓ (*chevron*) in the proper, slurred, descending position of the *Pralltriller* and ⁓ (*trilletto*) as a substitute for ***tr***. Furthermore, by using arrows, I have suggested that the Haydn ornament (~) was employed in the position of both turn and mordent. Symbols that occur rarely are in parentheses; symbols corresponding to small-note forms of the same ornament are placed together.

16. "The effect of the combined ornaments can be most easily realized by thinking of a short trill with a suffix" (§ 27).

17. An idiosyncratic term coined by C. P. E. Bach: a combination of *Schneller* (see embellishment no. 8) and *Doppelschlag*.

TABLE 2 SYMBOLS USED BY HAYDN TO DENOTE ORNAMENTS

Date	Sonata	C. P. E. Bach-Type Compound Trills		Bach's Short Trill (*Pralltriller*)	∿ as a Trill	*tr*, Long Trills: ∿∿∿ etc.	Turn	Haydn Ornament	Mordent	Slides	Compound Turns	*Anschlag*
1750s	13 G (autograph)					*tr* (*tr*∿)		(∾)→				
	11 B♭					*tr*		←∾→	(♬)	♬	(♬)	
1766	29 E♭ (autograph)			⁀∿ ⁀∿ (a)	∿	*tr* *tr*∿∿∿		←∾→		♬		
–1771	20 B♭, 31 A♭, 32 g			⁀∿	∿	*tr* (*tr* (b))	∾ (♬) (c)	←∾→		♬		
1771	33 c (autograph)	(d) (∿∾ ∾∿)	(∿∿∿)	⁀∿	∿	*tr* (∿∿∿)	∾	←∾		♬		
1773	36–41, *Esterházy* set (autograph)		(∿∿∿ ∿∿∿)	⁀∿	∿	*tr*	∾	←∾→	(∿̸) (e)	♬	♪∾	
–1776	42, 47, *Anno 1776* set			⁀∿	∿	*tr*	∾	←∾→	(♬)	♬	(♬)	♬
–1780	48–52, *Auenbrugger* set			⁀∿	∿ (♬) (f)	*tr*	∾	←∾→		♬	(♬)	♬
1783	54–56, *Bossler* set			⁀∿	∿	*tr*	∾/♬			♬	(♬)	
1789 –90	58 C, 59 E♭ (partly autograph)			⁀∿	(∿)	*tr*	∾/♬			(♬) ♬	(♬)	
1794	60 C, 61 D, 62 E♭ (partly autograph)					*tr*	∾/♬					

a. II, 19–20 etc., the longer *chevron* only in the *JHW*.

b. 20 B♭ II, 10, no autograph evidence; and II, 76, only in the *JHW*.

c. 32 g II, 52 ff., only. The reason for the small-note notation instead of the ∾ symbol is probably that here, for the first time in the movement, both the upper and the lower note of the turn had to be altered (E♭-D-C♯), and this is the only unambiguous notation.

d. The first position (*chevron* above a turn symbol) is in I, 8, only. The second one (turn above the *chevron*) is in I, 9. In I, 66, 68, the turn is an editorial addition. There is no satisfactory explanation of these two different double symbols. The first one is C. P. E. Bach's formula, which should be slurred (see 1 below). Haydn's notation, however, has no slur—neither in the autograph nor in the Artaria edition—thus suggesting an upper-note anchored ornament (see 2 below). The second combination means either the same ornament (see 3 below) or a version beginning with a turn. I suggest that it might be played with a thirty-second anticipation as well (see 4 below):

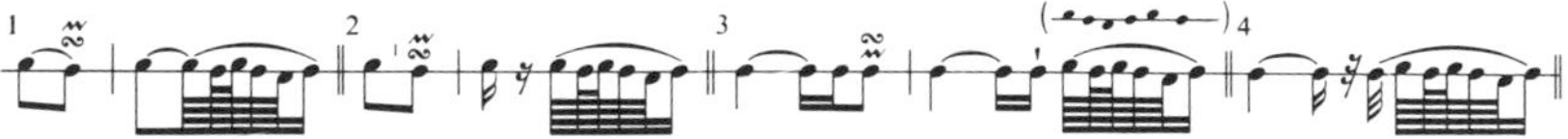

e. For example, 36 C I, 5; see the facsimile page in the *JHW*.

f. 52 G I, 18, only. This is Haydn's notation for a real *Schneller* with small notes as in C. P. E. Bach.

Extending the survey of the symbols Haydn used to all genres of his music would naturally result in a more reliable chronological ordering. Nevertheless, it is clear that Haydn confined himself to the use of the *tr* and the all-purpose Haydn ornament in the first decade of his composition of keyboard music, with scattered small-note indications for specific ornaments. Bach's *Pralltriller* appeared in the 1766 autograph of the Sonata no. 29 in E♭; the ordinary turn symbol appeared in the late 1760s (not yet in the 1767 autograph of the Sonata no. 30 in D); the first clear-cut ⁓ mordent symbol appeared in the 1773 set; and the three-small-note form of a turn first appeared in the *Bossler* sonatas (except the much earlier special use in 32 g).

Focusing again on the turn, the first difficulty is Haydn's own inconsistent notation. He often used clearly drawn ∾ and ⁓ signs or ⁓ and *tr* interchangeably in the same piece (see the examples in ex. 11); indeed, on a short note, all these signs signified a turn. The second difficulty derives from Haydn's very small and sketchy handwriting. It is not always easy to decide which symbol was used, especially if one has access only to a photocopy. There are different interpretations by individual urtext editors and different readings of uncertain cases. In Haydn's handwriting, (*a*) the conventional ∾ symbol looks more like ∼, ∼, or ∽; (*b*) the *tr* (with the designs t:, *tr*, +) sometimes approaches a scribbled Haydn ornament ⁓; and (*c*) the rare ⁓ symbol does not contrast much with the ⁓ sign. Haydn's own copyists learned to imitate the ⁓ master symbol, but foreign copyists and engravers in Vienna and abroad handled it carelessly, usually turning it into a mordent sign. Whenever a Haydn sonata survives only in such secondary sources—and this is the case for more than half his solo keyboard music—editors must depend on their musical sensitivity and expertise to decide whether to suggest the possible original in brackets.

For performers today, the crucial question is, naturally, whether to play all Haydn ornaments as turns automatically or whether to interpret the symbol from its context and choose between a turn and a mordent. The editors of the urtext editions of the sonatas are of the same opinion here. Christa Landon states that "the sign ⁓ is in the majority of cases equal to a turn (∾). . . . On the other hand it can be a mordent (⁓)." Feder suggests that the sign ⁓ "usually means a turn, but it can also be played as a mordent, depending on the musical context."[18] There are clever essays dedicated to this issue,[19] but no instructions are available in print for the performance of the individual sonatas.

I suggest that we consider a few phenomena with the help of the chronological diagram in table 2 above. First, as a general trend, the mordent was disappearing from use during the four decades of Haydn's sonata writing while the

18. Landon, in *WUE*, 1a:xviii; Feder, in *JHW*, 1:x.

19. For example, Christie Tolstoy's "The Identification and Interpretation of Sign Ornaments in Haydn's Instrumental Music."

Ex. 11. Turn, Haydn ornament, mordent, and trill used ambiguously in the text of Haydn's sonatas. *a,* Inconsistent notation in the autograph: (i), 29 E♭ I, 31 (exposition), 89 (recapitulation); (ii), 29 E♭ I, 43 (exposition), 95 (recapitulation); (iii), 41 A I, 2, 60; (iv), 44 F I, 13 (autograph), 71 (copy only); (v), 30 D II, 64; (vi), 29 E♭ I, 33. *b,* The source(s) differently interpreted by the editors of the urtext: (i), 33 c I, 59–60; (ii), 34 D I, 69–72. The ornaments above the rule are from the *JHW* (exact copies of the hardly legible signs of the autograph), those below the rule from the *WUE* (interpretation).

turn was becoming the central, irreplaceable ingredient of his late instrumental cantabile, more important than the trill. Second, the role of the ∿ as a master symbol was diminishing. The frequency of its use, particularly in the sonatas, can be seen in these phases: the problematic early phase, until ca. 1768–69, with the undifferentiated "Haydn sign"; the middle phase, with the joint use of ∾ and ∿; and a late phase of ♬♩ and ∾ turn notations, practically without the ∿ symbol[20] and with no mordent at all. As to the middle phase, one can assume that, as Haydn started to use the regular C. P. E. Bach–type keyboard turn (∾), his use of the ∿ symbol in the same piece was meant to express something else—a mordent. This is a reasonable assumption that seems to fit the sonatas transmitted in autographs or in other fairly reliable sources—in 31 A♭, 20 B♭, 32 g, 33 c, 36–41,[21] and 42–47,[22] ∾ = ♬♬, and ∿ = ♬—although several typically mordent-position, on-beat ∿ signs might be played as turns as well (e.g., 38 F II, 1; 46 E II, 1). The Artaria edition of the *Auenbrugger* sonatas (nos. 48–52) is less reliable,[23] and 34 D I has serious problems in this regard. I must admit that this plausible working hypothesis is somewhat undermined by the often-quoted evidence in the 1784 Piano Trio in F Major, XV:6 (III, 6), where in a unison statement of the theme the violin has ∿ and the piano ♬♩; that is, the Haydn ornament here is indeed a turn. In any case, the notation of the trios from the mid-1780s is another subject, and I still maintain the suggested differentiation in the solo sonatas listed above.

Now let us consider, independent of the sign, the proper rhythmic performances of the turn. In Haydn's music, there are four typical positions (see ex. 12).[24]

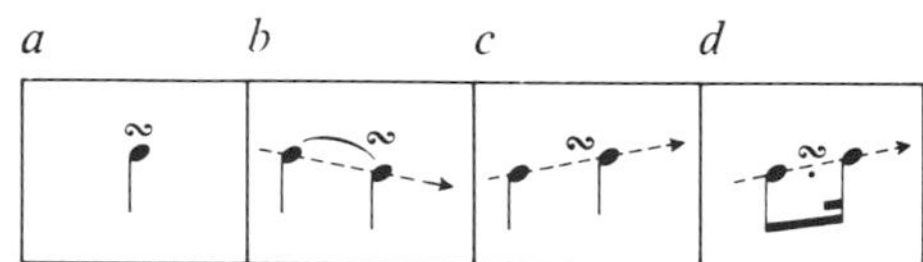

Ex. 12. Four positions of the turn in Haydn's music. *a,* First position, above a note. *b,* Second position, above a slurred note. *c,* Third position, before a note. *d,* Fourth position, above the dot.

20. It may be a coincidence that the ∿ disappears in the sonatas because Haydn continues to use it in other solo keyboard pieces (up to the 1793 autograph of the F Minor Variations, m. 5); there are many instances of its use in the piano trios, a few in string quartets written in 1790 (op. 64), etc.

21. Certainly, ∾ should stay in 41 A I, 36, 72–73 (∿ in *JHW,* ∾ in *WUE*).

22. There should be a turn in 44 F II, 5 (∿ in *JHW,* ∾ in *WUE*), and in 45 A I, 114; the ∿ as mordent does not fit the minuet cadence in 45 A, m. 223 (= III, 40), etc.

23. The ∿ signs are all turns in the second movement of 48 C; I prefer a turn in 49 c♯ I, 2–5 etc., and 50 D I, 35–36 etc.

24. It is essential to know that, owing to his studies with his father and to other experiences (but not with C. P. E. Bach), W. A. Mozart's use of the turn is considerably different from that of Haydn.

First position is a turn above a note (typically on the beat). The rhythm of this turn depends on the tempo and character of the piece, the instrument, and the performing style. In early sources (but not in sonatas), Haydn sometimes wrote it in an Italian notation (see ex. 13*a*). Several times, if he intended a "singing" turn, he wrote a less rapid appoggiatura-plus-main-notes formula (see ex. 13*b*).

Ex. 13. *a,* String Quartet III: 8 V, 18. *b,* 13 G I, 8; 32 g I, 1; 60 C I, 8.

Occasionally, it is not clear what Haydn had in mind when he put turns on an ascending set of notes where mordents might be more likely, as, for example, in the right-hand solo passage of the A♭ Major Sonata, no. 31 (see ex. 14*a*). Because of the step between a♭ and b♮, the first suggestion (i) sounds awkward; a voluntary upbeat slurring helps find sensible turns, with either an accented (ii), an anticipated (iii), or a grace-note (iv) rhythm.

An important subclass of Haydn's first-position turns is the snapped turn (*geschnellter Doppelschlag*).[25] This is a problematic group because Haydn adapted the small-note anticipation formula recommended by Bach (see the first theme of 39 D I; ex. 14*b*) but wrote it both with his late-style, four-small-note notation (see 59 E♭ I, 8; ex. 14*c*) and with normal-sized anticipation as well (43 E♭ II, 1; ex. 14*d*). I am convinced that these are chronological variants of the same idea and that all three can be played as a brilliant, on-beat ornament (see ex. 15).

Leopold Mozart described two of the four positions that I discuss. He called only the third-position turn *Doppelschlag* (chap. IX, § 27). The first-position turn-like ornament he called the "dritte Gattung der *Mordente*" (chap. XI, § 9–10), a "biting" prebeat ornament. His son used these two and, with a change of style, added the fourth-position turn above the dot, but he preferred a four-small-note form of notation (see *a* below) and had two favorite rhythmic variants in normal-sized notation (see *b–c* below):

The second position is absent in his music (see my "Wolfgang Amadeus Mozart 4-hangos ornamense" [W. A. Mozart's four-note ornament], in *Zenetudományi Dolgozatok 1983* [Budapest, 1983], 17–32). Those who know the 1979 Hungarian version of this book will recognize that I have considerably revised the section on the turn.

25. See Bach, *Versuch,* §§ 34–36.

a (i) (ii) (iii) (iv)

b (i) Allegro (ii) (Adagio)

c (Allegro) (i) (ii) (iii) (iv)

d

e Tempo di Minuet not recommended recommended

Ex. 14. *a,* 31 A♭ I, 29. *b,* "Snapped turn": (i), old-style notation (39 D I, 1 [1773]) and its rendition; (ii), new-style notation (52 G II, 6 [1780]), the same as C. P. E. Bach might have written, and its rendition. *c,* Small-note notation of the "snapped turn" (59 E♭ I, 7–8), with suggested renditions ([i]–[iv]). *d,* Normal-sized anticipation (43 E♭ II, 1). *e,* The suggested singing turn in the *Genzinger* finale (59 E♭ III, 16 [with renditions], 20).

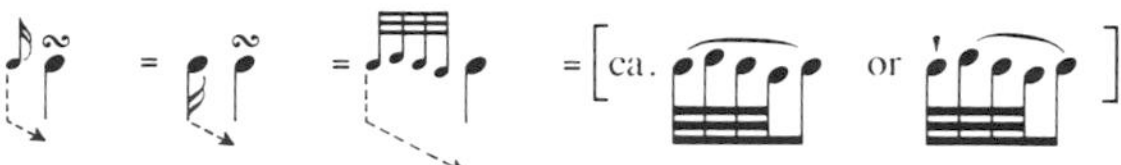

Ex. 15. Löhlein (*Clavier-Schule* [1st ed.]) gives this notation with a "snapped" staccato beginning of the snapped turn, which he calls *der vermehrte Doppelschlag.* Note that the first four notes were incorrectly printed as thirty-second notes in the first edition; they were corrected to sixty-fourth notes in the second edition.

In a minuet rhythm, there are special cases, mainly in connection with the upbeat third quarter, dependent on the slur or on the particular rhythmic context of the movement (see the suggested singing turn in the *Genzinger* finale,[26] shown in ex. 14*e*).

Second position is a turn above a note that is slurred to the previous one. This is a rare type in Haydn's style and sounds like a "delayed mordent" (see Türk's example, reproduced in ex. 16*a*), that is, a three-note ornament, an "inverted *Pralltriller*." This probably explains the controversial difference in notation between the exposition and the recapitulation of the A Major Sonata, no. 41, mentioned before. A slurred mordent in the context is just a slight variant of the second-position three-note turn (ex. 16*b*).

Ex. 16. *a,* Türk, *Klavierschule,* 4:3, 73. *b,* 41 A I, 18–19 (exposition), 72–73 (recapitulation).

One of Haydn's compound turns, a rare one appearing only in slow movements, belongs to this class. It is written with four small notes ( ) and stands for a turned appoggiatura (approx.). One has to play it on the beat, but since it is preceded by very short notes, the general impression is a free-style, improvisation-like, rich ornament, often in the guise of a trill, which may start before the stressed beat (see ex. 17).

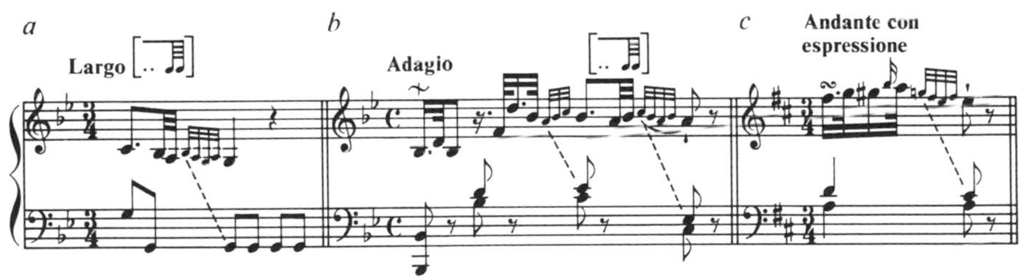

Ex. 17. *a,* 11 B♭ II, 4. *b,* 44 F II, 1. *c,* 56 D I, 73.

Third position is a turn before a note. In Haydn's sonatas, we find an old-style (diacritical) and a new-style (small-note) notation of this kind. The first one was introduced in the 1773 set (ex. 18*a*) and was in fact one and the same motive

26. The same rhythm was realized by Niemecz in the *Flötenuhr* transcription of the *Clock* Symphony minuet (see no. III.3).

in different sonatas. Here, a rendition such as suggested by Leopold Mozart gives a more natural rhythm than the orthodox C. P. E. Bach version. Moreover, owing to the octave shift, the compound notation of the E major recapitulation is a strong argument (ex. 18*c*).

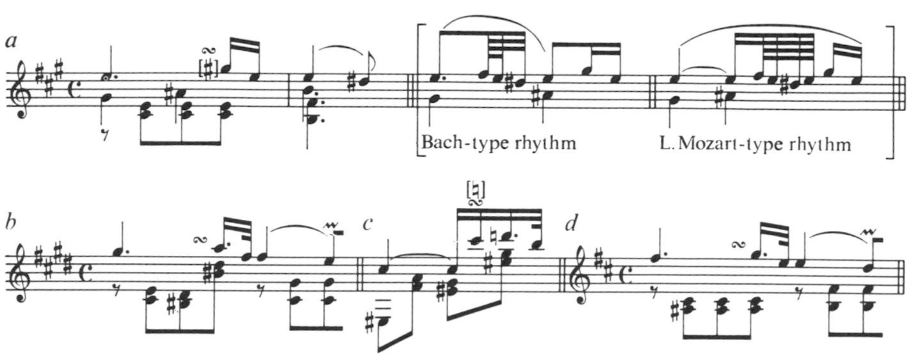

Ex. 18. *a,* 41 A I, 9. *b,* 46 E I, 9. *c,* 46 E I, 50. *d,* 47 b I, 50.

The new-style notation of a turn before a note looks like a first-position turn, but it appears on a very short note that is always on a weak beat. This was a practical notation for the dilettante because, as soon as the player learned that the three-small-note figure before a note had the same meaning as a turn symbol above the note, the beginning of the four-note turn was clear. In keyboard trios, Haydn introduced it earlier (XV:5, 1784); the first sonata that had this new form was 58 C (see ex. 19).

Ex. 19. 58 C I, 1. *a,* Old-style notation (reconstruction). *b,* New-style notation, full form and abbreviated form. *c,* Rendition.

Fourth position is a turn above the dot, that is, in the middle of a dotted-rhythm formula.[27] This is the most frequent position of the turn in Haydn's music. The problems are considerable, and a chronological orientation is absolutely necessary. There is a normal-speed basic form, mostly in common-time move-

27. In Haydn's time, it was indeed placed above the dot. In his letter of 10 December 1785 to Artaria, Haydn warned the engraver, "All the way through, the dots ought to be further away from the notes, so that the sign ∾ comes directly over the dot" (Haydn, *CCLN,* 51).

ments, with an "old-style" diacritical notation (ex. 20*a*), following C. P. E. Bach's model. Around 1780, but occasionally earlier too (see ex. 21*b*, 43 E♭), Haydn simplified this into a "new-style" notation that expressed the compound nature and the actual rhythm of this ornament in an easily intelligible way (ex. 20*b*). The performance of both forms should be practically identical, except there are hints in Haydn's late ornaments, written out in full with normal-size notes, that point to the triplet and not to the Bach-type square rhythm in the middle section.

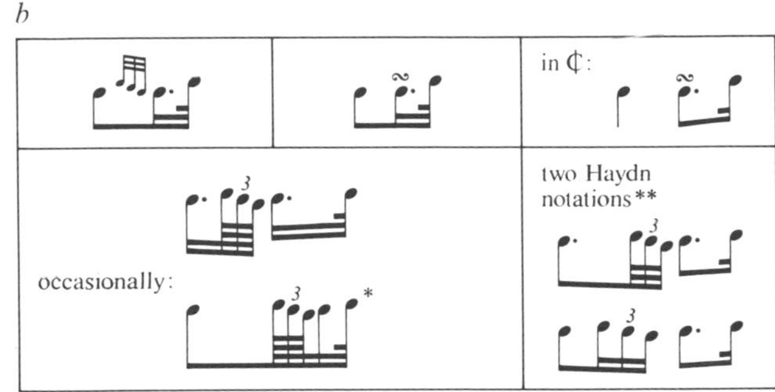

Ex. 20. *a,* Old-style notation. *b,* New-style notation (from ca. 1780 on).
* This rhythm occurs in a *Flötenuhr* realization, no. I.2, m. 15, of the undated clock. I think that a few unusual slurs by Haydn might have been understood in this way in the late eighteenth century, specifically if the slur gave a direct indication of down-bow and up-bow, as in the Symphony no. 99, II, 9:

** Both are quoted from piano trio movements—XV:11 I and XV:12 I.

The quasi-overdotted rendition of the notation (ex. 20*a*) is recommended whenever the piece has ♪. ♬ movement as the characteristic dotted rhythm. In very early sonatas with motion in even sixteenth notes (e.g., 6 C I, 14), there is no reason for the overdotted interpretation. The E Major Sonata, no. 15 (see ex. 21*a*), is a borderline case. The sources are confusing; the Haydn ornament probably belongs over the first note and represents a mordent. If it belongs over the dot, as the *WUE* suggests, I recommend an overdotting of the ♪. ♬ in the whole piece; in measure 23 it seems necessary. In any case, from the E♭ Major Sonata, no. 29 (1766), on, the old-style diacritical notation was used according to C. P. E. Bach's teachings.

The turn in a dotted-style movement often worries the modern performer who plays on an instrument with a heavy action. Should he soften the sharp ending of the turn in a minuet-like Moderato (ex. 22*a*) to conform to the rest of the bar? Or should he play a slightly overdotted but not necessarily double-dotted rhythm after the turned figure? In a quite different context, in which various *emp-*

Ex. 21. *(See legend opposite).*

findsam effects embellish the beginning of each measure (with some dotted rhythms too, but not an extended dotted style), the fourth-position turn may be played in a less regular manner (see ex. 22*b*).

Ex. 22. *a,* 20 B♭ II, 3: (i), proper rendition of the turn leading to controversial dotting; (ii), the conventional solution; (iii), the recommended solution. *b,* 45 A III, 1: (i), rendition according to C. P. E. Bach; (ii), recommended rendition.

We do not know much about the authentic Haydn rhythm of a fourth-position turn in a fast tempo in a situation where there are many notes. I am convinced that the smooth, legato performance following the tradition of W. A. Mozart and Clementi,[28] which eliminates the dotted element (see ex. 23*a*), does not apply to Haydn. Two special notations, one from the score of a string quartet[29] and another from the C♯ Minor Sonata (see ex. 21*c* above), suggest useful Haydn patterns (ex. 23*b–c*). The first one is an all-purpose substitute; the second

28. Clementi, *Introduction to the Art of Playing on the Piano Forte* (1801), facs. ed. (New York: Da Capo, 1974).

29. From the String Quartet in D Minor, op. 9:

◄ Ex. 21. Presumed changes in the rhythm of the fourth-position turns. *a,* Before 1773, according to C. P. E. Bach's suggestion: (i), 15 E I, 1, 23 (before 1766); (ii), 40 E♭ I, 1 (1773); (iii), 41 A I, 2 (1773); (iv), 37 E I, 1 (1773). *b,* From 1776, Haydn's presumed new rhythm; this presumption is based on the inconsistent notation in 43 E♭ I, 23 (exposition), 119 (recapitulation). *c,* From 1778–80, presumed simplified rhythm: (i), this presumption is based on the notation in 49 c♯ I, 1 (first theme), 12 (transition); (ii), in fast tempo probably already in 1776: 42 G I, 1, with suggested rendition.

can be the choice in a very fast tempo and whenever an eighth-note upbeat or eighth-note movement is dominant (see 42 G in ex. 21*c*).

Ex. 23.

With the introduction of the new-style compound notation (in Sonatas 48–56, 58–62), two further phenomena have to be taken into consideration: the augmented notation of the compound form in *alla breve* movements (see ex. 20*b* above) and the "broken" form, as I call it, that is, the second half of a full motive (ex. 24). The second phenomenon is a tricky formula that needs to be recognized and understood. This time the ∾ symbol or the three small notes must be played before the beat.

Ex. 24. "Broken" form of a fourth-position turn.

It is not always easy to recognize the "broken" turned figure because Haydn's notation (or that of the existing secondary sources) often produces a confusing and inconsistent picture. In the *alla breve* Allegro of the B♭ Major Sonata, no. 55, the different notations in measures 25, 29, and 68 (ex. 25) may all mean the same broken figure or perhaps a special variant of it: four notes before the beat but in triplet subdivision owing to the left-hand motion.

Ex. 25. 55 B♭ I, 25, 29, 68.

Triple meter can be the source of further complications when the fourth-position turn is no longer an old-style lasting one beat but a figure with the notation lasting two-thirds of a full measure. The *Genzinger* Sonata—the only one with three movements in triple meter—has numerous examples that have not yet been fully explained by performance-practice scholars; the ornaments are generally played in rhythms that are traditional, but not necessarily correct or characteristic. Example 26 presents several cases, some of which are not fourth-position turns. First, we must take into account the fact that in the Allegro first movement and in the Tempo di Minuet finale the characteristic dotted rhythm is while in the Adagio it is . Next, we have to consider the metric strength of the second beat in a triple meter. In the finale (ex. 26*a*), owing to the upbeat theme, the second beat is the weakest in the measure. Therefore, the turn in measure 7 is a regular fourth-position one (iii). The turn in measure 1, although usually played the same way (i), is not a fourth-position turn since the slurred upbeat and the two staccato notes form a motive and the supposed middle part of the turn is detached from the beginning of the figure. Thus, I prefer to play it on the beat, in a crisp way (ii). In the first Allegro (ex. 26*b*), (i) and (iv) are third-position turns; (iii) is a regular fourth-position turn, as in (ii), but they must be played in one of the "Presto forms," preferably not just as a sextuplet.

The Adagio e cantabile theme (ex. 26*c*) is of course a hard test. On a modern piano with a heavy action, cantabile primarily indicates beautiful legato; for such a legato, an abundance of ornaments and small-note embellishments is highly disturbing, from both a technical and a musical point of view. But this is not a legato piece, as Haydn carefully indicated by his articulation marks. It needs breathing space, rhythmic inflection, sophisticated ornamentation, and a constant feeling of surprise. The second beat of the first motive, all through the piece and with continual variations, is first and foremost a repetition of the first note in a more forceful, or more delicate, or more pleading way (see mm. 5, 27, etc.). Therefore, the role of the three-small-note turn in measure 1 is not, using Bach's terms, to "connect tones," as with the traditional renditions, but rather to "enliven tones," as I recommend. The turn has to be detached from the first d, and we have to take Haydn's slurs seriously, playing the slur-ending tones, e♭ and a, respectively, in a slight and a somewhat shortened manner.

Further dilemmas arise in slow movements in $\frac{6}{8}$ time written in the 1780s and 1790s; in Haydn's music involving the piano, this concerns only the trios,[30] the German lieder, and the English canzonettas. There are, however, two important piano-sonata themes from around 1771 that need to be discussed here. The first one is in the minuet-style Allegretto second movement of 32 g: a turned upbeat motive in triple meter (ex. 27*a*) with three forms (i–iii). Of these, (ii) is a typical third-position turn; the nondotted form in major is a slower turn (iii). The

30. See, e.g., XV:7 II, the anacrusis of m. 1.

Ex. 26. Problems of the rhythm of a turn in triple time: examples from the *Genzinger* Sonata. *a,* 59 E♭ III, 1–2, 7–8: (i)–(ii), renditions of the turn in m. 1; (iii), rendition of the turn in m. 7. *b,* 59 E♭ I, 33–35, 40–41, turns ([i]–[iv]) and their renditions. *c,* 59 E♭ II: (i), turns in mm. 1–2, with renditions; (ii), mm. 5, 27.

Ex. 27. *a,* Three forms of a turned upbeat motive in triple meter ([i]–[iii]) in 32 g II, 1–2, 7–8, 35–37, with possible renditions of (i): (1)–(2), anticipated snapped turn; (3), dotted style, with turn on the beat; (4), the recommended grace-note form of the snapped turn; (5), snapped turn on the beat. *b,* 20 B♭ I, 1–2, with rendition as suggested in *WUE* (i) and the recommended rendition (ii).

most frequent form (i) is a great problem for the pianist. It used to be played as an anticipated turn like renditions (1) or (2),[31] but this was probably incorrect. My suggestion (3) may be a bit crude, but it keeps the dotted-style rhythm. A

31. According to Christa Landon (see her note in *WUE*) and Paul Badura-Skoda ("Beiträge," 417), the small-note form in m. 52 denotes the correct execution—meaning the rendition (1) in ex. 27*a*. There is, however, no rhythmic evidence for this.

snapped turn on the beat (5) goes far beyond what the notation suggests, but recall what we have said about the notational experiments with this ornament (p. 63). The best way to play it is rendition (4). The second interesting case of a theme with turns is the B♭ Major Sonata, no. 20 (ex. 27*b*). Instead of the rhythm suggested in the *WUE* (i), the best way to play it on a harpsichord or fortepiano is probably the grace-note form of a snapped turn (ii).

There is a last group of problems concerning the rhythm of a turn. What is to be done if a dotted rhythm with a turn in the right hand is against a triplet accompaniment? (See 55 B♭ I, 25ff.; 59 E♭ II, 66ff.; etc.) Is a sharper or a softer dotted rhythm required? From where should the turn start? Those questions will be dealt with in section 10 below.

5. *The Mordent*

§ 1. "The mordent is an essential ornament which connects notes, fills them out, and makes them brilliant. It may be either long or short. The symbol of the long mordent is shown in Fig. LXXII [see ex. 28*a*]. Its execution may be lengthened (a) if necessary, but the symbol remains the same. The short mordent and its execution are illustrated in Example (b)."

§ 2. "Although it is customary to play the long mordent only over long notes and the short over short notes, the symbol of the long ornament is often found over quarters or eighths, depending on the tempo, and that of the short mordent over notes of all values and lengths."

§ 3. "Example (c) of Fig. LXXII illustrates an unusual manner of performing a very short mordent. Of the two tones struck simultaneously, only the upper one is held, the lower one being released immediately, there is nothing wrong in this execution, provided that it is employed less frequently than the other mordents. It is used abruptly only, that is, in unslurred passages."[32]

Ornaments depicted by an unambiguous mordent sign seldom occur in Haydn's autograph manuscripts (see sec. 4 above on the turn), but they do exist. The *JHW* edition of the piano sonatas disguises this by printing ∻ and ⩫ uniformly as ∻.[33] Nevertheless, in some cases there is a clear ⩫ shape symbol in Haydn's handwriting, as can be seen on the facsimile page of 36 C (m. 5) in the *JHW*.

Despite the striking notational inconsistencies of the B Minor Sonata, no. 47, the execution of its ornaments does not cause any difficulties, even though

32. Usually called the *acciaccatura*.

33. "Da Haydn die Zeichen ∻ und ⩫ nicht unterscheidet, wird hier immer das doppeldeutige Zeichen ∻ gesetzt" (*JHW*, 1:x).

Ex. 28. Mordent, *Anschlag*. *a,* Mordent, C. P. E. Bach's examples. *b,* Mordent, Haydn's examples: (i), 47 b I, 1, 9; (ii), 36 C I, 5, with rendition. *c, Anschlag,* C. P. E. Bach's examples. *d, Anschlag,* Haydn's examples (45 A, mm. 171, 178, 170, 280). *e, Anschlag* (*) in Haydn's normal-sized notation (51 E♭ I, 8).

the secondary sources have used ~ signs. The ornament is, according to Bach's classification, a short mordent started on the beat.[34] Incidentally, there seems to be no direct evidence to support the French-style prebeat-rhythm mordent in Haydn's music; in his "court style" harpsichord sonatas, however, there are mordents in a dotted-rhythm context that the prebeat rendition would fit well (see 36 C; ex. 28*b*[ii]).

In Haydn's own vocabulary, the three-note "short mordent" was called *Halb Mordent,* that is, half mordent.[35] The evidence is in two often-quoted documents. The first is the famous angry letter to Artaria (10 December 1785): "You should put instead of the sign ***tr:*** the following: ,[36] since the first one, as the engraver has done it, means a trill, while mine is a half-mordent [*Halb Mordent*]. If therefore, the engraver doesn't know signs of this sort, he should inform himself by studying the masters, and not follow his own stupid ideas."[37] The second is Haydn's instructions to Niemecz for the realization of the *Flötenuhr* fugue with a mordent on the first note of the theme all through. Haydn speaks of the "folgender Halbe Mordent" and gives an example with two thirty-second small notes.[38]

6. *The Compound or Double Appoggiatura* (Der Anschlag)[39]

§ 2. "Both types are clearly recognizable in the illustrations of Fig. LXXX" (see ex. 28*c*).

§ 3. "The first type is less rapid than the second, but both are played more softly than the principal tone, see Fig. LXXXI" (see ex. 28*c*).

34. The Largo of an early partita sonata, 11 B♭, contains (in m. 8 of the second movement), exceptionally, Bach's long mordent, in small notation, as if Haydn had only recently learned about it (perhaps in Bach's *Versuch*):

If the presumption stated in n. 13 of chap. 2 is true, i.e., if Haydn was reading through pt. 1 of Bach's *Versuch* in about 1762, this might suggest 1762 as the year of composition of the Sonata no. 11 in B♭. On the other hand, at least according to the secondary sources, for the autograph manuscript is missing, this sonata still has uniform eighth-note appoggiaturas, an *ante quem* 1762 indication.

35. I withdraw my hypothesis, outlined on pp. 60–61 of the Hungarian edition of this book, about the Leopold Mozart "third mordent" as a possible explanation of Haydn's *Halb Mordent.*

36. It is hard to decide whether Haydn wrote or ~ in this letter.

37. Haydn, *CCLN,* 51.

38. See *JHW,* 22 and frontispiece. The interesting thing about this case is that the two *Flötenuhr* realizations are different. The undated clock has a regular three-note short mordent but with an upbeat rhythm; the 1793 clock has an onbeat mordent of the two-note version, with immediate release of the lower note, as Bach suggests in § 3.

39. It seems advisable to stick to the German term instead of applying the English denominations. Marpurg and Hiller called it *Doppelvorschlag* (see Neumann, *Ornamentation,* 490–91).

§ 8. "It never appears in rapid movements but is well used in affettuoso passages."

This ornament appears very seldom in Haydn's sonatas. Its dynamics are unusual, for it must be played more softly than the principal note, although it is begun on the beat. When Haydn used a variant of this embellishment, written in small notes or regular-size notes (ex. 28*d–e*), he was careful to place a rest in the left hand during the unaccented ornament.

7. *The Slide* (Der Schleifer)[40]

§ 1. "The slide appears both with and without a dot. Its execution is suggested by its name. Melodies are made flowing through its use."

§ 2. "The undotted slide consists of either two or three small notes which are struck before a principal tone."

§ 3. "When it consists of two notes they are notated as small thirty-seconds in the manner of Fig. LXXXVIII [see ex. 29]. In an *alla breve* they may also appear in the form of sixteenths, as in the asterisked example. Occasionally the slide is indicated in the manner of Example (a), and frequently it will be found in large notation (b)."

§ 4. "The two-note slide is distinguished from the three-note in that (1) it is always used in a leap which it helps to fill in, as in Fig. LXXXVIII; the three-note slide, as we shall see presently [Fig. LXXXIX], performs other duties in addition to this one; (2) the two-note slide is always played rapidly, Fig. LXXXVIII (b), the three-note is not."

§ 5. "Fig. LXXXIX (a) illustrates the execution of the three-note type. Its place is determined by the character of the movement and the tempo."

Neither the somewhat obsolete sign for the two-note slide known from J. S. Bach's music (Fig. LXXXVIII a) nor the "inverted turn" sign invented by C. P. E. Bach for the three-note slide (Fig. LXXXIX b) found its way into Haydn's notation. Haydn uses the slide as a relatively rare embellishment for expressive passages. The two-note slide is generally used in sicilianos to achieve an archaic-pathetic effect (ex. 29*a*); otherwise, it is played relatively quickly, in agreement with Bach's teachings (ex. 29*c, d* [Allegro]). The three-note slide seems to have been used with essentially the same meaning from the Sonata no. 30 in D of 1767 (ex. 29*b*) up to the Variations in F Minor (ex. 29*e*) composed in 1793. A mature example (ex. 29*f*), from the Allegretto e innocente of the Sonata no. 54 in G Major (which, of all the so-called *Damensonaten,* was to create a prototype), suggests that Haydn was already ornamenting with the utmost care and precision

40. Bach's orthography reads *Schleiffer.*

Ex. 29. *Schleifer*. Figs. LXXXVIII–LXXXIX, C. P. E. Bach's examples. *a–f, Schleifer* in Haydn's notation: *a,* 19 e I, 1, and 38 F II, 1. *b,* 30 D II, 25, and 33 c I, 2. *c,* 31 A♭ I, 26. *d,* 59 E♭ I, 101, and II, 25. *e,* F Minor Variations, mm. 17, 44–45. *f,* 54 G I, 24.

at the time. Note the articulation involved; some of the ornaments connect while others separate neighboring tones.[41]

8. *The* Schneller[42]

§ 1. "Figure XCIV illustrates my unvariable notation of the short mordent in inversion, the upper tone of which is snapped [. . . *man schnellt*], the other tones being played with a stiff finger [ex. 30]. Its execution suggests that this ornament, not mentioned by other writers, might be called the snap. [Addition in the 1787 ed.:] In its employment as well as its shape it is the opposite of the mordent, but its tones are identical with those of the short trill."

§ 2. "The snap is always played rapidly and appears only before quick, detached notes, to which it imparts brilliance while serving to fill them out."

§ 3. "It is in effect a miniature unsuffixed trill. Unlike the suffixed trill, which is best followed by an ascent, the snap is better before a descent. Undoubtedly this is because its second tone and the principal tone resemble an inverted suffix. Nevertheless it is different from all trills in that it is never enclosed and never appears under a slur."

§ 4. "It must be assiduously practiced before it can be made to sound as it should. Because only the strongest, most dexterous fingers execute it effectively, it is often necessary to play the following tones with a finger that will not interfere with the staccato character of the ornament, as illustrated in Fig. XCV (a)" [see ex. 30].

Ex. 30. *Schneller,* C. P. E. Bach's examples.

41. There is an unusual upbeat-rhythm slide in the English edition by Caulfield of 60 C (ca. 1800), mm. 35–36 of the second movement (see *b* below), that was still regularly printed in Vienna in the form of an Adagio, issued by Artaria in 1794 as an independent piece (the same measures in this edition; see *a* below). I wonder whether Haydn changed his mind or whether the London engraver (editor) simply understood the notation in a different way in 1800:

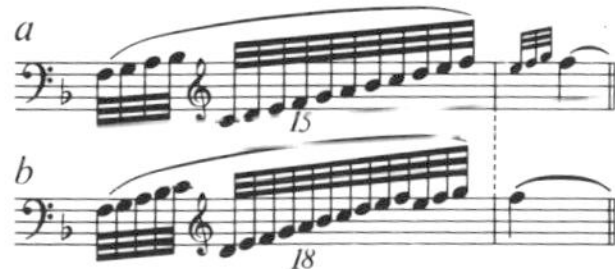

(*a*, Adagio, mm. 35–36. *b,* 60 C II, 35–36.)

42. Mitchell (in the *Essay*) and Neumann (*Ornamentation*) translate *Schneller* as "the snap"; the "Ornamentation" article in *The New Grove* translates *schnellen* as "to jerk."

It is possible that C. P. E. Bach's description of the *Schneller* as an "inverted mordent" inspired the most interesting thematic *Schneller* idea of Haydn's sonata output, written out in large-size notes (ex. 31*a*). At the exchange of hands in measure 17, the figure of the *Schneller* changes to a mordent.

Ex. 31. *Schneller* in Haydn's notation. *a,* 52 G III, 1, 17. *b,* 52 G I, 17–18.

In Haydn's entire sonata output, there is only one real *Schneller* in small notes, in the first movement of the same work (ex. 31*b*). It is unfortunate that Paul Badura-Skoda picked this very place to prove—with faulty reasoning—that in Haydn and Mozart the short trill (⁓ *Pralltriller*) "begins with the main note and consists of three notes."[43] This *Schneller* is an absolute rarity in Haydn's keyboard music. The only reason we need to form a clear notion of it is to avoid being taken in by the recent interpretations of theoreticians and performing artists who wish to start the short trill on the main note.

9. *The Elaboration of Fermatas: Cadenzas in the Sonatas*

§ 2. "*Fermate* are often employed with good effect, for they awaken unusual attentiveness. Their sign is a slur with a dot under it, which denotes that a tone is to be held as long as required generally by the nature of the composition."

§ 3. "At times a note without the sign may be held for expressive reasons. Aside from this, there are three places at which the *fermata* appears: over the next to the last, the last, or the rest after the last bass note. To be used correctly

43. See Paul Badura-Skoda, "Suggestions for Ornamentation," in *Haydn: 4 Keyboard Sonatas,* ed. Paul Badura-Skoda (Paris: Leduc, 1982), 11–12, enclosed booklet with English text. See also Badura-Skoda, "Beiträge." In "Suggestions," Badura-Skoda states that "the widespread present-day execution of this ornament with four notes and beginning on the upper auxiliary is quite wrong. In all of Haydn's and Mozart's keyboard music (and in J. S. Bach's as well) this figure is never once found written out in either small or normal notes, no doubt because those composers did not wish anything of the sort." On the contrary, Haydn wrote out the three-toned *Schneller* figure in small notes precisely because the *chevron* symbol (⁓) stood for a four-toned *Pralltriller;* he was obliged to use small notes to show that in this sonata he wanted to have, as an exception, an ornament with three notes in this place. Note that Haydn followed C. P. E. Bach's advice only superficially, since he used the ornament not on a staccato note (in WUE slurred). Rosenblum (*Performance Practices,* 257) suggests that "probably almost every trill on rapid, descending stepwise notes should be realized as a *Schneller*" (see also her fig. 7.72). This may be sound advice for the player of a modern grand piano, but no unambiguous source directly pointing to Haydn seems to support it.

the sign should be written at the beginning and again at the end of an elaborated *fermata*."

§ 4. "*Fermate* over rests occur most frequently in allegro movements and are not embellished. The two other kinds are usually found in slow, affettuoso movements and must be embellished if only to avoid artlessness. In any event elaborate decoration is more necessary here than in other parts of movements."

§ 6. "Those who lack the ability to introduce elaborations may apply a long ascending trill when necessary to an appoggiatura which stands a step above a final tone."

The eight small examples of fermatas in C. P. E. Bach provide little help for elucidating the cases found in Haydn. Türk's *Klavierschule* gives numerous examples of fermatas that are closer, in both time and style, to those of Haydn.[44] However, the *Klavierschule*, published in 1789, also gives suggestions, characteristic of the local German style and of clavichord thinking, that are alien to Haydn's music for fortepiano.

Türk's merit for us lies in his having clearly distinguished and described the function of three kinds of fermatas. They are (1) the fermata proper, a relatively short series of notes executed with the right hand only, outlining the chord of the left hand, marked with a fermata; (2) the *Übergang* (transition), a short passage leading up to the return of the main theme in rondos and other forms (the fermata and the *Übergang* may occur together);[45] (3) the *Kadenz*, that is, a cadenza before the end of the movement, for the right hand or both hands, leading into a full cadenza after a trill. This type was already much criticized in Türk's time because of its frequently excessive length.

Haydn's music for piano solo contains examples, some notated by the composer and some to be improvised, of each of the categories described by Türk—the smaller fermata, the *Übergang* leading to a reprise of a main theme, and substantial cadenzas coming at the end of the movement.[46]

1. Cadenzas to be improvised before the end of the movement occur in the slow movements of two early concert sonatas,[47] 30 D II, 112, and 31 A♭ II, 77.[48]

44. See Türk, *Klavierschule*, 313–22.

45. See ibid., 296.

46. For a partly different view of the treatment of cadenzas in Haydn's sonatas, see Vera Schwarz, "Missverständnisse in der Haydn-Interpretation."

47. The only forerunner among the divertimento sonatas is in the Adagio of 13 G, mm. 10 and 24. On my terminology *concert sonata, chamber, court sonata*, etc., see pp. 174–80.

48. Similar cadenzas in the slow movements of Haydn's string quartets dating from the same years are also meant to be improvised; see op. 9 d III, 73*; C III, 64*; G III, 69; and A III, 54*. (Contemporary cadenzas survive for the items marked with an asterisk; see the *JHW* score.) Haydn wrote out in full a small cadenza in op. 9 E♭ III, 44. Although he composed the necessary cadenzas and fermatas in the slow movements of op. 17, a good performer may nevertheless improvise at m. 89 of c III, mm. 16 and 38 of D III, and perhaps even in E♭ III; moreover, the recitative formulas of G III also invite improvised ornamentations and interpolations.

No cadenzas for these or similar movements by Haydn, written in Haydn's time, have come down to us. Present-day performers must write or improvise their own cadenzas, drawing on their own familiarity with the style (for which, above all, intimate knowledge of C. P. E. Bach's music can offer a helping hand), or accept the suggestions found, for example, in the *WUE*.[49]

2. A large-sized cadenza in concertante style before the end of a movement, notated by Haydn and dating from about 1780, appears in measures 48–49 of the second movement, Adagio, of 52 G. This cadenza has nothing to do with earlier practice but rather belongs to the novel effects of the mature Haydn. Just imagine the young amateur pianist of the salons attempting to perform a cadenza suitable for a concerto. The cadenza inserted into the reprise of the minor theme in the F Minor Variations is of an even more genuinely concertante style and dramatic quality. A thirty-seven-measure passionate fantasy[50] begins with a turn to G♭ major, the key of the Neapolitan sixth so important for the theme, just at the point when one expects the final phrase of the theme (m. 169). After the cadenza, the piece is crowned by twenty-four memorable coda measures. It is not surprising that a contemporary reviewer found that the Variations reminded him of free improvisation, were particularly difficult in technical terms, and made the most of the new instrumental capabilities of the fortepiano.[51]

3. A long, written-out fermata occurs in the first movement of 32 g, measures 66–70, just before the closing motives of the recapitulation, that is, at about the place a cadenza might occur. Marked *sempre più adagio,* it is the lyrical summit of the piece. Note that the coda of the opening movement of 48 C, beginning with a fermata in measure 151, starts as a pseudocadenza in a similar formal position.

4. Fully written-out fermatas before the recapitulation of the first theme, in fast movements, appear in two mature sonatas. In 59 E♭ I, 131, a *suo piacere* passage of about fifty notes occurs between two fermatas; it can be performed "at one's discretion" and is full of effects. In 62 E♭ III, there is a passage (mm. 195–203) containing five fermatas, a change to an adagio tempo, and ex-

49. Of the cadenzas written in the *WUE* for Sonatas nos. 30 and 31, the former is better; the latter is simply too short. In fact, both these movements could do with longer right-hand cadenzas. Unfortunately, any notated suggestion made by an editor, no matter how well intentioned, is likely to be considered by inexperienced musicians not so much a model as a recipe, an acceptable, organic part of the work that may be practiced and performed. Those who have not played enough music by C. P. E. Bach and Haydn to enable them to invent a small cadenza—or even to improvise one on the spot—might be advised to postpone a concert performance of these sonatas.

50. Originally, it consisted of only twenty-three measures; mm. 180–93 were inserted into Haydn's autograph score later. This inserted page may be studied in facsimile in Emanuel Winternitz, *Musical Autographs,* vol. 2, pl. 54. The nine omitted measures preceding the insertion of fourteen measures are included in the critical notes of *Haydn Klavierstücke,* ed. Franz Eibner and Gerschon Jarecki (Vienna: Wiener Urtext Edition, 1975).

51. Cited by Landon (*HCW,* 3:439) from the May 1799 issue of the *Allgemeine musikalische Zeitung.*

traordinary dynamic contrasts; the fermatas in measures 195 and 196 signify arpeggios of special notation. The passage in 43 E♭ III, 91–94, may be considered a preliminary study for the more elaborate one in 62 E♭.[52] The fermatas in the first movement of 54 G, a set of double variations, should be mentioned here. In measure 16, the *Übergang,* written in small notes, leading to the reprise of the theme can be further extended at the performer's discretion; the performer can also elaborate the fermata at measure 52. In measures 89–91, the fermata is embellished by Haydn himself.

5. Written-out adagio fermatas inserted into both the exposition and the recapitulation of sonata forms can be found in 33 c (I, 24–26, 87–89), 34 D (I, 52–53, 177–78), and 43 E♭ (I, 37–38, 133–34). Less developed variants include 49 c♯ (I, 85–86) and 20 B♭ (II, 33–35, 97–99).

In addition to these special cases, there are many very effective fermatas in Haydn's sonatas. Some movements, such as 51 E♭ I or 53 e I, are richly decorated with dramatic fermatas that do not need to be arbitrarily ornamented.[53] Small cadenzas may be improvised here only by artists with infallible taste who comfortably find their way in the style and function of the various Haydnesque forms. In the slow movements of sonatas 58 C (I) and 60 C (II), Haydn notated precisely what to play.

Leopold Mozart's teaching on the proper execution of fermatas, the length of rests, and suspensions and appoggiaturas is most interesting and useful, although he is primarily concerned with ensemble playing and performance by strings:[54]

§ 19. "It is true that such sustaining is to be made according to fancy, but it must be neither too short nor too long, and made with sound judgement. . . . Here it must be noticed in particular that the tone of the instruments must be allowed to diminish and die entirely away before beginning to play again. . . . The Italians call this sign 'La Corona'. [Addition in the 1787 ed.:] But, when this sign (which the Italians call 'La Corona') stands over or under a rest [*sospir*][55] or pause, the rest is silent for a longer space of time than the value of the bar demands. On the other hand, a pause over which this sign is seen is not held long,

52. Passages with fermatas and *adagio* markings occur in the outer movements of 35 A♭ (I, 98–100, and III, 208–10); regarding the authenticity of this sonata, see pp. 163–64.

53. The first movement of 31 A♭ is interesting in this regard. Some of its fermatas indicate expressive pauses that should probably be played without ornamentation (such as in mm. 17, 64, 69, 72, and 91), while other fermatas might welcome ornamentation (mm. 23 and 97). In the second movement, Adagio, of 53 e, improvisation is possible before the recapitulation in mm. 30–31; the cadential trill in m. 44 might also allow some improvisation, although in the rather poor surviving source material for this sonata there is no fermata sign in this measure.

54. See Mozart, *Violinschule,* 45 (pp. 46ff. of the 1948 English ed.).

55. According to Leopold Mozart, "One sort of rest is the 'Sospiro.' It is so called because it is of short duration" (*Treatise,* 38). Thus, in his terminology, sixteenth, eighth, and quarter rests are called *sospir,* the longer ones *pauses.*

but is often observed as little as if it were not present [see ex. 32]. . . . The conductor who beats time, or the leader, must be watched carefully, for such matters depend on good taste and right judgement." This advice holds equally well for reading rests with a fermata in Haydn's sonatas.

Ex. 32. L. Mozart's example of the execution of the fermata in the 1787 ed.

10. On Certain Dotted and Triplet Rhythms

The notation of rhythm in Haydn's time has two problematic areas that have provoked a good deal of speculation among performance-practice scholars. One concerns the duration of dotted notes. Are they to be executed strictly as written or with so-called overdotting, in which the shorter notes of dotted patterns in the same movement are played the same whether written as sixteenths or as thirty-seconds? The other area embraces the group of problems connected with triplet motion. Does the dotted rhythm accommodate the triplet? Is the rhythm of two- and four-note groups in a melody influenced by a triplet accompaniment?

Rhythm in eighteenth-century music was not only a matter of duration but also a component of style, closely connected with touch and performing style, as is shown by passages in Bach's *Versuch* and Türk's *Klavierschule.* In his section on performance, after describing the three major types of touch and remarking that unmarked quarters and eighths (*movimento ordinario;* in present-day usage, *nonlegato*) are sustained for only half their value, C. P. E. Bach adds:

§ 23. "Short notes which follow dotted ones are always shorter in execution than their notated length. Hence it is superfluous to place strokes or dots over them. Fig. VII [see ex. 33] illustrates their execution.[56] The asterisked example shows us that occasionally the division must agree with the notated values.[57] Dots after long notes or after short ones in slow tempos, and isolated

56. C. P. E. Bach wrote, "Bey Fig. VII sehen wir ihren Ausdruck." In reality, the first four examples of Fig. VII show only that no signs of articulation or touch are required for their notation. These examples have been omitted. The rhythm of the off beat of the first section in ex. 33 must be considered either an engraving error or, what is more probable, a demonstration of how both parts should be simultaneously executed in such a passage (here, thirty-seconds!) regardless of their notated value.

57. In the asterisked example, the convention of double dots does not prevail.

dots, are all held. However, in rapid tempos prolonged successions of dots are performed as rests, the apparent opposite demand of the notation notwithstanding. A more accurate notation would remove such a discrepancy. Lacking this, however, the content of a piece will shed light on the details of its performance. Dots after short notes followed by groups of shorter ones are held fully (Fig. VIII) [see ex. 33]."[58]

Ex. 33. C. P. E. Bach's examples.

In Bach's text, overdotting is touched on only incidentally, as something with which any reader would have been familiar.

Leopold Mozart discusses certain aspects of taste and aesthetics underlying the practice of overdotting and also presents a notational idea:

§ 11. "There are certain passages in slow pieces where the dot must be held rather longer than the afore-mentioned rule demands if the performance is not to sound too sleepy. For example (a) [see ex. 34]. . . . It would be a good thing if this long retention of the dot were insisted on, and set down as a rule. I, at least, have often done so, and I have made clear my opinion of the right manner of performance by setting down two dots followed by a shortened note (b)."[59]

Ex. 34. L. Mozart's examples.

As I will show, Haydn began using written-out double dots in his notation rather late, not before about 1780, with the beginning of the series of Artaria editions. The conventions of the time allowed his music to be properly read without written-out double dots as late as the 1760s or 1770s. The question arises, however, of how long the custom of overdotting continued. According to Türk,

58. In the 1787 edition of his book, Bach added that "when four or more short notes follow a dot they are to be played with dispatch, there being so many of them." This implies that overdotting is not required.

59. Mozart, *Treatise,* 41–42.

overdotting was self-evident as late as 1789—at least in northern Germany—and the major concern was whether the prolonged and ensuing notes should be slurred or detached, according to the mood of the piece:

§ 48. "Dotted notes especially in addition to the attention which must be given to the proper arrangement of note values as well as to heavy or light execution, require a very varied treatment according to the context in which they occur. It is customary, for the most part, to dwell on notes longer (and therefore to play the following shorter notes even more quickly) than the notation indicates. For example [ex. 35]. The realization of dotted notes as shown in (b) is generally chosen when the character of the composition is serious, solemn, exalted, etc., thus not only for an actual *Grave* but also for overtures or compositions which are marked *Sostenuto,* and the like. The dotted notes are executed in this case with emphasis, consequently they are prolonged. For the expression of livelier or more joyous feelings the playing must be somewhat lighter, approximately as in (c). The execution shown in (d) is particularly well-chosen for compositions which are to be played in a vehement or defiant manner or those which are marked staccato."[60]

Ex. 35. Türk, *Klavierschule,* 6:3, 48.

Probably owing to C. P. E. Bach's admonitions, Haydn notated several of his themes with dotted rhythms more precisely than many of his contemporaries did. To avoid a detached execution of the two notes of the dotted formula, Haydn added slurs, as, for example, in the first and third movements of the Sonata no. 33 in C Minor. When he had an elegantly crisp dotted style in mind for an adagio tempo, he also notated it unambiguously, as in the Adagio movements of 34 D or 36 C. With this in mind, the pianist may boldly exploit the wonderful contrasts (detached dotted figures up to the repeat sign, legato phrases in the subsequent measures) marked in the third movement, Tempo di Menuet, of 34 D.

Returning to the topic of overdotting, we must differentiate between those places where overdotting is an optional possibility and those where overdotting is essentially obligatory. The latter places, in some part, stem from matters of notational habit and convenience. Thus, the real meaning of the traditional notation shown in example 36 is beyond doubt.[61]

60. Türk, *School,* 350.

61. That this is not an accidental slip of the pen is borne out by the upbeats to mm. 1, 40, and 74 of the first movement of 20 B♭, which are written the same way.

Ex. 36. 20 B♭ I, 1, and 33 c I, 28.

Before discussing in some detail a few pieces in which overdotting is obligatory, let us examine a notational curiosity. Chronological study of Haydn's notation of dots, in the most authentic sources and in various genres, shows us that Haydn did not notate two dots following a note (i.e., written-out double dotting) until the 1770s, either because he was unaware of their existence or because he considered them superfluous. He could indicate sharp dotting by using a "shorthand" form (with one dot that, in some modern editions, is simply completed without editorial comment) or "compound" notations (either with inserted rests or with tied notes); otherwise, he left the simple dotted formula to be played by the musician with an awareness of the general style (see ex. 37).

before ca. 1780				after ca. 1780
shorthand:	compound:		or simply:	
[..]			[♩.. 𝅘𝅥𝅯]	

Ex. 37. Double-dotted rhythm.

In Haydn's sonatas, the rhythm ♩.. 𝅘𝅥𝅯 first appears in the third movement of 34 D, dating from about 1773 (?) and surviving only in secondary sources from 1778 on. Its next occurrence is in 1780 in the Adagio of 52 G. In his earlier sonatas, Haydn used ties to express double dots whenever it was absolutely necessary (e.g., 36 C II, 1).

The opening movement of 31 A♭, from about 1768–70, is an interesting example of what appear to be two kinds of dotted formulas, that is, dotted notes on two different rhythmic levels (see ex. 38).[62] Are there really two lengths of short notes (𝅘𝅥𝅯 and 𝅘𝅥𝅰) following a dotted note in this passage? Only if the present-day performer is incapable of detaching himself from the visual image of the mu-

62. This succession of dotted motives preceding a cadence—a notation of the acceleration of a cadential figure—is a well-known, usually improvised, ornamentation figure of eighteenth-century music, the ribattuta. Leopold Mozart recommended it in places like this (*a*, the written form; *b*, the same played with a ribattuta):

sic. There is only one ruling dotted rhythm in this piece; the dotted note is followed by a thirty-second note. The pianist is not only allowed to play it this way but is encouraged to enjoy the natural "scanning" of the rhythm. (In ex. 38, the notes marked with an asterisk are thirty-seconds; in the first theme, all the ♪.♬ patterns need to be double dotted.) Of the earlier sonatas,[63] the main theme of 16 D is to be read in accordance with this convention (see ex. 39).[64]

Ex. 38. 31 A♭ I, 31.

Ex. 39. 16 D I, 1.

The opening movement of the C Minor Sonata, sketched in 1771, is the first sonata movement in which three rhythmic levels of dotted motives appear in the notation (*a*, ♩. ♪; *b*, ♪.♬; *c*, ♬.). Haydn did not yet employ double dots in this movement. The exciting variety of doubly diminished rhythms is, however, only an illusion of the notation. In fact, the smallest dotted rhythm, *c*, represents the ruling dotted movement of the piece; *a* is only the individual head motive of the first theme, and the *b* level never quite sounds as written because the sixteenth notes are variously ornamented (delayed *Pralltriller* in m. 7, appoggiatura in m. 37).

The only Largo movement in the mature sonatas of Haydn is in 50 D, from the end of the 1770s. Headed *Largo e sostenuto*, in agreement with Türk's explanation, it is a test piece for the ability to read dotted notes properly. Hungarian musicians frequently refer to this movement as an example of Hungarian features in Haydn, calling it a derivative of the *verbunkos* or recruiting dance. In reality, it is much more French than Hungarian in style, a period piece to be performed with some kind of pompous embellishment. Can there be any doubt as to the

63. The main theme of the first movement of 28 D, of which only a fragment of the manuscript survives, should also be read so.

64. Of the later sonatas, I recommend double dotting the second beat of the first theme of 51 E♭ in mm. 1, 13, 32, and 48–49 and probably even in mm. 40–42.

need for double dots in the first measures (see ex. 40)? The rhythm marked with the asterisk causes some problems since there are even eighth notes in the movement (in the second and third beats of m. 3 and in mm. 7–8, 10, 12, and 16–17). Nevertheless, in the interest of a homogeneous rhythmic style, dotted notes followed by thirty-second notes can be suggested here as well as in measures 5[65] and 13–15.

Ex. 40. 50 D II, 1.

The closing motive of the first movement of the C♯ Minor Sonata also requires discussion under the topic of adjustments in rhythm. This theme appears in dotted rhythm in the exposition, without slur or staccato on the first three notes, and in simple pairs of sixteenths in the recapitulation, with slur and staccato for the first time (see ex. 41).[66] Given the apparent differences in articulation and the major-minor contrast, the performer may wish to render this theme with two kinds of character. This could probably be a mistake, however. Haydn used to write his recapitulations from memory, and he might have considered dots in such affective motives to be obvious; in the manuscripts of other works as well, he alternately wrote out dots fully or just started them as a kind of indication.

Ex. 41. 49 c♯ I, 31 (exposition), 95 (recapitulation).

65. For reasons of harmony, no dotting is required on the last eighths in the right hand of m. 10.

66. The last slur in mm. 95–96 and the third stroke in m. 96 are editorial additions in the *WUE*. The form of the leading voice in the right hand found in the recapitulation (stems drawn in the same direction instead of in opposite directions) seems to be different too. This, however, is a pseudo-deviation.

There is a very large range of optional overdotting, left to the taste and style of the performer, that does not necessarily modify written sixteenth notes to exact thirty-second notes. Any minuet, or middle or last movement in a minuet tempo, based on the combination of dotted and triplet rhythms (♩. ♪ and ♪♪♪) gains by being slightly overdotted (see, e.g., 43 E♭ II, 59 E♭ III). In movements of a pathetic affect, one could make greater use of overdotting to increase tension and thus avoid dependence on dynamic changes or other devices (see, e.g., the transitional Adagio of 45 A). When the right hand plays a noble dotted-rhythm cantabile melody over repeated notes, tasteful overdotting can hardly be rejected even if the sonata is an otherwise carefully notated one (see 59 E♭ II, 21–23, 41–42, 93–95). In example 42, the arrows indicate notes to be played approximately the length of a thirty-second note.

Ex. 42. 59 E♭ II, 21.

Overdotting can be a powerful tool in the hands of the performer. But I would hesitate to recommend the use of *notes inégales* as a rhythmic embellishment in Haydn's sonatas to any considerable extent. No theoretical or notational evidence seems to support the presumption that Haydn was still reckoning with this subtlety of Baroque performance. *Inégale* rendering might be appropriate, however, in the ♫ ♫ ♫ motion of early minuets not differentiated by any other rhythm.

The rhythmic problems arising from triplet accompaniments provide convincing proof that the written rhythmic values of the music of those days cannot always be reduced to a homogeneous and relatively simple arithmetic system. In the Adagio of 52 G, which was notated in 1780 with a comparatively great degree of precision, including double dots,[67] the present-day pianist has to make the following decisions in just the first eight measures (see ex. 43): (a) is either 𝅘𝅥𝅰 if analogous with (b) or 𝅘𝅥𝅯 if analogous with (c) (my suggestion is 𝅘𝅥𝅰); (e) is either 𝅘𝅥𝅰 because it is independent of the accompaniment or a sextuplet 𝅘𝅥𝅯 because it takes over the motion of the accompaniment (my suggestion is a sextuplet 𝅘𝅥𝅯);[68] if (e) is a sextuplet 𝅘𝅥𝅯, (d) anticipates the rhythm of (e) (sextuplet 𝅘𝅥𝅯) or remains invariably

67. According to the *JHW*, the Artaria edition has two dots in 52 G II, 31, but only one on the first beat of II, 3.

68. If the right hand does not merge with the sextuplet accompaniment, the performer should apply overdotting. However, m. 10 reinforces my suggestion that two thirty-seconds equal one sextuplet sixteenth.

♬ by analogy with (b). This should not be decided by whim. It is relevant that the upbeat here has a different function and articulation from the upbeat of measures 2–3; it introduces, for the first time in the movement, a beat embellished with a Haydn ornament. Naturally, it will have a greater accent and will change almost automatically to a kind of sextuplet-sixteenth rhythm.

Ex. 43. 52 G II, 1, 6, 8.

C. P. E. Bach did not dwell on rhythmic problems connected with accompaniments in triplet motion because the convention was self-evident. He simply stated:

§ 27. "The performance of other lengths against these notes [triplets] is shown in Fig. XII" (see ex. 44).

Ex. 44. C. P. E. Bach's example.

For Löhlein, it was similarly self-evident.[69] By 1789, a change in the tradition may have caused Türk to write as follows:

§ 64. "The playing of dotted notes against triplets also presents difficulties and is not to be expected of beginners in the most exact fashion. In example (a) [see ex. 45] the sixteenth note should be played only after the last note of the triplet and in such a fashion that between the triplets there should be no gap; generally, however, beginners play such a passage as in (b). For this reason, it would be better to take away some of the value of the dot and play the sixteenth note with the last note of the triplet, as in (c). This latter realization may have been what various composers had in mind in such cases. In compositions of vehement character, in which there are many dotted notes, the latter realization

69. Löhlein, *Clavier-Schule,* 70 (1765 ed.); 68 (1773 ed.).

would probably not correspond to the whole, but then, such pieces are not suitable for beginners."[70]

Ex. 45. Türk, *Klavierschule,* 1:4, 64.

In connection with Haydn's notation of triplets, two facts must be stated at the outset. (1) Haydn's notation is so dense and scratchy in his autograph manuscripts that using the vertical alignment of notes as a means of clarifying the rhythm is simply not possible. Nor is it clear that any eighteenth-century composer observed such a notational convention. The use of vertical alignment in the urtext editions represents not Haydn's notational practice but merely acceptance of the present-day rules of musical layout. (2) Certain triplet fragments and incomplete groups of triplets (e.g., ,) appear in Haydn's notation, while others (e.g., ,) do not.[71] As shown in example 46, Haydn notated the 2:1 proportion between note and rest with an approximately exact rhythm (i),

Ex. 46. *a,* 56 D I, 80. *b,* 33 c I, 36. *c,* 37 E II, 3. *d,* 38 F II, 18.

70. Türk, *School,* 101.

71. In 62 E♭ II, 4, 36, the proportion between rest and note notated as 1:1 most likely represents the proportion 2:1. As an earliest source, 61 D is known only from the Breitkopf & Härtel edition (1805), which is of poor source value in every respect. Consequently, we do not know if the notation of notes and rests in the left hand of mm. 100–101, where exceptionally there is a 2:1 formula of rest and note, was written so by Haydn or if his typical notation, as seen in m. 34, was altered by the engraver in mm. 100–101.

whereas he wrote notes in the ratio of 2:1 either as a dotted formula according to the notational custom of the Baroque gigue etc. (v) or with a rhythmic formula in which the written equal values were to be accommodated to the triplets (iii) and (vi). The way of playing triplet proportion in 33 c and 38 F is evident. The beginning of measure 4 (v) in 37 E can, however, be performed either with a triplet or with a dotted figure; its convincing force depends largely on the style of the performance.

Now let us consider the types of conflicts between triplet motion and other rhythms. The majority of cases can be arranged into two types.

The first category is triplet motion in the left hand in fast movements, that is, arpeggiated basses or *Harfenbässe.*[72] In Moderato or Allegro moderato movements, there are sixteenth-note triplets—for example, in the closing-theme area of 30 D I,[73] in the closing theme and above all the development section of 33 c I, and in the development of 41 A I. In faster movements and *alla breve* movements, there are eighth-note triplets, as in 48 C I,[74] in the second-theme area and the development of 55 B♭ I, and in the second-theme area of 61 D I. In the case of really fast triplet motion, four-note groups and dotted figures in the right hand live independent lives; rhythmic accommodation is out of the question. This is what Türk had in mind when he wrote about triplets of "vehement character." The triplet accompaniment should not cause the right-hand notes to be automatically overdotted unless the *anticipato* short note is the first member of a dense embellishment (e.g., a snapped turn).[75] As with many of his innovations, Haydn established this style of stormy motion in the left hand with a cantabile above it in the C Minor Sonata, no. 33. One notational problem is that several times (e.g., in the development section of 41 A I) Haydn notated the dotted rhythms in the right hand as a partial indication only, as it were a *simile* direction. In these cases, the dotting almost certainly needs to be continued (see ex. 47).

Ex. 47. 41 A I, 34.

The situation is more ambiguous if the triplets in the left hand are slower and there are occasionally simultaneous triplets in the left hand and right hand. In the middle section of the Adagio of 59 E♭, with its continuous sixteenth sex-

72. In Türk, *School,* 377, the triplet figure and the pattern that is now generally called the Alberti bass are both termed *Harfenbässe.*

73. Its prototype among the early divertimento sonatas is 13 G I.

74. An early example of this type is the Allegretto in $\frac{3}{4}$ of 14 C.

75. For the same reason, the short upbeat note in mm. 59–60 of 33 c I and mm. 25, 27, etc. of 55 B♭ I can be shorter.

tuplets, accommodating dotting is completely convincing. (In the *WUE,* the relevant notes in mm. 57, 59, 61, and 66–71 are vertically aligned.)[76] On the other hand, in the Tempo di Minuet of the same sonata, strong contrast between triplet and dotted rhythms is recommended since this helps establish the character and the flavor of the piece.

It is not clear how fast the first movement, marked *Andante,* of the D Major Sonata, no. 61, should be played—whether the Andante is *alla breve* or **C**—because the surviving sources are not good. Partly depending on the tempo, the movement may be executed in two slightly different styles. There are a few measures in which the rhythmic interpretation is evident; in measure 9 etc., the upbeat is a part of a triplet, while in measures 33, 38, etc., real dotted rhythm against triplets seems to be intended. As for the rest of the movement, the cantabile right hand may be played with its rhythm adjusted to the accompanying triplets,[77] in which case there emerges a nice contrast between the dotted first theme and the smooth cantabile idea; or it may be played as written, independent of the triplet accompaniment. Many present-day pianists tend to prefer the latter choice, perhaps partly because they attach greater importance to a homogeneous rendering of identical motives than to variation of character. I find this regrettable.

The second category is triplet motion in slow movements. Romantic and modern piano textures have accustomed present-day musicians to play patterns of three against four, four against five, and three against five with great accuracy and precision. This precision would hardly have been appreciated by the composers of the eighteenth century. Rhythmic patterns of three against two and three against four do occur in J. S. Bach's music when two previously presented materials are joined contrapuntally. But the next generation of musicians considered it more important to achieve a clear performance, governed by one will only—the leading melody or the leading rhythmic motion. This is especially true in slow movements. In the siciliano-rhythm Adagio of 38 F, it would be a vain achievement, alien to the style, to keep the rhythm of the right hand independent of that of the left; the adjustment is obvious (see ex. 48).

Ex. 48. 38 F II, 1.

76. In this respect, the arrangement of Haydn's autograph manuscript is completely irrelevant. See, e.g., the measures on the top staff on p. 12 of the facsimile edition (Graz, 1982) of 59 E♭.

77. If one uses overdotting in m. 37 etc. and a softer (5:1) dotting in mm. 12 and 16 and also in m. 33 etc., one might also, in m. 24, play the eighths in a ♪♩ triplet rhythm.

In slow movements, there would appear to be no general rule regarding the adjustment of dotted-note patterns to triplet patterns. The most interesting problem in Haydn's late sonata output is found in the first two variations (starting in mm. 21 and 41) of the first movement, Andante con espressione, of 56 D. The solution that I suggest is to play the dotted notes precisely as written, that is, in the proportion 3:1, in the first variation because the sixteenth-note triplet here is merely a figurative, ornamental rhythm. On the other hand, in the minor variation, I recommend a dotted sextuplet rhythm, in the ratio 5:1, all through (mm. 41–42, 49–50,[78] and 53), which is confirmed in measure 53 itself. Further, this more pathetic manner of dotting better suits the affect of the *minore* section.

Finally, let us investigate two additional interesting examples. The first shows a confusion in the interpretation of a figure in a relatively early sonata, 30 D from 1767, that seems to be inaccurately notated. The *WUE* gives two corrected readings (see ex. 49): one (*a*) is somewhat too simple; the other (*b*) appears probable but is most likely erroneous.[79] It is conceivable that Haydn used this approximate notation to write a triplet figure with a nice turn of phrase (*c*).

Ex. 49. 30 D II, 5. Haydn's autograph, with renditions. * *JHW:*

78. The last beat in the right hand of m. 50 may be executed in two different ways:

79. If Haydn had forgotten to write a trill in a regular manner in just one place, this solution might be conceivable. But the pattern occurs repeatedly in this movement.

The other case, even more striking, concerns the Adagio of the *London* C Major Sonata, no. 60 (see ex. 50). The preliminary edition and the definitive form represent two attempts at precisely marking an arpeggio that was meant to sound improvisatory. In the first version—which is, in fact, identical with reading *c* of example 49—the slowing down is notated, perhaps causing the c^2, played by the right-hand thumb, to sound too important. In the second version, the slowing down is entrusted to the performer, and this disturbing inner accent is avoided. How many masters before Beethoven had ever taken so much trouble over notating an arpeggio?

Ex. 50. *a,* First version, Adagio, m. 59. *b,* Second version, 60 C II, 59.

11. *Arpeggios and Passages in Small-Note Notation*

The widespread use of broken chords in the eighteenth century is, for the most part, not reflected in the notation because it was an assumed aspect of the playing technique. This is connected with both the construction and the sound ideal of the clavichord and harpsichord. If all the notes of a chord were played simultaneously, the pitches would lose definition. The resulting blunt sound might be useful for certain effects, but it was not the most subtle or the most euphonious sonority the instrument could achieve. A chord that was deliberately arpeggiated, upward or downward, created order in the sound image. Equally important, a harmony lasted longer when its component notes were played one by one.

Haydn seems to have profited very little from C. P. E. Bach's book with regard to notating arpeggiation. He never uses a downward arpeggio sign in his keyboard music. It will suffice, then, to cite just a few examples from Bach.

§ 26. "The usual signs of arpeggiation and their execution appear in Fig. XI [see ex. 51]. The asterisked example represents an arpeggio with an *acciaccatura*."

Ex. 51. C. P. E. Bach's examples (excerpts).

In the manuscripts of his keyboard music, Haydn uses a stroke between the note heads, rather than a wavy line before the chord, to indicate arpeggiation. He was not confusing an arpeggio with an acciaccatura in his notation but rather applying a kind of shorthand abbreviation.[80] When there is an arpeggio in both hands, one must decide if it should be played as one long arpeggio or two arpeggios played simultaneously. Urtext editions offer various suggestions in these matters, as in the case of the Neapolitan chord of the theme of the F Minor Variations (see ex. 52). In the autograph,[81] Haydn notated the arpeggios in the right and left hands independently, which seems to be reinforced by the ***fz***[82] written out in each of the parts. This has been literally transcribed with modern notational signs in the Henle edition. If the two broken chords are played together, as suggested by Bach, empty fifths and parallel fifths may occur. These would have been avoided by musicians in Haydn's era. Eibner's suggestion in the *WUE* is, after all, a reasonable interpretation, although, as far as the general impression of the notation of a long wavy line goes, it is farther from Haydn's manuscript.

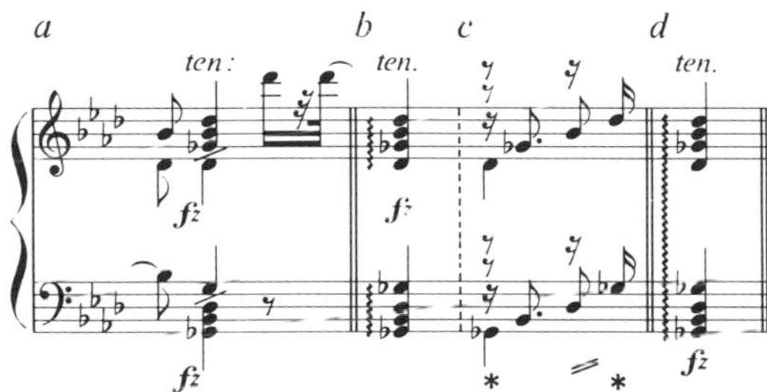

Ex. 52. F Minor Variations, m. 25. *a,* Haydn's autograph. *b,* Henle urtext. *c,* According to C. P. E. Bach. *d, WUE.*

When interpreting Haydn's arpeggios, the date of composition must never be left out of consideration. The pre-1780 sonatas were written for the harpsichord: arpeggios were marked only at thematically significant moments, and even then inconsistently and insufficiently. The notation of arpeggios in the pieces starting with Sonatas nos. 54–56 is much more precise. In the middle movement (E major, Adagio) of the *London* Sonata no. 62 in E♭, for example, the notation is very precise, with independent arpeggios in the right and left hands (see

80. Unlike C. P. E. Bach's asterisked example (see ex. 51), Haydn places the oblique stroke at the fourth of the chord, where there is the most room between the note heads, and not between the notes of the chord where a second must be introduced, which is already an acciaccatura.

81. For the facsimile of this page, see Winternitz, *Musical Autographs,* vol. 2, pl. 53.

82. See my discussion of writing dynamics for both hands, pp. 128 and 142.

ex. 53*c*). Example 53*a* shows an arpeggio in small notation;[83] in example 53*b* the arpeggiation in measure 3 can evidently be applied in measure 1 as well.

Ex. 53. *a,* 19 e III, 1. *b,* 37 E I, 1, 3. *c,* 62 E♭ II, 3.

The arpeggio as an idiomatic instrumental effect often suggested themes to Haydn, just as other instrumental effects did. The second themes of the first movements of 32 g and 44 F are real arpeggio themes, with approximate rhythmic notation (see ex. 54). An attempt at precise execution of the sixty-fourth notes among the thirty-seconds in the second theme of 32 g can produce only a grotesque effect.

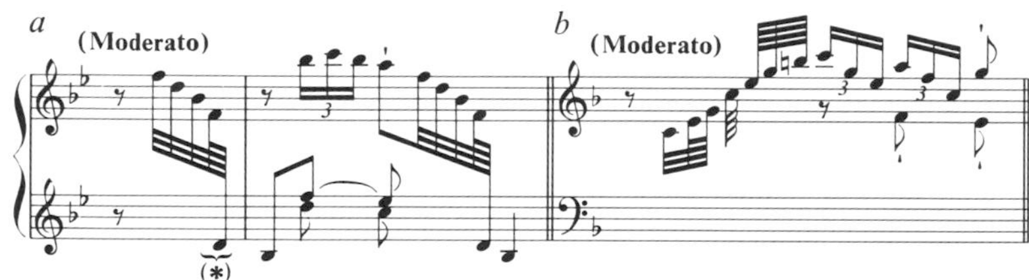

Ex. 54. *a,* 32 g I, 13. *b,* 44 F I, 15.

The most beautiful types of arpeggios occur at the ends of movements in Haydn's sonatas, once again thanks to C. P. E. Bach's inspiration. What is sought after, often, is a means to conclude a piece forcefully. This may be achieved by an abrupt slowing down, which Haydn expressed in his early sonatas by the direction *adagio* and in his later works by writing augmented rhythms. Regarding the resolution of a final pair of chords in a movement, sometimes the resolution must come without rallentando and with decisive force. This is indicated by the characteristic accent staccato, on the second note of a two-note slur. (In addition to ex. 55*b,* see the end of 33 c III.) More often, the end is arpeggiated, as at the end of 29 E♭ III (ex. 55*a*), or played with a real acciaccatura, as at the conclusion of the Andante of 58 C (ex. 55*c*). The *WUE* provides appropriate performance suggestions for these.

83. The arpeggio in the right hand may not be started before striking the bass in the left hand; in this situation, because of the e-b fifth, a full e-b-e^1-g♯^{1}-b^1 arpeggio rendition is suggested.

Ex. 55. *a,* 29 E♭ III, 136 (* *WUE:* Seconda volta). *b,* 20 B♭ II, 109. *c,* 58 C I, 134 (** *WUE:* acciaccatura).

Passages in small notes are essential elements of ornamentation in Haydn's keyboard style. These passages are sometimes long, sometimes short, sometimes scalar, and are generally diatonic and only rarely chromatic. In the late sonatas (as, e.g., in the embellished reprise of the Adagio of 62 E♭), these passages are the notational representation of an improvisatory and imaginative individual performance. The majority of Haydn's small-note passages should be played according to the eighteenth-century sense of *tempo rubato;*[84] the passage should occupy the time of the preceding normal-size beat or rest and conclude in time for the subsequent beat. The speed of execution depends on the tempo of the movement and on the dramatic or pianistic effect desired.

Since Haydn's writing of passages in small notes seems to be a sign of a more mature and less pedantic notation, the question arises whether some of the passages in normal-size notation in the earlier pieces may not be understood in the same manner—not as an evenly timed series of notes but as a right-hand passage with rhythmic flexibility within the beat. This possibility could be supported by many examples (see ex. 56).

Ex. 56. *a,* 36 C II, 41 (1773). *b,* 52 G II, 11 (1780).

84. "The so-called *tempo rubato* or *robato* (actually *stolen* time). . . . Commonly it is understood as a kind of shortening or lengthening of notes, or the displacement (dislocation) of these. There is something taken away (stolen) from the duration of a note and for this, another note is given that much more. . . . From this it can be seen that through this kind of execution the tempo, or even more, the meter as a whole is not displaced" (Türk, *School,* 374).

The reason for the normal-size notation of passages in the earlier sonatas is easily explained. Haydn did not write small-note passages under a rest in his keyboard music before the G Major Sonata, no. 52, of 1780. Had he written such passages, they probably would have been understood as an unusual ornament and would have been begun on the next beat. He did, however, write passages shortening the duration of a previous normal-size note (e.g., 39 D II, 21). Around 1780, while revising his notation in general, Haydn introduced these unorthodox ornamental passages, with eighth-note beaming that is not meant to suggest any kind of concrete rhythmic value.[85]

12. *On the Embellished Repeat*

Variation is imperative for repetition these days. It is expected of all performers.

—C. P. E. Bach, *Sonaten mit veränderten Reprisen*

Before embarking on what is perhaps the most exciting topic for present-day pianists, as a musicologist I feel obliged to state that most of my suggestions are based on indirect evidence. In Haydn's correspondence, and in the authentic references of his contemporaries, there is no mention of the necessity of playing ornamented repeats; nor is there any direct information regarding how or in which of Haydn's keyboard works ornamented repeats might have been played. To my knowledge, no eighteenth-century source survives containing an ornamented variant of any of Haydn's sonatas.

Does it follow that in the eighteenth century Haydn's sonatas were not executed with embellished repeats or added ornaments? On the contrary, they were most definitely played so. In an age when the title page of C. P. E. Bach's well-known set of piano sonatas announced that they had been composed *mit veränderten Reprisen* (with altered repeats), the *Veränderung* (a term implying alteration, variation, and embellishment alike) belonged to the basic vocabulary of musicality and taste. Both professional musicians and experienced amateurs embellished compositions more or less routinely; modest amateurs would have coveted this ability as much as they envied accomplished keyboard technique.

Türk's *Klavierschule* testifies to the complete confusion regarding ornamentation that reigned by the second half of the 1780s. He observes, "The main question: what can actually be varied? is difficult to answer without going into great detail and can perhaps not be answered to our full satisfaction. It may gen-

85. In his late sonatas, these passages are less of ornamental than of dramatic effect. See, e.g., the end of the first movement or the coda of the second movement of 59 E♭ or the two-hand, broken-chord passage at the end of the trio of the second movement of 62 E♭.

erally be observed, however, that only those places should be varied (but only when the composition is repeated) which would otherwise not be interesting enough and consequently become tedious."[86] Although some of his advice is still useful,[87] he was of course unable to give definitive answers to all questions concerning the embellished repeat. How could he have given a universally valid formula in 1789 when the practice of notating fully embellished versions varied from composer to composer?

As regards Haydn's piano sonatas, one must be aware, on the one hand, of the date of composition and the characteristics of the given sonata genre and, on the other, of the form and tempo of the movement. The main point is not whether repetitions should be embellished but whether ornaments in general should be added, changed, omitted, or varied, even at the first playing. In other words, is the notation of a given movement a "skeleton" notation or a fully detailed "definitive" notation?

Around 1770, the degree of sketchiness or detail of notation had less to do with the evolution of the sonata and more to do with the purpose or genre of a given group of sonatas. When a composer intended to perform a sonata himself or conceived it with the technically and musically skilled *Kenner* in mind, it was advisable and proper to leave room for a demonstration of the personality, taste, and improvisational ability of the player. On the other hand, the composer pleased the amateur, the *Liebhaber,* when he gave him sonatas that, when practiced carefully, might give the impression that the performer was able to execute, on his own, embellished repeats, variations, and attractive ornaments. Let us examine these two types in some detail.

A. The bulk of the mature, long, and technically demanding sonatas composed before 1773 (such as nos. 20 and 28–32, together with a few early pieces such as nos. 11 and 13–16) may be regarded as sonatas for professionals, notated somewhat sketchily; the individual performer is expected to execute ornaments, variations, and embellished repeats; this is not only possible but seems imperative, although not in every type of movement.

In several opening movements in a moderato or allegro moderato tempo,

86. Türk, *School,* 310–11.

87. § 24. "1. Every variation must be appropriate to the character of the composition. . . . 2. The variations must be of significance and at least as good as the given melody. . . . 3. Ornaments of the same sort, even if they are ever so beautiful and fitting, should not be used often. . . . 4. The elaborations must appear to have been achieved with ease rather than with effort. Therefore, they must be performed by the player with nicety and without affectation, even if they have cost him ever so much labor. . . . 5. Those passages which in themselves are already of striking beauty or liveliness, as well as compositions in which sadness, seriousness, noble simplicity, solemn and lofty greatness, pride, and the like are predominant characteristics should be completely spared from variations and elaborations, or these should be used very sparingly and with suitable discrimination. . . . 6. In general, the counting must be maintained in the strictest manner, even for the most extensive ornaments. . . . 7. Every variation must be based upon the given harmony. . . . 8. In pieces for the keyboard it is also permissible to vary the bass, but the basic harmony must be retained thereby" (ibid., 312–14).

Haydn built in repeats of the first themes similar to Bach's *veränderten Reprisen* (e.g., 20 B♭, 30 D). Nevertheless, the first movements of 20 B♭,[88] 28 D,[89] 29 E♭,[90] 30 D,[91] 31 A♭,[92] and 32 g[93] may be ornamented. It is unnecessary to force anything into the completely compact opening movement of 33 c, crammed as it is with original details. But the text of even this movement does not forbid the performer to embellish—or even to simplify the style.[94]

Any Andante or Adagio movement may be enriched by variants, ornaments, and embellished repeats, although 33 c II may be less amenable to alterations than 19 e I, 29 E♭ II, 30 D II, and 31 A♭ II.

Of the minuets and minuet-style movements, 19 e III and 20 B♭ II permit some ornamentation, whereas 28 D II offers few opportunities for it. Haydn composed an embellished repeat into the form of 32 g II; with the actual return of the theme, however, small variants can be effective.

The fast sonata-form finales (29 E♭ III, 31 A♭ III, 33 c III) do not seem to require ornamentation, although it should be noted that Haydn did provide a written-out embellished recapitulation in the C Minor Sonata. The rondo variations of 19 e II and 30 D III may benefit from a little ornamentation.

B. The sonatas written around 1773–80 (nos. 36–41 and 34,[95] 42–47, 48–52, and 53), collected in six-piece sets and intended for amateurs, are essentially of definitive notation. Their notation was, of course, not to be taken as gospel by contemporary professionals, nor should it be taken so today by pianists well versed in the style, particularly if they perform them on a fortepiano or a harpsichord; some adroit modifications and varied ornaments may work to their advantage. On the level of basic instruction, however, or when playing for one's own pleasure, one can dispense with such embellishments. Anyone who can perform with adequate ease and with the impression of spontaneity while playing the fully written-out embellished repetitions of the slow movements, the variation

88. In 20 B♭ I, e.g., in the dotted measures of the first theme, those passages around cadences (mm. 7–9) etc. may be decorated when they are repeated (mm. 20–24).

89. The first movement of 28 D survives only as a fragment.

90. In 29 E♭ I, e.g., the second statement of the first theme (mm. 7ff.), the second theme (mm. 19ff.), the repeated motives, and the closing section may be embellished.

91. In 30 D I, e.g., even the first phrase of the first theme, plus the ornaments, appoggiaturas, etc. of the closing theme group (mm. 33ff.), may be altered.

92. In 31 A♭, the first movement offers the most opportunities for embellishment and variation during both the first statement of the movement and its repetition (mm. 1–12, 23–31, etc.).

93. In 32 g I, only a few ornaments and alterations are justified, perhaps only in the transitions (mm. 5ff., 15ff.), in the first part of the development section, and in the *sempre più adagio*.

94. Rosen's argument concerning the contradiction between the ornamented repeat of the exposition and the unornamented recapitulation (*Haydn Studies,* 198) is not valid, for the simple reason that the entire second part after the double bar (i.e., the development and recapitulation) can and should be repeated also.

95. Sonata no. 35 in A♭, being a piece of dubious authenticity, does not figure in this survey. But, regardless of the composer, the two outer movements offer manifold opportunities for variation and ornamentation.

forms in faster tempos, the notated cadenza (52 G III), and the dramatic fermatas of the opening movements is capable of giving a perfect picture of these sonatas.

C. There is a third notational style, which Haydn used during the last ten years of his solo-keyboard composition (sonatas nos. 54–56, 58–62), that represents a higher level of development. Uniquely interesting, fully embellished returns and recapitulations occur in the so-called *Damensonate* types, which are genuinely on a *Kenner* level; in the concert sonatas, ranked among the outstanding achievements of contemporary piano writing; and in two other magnificent piano pieces, the Fantasy in C Major and the F Minor Variations. The double variations and the slow movements with variations written during this period (54 G I, 56 D I, 58 C I, the F Minor Variations, 59 E♭ II, 60 C II, and 62 E♭ II) have almost the appearance of anthologies of the most meticulously and individualistically notated ornaments of the time. They could have been written only by a great master who did not intend to present his treasures in concert personally. In this period, Haydn preferred to write embellished recapitulations in very fast tempos as well (54 G II, 55 B♭ II, and 56 D II). Other less elaborately notated movements—the sonata-form first movements with traditional repeat signs, the so-called scherzo forms with, for the most part, notated literal repeats,[96] a sonata rondo and an exceptional minuet finale—likewise do not require additional embellishments on the part of the performer.[97]

But even exaggerated or arbitrary ornamentation is more fitting than the mechanically exact repetition of an exposition. Great pianists of our age with perfect technical and artistic control are capable of playing precise repetitions of whole expositions or movements, and, unfortunately, they even seem to enjoy doing so. Many virtuoso pianists touring the world repeat the exposition of a Classical sonata form, if at all, only to ward off criticism rather than out of conviction.[98] For the star pianist, playing an exact repetition may be an easier feat than to perform two or more variants in an artistically convincing manner in each concert. Listeners may notice and find pleasure in performers' utmost command of the piece, in their ability to play it in exactly the same way. Such an approach seems senseless and impoverishing. If, in the interpreting artist's opinion, those sections of a sonata-form movement marked with a repeat sign can be performed in one single way only—either because its notation is so strictly fixed or because the pianist's ability at improvisation or memory cannot be depended on—the repeat might be better omitted altogether.

96. Compare 60 C III and 61 D II; the first part of the latter contains repeat signs.

97. Here, too, exceptions may be made by experts specializing in the performance of Haydn's music, who may exchange for a written-out ornament one of equal value more suited to their personal taste at the moment.

98. The repetition of the longer, second half of a Classical sonata-form movement is beginning to be heard more often in today's performances, although still in a minority of instances.

How does one learn appropriate embellishments and variations for Haydn's sonatas? Scholars, in conjunction with those performers who profoundly study the historical instruments and style, precede us as pioneers. The simplest way to learn about ornamentation is to gather ideas from sample performances, live or recorded, considering them as models or as sources of inspiration. Musicians can be more easily convinced by their ear, their intuition, and their subconscious analyses. Unfortunately, however, this would lead no farther than simple imitation in many cases. Pianists need to know the value and relevance of the sources from which they intend to learn the taste of a bygone era.

There are, to simplify, two kinds of sources on which the present-day pianist may rely.

1. At least some of Haydn's sonatas give primary information on how Haydn imagined and wrote an embellished repeat or an ornamented recapitulation. Compare, for example, the following sets of measures from the Andante of 58 C:

1–2 and 73–74	or
3–4 and 75–76	14–17 and 69–72 and 85–88
18–19 and 89–90	or
20–21 and 91–92	9–10 and 64–65
56–57 and 121–22	etc.
58–59 and 123–24	

(On the variation technique of 56 D I and 59 E♭ II, see pp. 339–45.) For examples of Haydn's varied repetitions in a faster tempo, study 54 G II (cf. mm. 1–10 with 49–58 and 59–68 and mm. 11–24 with 69–82) and 55 B♭ II (cf. mm. 1–8 with 70–77 and mm. 9–30 with 100–121). In the case of minuets, compare the first part and the return of 44 F III.

The safest method of self-education is to memorize the basic and the ornamented forms and play them side by side, to reduce them to their skeletal forms—melody and harmony—and to decorate them step by step again to arrive at the degree of embellishment conceived by Haydn. The chief advantage of this process is that Haydn's most characteristic, reflex-like devices will gradually become incorporated into one's stock of ornaments. From this point on, we may safely rely on our own improvised attempts at embellishment. The worst that might happen is that we unconsciously borrow from another of Haydn's sonatas. It is easier to improvise the ornamental components of an embellished movement by Haydn if the suitability and frequency of the ornaments has already been observed in other works.

2. Secondary information is available in greater abundance. On the one hand, eighteenth-century theoretical works and treatises written for beginning players and students of composition offer numerous examples of the manner in which an interval, a scale, or a motive may be ornamented. Our vocabulary of

ornaments should contain at a very minimum *groppo, Zirkel* (circle), *Halbzirkel* (half circle), and *tirata.*[99] On the other hand, the sonatas, rondos, and other pieces *mit veränderten Reprisen* by C. P. E. Bach demonstrate the difference between simple and varied form almost as methodically as a tutor. Of course, sonata-form movements and variation forms of many other composers can show us both similar trends and a variety of individual ways of ornamentally executing keyboard music.

What is the value of these indirect sources? To be sure, whenever ornaments are used, the selection, their extent, and the possible place of their application in Haydn's music should always be weighted with critical acumen. This notwithstanding, it must be stated that no one unfamiliar with Carl Philipp Emanuel Bach's music can be a sovereign interpreter of Haydn's keyboard works.

99. See Mozart, *Treatise,* 211–14.

Five

NOTATION *and* PART WRITING

AS REPRODUCED IN PRESENT-DAY URTEXT EDITIONS, Haydn's personal manner of notating music differs from the notation of a later period in several aspects. Moreover, his notation differs even from that of Classical music familiar to us through the urtext editions of Mozart and Beethoven sonatas. The first question we might raise, on seeing two or more independent voice parts on the same staff and independent dynamic and articulation marks on the two staves, is whether these features have any real bearing on the music. And occasionally, when a comparison of the *WUE* with the *JHW*—or of either of these editions with a facsimile edition of the manuscript—reveals small deviations in the notation, one wonders about the cause of these deviations.

Haydn was conservative in his notation; for several decades, he seemed satisfied to adhere to habits acquired in his youth. In his maturity, however, he suddenly embarked on decided notational innovations and experiments. In his keyboard compositions, he abandoned the use of the old-fashioned soprano clef that he had long insisted on and replaced it with the G clef surprisingly late.[1] The G clef accommodated the expanded upper range found in the C Major *London* Sonata, no. 60, just as the old-style clef had fit the notation of the range F_1–f^3 (see ex. 57).

1. The manuscript fragment of the piano trio (XV:5) of 1784 is the first keyboard part that Haydn notated in G clef. In his sonatas for solo keyboard, he continued using the soprano clef as late as 1789, in the now-lost manuscript of 58 C, as Christa Landon infers from indirect evidence (see the foreword to the third volume of the *WUE*). The earliest surviving autograph manuscript of a piano sonata written in G clef is that of the *Genzinger* Sonata, no. 59, dating from 1789–90. In the earlier keyboard works, high parts to be played by the left hand were notated in soprano clef, not G clef.

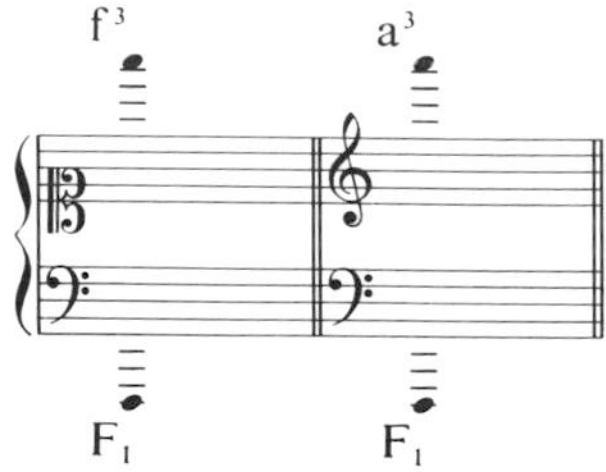

Ex. 57. The range of the C Major *London* Sonata, no. 60.

Polyphonic notation, in which the stems of two-part passages or of two- or three-toned chords written on the same staff were drawn in opposite directions as if they represented independent voices, reflects traditional Baroque practice. Musical common sense (because the careful notation of independent parts is a necessity) and the visual motivation of indicating voices consistently go hand in hand here.

If we scrutinize the first theme of the C Minor Sonata, no. 33, as printed in the *WUE,* we find some truly polyphonic writing together with some apparently ornamental pseudo–part writing.[2] (Note that the *WUE* version already uses a slightly simplified notation[3] compared to the *JHW* text; e.g., Haydn notated the voices in the left hand of mm. 7–10 independently.) Haydn's notation presents the strict three-part texture of the first theme as clearly as if it were written in score; a string trio could easily sight-read it. Nevertheless, an exacting musician might question the part writing at the end of measure 2 (ex. 58). The beams suggest that the middle part (II) takes the place of the soprano (I), while the bass (III) goes up into the middle voice. Does the original soprano part continue its own voice an octave lower?

Ex. 58. 33 c I, 2–3.

2. For an analysis of the motivic construction of the C minor theme, see p. 250.

3. Outlining the editing principles of the *WUE,* Christa Landon states, "We have kept Haydn's notation in 'parts' where understanding of the musical content appeared to be clarified thereby."

The case becomes simpler if we consult the autograph fragment of 1771,[4] which is sketch-like and contains slurs and dynamics only sporadically. Haydn used a Dorian key signature and a soprano clef. The passage under discussion receives another meaning in this clef (see [1] in ex. 59). Since the notes of measure 3 are above the third line of the staff, the stems must be drawn downward. Although Haydn could have written the voice leading more precisely (using a beam with the shape ⅂ for the middle voice's d¹-e♭¹ on two staves or using only flags and no beams for the eighth notes in the second half of m. 2), he clearly found this unnecessary.

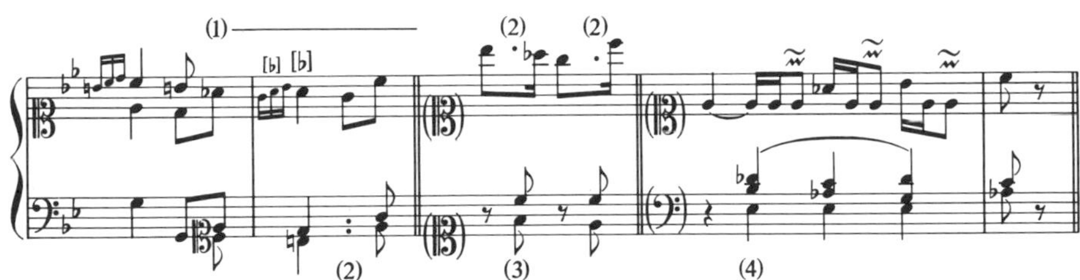

Ex. 59. Measures 2–3, 7, 9, from the autograph fragment of 33 c, showing Haydn's use of clef and key signature and his habit of placing dots and drawing stems.

While on the subject of Haydn's writing habits, it is worth noting that, with meticulous care, he consistently placed the dot in the place where its time value started, at a relatively great distance from the note head (see [2] in ex. 59), and that he also notated the seventh measure polyphonically (see [3] in ex. 59), just as he did the chords of the transition after the first theme (see [4] in ex. 59).

Haydn's notation of keyboard music in a polyphonic way reinforces our awareness that most of his music for harpsichord and fortepiano is composed in a strict part-writing texture.[5] Most of the movements written before his experiences in London are a composite of three- and two-part textures. The principal part carrying the melody and also the accompanying lower voice or voices are all of clear melodic and motivic construction. The ideal is that of chamber music with more or less equal, linear parts. The strict part writing may occasionally be broken (chords of several parts used as special "harpsichord" accents will be

4. In the possession of the Bibliothèque Nationale, Paris. The first page has been reproduced in several books, e.g., *JHW,* 18:2.

5. It is a pity, therefore, that urtext editions sometimes modernize Haydn's notation of stems. It must be admitted, however, that neither the engravers of Haydn's own time nor Haydn's own copyists faithfully reproduced it. Only surviving autograph manuscripts can be used as a source of a trustworthy reconstruction, and even these show inconsistencies. Compare mm. 1–2 and 5–6 or 11 and 142 of the second movement in the facsimile edition (Graz, 1982) of the autograph of the *Genzinger* Sonata.

treated in more detail later on); it may sometimes widen out to a four-part fabric[6] or, even more frequently, become condensed into a single voice in the right hand. But, in the sonatas written up to 1790, the majority of themes and transitions feature clear part writing, particularly in their initial presentation. Indeed, the strategy of alternating three- and two-voice sections with other textures and types of motion is a major means of articulating the form of the exposition in a number of sonatas.

The strict part-writing ideal in Haydn's keyboard music may have had two sources. First, his initial keyboard experiences came from playing harpsichord and organ. On these instruments, a fourth voice added for harmonic reasons to a three-voice texture (i.e., a melody with two accompanying parts) would result in a significant increase in volume, perhaps producing a strong accent at an inappropriate moment. Second, Haydn, who was an instinctively polyphonic composer, preferred creating the feeling of full harmony with rather few voices or instruments.

As Haydn gradually came to know the dynamic possibilities of the fortepiano, his strict contrapuntal notation became more flexible (1783–84, the *Bossler* sonatas, nos. 54–56, and the piano trios). Yet, even in the *Genzinger* Sonata, no. 59 in E♭, written for the Schanz piano that Haydn enthusiastically praised, most of the accents are created with the help of melodic and harmonic turns, ornamentation, rests, new textures, changes of register, and reinforcement of chords, that is, by means appropriate to music for the harpsichord[7] rather than by touch and dynamics proper to modern piano playing.

The free style of part writing of the first and second movements of the E♭ Major Sonata, no. 62, provides the chief compositional evidence of the superiority, in terms of action and dynamic capability, of the English instruments with which Haydn became acquainted in London. In this sonata, everything is present: from two to eight voices, in *forte* and *piano,* merging with *crescendo,* and, as an unexpected contrast, a phenomenal sense of novelty. Moreover, instead of the earlier cantabile themes of extremely sophisticated phrase construction (see the main themes of the first and second movements of 59 E♭), here Haydn composed much more direct first themes of concerto style and effect.

The stylistic differences in the part writing of the last two sonatas in E♭ major, nos. 59 and 62, are abrupt and enormous. The pieces of the 1780s are, in this respect, masterworks of a pre-Mozartian ideal; the best movements of the *London* sonatas point far beyond the qualities of the sonatas of Mozart and anticipate Beethoven.

6. For example, 31 A♭ II, 14ff. and 53ff.

7. In 59 E♭ I, those few moments that are not in two or three voices are worth special study, for they seem to call attention to either an important accent or a special kind of touch.

 *Six*

Touch *and* Articulation

The fact that C. P. E. Bach's *Versuch* deals primarily with performance on the clavichord, which was the ideal instrument for his own style of composing and playing, does not dissuade me from taking his teachings on touch and articulation as a starting point. With the exception of the *Bebung,* which can be played only on the clavichord, Bach's explanations have considerable importance and illuminative force for Haydn's music. Bach avoided Italian terms, but he did carefully describe the three basic kinds of touch—staccato, legato, and portato:

§ 17. "When notes are to be detached [*gestossen*] from each other strokes or dots are placed above them, as illustrated in Fig. I [see ex. 60]. . . . Notes are detached with relation to: (1) their notated length, that is, a half, quarter, or eighth of a bar; (2) the tempo, fast or slow; and (3) the volume, forte or piano. Such tones are always held for a little less than half of their notated length. In general, detached notes appear mostly in leaping passages and rapid tempos."

§ 18. "Notes which are to be played legato [*Die Noten welche geschleift werden sollen*] must be held for their full length. A slur is placed above them in the manner of Fig. II. The slur applies to all the notes included under its trace. Patterns of two or four slurred notes are played with a slight, scarcely noticeable increase of pressure on the first and third tones. The same applies to the first tones of groups of three notes. In other cases only the first of the slurred notes is played in this manner. It is a convenient custom to indicate by appropriate marks only the first few of prolonged successions of detached or legato notes, it being self-evident that all of the tones are to be played similarly until another kind of mark intervenes. The slurred tones of broken chords are held in the manner of Fig. III."

§ 19. "The notes of Fig. IV are played legato [*werden gezogen*], but each tone is noticeably accented. The term which refers to the performance of notes that are both slurred and dotted is *portato* [*das Tragen der Tone*]."[1]

§ 21. "The notes of Fig. V are played in such a manner that the first of each slur is slightly accented. Fig. VI is played similarly except that the last note of each slur is detached. The finger must be raised immediately after it has struck the key. The *portato* and vibrato of Fig. IV apply only to the clavichord;[2] Fig. V–VI may be played on both the harpsichord and the clavichord, but more effectively on the latter."

§ 22. "Tones which are neither detached, connected, nor fully held are sounded for half their value, unless the abbreviation *Ten.* (hold) is written over them, in which case they must be held fully. Quarters and eighths in moderate and slow tempos are usually performed in this semidetached manner. They must not be played weakly, but with fire and a slight accentuation."

Ex. 60. C. P. E. Bach's examples (*Versuch,* 1753 ed.). Fig. I, *Stossen* (staccato). Fig. II, *Schleiffungen* (legato). Fig. IV, *Gezogene Noten; das Tragen* (portato).

In the supplement to the third edition of his book (1787), C. P. E. Bach gave two further pieces of advice useful to present-day pianists (see ex. 61).

§ 18. "Passages in which passing notes or appoggiaturas are struck against a bass are played legato in all tempos even in the absence of a slur (a). As illustrated in the example marked N.B., the same remark applies to basses which are similarly devised. . . . Successions of thirds like those in (b) would be always impossible to perform in a fast tempo. . . . However, played in the manner of the asterisked example with the quarters held for their full value, the desired effect can be easily produced on the clavichord as well as the harpsichord."

Ex. 61. Additions to the 1787 ed. of C. P. E. Bach's *Versuch*.

1. Türk speaks of *appoggiato*.
2. Fig. IV (b) refers to *Bebung;* this musical example has been omitted here.

While Löhlein did not differentiate between staccatos marked with a dot and those marked with a stroke (neither in the first edition of 1765 nor in the revised second edition of 1773 of his *Clavier-Schule*), Türk's book contains an interesting small addition to what has been said about staccato.

§ 36. "The signs at (a) and (b) have the same meaning, but some would like to indicate by the stroke (a) that a shorter staccato be played than that indicated by the dot (b)" (see ex. 62).[3]

Ex. 62. From Türk, *Klavierschule,* 6:3, 36.

Having surveyed the discussions of C. P. E. Bach, Löhlein, and Türk, let us go back to some sources from the 1750s that were not specifically concerned with keyboard playing but that explained staccato, legato, and other signs either in a more general framework or with reference to string instruments. It is worth repeating that the instrument of the young Haydn was, first and foremost, the violin. Moreover, Haydn's use of articulation signs was the same whether he wrote for piano, violin, or other instruments.

Quantz's book is useful in furthering the present-day performer's understanding of Haydn's staccatos (even if Haydn did not make direct use of Quantz himself). It establishes a difference between the staccato stroke and dot with regard to bowing, and it makes a subtle differentiation between a series of staccato strokes and a staccato stroke placed above an individual note, the latter meaning a kind of marcato. This usage was observed by Haydn. I will not quote here Quantz's discussion of the relation of the length of the staccato note to the tempo of the movement. Other points that he makes are as follows:

27. "In playing staccato the bow must be detached a little from the strings.[4] . . . If a little stroke stands above only one note . . . it indicates not only that the note must be played half as long,[5] but also that it must at the same time be accented with a pressure of the bow. . . . If dots stand above the notes they must be articulated or attacked with a short bow, but must not be detached. If a slur is added above the dots, all the notes within it must be taken in one bow-stroke and stressed with a pressure of the bow."[6]

Leopold Mozart did not use the term *staccato,* but he did describe staccato

3. Türk, *School,* 342.
4. Quantz later added ". . . only on those notes in which time permits" (*Playing,* 232).
5. In general, Quantz suggests that "they must sound half as long as their tone value" (ibid., 232).
6. Ibid.

playing, discussing the meaning of the staccato markings shown in a musical example.[7] The dot appeared in Mozart's book, as in Quantz's, just at the description of what was later called *portato playing* and, moreover, with some remarkable examples:

§ 17. On the dot under the slur, "This signifies that the notes lying within the slur are not only to be played in one bow-stroke, but must be separated from each other by a slight pressure of the bow [ex. 63*a*]. If, however, instead of dots small strokes be written, the bow is lifted at each note, so that all these notes within the slur must be taken in one bow but must be entirely separated from each other [ex. 63*b*]."[8]

Ex. 63. Staccato and portato playing of staccato dots according to L. Mozart's description.

We may now turn to the interpretation of the signs that Haydn used to notate articulation. Haydn's notation was consistent with the small-dimension articulation of the time; he used no idiosyncratic signs for touch proper or phrasing. One should not forget the following:

a) The majority of Haydn's keyboard sonatas are composed for the harpsichord, an instrument essentially incapable of producing the dynamic subtleties possible on the clavichord or the fortepiano. Thus, the notation can suggest the musical character primarily by means of articulation signs, such as slurring or sharply detaching a series of notes. These notations may be read in essentially the same manner whatever the instrument.

b) Haydn did not use phrasing signs such as slurs extending over several measures or "double-layer" slur combinations, that is, signs adopted by composers of nineteenth-century keyboard music for showing the middle-dimension phrase structure of musical sentences. Haydn could assume that the readers of his music were familiar with the musical grammar of the time. A richly articulated rhetorical rendering, fully supplied with internal punctuation, formed one of the basic constituents of good musical taste.

Three further notational conventions of Haydn's time need to be understood by the modern performer. Even the best modern urtext editions cannot aid the performer in these instances without departing significantly from Haydn's notational practice and becoming not urtext editions but performing editions.

7. Mozart, *Violinschule,* 47.
8. Mozart, *Treatise,* 45.

These conventions, discussed below, must be comprehended in every case and carefully applied in a given context:

1. The composer was expected to supply articulation marks for only the first of a series of similar figures or at most for a measure. The performer would continue *simile* even if the word itself was not written out. Likewise, once an articulation was written in a detailed manner, for example, in the exposition, it was sufficient to refer to it by way of abbreviation in later, analogous measures.

2. In general, the largest unit over which articulation was marked did not exceed one measure. Of course, short slurs tying the two notes of a syncopated motive could extend over the bar line, there being no other way to indicate such a figure. And in certain cases a traditional writing habit of Haydn's produced unorthodox notation.[9] Normally, however, the slur ended before the bar line. Nevertheless, the performer must consider whether a legato passage is to continue uninterrupted by the bar line.[10]

3. Right- and left-hand parts appear in Haydn's notation as if they were polyphonically independent; in the autographs of his late fortepiano music, he also wrote dynamics in this independent-voice manner. The bass part is generally accompanimental and supporting, while the upper part is the melodic, leading part. Certain articulations written in the upper part do not necessarily apply to the lower part as well. Making things even more complicated, we may note that a difference in the notated articulation of the two hands, such as staccato in one hand with no notated articulation in the other hand, does not necessarily mean that the two parts should be sharply and consciously distinguished.

"Ordinary notes" and tenuto. In addition to these three well-documented notational conventions, there is a fourth area with great potential for ambiguity. Unmarked notes and figures, called "ordinary notes" by Türk and *movimento ordinario* (*mov. ord.*) notes by Marpurg, raise several fundamental questions. For how long and with what articulation should a single unmarked note be played? What information is implied in the notation? Which of the Baroque performance traditions were still valid in Haydn's time? To demonstrate the significance of this problem, let us examine three examples (ex. 64*a, b,* and *c*). Haydn wrote down three themes two times, and in each case the notation is slightly different. The discrepancy in examples 64*a* and *b* has nothing to do with chronology; the versions in the *EK* simply reflect the way Haydn remembered the thematic incipits when writing them down sometime later. In example 64*c*, however, an "old-style" notation and an "edited" later form are displayed side by side.

9. The right-hand slurring in 49 c♯ II, 68–69, 72–73, 76–77, 78–79, etc., is the first sign of a later style of notation giving indications of phrasing.

10. A good example is 33 c II, 1–2, 9–10, left hand.

Ex. 64. Discrepancies in Haydn's thematic incipits. *a,* 16 D, and the same in the *EK.* *b,* 29 E♭, and the same in the *EK.* *c,* 33 c, 1771 and 1780 versions.

For Haydn's contemporaries, minor divergences in notation were not particularly disturbing. For one thing, they were reading the music in the spirit of certain accepted conventions. They interpreted the written music in agreement with these conventions and varied their interpretation according to their own taste and capabilities. For us, however, the divergences provide evidence for formulating or reexamining certain assumptions. In example 64*a,* the "harpsichord-legatissimo" performance of the accompanimental figure in the left hand is precisely notated in the *EK;* this may justify a similar rendering in other movements by Haydn. The "edited" version of the theme of the C Minor Sonata (ex. 64*c*) verifies the *mov. ord.* (i.e., shortened) execution of the high C's in the left hand. By adding slurs at the same time, the notation specifies an articulation that would not otherwise be self-evident. The case shown in example 64*b* is certainly instructive. When entering this incipit into the *EK,* Haydn could presumably remember no more than the motivic structure. He forgot that, owing to the written-out ties in the original form, the B♭'s in the right hand are "quasi tenuto," held out to their full value, in contrast with the G's in the left hand, which are *mov. ord.* tones to be played shorter than their written value.

These examples reveal that not all the "ordinary notes" in Haydn's sonatas should automatically be played shortened and detached. There are figures that had been conceived as connected but in Haydn's old-style, basically Baroque notation were not marked with slurs. Nevertheless, most of the notes that are not marked with slur or staccato signs can be categorized as *mov. ord.* notes and should sound for less time than their written value. The numerous *tenuto* or *tenute* inscriptions substantiate the validity of the *mov. ord.* convention. The *tenuto* marking instructs the player to hold an "ordinary note" for its full written value. I would say that a note marked with a tenuto is, in fact, a "one-note legato." In certain cases, the tenuto was the only means of indicating that an individual note must be held for its full value.

The examples collected in example 65 show the various functions of the tenuto. Case *a* is actually misleading because the slur and the tenuto occur together;[11] form *b* is the unambiguous notation of "chord legato." The instructions ensure that the broken chord will be sustained in Türk's manner[12] (*c, j*) and that the tenuto signs will remain valid, in the sense of *simile,* for a longer section (*d–e*). Cases *f–g* include instructions to prevent the separation of phrase ends, a natural interpunctuation; this must have appeared very modern in 1780. In example *h* the tenuto guarantees bringing out the melody, while in *i* it facilitates proper voice leading. Finally, in case *k,* the leap of almost four octaves in the right hand and the resulting sustained low E almost amount to a change in meter or, in other words, to a written-out slowing down of the tempo at the end of the movement.

In the framework of the more modern notation emerging in about 1780, an interesting phenomenon appeared that I call the "approximative notation" of the generation of Haydn and Mozart. This notation of certain themes and sections of movements was characterized by fewer *mov. ord.* notes and a strikingly large number of short rest signs between the notes, the so-called *sospir* (as, e.g., in the theme of 56 D I). The occurrence of an abundance of *sospiri* must have given contemporary music readers the impression that they had come on a new-style, more detailed rhythmic notation, one that had to be precisely realized.

In addition to issues connected with *mov. ord.,* several other aspects of Haydn's use of articulation signs require careful study. These include the two kinds of staccato signs (the stroke and the dot), the difference between staccato and portato, and the various legato and staccato combinations. As with other notational matters, a knowledge of the chronology of the works is important, for Haydn's writing habits and preferences underwent several developments and changes that can be traced clearly.

11. The fragmentary autograph draft of 1771 (for the facsimile of p. 1, see *JHW,* 18:2) suggests that Haydn had first written a slur above the four chords, then substituted the term *ten.* without erasing the slur. The *ten.* is a clearer indication because of the repetition of the note e♭². The recapitulation is no longer preserved in the autograph manuscript, but in the 1780 first edition corrected by Haydn the analogous place has a *ten.* without a slur, as ex. 65*b* shows.

12. "If the notes of a broken chord are to be held, this can be indicated by the word *tenuto* (abbreviated *ten.*)" (Türk, *School,* 284).

Ex. 65. *a–c,* 33 c I, 18, 81, 25. *d,* 38 F I, 38. *e,* 39 D II, 9. *f,* 49 c♯ III, 1. *g,* 50 D II, 4–5, 9, *h–j,* 52 G II, 14, 16, 50. *k,* 62 E♭ II, 51.

Staccato stroke, staccato dot. Except for a small, well-delineated group of cases, Haydn used a small stroke for marking staccato, in all kinds of combinations and tempos, in all his autograph manuscripts, from the very first up to the last. An individual staccato stroke is primarily an accent indicating a stressed short tone; a set of strokes signals short notes and a clearly articulated and accented performance as well. Example 66 gives excerpts from an Adagio dating from 1773 and an Allegro movement from about 1794 to illustrate the variety of pianistic shades of performance possibilities expressed by the staccato stroke. We find a terse cantabile phrase ending with the right hand removed (*a, c, h*); clipped points of sound in a slow tempo (*b*), nervous points in a virtuoso tempo (*i*), slightly agitated alternation between two notes (*g*), and pointed rhythmic stress (*k*); and graceful staccato passage from the wrist (*l*) and warm, declamatory execution (*f*). Sometimes the staccato expresses the phrasing proper, as one to three staccato-legato notes (*d*), but in other instances it primarily assumes the value of an accent (*e*).

Ex. 66. (a)–(h), 36 C II. (i)–(l), 60 C I.

In the manuscripts of Haydn's solo piano works, the dot occurs exclusively over a series of notes, usually in tone repetitions but later and more rarely above scale passages.[13] Haydn scholars have been engaged in a dispute over the possibility of attributing the alternate appearance of staccato dot and stroke to writing

13. Staccato dots above individual notes are found, however, in Haydn's mature string quartets (e.g., op. 71 B♭ I, 6; see *JHW,* 12:5). I am inclined to term these signs—in agreement with Nikolaus Harnoncourt's remarks on *Idomeneo* ("The Performance of 'Idomeneo,'" pp. 12–13, in the commentaries to the recording, Telefunken 6.35547, 1980)—*dolce staccato.*

with a quill.[14] The concrete evidence in the manuscripts, however, negates the possibility of an extramusical cause. The dots, as they first emerge in the authentic sources of Haydn's sonatas (1767: 30 D II, first theme; 1774: 44 F I, first theme, left hand; see ex. 67), always appear in conjunction with staccato strokes.[15] The only plausible interpretation is that in these cases the dot is a less sharp staccato than the stroke and that an accent, as a second meaning, is not involved. The dot may indicate a kind of articulation that was later notated as portato.

Ex. 67. *a,* 30 D II, 1. *b,* 44 F I, 1.

The autograph fragment of 44 F, dating from 1774, is a key work in Haydn's development of newer, subtler notational processes. This work may have already been conceived with the fortepiano in mind, an idea that is reinforced by the details shown in example 68.[16]

14. To make a dot (or to draw empty note heads) with a quill that easily got stuck on the knotty surface of contemporary handmade paper was difficult and involved the risk of leaving a blot. Below is an enlarged representation of how Haydn typically notated half notes (*a*) and staccatos (*b, c*). The half note was drawn on the basis of Winternitz, *Musical Autographs,* 1:29, and the staccatos by analyzing Haydn's autograph manuscripts in Budapest:

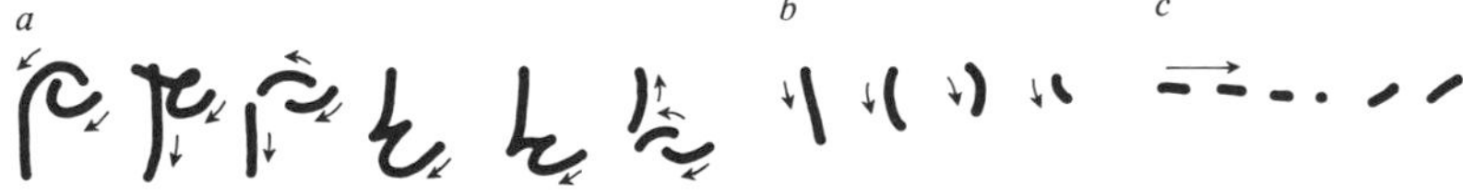

These examples suggest that the two kinds of staccato are the outcome of two possible types of rather fast gestures: the stroke is drawn with one quick movement for each mark, whereas a series of dots is produced with a continuous movement. Staccato strokes drawn very quickly in a series are sometimes, as an extreme, reduced to dots. This leads inexperienced urtext editors to complain that one cannot always distinguish the stroke from the dot. In my experience, however, genuinely ambiguous staccato signs are very rare in Haydn's autograph manuscripts.

15. If the hypothesis of the quill were true, Haydn could have written dots in the right hand as well as in the left hand of the first theme of 44 F. The differences in articulation, however, denote differences in musical content. The right hand presents a genuine rhythmic motive, while the left hand is just the customary drumming bass (Türk, *School,* 370), an imitation of a typical orchestral bass of an Allegro movement.

16. Using the same contemporary authentic copies, the *WUE* places staccato dots above the f^1's in 44 F I, 3, while the *JHW* puts staccato strokes in parentheses.

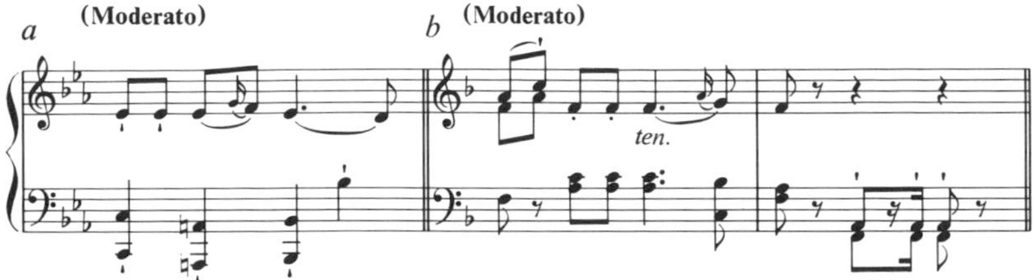

Ex. 68. *a,* 40 E♭ I, 2 (1773). *b,* 44 F I, 3 (1774).

Staccato and portato. Several examples suggest that slower scale passages in Haydn's sonatas, whether marked with a series of staccato dots or with slurred staccato dots, are meant to be played the same way, that is, as genuine portato (ex. 69).[17] On the other hand, the examples taken from the Adagio of 62 E♭ (reproduced here exactly in agreement with Haydn's original manuscript) point to the role of the staccato stroke (i) as an accent sign, as opposed to staccato dots. The staccato stroke is the softest accent sign found in Haydn; the marcato sign > (ii) emerging in his late manuscripts calls for a stronger accent. The strongest accent of all is ***fz***, used from Haydn's youth on.

Ex. 69. *a,* 44 F II, 8. *b,* 62 E♭ II, 4, 14. *c,* 39 D II, 13. *d,* 51 E♭ I, 14.

17. Precisely because Haydn had already experimented with a sort of portato expressed by means of staccato dots in 30 D II, I consider it a mistake to play the first measure of 32 g I as portato, as printed in the *WUE* and heard in many performances. Experimenting at the harpsichord or fortepiano, one must search for a kind of noble staccato (perhaps by playing the four staccato notes with the same finger?), producing something that Haydn might have considered appropriate to such an exceptional theme.

In the *London* Sonata no. 60 in C, the Adagio in F major, which is extant in two versions, proves to be an indispensable work with regard to interpreting existing signs and deducing proper articulations from them. The sonata version is more precisely notated (ex. 70*b*). It reveals that one should not always read the articulation literally, restricting it to a certain group of notes; it also suggests that a ***fz*** in the right hand with a slur in the left gives the exact articulation of the whole area as intended by Haydn.

Ex. 70. *a,* Adagio, m. 9. *b,* 60 C II, 9 (* ***fz*** in the next measure already written out).

This late Adagio for fortepiano exemplifies the rare subtleties of piano playing that Haydn became capable of notating. For example, when a scale passage is restated in octaves, the change in sonority is reinforced by a change in articulation (see ex. 71).

Ex. 71. 60 C II, 18, 20. (* *JHW:* no slur.)

Legato-staccato combinations. A great number of motives and figures in Haydn's keyboard works end on notes marked with staccato signs. Their proper articulation and varied execution constitute a cardinal point in the lively performance of his music. Haydn's style, in contrast to the more Italianate style of his Viennese contemporaries, is characterized by a number of rests, caesuras, and detached notes that express the clear articulation of the melody and the clear-cut accompanying texture. Both the variety of textures in his scores and the details of articulation seem to underline this impression.

The selection in example 72 is drawn from one sonata in harpsichord style, 36 C (1773), and one in fortepiano style, 59 E♭ (1789). In the finale of 36 C, the short, snapped character of the ending notes of the two-note slurs throws an accent onto the beginning notes. The same effect may be found in measure 15, in spite of the sixteenth-note triplet embellishment; writing a slur over this group of notes would be superfluous because the tempo precludes any other articulation. The cleverness of the notation of the superimposition of upbeat and downbeat motives in measures 31ff. lies in the fact that, for the sake of the proper accent on the beat, Haydn departs in the left hand from the established staccato at the end of the slur. The opening movement of the *Genzinger* Sonata, no. 59, makes equally fine distinctions for the fortepiano. As an experiment, it is worth playing the ends of the slurs (marked [i] and [ii] in ex. 72*b*) as written, with the articulations reversed, with staccato notes at the end of all slurs, and with no staccatos. In the same sonata, we see clear combinations of marcato staccato strokes, nonlegato passages, and legato articulations.

Ex. 72. *a,* 36 C III, 1, 15, 31. *b,* 59 E♭ I, 12, 21.

On conventions of writing slurs. The courageous pianist who does not hide his phrasing beneath a generalized, pedaled legato needs his musical intuition and good taste to discover the proper slurring, accentuation, and declamation in each phrase he plays. Haydn, like his contemporaries, was inclined to slur entire groups of notes routinely, that is, to place a slur, mechanically, above groups of four sixteenth notes joined by a beam (36 C II, 13ff.; 62 E♭ I, 6ff., left hand, etc.). These passages were probably meant to be played with a continuous legato, in which the first notes under the slurs were slightly accented, in agreement with C. P. E. Bach's teaching. There is some danger, however, in assuming that an articulation mark is routine or is to be routinely continued; in reality, a unique musical idea may be concealed. To what extent, for example, are these two passages from the exposition of the Sonata no. 33 in C Minor analogous (see ex. 73)?

Ex. 73. 33 c I, 11, 14.

It is obvious that the sections of four eighth notes in the two passages (marked with a wavy line in the example) are dissimilar in character. But what is the articulation of the two upbeat eighth notes (marked with an asterisk) in measure 10? Are they legato, like the succeeding four notes? The melodic declamation in measure 10 may be displayed more beautifully if these two notes are played nonlegato, but a syncopated two-note slurring of the ***f*-*p*** groups in measures 13–14 is natural. The other question is whether the sixteenth notes in measure 11 (marked with two asterisks) should be played legato. The corresponding group of notes, in measure 14, is marked with a slur. However, the rhythmic function of the group of sixteenth notes is not the same in both passages: in measure 11, they lead to a *forte* passage in the next measure; in measure 14, they continue into a lyrical theme. Thus, there is no necessity to articulate these two groups of notes the same way.

The slurs of articulation in the late, mature notation of Haydn must, however, be given full credence. Haydn did not have in mind a cantabile piano technique made up of large legato slurs. Instead, his works speak with the noble diction of a series of precisely shaped and emotionally rich units—sigh motives, scale passages, melodic circles, and other melodic turns. For example, the beauty and complexity of the Adagio theme of the *Genzinger* Sonata does not emerge if it is played as if bound by one single comprehensive slur; one wants to hear the choreography of the motives unfold. How beautiful it is that the first dotted motive begins by disentangling itself from an ornament while the second begins frankly on the principal note, that the first motive ascends and the second changes direction and descends (see ex. 74).

Ex. 74. The Adagio theme of the *Genzinger* Sonata. *a,* Anachronistic ideal of legato. *b,* Motive-by-motive legato performance.

Independent articulation in the two hands. Haydn's pianistic style shows numerous cases of both real and pseudo asynchronisms in the two hands. It would be a mistake to simplify the notation and insist on uniform synchronous touch. When the music in the right and left hands is similar with regard to both rhythm and texture, then apparently different articulations in the two hands (such as the presence or absence of a staccato stroke at the end of a slur or over a chord) are not really asynchronous. Haydn often considered it sufficient to notate articulation signs in the right hand alone (see, e.g., 59 E♭ II, 36, 123–24). But when a contrapuntal concept, an independent rhythmic design or accentuation, can be easily recognized in the motives, the performer would do well to find a tasteful solution to the problems of asynchronous articulation, although it must be said that such passages will sound less clumsy and more natural on period instruments than on the modern piano.

Indeed, explanations for some asynchronous articulations may be sought in the capabilities of the instrument itself. Although the bass of the eighteenth-century harpsichord and fortepiano is clearer than that of the modern piano, notes played two or three octaves apart, even with identical staccato touches, will sound for different lengths of time. Composers either accepted this circumstance, finding no contradiction in the longer resonance of the bass of the chord—the typical attitude[18]—or did their best to make all notes of a chord sound for an equal length of time by turning to a device such as placing a stroke above a bass note. The three examples given in example 75 represent three different approaches. In example 75*a,* the marcato-staccato in the left hand of the D Major *Esterházy* Sonata, written for harpsichord, is an attempt at such a "correction"; it can be played as a brilliant effect on the fortepiano as well. In example 75*b,* the first theme of the *Genzinger* Sonata shows a genuinely asynchronous notation. The precise touch of the eighth notes of the left hand must be chosen independently of the marcato-staccato in the right hand. In example 75*c,* the passage at the end of the exposition of this sonata offers a natural compromise. The final chord is to be played short in both hands. The left-hand chord will naturally sound longer, which should by no means induce us to play the right hand with a

18. Editors of eighteenth-century symphonic scores are well aware of the frequency of notational idiosyncrasies such as writing closing chords on the beat in eighth notes in the upper voices while giving the string bass quarter notes. Such a notation is, in fact, not careless but rather pragmatic.

softer, nonlegato touch. On the contrary, the final chords of both hands must be executed marcato.

Ex. 75. *a*, 39 D III, 1. *b*, 59 E♭ I, 1. *c*, 59 E♭ I, 63.

While at first glance Haydn's notation might seem insufficient, in fact it contains splendid pianistic ideas. The discovery of this is one of the intellectual adventures of playing Haydn's music on an accomplished artistic level. Haydn relied on the player as his partner in the presentation of his work with persuasive power. The performer who shares this belief will be convinced that it would be a loss to unify or simplify the five or so variants of touch and articulation in even a short and almost monothematic contredanse-like finale such as is shown in example 76.

Ex. 76. 38 F III, 1, 9, 33, 35, 41.

Seven

HAYDN'S NOTATION *of* DYNAMICS *and* ACCENTS

HAVING REACHED THE DIFFICULT SET of problems connected with reading the dynamic marks and accent marks in Haydn's notation, we must first attempt to separate two matters clearly. One is the study of the intended meaning of the signs, in eighteenth-century notation in general and in Haydn's keyboard writing in particular. The other is the application of this study by modern-day players who aspire to find and bring out the true message in Haydn's works, regardless of their choice of instrument or performance situation. In this book, I have chosen to limit my remarks to the first problem, leaving the adaptation of this information to performers and teachers who are willing to guide and reinforce their insights with the help of scholarly findings.

A few preliminary remarks regarding the notation of dynamics and accents in Haydn's time may be useful here.

1. The character of a given movement must condition the player's response to dynamic marks; detailed elaboration of dynamics cannot take place until the general affect and overall style of a piece has been ascertained. In the eighteenth century, there was no autonomous dynamic structure; "consistency" of dynamics in a performance was neither an aim nor a merit.[1]

2. Any dynamic mark or accent mark is relative. It is affected by the tempo,

1. After describing the grades of dynamics, C. P. E. Bach states, "It is not possible to describe the contexts appropriate to the forte or piano because for every case covered by even the best rule there will be an exception. The particular effect of these shadings depends on the passage, its context, and the composer, who may introduce either a forte or a piano at a given place for equally convincing reasons. In fact, complete passages, including their consonances and dissonances, may be marked first forte and later piano. This is a customary procedure with both repetitions and sequences, particularly when the accompaniment is modified. But in general it can be said that dissonances are played loudly and consonances softly, since the former rouse our emotions and the latter quiet them" (*Essay,* 163).

the style of the movement, the thematic environment, and the harmonic progression, among other factors.[2] A direction serves primarily as a recommendation.

3. A healthy *forte* volume, adjusted to the style of the movement, is proper for the beginnings of movements, even Adagios, unless an explicit *piano* advises the contrary.[3]

4. In eighteenth-century sources, it is not necessarily the case that a given dynamic marking controls a passage, inflected by accent marks within the overall dynamic, until replaced by another dynamic marking. That is, in a series such as ***f*-*p*-*fz***, it is not clear whether the dynamic level after ***fz*** should be ***f*** or ***p***. The unclear interrelation between markings for dynamic level and markings for accent results in many ambiguous readings. Editors of the modern urtext editions have tried to reduce the possible confusion by adding explanatory directions in brackets.

5. One cause of serious difficulties in reading Haydn's autograph manuscripts is his almost indistinguishable graphic form of the ***f*** dynamic mark and the ***fz*** accent mark, *for:*, *for*, *forz:*, etc. The experience and intuition of scholarly editors, who have done textual analyses of a large number of autograph manuscripts and of contemporary texts sometimes corrupted by copyists or printers, can be of help in the interpretation of these signs. Facsimile editions of autograph manuscripts are a dubious guide for someone who lacks a thorough preliminary grounding in the notational problems and writing habits of a given composer.

6. In his keyboard music, as a rule, Haydn marked the dynamic levels of the right and the left hands separately, in a part-writing manner, with a multitude of asynchronous places resulting. In secondary sources, including a considerable portion of the contemporary prints, this feature disappeared. It cannot be reconstructed unless additional sources become available. Thus, the synchronous dynamic markings placed between the two staves in the modern urtext editions do not necessarily signify a more developed, modern notation on Haydn's part.[4]

7. The notation of expression marks underwent considerable evolution and refinement during the five decades of Haydn's activity as a composer. Consequently, in his music dating from various periods, different signs may be used

2. Leopold Mozart (*Treatise*, 218–23) described special situations that call for stronger or weaker notes. In his examples, he uses ***f***, ***p***, and ***fp*** signs. Altered notes, long notes occurring between short values, syncopated notes, and emphasized high notes in gay movements all need to be stressed. Mozart also described, in full detail, the notes that are generally stressed in the various meters, "which the Italians call *Nota Buona*."

3. See the entry "Forte" in Heinrich Christoph Koch, *Musikalisches Lexikon* (Frankfurt, 1802), 589–90. There are authentic *piano* effects at the beginning of fast movements in Haydn's piano sonatas 50 D III, 53 e I, 60 C III, and 62 E♭ III and at the head of slow movements in 54 G I, 56 D I, and 62 E♭ II. The editorial directions of *piano* in the *WUE* at the beginnings of 59 E♭ II and III are in fact disputable suggestions.

4. It is a pity that the printed score, edited by O. Brusatti, attached to the facsimile edition of the autograph manuscript of the *Genzinger* Sonata does not follow Haydn's original notation of dynamics (see, e.g., I, 20–24).

for the same effects. For example, to get a strong accent on one single note, Haydn marked ***fp*** or ***fz*** before his journeys to London but used a marcato (>) or even marcatissimo (∧) sign in his late scores.

In the notation of Haydn's solo keyboard music, we may distinguish the period of harpsichord dynamics from that of fortepiano dynamics (33 c, 20 B♭, and 44 F are exceptional cases).[5] The dividing line is the 1780 edition of the *Auenbrugger* sonatas (nos. 48–52 and 33) by Artaria in Vienna. Owing to their large number of dynamic markings and accent signs, the majority of movements in these sonatas can be played correctly, with the nuances suggested by Haydn, only on the fortepiano.

Dynamics and accents in the sonatas composed for harpsichord. Some slips of the pen in keyboard manuscripts from around 1770 suggest that the limited dynamic capabilities of the harpsichord, compared with the flexible dynamics of stringed instruments, required a certain restriction of Haydn's fantasy. The *forte* on an inflected note of 31 A♭ I, 75, and of 37 E I, 41, is supposed to produce a genuine *forzando* accent; the *piano* of 37 E III, 29, suggests an echo.[6] On the other hand, Haydn used plenty of compositional devices to write dynamic effects into his harpsichord music.

Quantz gives useful advice for counterbalancing the disadvantages of a one-manual harpsichord. He states, "Passages marked Piano on this instrument may be improved by moderating the touch, and by decreasing the number of parts, and those marked Forte by strengthening the touch and by increasing the number of parts in both hands." Later he observes, "Fortissimo may be attained by quick arpeggiations of the chords from below upwards."[7]

From Haydn's sonatas a whole collection of examples could be compiled of ingenious effects of dynamic changes or accents based on a sudden alteration of texture in a context that otherwise maintains a strict number of parts, in agreement with Quantz's advice. Trying these on a harpsichord might encourage modern pianists to apply appropriate dynamic contrasts on their own instruments. It is a commonplace to begin a keyboard movement *forte* with a many-voiced chord.[8] But the subtly composed design for a principal accent, resolution, and secondary accent resulting from the manipulation of number of voices, as it was presented in a 1773 sonata, bears the imprint of Haydn's genius (see ex. 77).

5. The Sonata no. 35 in A♭ proves to be problematic in this respect too, for it does not fit into its supposed chronological environment. This work may not be by Haydn, and I will not treat it in full here.

6. We may not assume that Haydn had a two-manual harpsichord in mind. For that matter, C. P. E. Bach states, "If the Lessons are played on a harpsichord with two manuals, only one manual should be used to play detailed changes of forte and piano. It is only when entire passages are differentiated by contrasting shades that a transfer may be made" (*Essay,* 164).

7. Quantz, *Playing,* 253, 259.

8. In this regard, it is worthwhile comparing the first themes of 15 E I, 37 E I, and 44 F I.

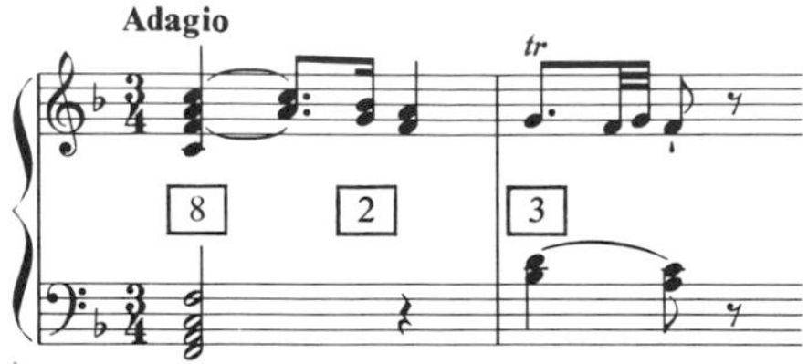

Ex. 77. 36 C II, 1. (Number of voices given in boxes.)

The arpeggio ***ff*** effect suggested by Quantz provides a dramatic flourish in the final measures of 46 E I (see ex. 78). (See also the eight-voice chord of 40 E♭ I, 67, with the subsequent passage of similar dynamic impact.)

Ex. 78. 46 E I, 64.

The well-timed exploitation of the extremes of the five-octave range was an important means by which Haydn achieved strong accents. The octave doubling of the bass or a full-voiced chord in the bass register produced an accent on the harpsichord as dramatic and forceful as a ***ff*** struck on a modern piano (see ex. 79).

Ex. 79. *a,* 30 D I, 22. *b,* 47 b I, 12.

In the first movement of 32 g, probably the most expressive among Haydn's sonatas conceived for harpsichord, the composition of the accents is so idiomatic—for example, measures 25–26, in which, without increasing the number of parts, a strong accent is achieved by an abrupt expansion of the range in both directions, further emphasized by a broken chord in the right hand, relaxing into the cadence (see ex. 80)—that it is by no means easy to find an equivalent for it on the modern piano.

Ex. 80. 32 g I, 25.

One cannot sufficiently marvel at Haydn's variety of means, both acoustic (volume and range) and psychological (degree of dissonance or consonance), for formulating subtly differentiated accents in a complex theme such as the first theme of the G Minor Sonata (see ex. 81). Such a theme once again cautions us against applying stylistically inappropriate techniques, which would simplify and distort Haydn's expressive message when performing on the modern piano.[9]

Ex. 81. 32 g I, 1. (* Left hand: register accent. ** Right hand: appoggiatura in the melody. *** Increasing number of parts and syncopation.)

Ambiguous cases for harpsichord or fortepiano. The Sonata no. 33 in C Minor has been much analyzed and variously interpreted over the years. It seems to represent an experiment in genuine fortepiano style. Written in 1771,

9. Equalizing the "unevenness" of the various registers of the modern piano, which can be achieved by skilled players intent on doing so, is certainly counterproductive in performing Haydn's keyboard works.

the date of its autograph fragment,[10] it is a fantastic tour de force among the sonatas written for harpsichord. Unfortunately, the autograph fragment does not unequivocally reveal how many of the expression marks—or indeed how much of the sonata itself—were part of the original 1771 conception. The fair copy was sent by Haydn to his publisher, as the sixth and final item in the *Auenbrugger* group of sonatas only on 31 January 1780.[11]

Some ***f*** and ***p*** directions can also be found in the text of the Sonata no. 20 in B♭, which originates by and large from the same period. These markings, however, seem to be simple echo passages that may, incidentally, indicate a two-manual harpsichord. If this is so, it would be the only such case in Haydn's entire sonata oeuvre.[12]

Finally, the Sonata no. 44 in F Major, which Haydn sketched (as a fragment

10. The argument emerges from time to time in the Haydn literature that, in the crumpled, worn manuscript, preserved in Paris, the final digit in the upper-right-hand corner of the title page cannot be read clearly enough for certainty of dating (see Brown, *Keyboard,* 120). Nevertheless, the 1771 dating of the manuscript is generally accepted as accurate.

11. No comprehensive study of this subject is available. My own observations may be summed up as follows.

a) The autograph manuscript of 1771 is only a draft. Pages 1–2 of the first bifolio contain the complete exposition, which has the appearance of a fair copy (it has the typical heading: title, *In Nomine Domini,* signature, and date), plus the first nine measures of the development section in a much sketchier handwriting. The rest of the first bifolio is blank except for a sketch, in two versions, for the last measures of the opening movement. The rest of the development and the recapitulation may have been finished in Haydn's head, but there is no evidence that he wrote out a complete movement in 1771. Page 1 of the other surviving bifolio is blank; pp. 2–4 contain the third movement up to m. 130, as much as this sheet could hold, again in a fair-copy-like handwriting. One may assume that the last page, with the end of the third movement, and an intermediate page or bifolio, containing the beginning of the second movement, are lost. At any rate, what exists now is an autograph fragment. In order to give the first movement to a copyist or an engraver, Haydn would have had to write the movement out in full once again, filling in the missing sections, mechanical though that work may have been for him. The question is when between 1771 and 1780 he did this.

b) The inscription on the title page in Haydn's hand is *Sonata p[er] il Clavi Cembalo.* The dynamic markings in the autograph draft, which, despite the title, go beyond the possibilities of performance on a harpsichord, can be studied better in the *JHW* than in the *WUE;* in the *JHW,* those expression marks taken over from the 1780 Artaria edition are clearly placed in parentheses. It is essential to observe that the only *cresc.* direction (I, 61) is, of necessity, missing in the autograph, which goes only as far as m. 37, the end of the exposition. (This counters one of Eva Badura-Skoda's arguments; see *Haydn Studies,* 216.) In addition, the following dynamics are missing in the autograph—***f*** in I, 1, ***fz*** in I, 29, and ***ff*** in I, 31. And the ***f(z)*** in the left hand of I, 45, was ***ff***. The second movement, for which we have no source dating from 1771, seems to be conceived straightforwardly for harpsichord. The only dynamic marking in the third movement that appears in the autograph fragment is the ***f*** in III, 78; all other markings were taken over from the Artaria edition.

c) Strictly speaking, the 1771 fragment does not contain any signs that would exclude the possibility of performing this piece on the clavichord or that would demand performance on a fortepiano instead of a clavichord. E. M. Ripin has stated that, "in the hands of an accomplished performer, there is no problem in doing this sonata justice on the clavichord" (*Haydn Studies,* 305). A. Peter Brown also thinks that the sonata was composed for the clavichord (*Keyboard,* 161).

12. The original manuscript of 20 B♭ survives only as a fragment, beginning at m. 40 of the second movement, with just a single ***p*** in II, 42. There is, however, no reason to doubt that the alternating ***f*** and ***p*** directions of the first movement were written in the missing autograph.

similar to that of the C Minor Sonata) in 1774,[13] represents a special case. In the sonata's elaborated form, dating from 1776, the ***f-p*** series in measure 10 of the first movement and the ***p-cresc.-f*** series in measures 21–23 again show a clear attempt to break away from the harpsichord idiom.[14]

Catalog of dynamic markings and accent signs in the sonatas for fortepiano. The *Auenbrugger* set of sonatas published in 1780 marks the beginning of the rapid crystallization of Haydn's idiomatic writing for fortepiano. Unfortunately, the primary and sole contemporary source for the *Auenbrugger* set (nos. 48–52, 33), inscribed *per il Clavicembalo, o Forte Piano,* is the first edition by Artaria. Here, as in the first edition of the *Bossler* sonatas (nos. 54–56), the piano appears only in second place. Likewise, the first printings of 53 e and 58 C are editions with fairly sloppy texts. In her preface to the *WUE,* Christa Landon asserts that, partly owing to their lack of understanding, Haydn's early publishers confused his ***fz*** inscriptions, intended as accents, with his ***f*** and ***ff*** marks, intended to indicate basic dynamic levels; she adjusts her urtext edition accordingly. (In the case of 58 C, the placement of signs under wrong notes in the first edition might also have been caused—at least in part—by the imperfections of the cheaper method of setting the music by movable type rather than engraving.) Considering the textual difficulties caused by the missing manuscripts of 60 C and 61 D, the only solo fortepiano compositions with completely reliable sources remain the F Minor Variations and the two large E♭ major sonatas (59, 62), which survive in both autograph manuscripts and editions supervised by Haydn. Thus, the musicologist and the pianist seriously concerned with the matter of authentic dynamic markings must take these works as the starting point. Here, in addition to the available facsimile editions, it seems indispensable to consult the *JHW* urtext in disputed cases, for the *JHW* follows the sources more scrupulously and provides more reliable evidence in certain aspects.

The number of fundamental dynamic markings that Haydn uses in the sonatas (***ff***, ***f***, ***p***, ***pp***) is not large compared, for example, with those in Türk's *Klavierschule* or in W. A. Mozart's notation. Nevertheless, the interpretation of certain signs leaves some room for speculation. Some of the explanations I give below are still in the stage of investigation and for the time being should be looked on as hypotheses.

Naturally, ***f*** and ***p*** are the two predominant dynamic levels. Several ex-

13. The first one and a half pages of the bifolio contain the exposition of the first movement; the rest of the bifolio is blank. The inscription reads *Divertimento da Clavicembalo.* This draft does not contain any dynamic markings, unlike the version disseminated by a professional copying workshop in Vienna as a part of the *Anno 1776* series. Although autograph proof of these markings in Haydn's hand has not survived, it is evident that the dynamics must have been added by Haydn in his final revision of the composition.

14. A. Peter Brown speaks of "elements of fortepiano style" in connection with this movement (*Haydn Studies,* 396).

tremely forceful and dramatically effective movements (e.g., 53 e I, 55 B♭ I, 59 E♭ I–III, 62 E♭ I) manage to make do with only these dynamic markings plus expressive accent marks. When an entire movement is meant to remain, harpsichord-like, at a fundamental *forte* level, there are no markings of dynamic level at all (see 49 c♯ III, 50 D I, 51 E♭ III, 53 e III, 56 D II,[15] 61 D II). An indication of *mezza voce* as a dynamic level, the only ***mf***-like dynamic that Haydn notated, appears in just one mature work for piano solo, in the theme and reprise of the F Minor Variations—and even here in only one of the authentic sources of the work, the Elssler copy.

Unlike the more elaborate indication of dynamics in Haydn's symphonies or quartets, in the sonatas ***ff*** and ***pp*** are held in reserve for special effects and short sections. It seems to me that, as a useful working hypothesis, both the ***ff*** and the ***pp*** places in Haydn's sonatas may somehow be connected with the possibilities of altering tone color on the fortepiano of his time by the use of pedals. The ***ff*** appears unambiguously to mean the raising of the damper, that is, the *Fortezug* (the predecessor of the right pedal on present-day pianos). The ***pp*** seems to suggest the use of the *Pianozug* (*Moderator* or other piano registers, the left pedal on modern pianos) but sometimes involves the use of the *Fortezug* as well. We have no evidence regarding what would have led Haydn to indicate "pedaling" through dynamic markings from 1780 on. However, a systematic survey of all the ***ff*** and ***pp*** markings in Haydn's sonata output—taking into account the possibility of error in the sources and in the urtext editions based on them—certainly suggests that these signs were intended to mark an effect, a change in timbre, rather than a dynamic level per se. Later indirect evidence, supplied by data published in Vienna in 1801, seems to reinforce such a theory. Andreas Streicher describes, among other things, the abilities of accomplished fortepiano players. By raising the damper at *fortissimo,* they practically convince us that they are playing on the organ or are in command of an entire orchestra; at *pianissimo,* they produce by similar means the soft sounds of a glass harmonica.[16]

Apart from two exceptions (33 c I, 62, and 62 E♭ III, 202), ***ff*** markings do not appear in Haydn's sonatas at the ends of crescendos;[17] instead, they present

15. The last two measures in 56 D II are *piano.*

16. "Bey *Fortissimo* täuschte er [der wahre Künstler] uns durch das Hinaufdrücken der Dämpfung, dass wir glaubten, eine Orgel, die Fülle eines ganzen Orchesters zu hören. Jetzt im *Pianissimo* zaubert er uns durch eben dieses Mittel den sanften Ton des [Glas] Harmonica her" (Andreas Streicher, *Kurze Bemerkungen über das Spielen, Stimmen und Erhalten der Fortepiano* . . . [Vienna, 1801; reprint, The Hague, 1979], 16).

17. It is evident that, in the combinations ***f***-*cresc.*-***ff*** (33 c) and ***f***-*più forte-fortissimo* (62 E♭), the damper must be raised at the sign ***ff***. The passage in the Sonata no. 62 is written with small notes and is so crammed in the autograph that the *fortissimo* appears to begin in m. 201 (a placement somewhat exaggerated in the *JHW* as compared to the *WUE*); nevertheless, it clearly belongs to the chord in m. 202.

themselves as real surprises, as local effects separated from their environments. For that matter, the places authentically marked with ***ff*** signs would not need to be played with a more forceful attack than those places marked ***f*** since they generally are such full chords that on the fortepiano of Haydn's time they would have automatically produced a louder sound. Yet the raised damper let the sound ring more fully, decay more slowly, and contrast in timbre.

The authentic ***ff*** signs are cataloged in table 3. The signs that are printed as ***fz*** in the *WUE,* probably erroneously, are marked. Whenever a dynamic marking follows immediately after the ***ff***, this too is noted in the catalog. In addition, I have made the following classification of types: type A, one chord or a chordal repetition; type B, a single "spot"; type C, a more complex area in which the damper has to be changed; and type D, unison or single notes. Some examples are shown with music in example 82.

The major difficulty with my hypothesis that ***ff*** means *Fortezug* (i.e., to raise the damper pedal) is the lack of references for releasing the pedal or for changing it with the changes of harmony. (On modern pianos, the problem is magnified because, if the pedal is depressed fully, sounds blend together to a greater extent and for a longer duration than they would on a fortepiano.) Another challenge to the theory comes from the *Genzinger* Sonata, 59 E♭, surviving in an autograph manuscript that contains no ***ff*** signs whatsoever. However, almost all ***f*** directions in this work appear at typically *Fortezug* places.[18]

Careful scrutiny of the places in the piano sonatas marked ***pp*** makes an even more convincing case for the idea that these markings imply a change of timbre more than simple gradations of volume. If we disregard the editorial ***pp*** directions, placed in parentheses in the urtext editions, we find that the remaining places with authentic ***pp*** marks—cataloged in table 4[19]—are either echoes at the ends of sections or movements or other effects and spots of a parenthetical nature. It is true that only two of those places marked ***pp*** are authenticated by Haydn's autograph manuscripts (59 E♭ II, 123, and the end of the F Minor Variations),[20] but the other places certainly do not appear to be merely engraving errors in the contemporary first editions. In table 4, the letters *P* and *F* indicate places where, in my opinion, it would be suitable to use the *Pianozug* and/or *Fortezug* registers

18. The most typical *Fortezug*-like places in the *Genzinger* Sonata are the following: I, 122, 131, 183, 210, 212, 217; II, 57, 59, 61, 65, 78, 108, 114, 119; III, 85 (II, 78, and III, 85, are given as ***fz*** in the urtext editions, but my reading of these places in the facsimile edition of the autograph is ***f***). The rest of the ***f*** positions may also be imagined as *Fortezug* effects, occasionally with changes of pedal: I, 57, 62–63, 182, 188–89, 200; III, 28–29, 36ff., 44ff., 67.

19. The Sonata no. 35 in A♭, whose authenticity I doubt (see pp. 163–64), contains three ***pp*** positions: I, 54; I, 140 (*WUE:* I, 147); and II, 221. All seem to be *Pianozug.*

20. The ***pp*** in mm. 201ff. of the F Minor Variations appears neither in Haydn's autograph manuscript nor in the Elssler copy. N.B.: Various editions of the F Minor Variations give a ***ff*** for mm. 185–99. However, this ***ff*** does not appear in the autograph manuscript or in Essler's authentic copy.

TABLE 3 AUTHENTIC ***ff*** SIGNS

	See Ex. 82	Direct subsequent dynamics	Type
33 c:			
I, 31*		***ff-p***	B
I, 62†		—‡	C
I, 92†		***ff-p***	B
48 C:			
I, 43§		***ff-p***	D
I, 151	*c*	***ff-p***	A
III, 34		—	B/C
49 c♯:			
I, 9§		—	B
I, 26§		—	D
II, 20§		—	A
II, 28§		—	A
50 D:			
II, 16§	*a*	—	A
51 E♭:			
I, 55	*d*	—	B
II, 11, 24		***ff-p***	C
52 G:			
I, 95	*e*	—	B
54 G:			
I, 63, 64§		—	A
I, 84		***ff*** *calando***	B
II, 10§		—	D
56 D:			
I, 18–19§	*f*	***ff-p***	AAA
I, 88§		***ff***>	A
58 C:			
I, 106		***ff-p***	C
II, 193		—	C
60 C:			
I, 100	*b*	***ff-p***	A
62 E♭:			
II, 10		***ff*** *dimin.*	C
III, 48, 250		—	A
III, 178		—	A
III, 201–2	*k*	***p****-più forte-fortissimo-****p***	A

Note: For definitions of types, see the text.

* Missing in the 1771 autograph.

† This part of the movement exists only in the 1780 edition.

‡ The ***p*** in m. 65 of 33 c I should probably not be considered a direct subsequent dynamic. Presumably, the dampers are raised for m. 62 only.

§ In the *WUE*, ***fz*** or ***f***(*z*).

** The *calando,* in Haydn too, probably combines getting softer and getting slower (see also Rosenblum, *Performance Practices,* 74ff.).

TABLE 4 AUTHENTIC ***pp*** SIGNS

	See Ex. 82	Direct subsequent dynamics	*Piano-zug?*	*Forte-zug?*
33 C:				
I, 76*		—	P	F
I, 88		***pp-f***	P	F
48 C:				
I, 45–50		***pp-f***	P	—
I, 135–40				
49 c♯:				
I, 33		***pp*:‖**	P	(F)?
50 D:				
II, 14	*a*	***pp-ff***	P	(F)
51 E♭:				
I, 23–24	*g*	***pp-f***	P	F
I, 71–72				
II, 26		—	P	F?†
54 G:				
I, 14–15	*i*	***pp-f***	P	(F)†
I, 72		—	P	(F)
I, 91		—	P	F
56 D:				
I, 20		***pp*:‖**	P	F
I, 105		***pp*‖**	(P)?	F
58 C:				
I, 10		***pp*:‖**	P	F
I, 16	*j*	***pp-f***	P	(F)
I, 22		***pp-f***	P	F
I, 54–55		***f*>*pp*<**	P	F
I, 65		***pp-f***	P	F
I, 134		***pp*‖**	P	F
C Major Fantasy:				
116		—	—	(F)?‡
464		***pp-f***	(P)	F
59 E♭:				
II, 123		***pp*‖**	P	F
F Minor Variations:				
232	*h*	***pp*‖**	P	F
60 C:				
I, 73–74§		—	P	F
I, 120–23				
II, 62		***pp*‖**	P	F

* This part of the movement exists only in the 1780 edition.

† In staccato context.

‡ It is technically impossible to use a *Pianozug* operated by a hand stop in this place. The application of *Fortezug*, even with a change every two measures, will produce a blurred sound in the chromatic passage.

§ With *open pedal* instruction and wavy line.

Ex. 82. (*See legend on facing page*).

Ex. 82. *a,* 50 D II, 14. *b,* 60 C I, 100. *c,* 48 C I, 150. *d,* 51 E♭ I, 55. *e,* 52 G I, 96. *f,* 56 D I, 18. *g,* 51 E♭ I, 20. *h,* F Minor Variations, m. 232. *i,* 54 G I, 14. *j,* 58 C I, 16. *k,* 62 E♭ III, 200.

of the fortepiano. In fact, most of the places marked ***pp*** may be realized with the *Pianozug* (*Moderator*) hand stops available on even small square pianos. In only a few places (e.g., 56 D I, 20, 105, and m. 116 of the C Major Fantasia) does the use of hand stops seem inconvenient. When he was writing these works in Vienna, Haydn was still unfamiliar with the construction of the English piano, which produced *una corda* and *due corde* effects by means of foot pedals. Streicher's suggestion that passages marked ***pp*** may be played by using the *Fortezug* while playing very softly, producing a sound similar to that of the glass harmonica, is not always applicable in Haydn's sonatas. For example, the long passage of 48 C I, 45–50, with its many staccato notes, makes no sense if played with the dampers raised. I would be wary of calling any of the other places rich in staccato, and those indicated in the list with an *F* in parentheses, textures amenable to raising the dampers.

Concerning the famous *open Pedal* passages in the first movement of 60 C (mm. 73ff., 120ff.), which are also marked *pianissimo,* several explanations have been put forward.[21] One interpretation of these places calls for the raising of the dampers (*Fortezug* being the equivalent of the right pedal) of the fortepiano. Even on the older instrument this would have produced a blurred sound, although one less unpleasant than that produced on the present-day piano. Another interpre-

21. Two well-known interpretations are Franz Eibner's ("Registerpedalisierung bei Haydn und Beethoven") and Christa Landon's (in Anhang [app.] II to the revised edition of the *WUE* [3:124]). In their reading, the direction means to raise the dampers. (See also Brown, *Keyboard,* 159; and Rosenblum, *Performance Practices,* 127.)

tation, suggested by H. C. Robbins Landon,[22] is that this is an *una corda* effect. The fortepiano by John Broadwood and Son dating from 1794 (see fig. 4 above) was fitted out with two pedals: the wooden pedal reaching out slantwise from the right leg of the instrument served as a damper pedal; the left-foot pedal provided an opportunity for playing *due corde* or *una corda* in two successive stages by shifting the hammers. My interpretation is that in these two places the joint use of both pedals is implied. By the way, it is far from proved that the *open Pedal* inscription after the ***pp*** sign stems from Haydn's hand.[23]

Crescendos and diminuendos, the next category of Haydn's signs to be discussed, are in fact the most interesting dynamic markings since their presence offers the surest evidence that a piece was no longer written for harpsichord. In comparison to the sparse markings of the *Auenbrugger* and *Bossler* sets and of 53 e, the first movement of 58 C (1789) shows a great leap forward both quantitatively and qualitatively. Before this movement, the direction *cresc.* appeared in the keyboard sonatas only in a completely written-out form and often without the final dynamic to be attained by the crescendo. Instead of *diminuendo,* the equivalent terms *perdendosi* and *calando* were used or else three tiny > signs.[24] In the C Major Sonata, no. 58, long and short < and > signs can be found as well as *crescendo* instructions with specified target dynamics and, even more striking, a one-measure < > (I, 58).[25] In the C Major Fantasy of 1789, Haydn's famous idea of the obligatory holding out of the octave in the bass, marked with a fermata, until the sound dies away completely (*tenuto intanto, finché non si sente più il suono*)[26] appears twice (in mm. 192 and 302).

The three late compositions for solo piano surviving both in autograph and in relatively authentic contemporary editions (59 E♭, 62 E♭, and the F Minor

22. "Of course, what Haydn wanted [in 60 C I] is the *sopra una corda* effect. In bars 73–4, the *sopra una corda* pedal is, obviously, lifted at once after the third note of bar 73; but in the next section (bars 120–123), Haydn presumably wants the pedal gradually lifted at the beginning of bar 124, in such a way that the semiquavers sound normally 'pianissimo'" (Landon, *HCW,* 3:445).

23. Evidently, Haydn left the manuscript of this sonata in London with Mrs. Bartolozzi (Therese Jansen), the dedicatee, who kept the work in her repertoire but delayed its publication for some six years (see Landon, *HCW,* 3:440–42). Because of the irregular notation of *cresc.-dim.,* which I will treat later, and for other reasons as well, I surmise that 60 C was printed on the basis of Haydn's authentic text, although slightly modified (edited) with regard to expression marks and notation in London in the 1800s. It could be that the words *open Pedal* and the crossed wavy line ( ) were added by Mrs. Bartolozzi, or by the engraver, in place of Haydn's original instructions, if there were any.

24. *Perdendosi* appears in 53 e II, 7, *calando* in 54 G I, 79, 88, and 55 B♭ I, 95, and the three tiny > signs in 54 G I, 96, and 56 D I, 77, 88.

25 The small > sign, applied in the sense of accent, and the *cresc.* without target dynamics but running up to a rest or a *subito p* appear here too.

26. The advice given in the *WUE* by Eibner and Jarecki, that this instruction should not be taken literally since even on a fortepiano made in 1784 it took a full fifteen seconds before the sound died away completely, is a complete misunderstanding of Haydn's intention and humor.

Variations) contain a relatively small number of *cresc.*, <, and > directions; these directions are, however, timed to appear at decisive points. In these works, rising and falling waves of sound are missing.[27] Moreover, the marking *dim.*, written as an abbreviated word, is unknown in the authentic sources of Haydn's sonatas. This leads me to the assumption that the *cres.-dim.* markings of the C Major *London* Sonata, no. 60, present in large number,[28] may have been transformations of the < > signs of the lost source.[29]

When it comes to recognizing and properly interpreting the varying grades of accent signs in all Haydn's genres, including his piano music, present-day performers find themselves on slippery ground. The very signs are not without problems. The ***fz*** or ***forz.***[30] indications definitely signify accents of a forceful and marcato nature. The short > marcato sign gained ground so late in Haydn's notation that it occurs in only two of the *London* sonatas (62 E♭ II, 4; 61 D II, 31–32, 67–68).[31] The adjacent ***f***-***p*** generally stands for a ***fp*** accent; frequently, ***f*** alone stands for the same thing. Naturally, all the accents created by a special texture, special register, or increased number of parts, which Haydn established in his harpsichord style, continue to exist in his writing for fortepiano. And the majority of the isolated (one-note) staccato strokes seem to mean not only shortness but accent as well.[32] After carefully studying the facsimile edition of the manuscript of the *Genzinger* Sonata, 59 E♭, it becomes apparent that the position of the staccato strokes at the beginning of the opening movement (I, 1, 2, 4, 5, 6, 12, above the right hand, i.e., on the wrong side of the note in an emphasized

27. The small adagio cadenza of 62 E♭ III, 199–203, has a very precise direction: ***f*** . . . *più forte* . . . *fortissimo*// ***p***. There is no diminuendo, and the ***p*** is a true *subito piano*.

28. 60 C I, 34, etc. Independent *dim.* directions occur in II, 1, etc., and III, 64, etc.

29. In II, 4, of 60 C they appear so.

30. Haydn did not write out the words *sforzando* and *sforzato* in full.

31. The > sign can be found in the autograph manuscript of 62 E♭ II, 4; in mm. 41–44 of the finale of 61 D, the *WUE* prints normal > accents, while *JHW* prints a Schubert-like short, two-note > sign. The numerous > marcato signs of the second movement of 61 D originate in the first edition only. Haydn started to use the ∧ (marcatissimo) sign only in his last scores. It was entered into the Adagio theme of the String Quartet in G, op. 77, written in 1799, as a later addition (the beginning of the second movement is reproduced below). (See my facsimile edition of the autograph score, *Joseph Haydn: String Quartet in G* [New York: Belwin & Mills, 1972], or the second edition, *Joseph Haydn: Zwei Streichquartette Op. 77* [Editio Musica Budapest, 1980]). The autograph notation of this theme shows intriguing experimentation with phrasing in addition to small-scale articulations. The marcatissimo sign is obviously an indication of bowing, too (i.e., m. 1 = up-bow, m. 2 = starts with down-bow):

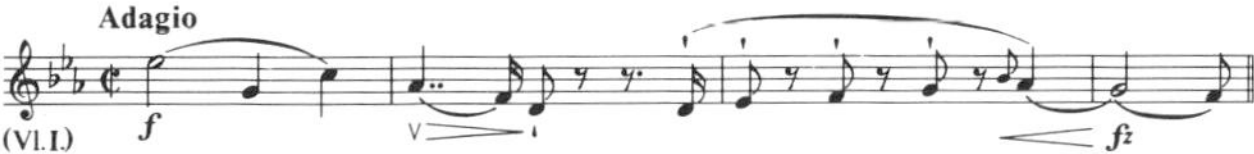

32. Sometimes the staccato stroke should by no means be performed staccato in the modern sense but unambiguously as marcato, as, e.g., in 53 e II, 12.

way) visually suggests an overall accent rather than staccato. In example 83, there are some samples of different types and grades of accents taken from the Adagio of this same 1790 sonata.

Ex. 83. 59 E♭ II, 36, 21, 7, 15, 11.

Yet even the *Genzinger* Sonata, of truly mature notation and surviving with an absolutely reliable author's text, leaves open fundamental questions. Does the ***fz*** accent apply to both hands? (In I, 3, and 7, it probably does not; in I, 20 etc., it probably does).[33] Is the ***fz*** followed by a *forte* dynamic level? (In I, 117–21, the series of ***fz*** are perhaps meant to be accents within the fundamental dynamic level of *piano;* this level changes only with the ***f*** written in m. 122.) What is the correct dynamic level after a ***p*** that has been written for its own special effect? (At I, 24, after the ***p***, forte seems naturally restored, although this is not indicated. At II, 8, ***p*** leads back to the basic dynamic level, which is not, in my opinion, ***p***, the level suggested by the editors of the *WUE,* but rather a healthy singing tone.) And we have not even considered the nuances of smaller accents evident from the harmony (small appoggiaturas, the majority of notes enhanced by small embellishments, dissonances) and the accent conventions deriving from rhythm (the so-called good notes of the measures, syncopated notes, etc.). Knowledge of these matters was expected of musicians with good taste in Haydn's time as a matter of course. Musicians of our time who feel on safe ground in this respect should show greater courage in performing Haydn's music in a richly accented manner. It is the lesser of two evils if the pianist's interpretation is initially considered Romantic than if the listener leaves an overpolished presentation with the impression that Haydn is at times boring.

33. In the facsimile edition, I, 138, contains a ***fz***, but the parallel and analogous places, I, 3 and 7, and I, 134, do not, although this may be inadvertent. On the other hand, independent right-hand–left-hand ***fz*** signs do occur at I, 20–22 and 117–20.

 *Eight*

THOUGHTS *on* TEMPOS *in* HAYDN'S STYLE

IN OUR DISCUSSION SO FAR, we have by no means exhausted the valid, valuable information to be found in the theoretical books and treatises of Haydn's time. General practical advice as well as essays on correct and beautiful execution are even more important for grasping the spirit of the style than minute explanations of small embellishments. This is particularly true if the eighteenth-century wording and terminology are properly understood and the suggestions are not considered obligatory rules taken out of context. I recommend to those teachers and performers who are not content with a partial and fragmentary knowledge of eighteenth-century style that they read extensively (if possible in the original) the relevant portions of C. P. E. Bach, Leopold Mozart, Quantz, and other literature in this special field.[1]

The process of acquiring a reliable knowledge of authentic performance practice takes place in many stages. Reading and assimilating the available literature and applying the information to the performance of Haydn's works is, in fact, just one step in this process. Frequent analysis and experimentation keep us moving forward. Examples and counterexamples must be sought to test better and bolder solutions. At the same time, one must remain alert and sensitive to the overall development of Haydn's style and the restriction of genre governing a given opus. In addition, it is worth heeding the insights of other artists, particularly those experimenting on instruments of Haydn's time.

1. C. P. E. Bach, "Performance," in *Essay,* 147–66; Quantz, "Of the Manner of Playing the Adagio," "Of the Keyboard Player in Particular," and "How a Musician and a Musical Composition Are to Be Judged," in *Playing,* 119–35, 162ff., and 295ff.; L. Mozart, "Of Reading Music Correctly, and in particular, of Good Execution," in *Treatise,* 215ff.

In the matter of choosing proper, authentic tempos, present-day musicians should seek reliable data that may assist them. Although this problem cannot be avoided in this book, we should in fact be less interested in how fast an allegro or an adagio was played in Haydn's time than in subtle alterations of the tempo—how adherence to the beat and the written rhythmic values between the beats were judged. The following discussion is meant to reinforce the realization that the virtues needed for a musician interpreting Haydn are not identical with many of the internationally acknowledged pianistic ideals of the 1960s and 1970s. Precision, technical perfection, and utmost fidelity to the written musical text are praiseworthy only to the extent that they contribute to a performance that is rich in detail, is full of fantasy and good taste, and gives expression to the genuine emotional content of the piece. At the other extreme, in the 1980s wave of performances striving to be historically accurate, interpretations of Haydn's music have emerged that, through arbitrary rubatos that almost completely give up the beat, represent a mannerism of style quite uncharacteristic of Haydn. It is worth carefully weighing the advice given by C. P. E. Bach in this matter: "Good performance, then, occurs when one hears all notes and their embellishments played in correct time with fitting volume produced by a touch which is related to the true content of a piece. Herein lies the rounded, pure, flowing manner of playing which makes for clarity and expressiveness."[2]

The greatest difficulty, undoubtedly, comes from the need for a revision of our present concepts of tempo and meter. Numerous rules and warnings, accepted by consensus, caution against the rigidly even execution of a movement within a chosen tempo. C. P. E. Bach admonishes that "the metric signature [*Schreib-Art*] is in many cases more a convention of notation than a binding factor in performance."[3] He argues that *recitativo accompagnato* provides the best evidence of how often the values of written music had to be changed to comply with changes in affect. Elsewhere, he points out that, for the sake of expression in performance, certain notes or rests must be held longer than indicated in the music. He illustrates this point with a series of examples (see ex. 84) marked with a cross at the places where the musical time needs some expansion. Bach asks only that "every effort . . . be made despite the beauty of detail to keep the tempo at the end of a piece exactly the same as the beginning."[4]

2. Bach, *Essay*, 148.
3. Ibid., 153.
4. Ibid., 161 (supplement to the 1787 ed.).

Ex. 84. C. P. E. Bach's example: notes and rests held longer in the interest of expression.

Several other musical situations typically call for a change in the basic tempo. C. P. E. Bach mentions that "passages in a piece in the major mode which are repeated in the minor may be broadened somewhat on their repetition in order to heighten the affect."[5] Türk discusses several situations in which the strict tempo gives way to a beat that is somewhat held back. Sometimes these passages have clear notational signals—embellishments engraved in small notes, marked *senza tempo,* or the notes connected to a fermata, for example. Less obvious cases requiring a relaxation of tempo are given in example 85(a), a passage leading up to a theme, and (b), in which "a languid musical thought also can be played in a somewhat hesitating manner when it is repeated."[6]

Ex. 85. Türk, *Klavierschule,* 6:5, 69.

Two essential sets of rules, derived from the relation between musical performance and speech, require mention here.[7] (These rules are not discussed in detail by C. P. E. Bach or Türk but are mentioned by systematic writers on theory such as Marpurg or sometimes described under other headings, such as *Pause,* i.e., silence.) The structure of a musical phrase is compared to the grammatical structure of a sentence in a written text; the full cadence was analogous to a

5. Ibid.

6. Türk, *School,* 361. The inscription *tempo rubato* does not appear in Haydn's sonatas, although there are many places in his music that would have been played that way by his contemporaries. As a matter of fact, the term *tempo rubato* (stolen time) was imbued with an astonishingly large number of possible meanings, discussed in treatises of Haydn's time. C. P. E. Bach described it, specifically, as the performance of rhythms divided by five, seven, eleven, etc. to be played simultaneously with and against the simple rhythmic values of the measure (*Essay,* 162 [1787 supplement]). Türk used the word to signify, among other things, a separation of the voices by means of anticipation or retardation applied to one voice only. Today, this is considered simply syncopated motion and is often played, unfortunately, in a rather even and mechanical manner (as, e.g., in 33 c II, 16–19, etc.; cf. n. 84 of chap. 4, p. 99).

7. Especially useful for an understanding of these matters is Vera Schwarz's "Missverständnisse in der Haydn-Interpretation."

period, the half cadence to a comma. After a full cadence, a sensible and proportional rest was needed, as if taking a breath at the end of a sentence, even in cases where no rest or caesura was notated in the music. Phrase construction in Haydn's music is easily recognized by musicians with a thorough grounding in harmony. Because of the great number of rests and other means of articulation in Haydn's sonatas, it is rarely necessary to violate the length of the measure in order to achieve a well-articulated performance of his themes.

Present-day musicians may find their intuitions less reliable for discerning the other eighteenth-century set of rules for division and accentuation. These are derived from the art of rhetoric, a discipline not much cultivated today. Players who wish to specialize in the performance of Haydn's music would do well to study a systematic survey of the musical equivalents of the rhetorical figures.[8] Beyond this, we must trust that Haydn's notation in itself—particularly in the years of the late, mature fortepiano writing—sufficiently calls attention to figures that imitate unusual rhetorical formulas.

To illustrate some of these ideas, let us study the first ten measures of the *Andante con espressione* theme of 58 C (see ex. 160, p. 336). The grammatical structure is far from customary. The full cadence at the end of the phrase is approached by a path that leads through three interrogatory and one exclamatory accent. Moreover, the music is full of dynamic instructions that contradict the "natural" rules of performance. The first five measures contain three interrogatory accents, each with a different set of dynamic indications. The first is a confident question that stops short and dies away; the second question is circumlocutory, increasing in nobility, while the third is merely a short, whispered one. These opening measures are not primarily rooted in purely musical thinking but rather are a fascinating demonstration of musical rhetoric. Anyone who takes Haydn's rhythms, dynamics, embellishments, and extensive use of registral contrasts seriously cannot be a slave to the beat of the metronome but must declaim with utmost rhythmic freedom and great expressive force.

Coming to issues of tempo proper, to the concrete meaning of various tempo indications in Haydn and the relation between different tempo indications, I must admit that my approach to this important problem is guided by highly subjective reflections. This subject is, in part, simpler than we tend to think it is now and, in part, so complex that no simple formula can be given. In the last analysis, it suffices to take C. P. E. Bach's advice literally: "The pace of a composition, which is usually indicated by several well-known Italian expressions, is

8. I recommend, for a first orientation, the article "Rhetoric and Music" by George J. Buelow in *The New Grove Dictionary of Music and Musicians*, vol. 15, pp. 793–803. A useful but somewhat more tiresome method is to follow the suggestions of Peter Cohen and acquaint oneself with the practical application of the affects through an analysis of the text of Bach's *Versuch* (Cohen, *Theorie und Praxis*, 113–84). A more recent treatment of the subject is found in George Barth, "The Fortepianist as Orator: Beethoven and the Transformation of the Declamatory Style" (D.M.A. diss., Cornell University, 1988).

based on its general content as well as on the fastest notes and passages contained in it."[9]

Bach condemned certain keyboardists of his time for trying to appear virtuoso by playing too fast and too mechanically. He warned against using the facility of the clavichord, the instrument then capable of the briskest motion, for its own sake. He also appealed to players not to neglect studying the art of well-trained singers because in that way "the keyboardist will learn to think in terms of song."[10]

According to Bach's teaching, the Italian terms could supply us with some basic information about the general character of the piece. A long-standing problem for students of performance practice, however, is that different eighteenth-century manuals either contain contradictory advice or cover the subject in such varying detail that it is impossible to compile and collate the data into a single reliable table. The eighteenth-century source that seems the most precise, Quantz's book, is in fact a considerable simplification made for the sake of students.[11] Some theoreticians appear to offer tremendous help by ordering the tempo indications into graduated categories. Disappointment ensues when it emerges that the interpretation of the author of the treatise does not coincide with that of the composer we are studying.[12] Donington's *The Interpretation of Early*

9. Bach, *Essay,* 151.

10. Ibid.

11. Quantz establishes four categories of tempo. He uses the pulse of a human being at rest as a fundamental beat and determines what rhythmic value would be equivalent to that beat in the various categories: *allegro assai* = 𝅗𝅥; *allegretto* = ♩; *adagio cantabile* = ♪; *adagio assai* = 𝅘𝅥𝅯. This correlation between tempo markings and pulse (which present-day convention renders as a metronome marking of ca. 80) postulates an eightfold difference of speed between the fastest and the slowest tempos and was already disputed by many in the eighteenth century (e.g., Türk, *School,* 108), although its pedagogical value was acknowledged. Unfortunately, the basic tempo categories in Haydn's music are not the same as the four Italian tempo indications given by Quantz. Nevertheless, some of Quantz's explanations are of cardinal importance for the understanding of Haydn's tempos.

According to Quantz, the smallest note values in the allegro assai category (which includes allegro di molto and presto) are the 𝅘𝅥𝅯𝅘𝅥𝅯𝅘𝅥𝅯𝅘𝅥𝅯 and the ♫ triplet. In the allegretto category (including allegro moderato etc.), the smallest note values are the 𝅘𝅥𝅰𝅘𝅥𝅰𝅘𝅥𝅰𝅘𝅥𝅰 and the 𝅘𝅥𝅯𝅘𝅥𝅯𝅘𝅥𝅯 triplet. Simple arithmetic shows that these values are equally fast.

In the search for a precise place for allegro and vivace (halfway between the first and the second categories), Quantz (*Playing,* 286) considered the standard pulse to be equal to a note value of ♩. in 4/4 meter; in 2/4 and 6/8, the standard pulse gave the time needed for one complete measure (𝅗𝅥 and 𝅗𝅥. values, respectively). It follows from this that the same designation in fact indicates a faster tempo in the "smaller" meters. This seems to hold true exactly for Haydn's music.

12. Leopold Mozart (*Violinschule,* 50) described the fastest categories as follows. The fastest tempos are those marked *prestissimo* and *presto assai. Presto* and *allegro assai* are slower, *molto allegro* is still slower, and *allegro* is the slowest of the fast tempo markings. For Leopold Mozart, *vivace, spirituoso,* and *animoso* occupy a place between fast and slow tempos. Unfortunately, these categories do not offer much help to the performer of Haydn's sonatas. The rhythmic vocabulary and passage work of Haydn's Allegro assai, Allegro molto, and Allegro di molto movements (30 D III, 60 C III, 29 E♭ III, and 55 B♭ II) are natural if executed at about identical speeds. Moreover, sonata movements that Haydn marked *Vivace assai* and *Vivace molto* (56 D II and 53 e III) belong essentially to this same category of tempo.

Music can be of considerable help in establishing an initial orientation, and Rosenblum's "Choice of Tempo" offers a useful survey of contemporary opinions.[13]

In connection with the Italian tempo indications of Haydn's music in general and his sonata output in particular, several matters must be discussed that are not dealt with in the contemporary treatises. Here, knowledge of the wealth of formulas in Haydn's music and the notational differences of his stylistic periods may come to our assistance. Some issues are the following.

1. Is it possible that, in movements composed by Haydn up to ca. 1780 in $\frac{4}{4}$ and $\frac{2}{4}$ meter having a tempo indication of *moderato* or *allegro moderato,* the ♪ goes at approximately the same speed as the ♩ in minuets and minuet-like compositions? The notation of certain stereotypical motives leading to cadences renders this likely (see ex. 86).

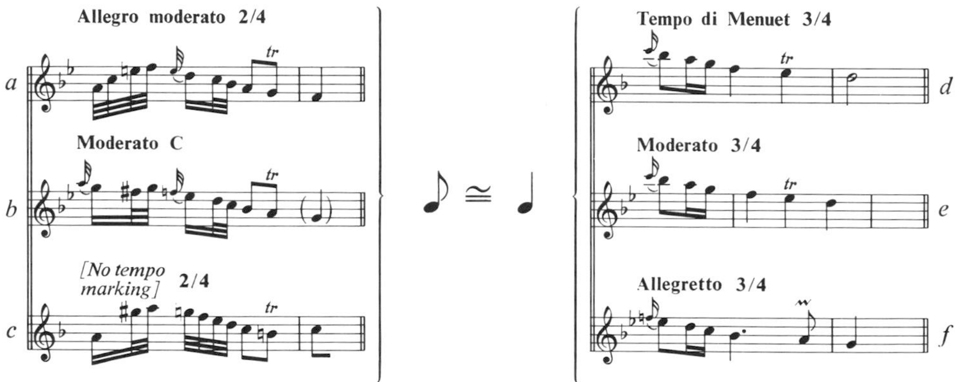

Ex. 86. *a,* 20 B♭ I, 38. *b,* 32 g I, 75. *c,* 38 F I, 43. *d,* 34 D III, 31. *e,* 20 B♭ II, 10. *f,* 32 g II, 23.

2. Is it possible that in a movement in $\frac{3}{4}$ meter the ♩ will be faster than in a movement in **C** or $\frac{2}{4}$ with the identical tempo indication? Probably yes. Let us compare the allegro moderato of 43 E♭ I (in $\frac{3}{4}$) with the other allegro moderatos or the presto in 61 D II with the presto in $\frac{2}{4}$ of 62 E♭. A relation of speed such that 𝅗𝅥. in $\frac{3}{4}$ is equal to 𝅗𝅥 in $\frac{2}{4}$ seems likely.

3. Does Haydn show an inclination to connect certain tempo indications with certain meters? In the sonatas, we see presto associated with $\frac{2}{4}$, allegro moderato or moderato with **C**, and andante with $\frac{3}{4}$.[14] (See table 9 below.)

4. Is a minuet by Haydn faster or slower if the word *Moderato* is added to the title *Menuet?* In 49 c♯ III, the cadential formulas, quarter-note repetitions, and other features suggest that, in spite of its serious character, the moderato

13. Robert Donington, *The Interpretation of Early Music* (London, 1963); Sandra P. Rosenblum, "Choice of Tempo," in *Performance Practices,* 305ff.

14. On the other hand, Haydn uses allegro freely in all meters.

minuet may perhaps be somewhat livelier than a simple *galant* minuet such as 43 E♭ II or 44 F III. The same is true of some minuet movements in the string quartets.

5. In Haydn's musical output, how much faster is a ♩ in ¢ than a ♩ in a movement with an identical tempo indication but a meter indication of **C**? Is it really twice as fast?[15] Or is it 50 percent faster, as Isidor Saslav's investigations of Haydn's string quartets suggest?[16] The number of movements in Haydn's sonatas with a trustworthy indication of ¢ is not great enough to increase our knowledge by very much. There are only two genuinely *alla breve* movements, 48 C I (Allegro con brio) and 55 B♭ I (Allegro). In addition, there is a Moderato (35 A♭ I) that is presumably not authentic, an Andante in **C** or ¢ (61 D I), and a somewhat simple Adagio (48 C II).

As we attempt to find solutions to questions such as these, using data drawn from the complete output of sonatas and from other genres in which Haydn composed as well, we will elucidate some of the characteristic features—and some of the oddities—of Haydn's tempo indications. Of course, in a mature interpretation of a Haydn sonata, tempos will be influenced, in equal measure, by the basic pulse of the piece, the overall character of a given movement, the entire set of rhythmic and motivic constituents of a movement, the instrument to be played and other conditions determining the acoustics, and the performer's decisions based on past study and on intuition of the moment.

If a performer becomes discouraged because serious and well-intentioned study of a sonata still leaves many unsolved problems, I offer another suggestion. Remember that Haydn raised and answered artistic questions not only in individual works but also in sets or groups of works. Consequently, if we are keen on finding reliable answers, sometimes we must search for counterparts, analogies, and variants in a stylistically corresponding group of works or movements. The following chapters are dedicated to the study of styles, types, and variants of groups of works.

15. Quantz, *Versuch,* 263; Türk, *School,* 109.
16. Isidor Saslav, "Tempos in the String Quartets," "The *alla breve* 'March.'"

PART II

Genres *and* Types

Nine

EARLY DIVERTIMENTO *and* PARTITA SONATAS

1. *Authentic and Doubtful Works: Types, Chronology*

NOT ALL THE SONATAS published as works of Haydn's in the two complete editions demand or benefit from equally intensive study. For one thing, we will always be uncertain about the authenticity and dating of several early sonatas; for another, the compositional skill and presence of Haydn's personality is so weak in many of these early pieces that they do not deserve a full-scale comparison with the mature sonatas from about 1765 on.

Volume 1a of the *Wiener Urtext Edition* contains eighteen sonatas; the first volume of the *Joseph Haydn Werke* contains eighteen sonatas plus a few individual movements from the same period. Ignoring three pieces in the *JHW* that are not sonata movements,[1] and recognizing that each editor rejected one sonata from the other's list (in the *WUE* Christa Landon rejects Hob. XVI:16 E♭, which is printed in *JHW* as no. 1, while in the *JHW* Georg Feder rejects *WUE* 5 G as a later compilation),[2] we have nineteen early Haydn sonatas. Neither editor insists that all the early sonatas that he or she prints are unequivocally by Haydn. Indeed, only the four sonatas whose thematic incipits were written into the *EK* by Haydn himself—9 D, 13 G, 14 C, and 16 D[3]—can be considered absolutely authentic. (The first three movements of 13 G are also preserved in an undated but signed autograph manuscript.) In table 5, these four sonatas are placed within boxes.

Christa Landon's pioneering attempt to devise a new chronological numbering of the sonatas was based on the oversimplified hypothesis that very short

1. Allegro molto in D (Hob. deest), Aria in F (Hob. XVII:F1), and Minuetto in F♯ (Hob. IX:26).
2. See *New Grove Haydn*, "Work-List," W.1, *13b*, and X.1, *1–2*.
3. Concerning the *EK* entries, see pp. 160–62.

TABLE 5
A SURVEY OF THE EARLY SONATAS: AUTHENTICITY, CHRONOLOGY, SUGGESTED CORRECTIONS

Date (see *New Grove Haydn* "Work-List")	"*Kenner*"-Type Sonatas (No. in *JHW*)	"*Liebhaber*"-Type Sonatas (No. in *JHW*)
ca. 1750–55 (?)	[No. 1 = Hob. XVI:16 E♭]*,† [No. 2 = *WUE* 8 A]*,† No. 3 = *WUE* 12 A [I:?]†	[No. 1 = *WUE* 10 C]‡
ca. 1755 (?)	[No. 8 = *WUE* 17 E♭*,†	
Before 1760 (?)	No. 4 = *WUE* 15 E No. 7 = *WUE* 11 B♭ No. 6 = *WUE* 13 G †† No. 5 = *WUE* 16 D	No. 2 = *WUE* 2 C No. 3 = *WUE* 1 G No. 4 = *WUE* 3 F§ No. 6 = *WUE* 4 G**
?		No. 5 = *WUE* 6 C (*WUE* 5 G II–III) [No. 7 = *WUE* 7 D]*
	[1762?] [early 1760s]	[early 1760s]
ca. 1764 (?)	[No. 9 = *WUE* 18 E♭]*,†	
ca. 1765 (?)		No. 8 = *WUE* 14 C ‡‡ No. 9 = *WUE* 9 D

* Doubtful, according to Christa Landon.
† Doubtful, according to Georg Feder.
‡ Thought doubtful by Georg Feder in the *JHW*.
§ A *Divertimento con violini* version exists in Elssler's copy.
** Movement III is movement I in the pasticcio sonata *WUE* 5 G.
†† I, III, and II printed in a harpsichord-violin-Basso version in 1767; see Hob. XIV:6.
‡‡ Movement I in a baryton trio version too; see Hob. XI:37 I.

pieces preceded more developed ones. Georg Feder constructed a historically well-founded alternative classification of the early sonatas into two types. The first, *für Kenner* (for connoisseurs), contains extended, technically demanding sonatas. The second, *für Liebhaber* (for amateurs), consists of shorter and easier divertimento-like sonatas, probably written for students and dilettantes. These "nine early sonatas" and "nine small early sonatas" might have been written at about the same time, as two subgenres of the solo keyboard sonatas. I question some aspects of this essentially sound classification. For example, stylistic analysis leads me to believe that the "small" no. 5 (*WUE* 6 C) belongs to the *Kenner* type, before 15 E. Moreover, in the *New Grove Haydn* "Work-List," Feder slightly revised the chronological sequence suggested in the *JHW*. The "Work-List" gives approximate dates only and is, for now, probably the last word on this aspect of Haydn source research.

However, on the basis of stylistic and notational considerations rather than any new sources, three or four dates might still be reconsidered, as indicated in table 5. The most mature "small" early sonatas (14 C, 9 D) as well as the very individual opening movement of *Kenner* type 16 D may well belong to the early 1760s.[4] (Concerning the possibility of dating 11 B♭ around 1762, see n. 34, chap. 4.) In short, probably three or four of Haydn's early sonatas were composed during his first years of employment as the Esterházys' vice-kapellmeister, while the rest are connected with his early teaching years in Vienna.

There is no consensus regarding the authenticity of those sonatas whose attribution to Haydn is based on secondary sources or on indirect evidence such as the thematic catalogs published by Breitkopf.[5] Christa Landon thought 7 D, 8 A, and the two *Raigern* sonatas (17 E♭ and 18 E♭) doubtful. Carsten E. Hatting's study attributed 18 E♭, in its three-movement form, to Mariano Romano Kayser.[6] Georg Feder noted in the *JHW* that Hob. XVI:16 E♭, 5 G (as a sonata), 8 A, 10 C, and probably 12 A I were doubtful attributions to Haydn; in the *New Grove Haydn* "Work-List," he added 17 E♭ and 18 E♭ to this category. Brown, Larsen, and Landon all considered 8 A and the two *Raigern* sonatas doubtful attributions to Haydn.[7] Scott Fruehwald, who applied a so-called profile analysis, reinforced the doubt about 8 A and 10 C but arrived at the surprising conclusion that 17 E♭ and 18 E♭ were authentic.[8] A. Peter Brown's most recent authenticity survey placed 7 D, 8 A, 10 C, 17 E♭, and 18 E♭ I–II among the "plausible" sonatas that "have weaker stylistic associations and/or the sources are not particularly strong, yet there is no reason to exclude them from the canon."[9] In table 5, I have bracketed those seven of the nineteen sonatas that I consider to be doubtful attributions and that, consequently, I will not analyze in parts II and III of this book.

4. H. C. Robbins Landon suggests that 15 E "belongs to the early Eisenstadt years" (*HCW*, 1: 222), but I doubt this. The suggested chronology in Brown's *Keyboard* (table IV-5, p. 123) puts 14 C, 9 D, and 16 D between ca. 1761–62 and ca. 1767.

5. Those questionable sonatas are nos. 8 (Breitkopf 1763); 1–3, 13 (Breitkopf 1766); and 5–6, 12, 15–16 (Breitkopf 1767). The next incipits of Haydn sonatas are found in Breitkopf 1776: the *Esterházy* sonatas, nos. 36–41.

6. The additional movement is included in the *Kritische Anmerkungen* of the *WUE*, pp. 103–5.

7. A. Peter Brown, "The Solo and Ensemble Keyboard Sonatas of Joseph Haydn," 21–22. In his *Keyboard*, Brown states, "Today I consider his authorship plausible" (p. 422). See also Larsen, *3HC*, xviii; Landon, *HCW*, 1:224–25.

8. Scott Fruehwald, "Authenticity Problems in Franz Joseph Haydn's Early Instrumental Works." Fruehwald did not include Hob. XVI:16 E♭ and *WUE* 12 A in his analysis.

9. Brown, *Keyboard*, 110.

2. *Composite Forms and Styles*

Regardless of the total number of their movements, all the early sonatas contain a minuet, usually as a middle movement, but sometimes as a finale. The variety of tempo, meter, form, and style used in these sonatas is small. Each has at least one movement in sonata or sonatina form; only five of the twelve sonatas generally accepted as authentic include slow movements. The relation of these features to the lighter mood of the newer divertimento and similar genres is obvious. In addition to the invariable presence of the minuet, there is a preponderance of movements in 2/4 or 3/8 meter.[10] In Haydn's music, these meters always coexist with short motives and a simple style.

The arrangement of tempos, forms, and styles of movements in the twelve early sonatas reveals Haydn's favorite multimovement patterns, separated from their individual variants and from experimental forms:

Three-movement main type (6): (2 C, 3 F, 4 G), 6 C, 15 E, 16 D	allegro[11]–minuet–finale
Variant of the above type (1): (12 A)	slow–minuet–finale
Three-movement secondary type (2): 11 B♭, 14 C	allegro–slow–minuet
Four-movement type (2): (1 G), 13 G	allegro–minuet–slow–finale
Two-movement type (1): 9 D[12]	allegro–minuet

The sonatas in parentheses (nos. 1–4) are miniatures, often showing a somewhat limited compositional technique; they represent only proto-forms of a type. 12 A, with its archaic slow opening, also belongs in this category.

Signs of Haydn's increasingly self-confident personal style are found in those opening sonata-form movements that have expanded to sixty to eighty measures, are in 2/4, with *moderato* replacing the more usual *allegro* tempo indication, and with a rich rhythmic vocabulary (♪. ♬ and ♬. ♪ with ♬♬ and triplet ♪♪♪ motion). 6 C I is the prototype, which Haydn corrected and quickly revised in 15 E I and especially in 16 D I. Even with a real slow movement still lacking, the three-movement main type represents a well-shaped keyboard work in every respect. A careful reading of these scores, with a thoughtful elaboration of the details of performance (on clavichord, harpsichord, fortepiano, or modern piano), is an excellent preparation for the study of Haydn's mature sonatas. In the open-

10. Of thirty-seven movements, thirteen (35 percent) are in 2/4, twelve (32 percent) are minuets, six (16 percent) are in 3/8, four (11 percent) are in 4/4, and two (5 percent) are in 3/4 but are not minuets.

11. The word *allegro* is used here to stand for a quick, sonata-form first movement, regardless of the specific tempo indication.

12. *New Grove Haydn* "Work-List" (W, *4*), "orig. III apparently lost"; and *JHW* (vol. 18, pt. 1, p. ix), "dritter Satz fehlt," which is a presumption without foundation.

ing Moderato, one can shape the nuances of declamation and fine articulation; the minuet offers a fine opportunity to play eloquently and beautifully in different styles; in the finale, technical finesse can be combined with a clear presentation of the musical sentences and phrase structures.

The two significant sonatas that make up the three-movement secondary type, with slow middle movements, are strikingly different from one another in style. 11 B♭, a serious *Kenner*-type partita,[13] as it may be called, seems to be a reaction, in a somewhat tentative manner, to a fresh outside influence, probably C. P. E. Bach's north German keyboard music. The fantastic rhythmic arabesques and the ornamentation in the G minor Largo movement are unlike anything else Haydn was writing at the time. 14 C, on the other hand, begins with a true "sonata facile" Allegretto with rolling triplets in $\frac{3}{4}$ meter. Not until 1773 did Haydn write another first movement in sonata form in $\frac{3}{4}$ that has come down to us.[14] The piece might reflect an as yet unidentified outside influence. The middle movement ($\frac{2}{4}$, Andante, with ♪.♬, ♬♬, and ♪♪♪ motion) is the forerunner of a characteristic later movement type in Haydn (29 E♭ II, etc.).

The single four-movement partita sonata proper, 13 G,[15] is an important work. It is the first sonata with an Allegro opening movement in common time that uses ♪.♬, ♬♬, and ♪♪♪ motion. Haydn returned to this same style and rhythmic vocabulary in the second half of the 1760s for Moderato opening movements in common time. An elegant minuet and a sparkling Allegro molto finale (in $\frac{3}{8}$) place this work on a higher level than most of the sonatas composed before 1760. Its third movement, an Adagio in $\frac{4}{4}$ in G minor, lacks self-assured, idiomatic keyboard writing, but it introduces a "concertante style" solo movement with two cadenzas to be improvised. Despite all its interesting features, this sonata represents the end of a tradition; it is the last four-movement piano sonata by Haydn.

The single two-movement sonata, 9 D, is notably innovative, although its minuet does not go beyond the average. The first movement is a small masterpiece (see pp. 223–27), and the two-movement structure foreshadows Haydn's most original piano-sonata and -trio type: a $\frac{4}{4}$ Moderato or Allegro moderato sonata-form movement set against a $\frac{3}{4}$ minuet, Tempo di Menuet, or hybrid varia-

13. I use the terms *partita* and *divertimento* sonatas to indicate contrasting styles, partly on the basis of the use of these titles in contemporary sources. Regarding this, see Feder's "Work-List" in *New Grove Haydn* and Christa Landon's *Kritische Anmerkungen* to the *WUE*. There are, of course, many counterexamples such as the *parthia* or *partita* titles for very short and easy works (1 G, 2 C). It is significant that Haydn himself called 13 G *Partita per il Clavicembalo Solo* in the autograph score but *Divertimento per il Cembalo Solo* in his *EK* entry. In his *EK* listing from around 1767–70, Haydn uniformly called his sonatas *divertimentos*. See also James Webster, "Towards a History of Viennese Chamber Music in the Early Classical Period," *Journal of the American Musicological Society* 27, no. 2 (Summer 1974): 212ff., esp. 219.

14. One of the $\frac{3}{4}$ incipits of the six lost sonatas, 26 C, had a triplet sixteenth motion.

15. The finale does not exist in Haydn's autograph (regarding the finale inscription, see Hoboken, *Joseph Haydn,* 1:739). A three-movement form of this sonata (I Allegro, II Adagio, III Menuet) was printed in 1767 by Hummel as an accompanied sonata, i.e., a piano trio.

tion form with minuet character (20 B♭, 28 D, 32 g, 40 E♭, 61 D; among the piano trios, Hob. XV:8 B♭, 11 E♭, 17 F).

3. *Variety of Minuet Types*

The two contrasting types of early sonatas, *Kenner* and *Liebhaber,* differ primarily in the length and the technical and intellectual difficulties found in their opening sonata-form movements. The bridge between these two types of sonata is their minuet movements. Neither in length nor in style can we find any well-marked contrast between the minuets of nos. 15, 13, 11, and 16, on the one hand, and nos. 3, 4, 6, 14, and 9, on the other. I believe that, without ignoring the preference for minuet movements in Viennese practice, the principal impetus for Haydn's composition of so many minuets, either as middle or as final movements, is his early mastery of this form. Haydn willingly wrote minuets in his early piano sonatas because he was already familiar with many types of Menuet and Trio and was developing several individual types of his own.

The seven longer and more mature minuets of the early sonatas are not only very fine works but clearly profiled ones. All but one of the trios are in minor, and all show Baroque harmonic and rhythmic features, which were still common in Vienna in the 1750s. The minuets proper, on the other hand, are very individual, as a study of their rhythmic vocabulary indicates. Characteristic "rhythmic codes"—the dominant rhythmic patterns of the movement—help us explore variants and contrasting styles; they will be useful in the analysis of Haydn's mature sonatas as well. The seven "codes" of the seven minuets are all different (ex. 87) and presage the various types that we will find in the later, more mature sonatas.

		MENUET			TRIO	
6	ʼ		C	c		three-movement form: middle movement
15	ʼ		E	e		
16	ʼ		D	d		
13	ʼ		G	g		four-movement form: middle movement
11	ʼ		B♭	b♭		three-movement form: finale
14	◡		D	d		
9	ʼ		D	=D		two-movement form: finale

ʼ on-beat, ◡ up-beat } beginning

Ex. 87. Rhythmic "codes" of the Menuets.

Ten

The Mature Solo Piano Sonatas: A Survey *with* Historical Hypotheses

1. *The Beginning of the Period*

THE MUCH-DEBATED E Minor Sonata, no. 19 (which survives, in controversial forms, in two keys),[1] is chosen by the editors of both urtext editions to mark the beginning of a new set of mature sonatas. Both editors suggest that the sonata was composed around 1765, but it must not be ignored that this sonata was not registered by Haydn in the *EK* circa 1767–70 (see below). If the three-movement form in E minor is not a fragment, its use of an opening Adagio follows an older, Baroque tradition. In fact, both the first and the second movements are written in a notably retrospective manner. Nevertheless, owing to the dimensions of the three movements and to the style of the sixty-eight-measure-long sonata-like form of the minuet without trio, I am inclined to believe that 19 e is the beginning of a new approach rather than the last link in the chain of early divertimento sonatas.

The E♭ Major Sonata, no. 29, dated 1766, gives a clearer example of a new-style sonata concept. Admittedly, the change in the solo sonata is not as dramatic as in the string quartet genre, in which the early five-movement divertimento

1. The three-movement version in E minor, the only one with which this book will deal, survives in one contemporary copy. Feder ("Probleme," 99) suggested that the three-movement form might represent a fragmentary version whose first movement could have been the lost *Divertimento per Cembalo Solo* in E minor. Only the incipit of this piece is known from the *EK* (see *WUE* no. 25 = Hob. XVI:2e = *JHW,* vol. 18, pt. 1, p. 180). In such a case, the present movements I and II of 19 e could have formed movements II and III in an allegro-slow-finale three-movement structure. An argument against Feder's suggestion is that there is no other example in this style period of a sonata by Haydn in which the opening movement and the following Adagio are in the same minor key. Concerning the other version of the sonata (*WUE* 57 F), see n. 8 below. For a detailed review of the sources and different combinations of movements, see Brown, *Keyboard,* 71–73.

form metamorphosed, a decade later, into the more sophisticated four-movement concept of op. 9. Seven sonatas from the late 1760s are lost; since we do not know their music beyond their short incipits,[2] we may be misreading some of the trends. It is certain, however, that around 1765 Haydn created some ambitious, large-scale solo keyboard pieces (the G Major Capriccio, 1765; Twenty Variations in A Major, ca. 1765, in several versions and in G major as well). At the same time, presumably, he began to write sonatas of considerable length, in an advanced style, of which 29 E♭ of 1766 is the first extant example. The sonatas that followed from 1767 to ca. 1771–72—30 D, 31 A♭, 28 D, 20 B♭, 32 g, and 33 c is their presumed chronological sequence[3]—form a highly unusual group of significant compositions. They were written not as an opus of six but rather one or two per year. Haydn research has not revealed any specific biographical motivation for the composition of these works. Were they written for pupils or for performance at Eisenstadt, Eszterháza, or Vienna? If so, who were the pupils or performers? No plans for the distribution of manuscript copies or for immediately printing these works can be discovered. They represent a true workshop atmosphere of inner motivation.

The entries of sonata incipits in the *EK* deserve a close analysis here.[4] Table 6, which distinguishes between Haydn's regular entries and his additions, will serve to remind us of the sequence of thematic incipits of the solo sonatas. A study of the sequence of the entries as revealed on the facsimile pages, and of the entered works themselves, leads me to certain hypotheses. The first and most important of these is that there are indeed chronological layers here. Apart from the nonthematic addition of the *Esterházy* and *Anno 1776* sets on *EK* 20 (*6 gedruckte Sonaten V, 774* and *6 Sonaten von Anno 776*), these being later entries from the 1770s, there seem to be two or three layers of thematic incipits. The first layer starts with two lost sonatas, 21 d and 22 A. It begins at the bottom of *EK* 20, after concertos and concertinos, and continues on the right-hand side of *EK* 21 with five more incipits. These seven works, designated by Haydn *Cembalo solo* or, in the cases of 30 D and 23 B, just *Cembalo*, make up the first layer. Two of these are dated (29 E♭, 1766, and 30 D, 1767), while the others are probably

2. Since the recently "rediscovered" six Haydn sonatas are forgeries, of the seven lost sonatas (Hob. XVI: 2 a–e, g–h; *WUE* 21–27), we can only study short thematic incipits of two to four measures as cataloged by Haydn in the *EK* (see *WUE*, 1b: 132–33; *JHW*, vol. 18, pt. 1, p. 180). Judging by the two-part texture and the motives of the incipits, 21 d and 25 e seem to originate before 1766. However, 27 A cannot be earlier than 1768 since the right hand goes as high as e^3 in m. 2, a step higher than the top note of the instrument Haydn used until 1768. The texture of 22 A and 24 B♭ suggests the workshop sonatas of 1767–71, but in rhythm and meter these works are more like early sonatas such as 15 E and 16 D. 23 B in *alla breve* and 26 C in triple meter with stormy left-hand motion are so unlike any other solo keyboard work from the period 1760–73 that one cannot begin to guess their date or stylistic type from such short incipits.

3. Another possible order for the last three sonatas is 33 c, 32 g, 20 B♭.

4. The sonatas are called *Divertimentos* in the *EK*. See Larsen's revised edition, *3HC*, ix–x and xvii and the facsimile pages *EK* 20–23, or their reproduction in Brown, *Keyboard*, 16–19.

TABLE 6 THE SEQUENCE OF THEMATIC INCIPITS OF THE SOLO SONATAS

	Additions	Regular Entries		Additions	Regular Entries
EK 20:			*EK* 21:		
		XIV:1			30 D
		XVIII:3			23 B*
		XVIIa:1			24 B♭*
	(36–41)	21 d*		16 D	25 e*
	(42–47)	22 A*			29 E♭
EK 22:			*EK* 23:		
		31 A♭			XIV:2
		26 C*		XIV:3	
	XVIII:4	27 A*			XIV:4
		14 C			28 D
		9 D			13 G
					XVII:2

Asterisks mark works that are now lost; numbers in parentheses are sonatas listed without incipits.

earlier works (nos. 21–22, 24–25?).[5] The sonatas on *EK* 22 are all marked *Clavicembalo solo*. Two of the works require a keyboard that extends above d³ (31 A♭ and the lost 27 A with e³ in its incipit) and thus may be dated after 1768. But this second layer also includes early pieces (14 C, 9 D). A third group, marked *Cembalo solo* again, begins on the middle of *EK* 23, after accompanied keyboard works. This is clearly an additional entry, from around 1768–69, of one new and one old piece (28 D after 1768 and 13 G before 1760). The later entry of 16 D as a *Cembalo solo,* on the left-hand side of *EK* 21, probably belongs to the third layer as well. It appears that Haydn ceased entering keyboard-sonata incipits around 1769, for 20 B♭ and 32 g (ca. 1770–72) and 33 c (1771) are lacking.

Another hypothesis is that Haydn wrote the incipits from memory.[6] In all cases but two among the solo keyboard sonatas, the existing sonatas show considerable notational deviations from the autograph incipits in the *EK*. There is a different notation of the left hand in 16 D, of a right-hand rhythm in 29 E♭ (see ex. 64 above), of left-hand content in 13 G, and of ornamentation in 31 A♭. Certainly, Haydn did not have Breitkopf's yearly thematic indexes at hand. Eight

5. The lost sonata 23 B may be linked with a piano work in B major that Haydn might have written in 1770 when he was ill (see Griesinger, 18), but this is an unsupported conjecture.

6. The -●- sign in the *EK* marks those works that were no longer available at the preparation of the *HV* list in 1805: XIV:1, XVIII:3, XVIIa:1, 21d, 22A; 23B, 24B♭, 25e, 16D; 26C, 27A, 14C, 9D; XIV:2–4, 28D, 13G, XVII: 2.

early sonatas listed under Haydn's name in the indexes from 1763 to 1767 are absent from the *EK*. As we have seen, Haydn entered fifteen sonatas in the *EK*, of which seven whole sonatas and the first movement of 28 D are now lost. How many authentic sonatas written prior to 1770 did he neglect to enter? I think that only a few notable pieces escaped Haydn's memory. He might easily have forgotten the short, early divertimentos (nos. 1–4, 6), or he might not have considered them important enough for such a list. Conspicuously absent, however, are 11 B♭, 15 E, 12 A (if authentic), and 19 e (if the work existed as a three-movement solo sonata at that time). Also disturbing is the absence from the *EK* of a significant nonsonata keyboard work, the G Major Capriccio of 1765. A. Peter Brown's suggestion that some keyboard works might not have been listed in the *EK* because there was no occasion to use them in the service of the prince does not seem to be sufficient.[7]

If Haydn wrote the *EK* incipits from memory, can we assume that he did not possess the manuscripts of those sonatas? Can we connect the loss of sources—entirely lost sonatas or missing autographs—with the misfortune of Haydn's house burning down in 1768 and again in 1776? The list of existing autographs of sonatas given in table 7 casts doubt on such an explanation. The survival rate of autograph manuscripts of sonatas written after 1776 is not better than for those written before the fires. Altogether, there are five complete autographs (designated in the list by italics), spanning four decades. Moreover, none of the incomplete autographs show any marks of burning.

The work of Hoboken and others has not succeeded in identifying the eighteenth-century owners of all the autographs we have today. We can only assume that they were preserved by chance, some by publishers, some by musicians associated with Haydn. At the time of his death, only the autograph of 29 E♭ (1776) was in Haydn's own collection.

2. *The Authentic Sonatas and Their Chronology*

Thirty-seven sonatas are collected in volumes 1b, 2, and 3 of the *Wiener Urtext Edition*. One of them, 57 F, will not be discussed in this book. It is an apparently authorized but nevertheless doubtful version of 19 e; its first movement, a Moderato, is almost certainly not by Haydn.[8]

7. Brown, *Keyboard*, 114.

8. The second and third movements of 57 F are unquestionably works by Haydn, although there are problems regarding the authenticity of the key and the arrangement of these movements. The first movement, however, raises doubts on another level. The musical quality and the total stylistic picture of this sonata-form movement ($\frac{3}{4}$, Moderato) is so far below Haydn's level at any period that I cannot accept it as a work of his. (One cannot be swayed by H. C. Robbins Landon's arguments in *Essays on the Viennese Classical Style: Gluck, Haydn, Mozart, Beethoven* [London: Barrie & Rockliff, 1970], 63: "It is Haydn . . . every genius has an off-day, even the greatest ones"; or in *HCW*, 2:643.) One might well ask how it was possible for Haydn's publisher, Artaria, to print such a potpourri

TABLE 7 EXISTING SONATA AUTOGRAPHS

Before 1760 (?)	13 G	IV missing
1766	*29 E♭*	
1767	*30 D*	
First Fire		
Ca. 1768–71	28 D	I missing
Ca. 1770–72	20 B♭	Fragment of II only
1771	33 c	Draft of I and fragment of III only
1773	36 C	One folio missing
	37 E	
	38 F	The end of III missing; missing bifolios
	41 A	II missing
1774	44 F	Draft of I only
Second Fire		
1789–90	*59 E♭*	
1794	*62 E♭*	

Note: Sonatas printed in italic exist in complete autographs.

I have my doubts about the authenticity of the A♭ Major Sonata, no. 35, as well. Neither Christa Landon nor Georg Feder seems to have suspicions about this work. However, the differences between their chronological placements of the work suggest some difficulty. 35 A♭ was printed in London in 1783, in an unauthorized edition, together with two authentic sonatas.[9] It hardly fits into the

sonata, presumably without even paying him. Only a few months before the publication of 57 F, Haydn had also failed to protest when Artaria published 20 B♭ and 30 D together with a spurious sonata in B♭ major (Hob. XVI:17, probably by J. G. Schwan[en]berg). Haydn's correspondence provides some explanation. In October and November 1787, Haydn and Artaria quarreled because the engraving-correcting-printing process of the String Quartets op. 50 in Vienna was so slow that Forster in London brought out his edition before Artaria. Haydn's letters from May and August 1788 show that during these months he did not offer Artaria new works. The publisher, making the best of a bad situation, brought out works of doubtful origin based on "illegal" sources—probably copyists associated with Haydn. These works appeared without Haydn's consent and, of course, without his supervision. In short, 57 F is probably a pasticcio sonata with a first movement not by Haydn. Of similarly doubtful authenticity are the "sonata for violin and piano" versions of several of Haydn's solo keyboard sonatas, the arrangers of which are unknown.

9. It was printed as part of *A Fifth Sett of Sonatas for the Piano Forte or Harpsichord*, by Beardmore & Birchall (London, 1783), together with 34 D and 53 e (see Hob. XVI:43). Among the few existing manuscript copies, there is no authenticated one. Haydn had no direct connection with this publisher, whose source could only have been an unauthorized copy. The version of 35 A♭ that was printed by André in 1786 as a sonata for violin and piano in G major (Hob. XVI:43) is, in my opinion, an adaptation by the publisher. It is most unlikely that 35 A♭ is an authentic violin sonata by Haydn.

supposed chronological evolution of forms and styles among the Haydn sonatas. Christa Landon's dating, circa 1771–73,[10] is not convincing, but neither is Feder's choice of the early 1780s.[11] In full agreement with James Webster's formulation that "no evaluation of 'good' sources and no critical analysis of style is an infallible means of determining authenticity,"[12] I maintain that, considering the source situation, formal characteristics, and certain alien features of style (of which a few will be mentioned later), 35 A♭ should be considered a composition from the early 1780s, a good work in general with an extremely well-done "à la Haydn" rondo, but not a work by Haydn.[13] Nevertheless, scholarly tradition and a respect for the opinions of others compel me not to exclude 35 A♭ from the following stylistic investigation completely.

The dating of 34 D is also a matter of debate. I prefer Christa Landon's dating, circa 1771–73, to either of Feder's—contemporary with the *Anno 1776* set (*JHW*) or prior to 17 January 1778, the date of a manuscript copy ("Work-List").[14] Indeed, 34 D might have been ousted from the group of *Esterházy* sonatas of 1773 by the more interesting 39 D, which contains a novel first movement, Allegro in $\frac{3}{4}$. Haydn always avoided putting two works in the same key in his authentic chamber music and sonata "opus" assemblings.

To sum up, we will deal with thirty-six mature sonatas, written between 1765 and 1794. Composed over a span of thirty years, they form a striking parallel with the eighteen mature piano sonatas composed by Mozart over a span of fifteen years, that is, from 1775 to 1789. Figure 8 gives a chronological picture of the output of mature solo sonatas, violin sonatas, and trios by Mozart and Haydn. It shows that the first sets of "public" sonatas by Haydn appeared by and large parallel to but independent of the sonatas Mozart wrote during his travels.

10. Apart from the general stylistic impression, there are two features that argue against this dating. First, eighth-note triplet motion does not appear in opening, sonata-form movements in *alla breve* before ca. 1780, when Haydn revised the tempo concept of his first movements (see p. 219). Second, finales with *Rondo/Presto* inscriptions are present in his instrumental genres no earlier than the String Quartet op. 33 (1781).

11. The pianistic style of the opening movement is less ingenious and generally far below the level of other works in the same category, such as 48 C. I can hardly believe it to be a work written by Haydn at the same time as the *Auenbrugger* sonatas or the *Russian* quartets. The second movement, with the minuet and trio both in major, would also be atypical for a work by Haydn written around 1780. The third movement is the outstanding movement of the sonata and the most Haydnesque. Of special interest is the critique of the Le Duc edition of Sonatas nos. 35, 34, and XVI: 15 that appeared in *Cramer's Magazin der Musik* in 1787. The reviewer sets forth in detail his doubts about the authenticity of the set (see Landon, *HCW*, 2: 703). Strangely enough, the reviewer liked the first movement of 35 A♭ best.

12. James Webster, "External Criteria," 77.

13. The authenticity of 35 A♭ could be proved if one could find a Haydn autograph or else a manuscript of the work written by a copyist known to be supervised by Haydn, with unambiguously typical notational details.

14. The variation form of the third movement, Tempo di Menuet, corresponds to a similar movement in 37 E. The opening movement, which is a novel, attractive $\frac{2}{4}$ Allegro, the style of the slow movement in minor, and its *attacca* ending all resemble the 1773 sonatas.

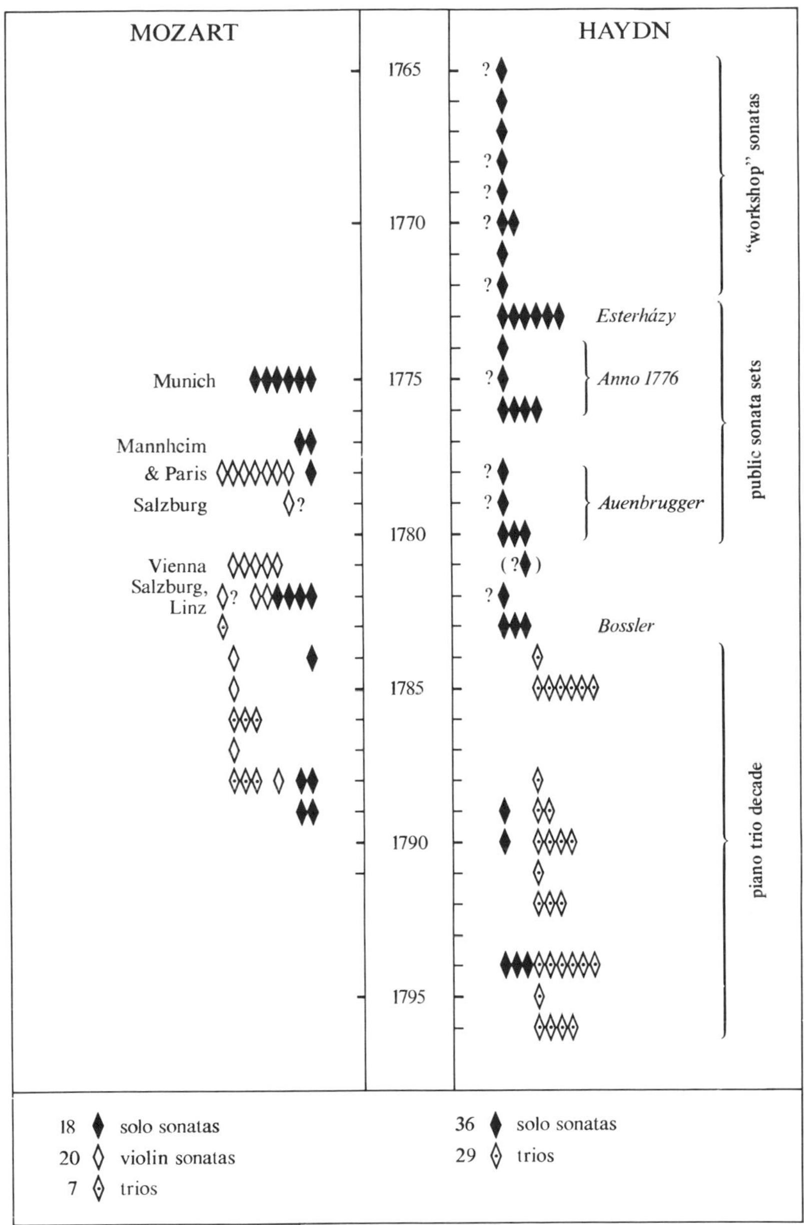

FIGURE 8 Chronology of the mature solo, duo, and trio sonatas by Mozart and Haydn.

It also shows that, from 1785 on, Haydn only occasionally composed solo keyboard sonatas; 1785–96 was the decade of what Haydn termed the *accompanied sonata,* which we call the *piano trio.*

3. *Style Periods and Sets of Sonatas Reflecting the Social Background*

Haydn's pragmatic way of thinking showed itself clearly in his careful consideration of the proper distribution of his works. Thus, before turning to purely musical issues, we would do well to ask a few sociological questions.[15] Why did Haydn write solo keyboard sonatas when he did? How and to what extent was he concerned with the interests of the publishers and purchasers of his music? To what extent were musical decisions such as number of pieces or selection of keys in an opus influenced by editorial expectations? Which were the preferred genres for distribution in different countries? How much time elapsed between the composition and the publication of a work?

This last question is a key issue for a proper understanding of musical patronage and the distribution of music in the eighteenth century. The printing of a piece of music did not automatically mean great value or high recognition. Since the expenses of engraving or typesetting a piece of music could be recovered only by the sale of a large number of copies, publication was a kind of indication of the popularity of a composer or genre.[16] A quite different consideration, one often ignored, also entered into the decision about whether to print a work—whether it was desirable that a given work be circulated further than the composer and his employer or patron. From the 1760s to the 1790s, music written primarily for the dilettante who played clavier, sang lieder, or took part in the performance of chamber music or chamber orchestral works was offered for sale in printed copies. These dilettantes were also the main audience for the immense number of printed arrangements for popular instrumental combinations. If, on the contrary, a new work was technically difficult music for professionals, or if the composer intended to perform an innovative work himself and hoped to keep it out of the hands of his rivals, naturally he withheld it from print. Thus, the majority of Mozart's great piano concertos were not published before his death,[17] while the

15. The survey in William S. Newman's *The Sonata in the Classic Era,* 55–79, is very useful on a general level. When dealing with a specific composer, however, we have to go into further details.

16. In the leading genres, the number of printed compositions of extremely poor quality is quite low. The percentage of occasional festival pieces or pieces printed to gratify the vanity of dilettante composers is negligible.

17. Of the twenty-three piano concertos written between 1773 and 1779, only six were printed in Mozart's lifetime. The two Artaria sets (K. 413 A, 414 F, 415 C, composed 1782–83, published 1785; and K. 595 B♭, composed January 1791, published August 1791) belong to the easier, "for the dilettante" type of concerto. The Paris publications of K. 451 D, *Ployer* (1784), and the early K. 175 D (1773) were in some sense fortuitous. Mozart's great "composer's concerto" types became known to a wider public only between 1792 and 1802.

charming but much less revolutionary D Major Concerto by Haydn, with its attractive Hungarian finale (XVII:11), was printed in Vienna, Paris, London, and Mainz in the one-year period from 1784 to 1785. This should be attributed, not to a tragicomic error in judgment, or to the vulgar musical taste of certain audiences, but rather to the different sociomusical functions of two basically different types of concerto.

Figure 9 compares the dates of composition and publication of Haydn's mature sonatas.[18] After separating authorized editions from printed ones based on copies made without Haydn's approval, certain chronological trends emerge.

The only sonata written before 1773 to be published with Haydn's approval was 33 c, included in a set of sonatas printed nine years after it was composed.

Sonatas written from 1773 to 1784 were obviously intended as "public" works from the very beginning, with a clear conception of the taste, preferences, and instruments available to the musical public of Vienna. In particular:

a) The six sonatas written in 1773 (the *Esterházy* sonatas, nos. 36–41) were published in February 1774 in Vienna by Kurzböck. At that time, there was no one in Vienna who specialized in music publishing. This was the very first work to appear in an edition authorized by Haydn.[19] It is possible that the impetus for publication came from Prince Nikolaus Esterházy, who might have subsidized the costs. The visit of Empress Maria Theresa to Eszterháza in September 1773 may have provided motivation for the music-patron prince and his kapellmeister to bring out an edition of sonatas with an eloquent Italian dedication to the prince himself.[20]

b) Sonatas nos. 42–47, composed around 1774–76, were probably planned by the composer to be distributed in manuscript copies made in Vienna in 1776 by a professional copyist's workshop.[21] Haydn's entry in the *EK* gave rise to the name *Anno 1776* sonatas. The first edition by Hummel was published without Haydn's knowledge or consent.

c) Sonatas nos. 48–52, written around 1778–80, supplemented by 33 c of 1771, were printed by Artaria, Haydn's principal publisher for the next ten years and the first person to establish a tradition of large-scale music publishing in Vienna. The set was dedicated to two skillful clavier players, the Auenbrugger sisters, hence the title *Auenbrugger* sonatas. This was the second authorized edition of Haydn's sonatas.

d) In 1784, Sonatas nos. 54–56 were published by Bossler in Speyer, hence

18. In fig. 9, the date of composition is represented in a necessarily simplified way. For more details, see the Catalog of the Sonatas.

19. Jens Peter Larsen, *Die Haydn-Überlieferung* (Copenhagen, 1938), 103.

20. The text of the dedication is printed in *JHW*, vol. 18, pt. 2, p. vii; Landon, *HCW*, 2:334; and Brown, *Keyboard*, 21.

21. There was a numbering of the sonatas in Haydn's fair copy, but it cannot be reconstructed from the extant copies. See Christa Landon's *Kritische Anmerkungen*, p. 58. The generally accepted sequence of nos. 42–47 is that of the Hummel edition (1st ed., Berlin and Amsterdam, 1778).

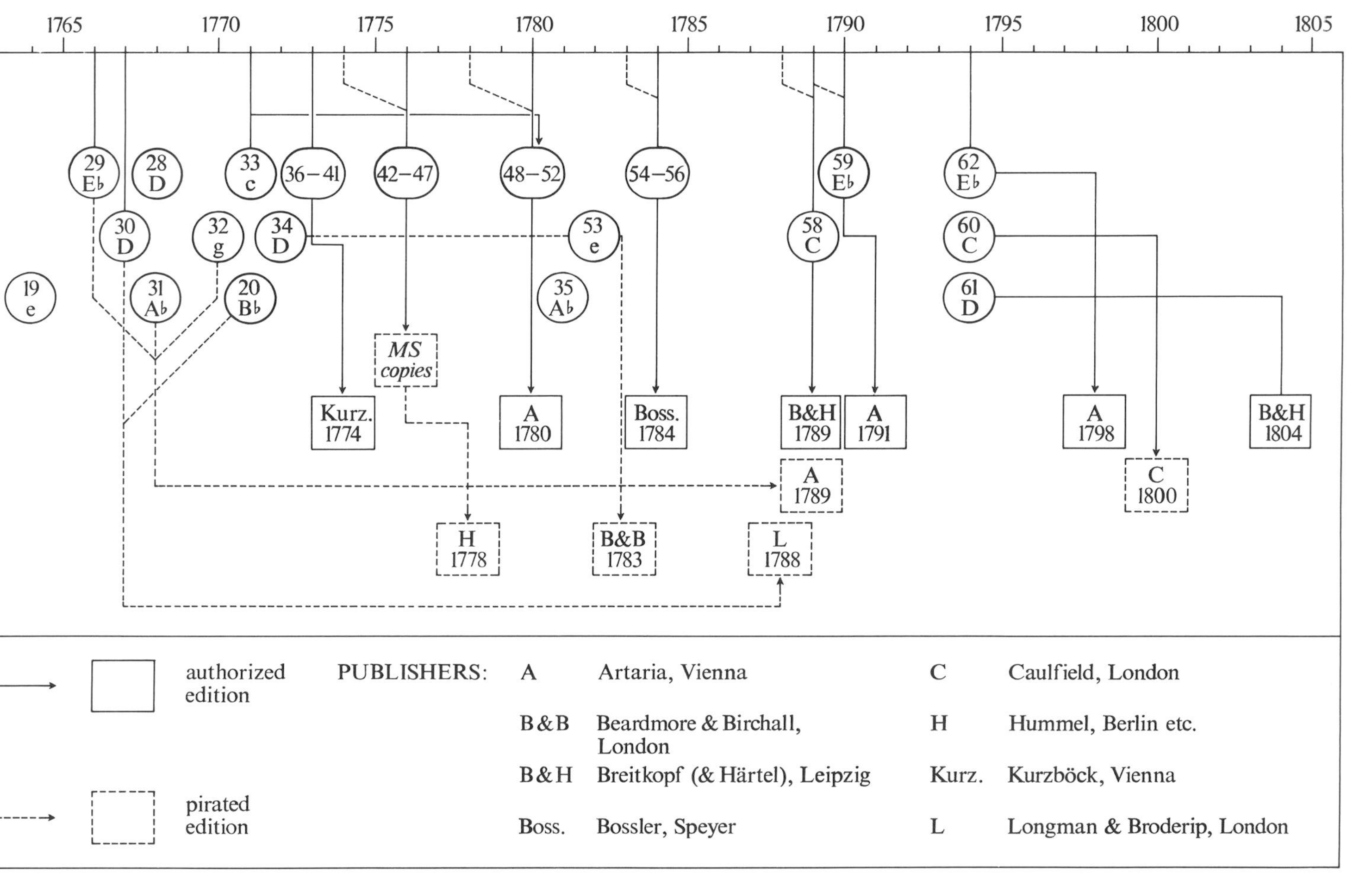

FIGURE 9 A survey of the date of composition and first edition.

the name *Bossler* sonatas. They were written as a kind of wedding present for Maria Hermenegild, née Princess Liechtenstein, who married the future Esterházy prince Nikolaus II. This edition was not supervised or corrected by the composer. Nevertheless, it may be included among Haydn's authorized editions since it had to be made with his consent, probably from his manuscript.

Between 1783 and 1790, reflecting the increasing popularity of Haydn's music throughout Europe and the decreasing number of new works for solo keyboard written by him, unauthorized editions proliferated. Usually, these were arbitrary compilations of sonatas by Haydn, mostly written fifteen to twenty years earlier, often supplemented by spurious works. Some were printed in London, some in Vienna by Artaria, who had had a serious, although not permanent, falling out with Haydn.[22] The two new sonatas that Haydn composed during this period, 58 C and 59 E♭, were commissioned works that were published immediately.

The last three sonatas were composed around 1794 in London. At least two of them, 60 C and 62 E♭, truly concert-style works, were addressed to the keyboard virtuoso Therese Jansen Bartolozzi. Haydn probably did not have a free hand in the publication of these works, which explains their delayed edition.

A complete survey of the contemporary printed editions of Haydn's sonatas, either in sets or as individual works, would give a clearer picture of their dissemination and reception in the leading musical centers in Europe. In the last quarter of the eighteenth century, music engraving and printing was concentrated in a few cities, Paris and London chief among them. Other important cities as far as Haydn was concerned were Amsterdam and Berlin because of Hummel, Leipzig because of Breitkopf (later Breitkopf & Härtel), and, beginning as early as the 1780s, Vienna. Arrangements for the international exchange of engraved plates and for mutual representation of the repertoire was customary, as was strained business rivalry between competing firms in the same city. Music publishers in Paris and London who wanted to be the first to print a new work by Haydn competed with one another and depended on their connections in Vienna. Rivals might already have the engraving in progress, and publishers had no choice, if they wanted the set to look different, but to bring it out with a different "oeuvre" (opus) number or perhaps with a different sequence of the pieces.

We do not have documentation for every contemporary edition and version of Haydn's sonatas.[23] Moreover, we will never know precise numbers of copies printed, sold, and reprinted in certain cities.[24] But even a simplified survey of the

22. See n. 8 above.

23. Even with the addenda and corrigenda in vol. 3, the Hoboken catalog is not the last word in every detail, as the critical commentaries of recent volumes of the *JHW* demonstrate.

24. If the copies of a printed edition sold out, new copies could be printed from the original plates. The original plates could also have misprints corrected or new performing signs or instructions introduced at the direction of the composer. In general, the publisher had no interest in advertising that a

early printed editions of Haydn's sonatas, as they appeared in certain cities, provides useful information (see fig. 10). We see, for example, that the *Auenbrugger* sonatas were the first authorized set to be published, within two years, in Vienna, Paris, London, and Amsterdam. In effect, these sonatas were quickly available throughout Europe, probably from Madrid to St. Petersburg, because the leading firms in the cities listed also had business associates in other countries. Figure 10 also shows that, in London and Paris in the 1780s, a good deal of music was printed under Haydn's name, including suspicious, doubtful, and illegally smuggled-out pieces; this was, in fact, the golden age of Haydn's piano sonatas as far as the public was concerned. Of course not all the sonatas were received with equal enthusiasm, and the judgment of Haydn's time does not always coincide with our estimation today. The *Genzinger* Sonata, 59 E♭, was the last sonata to have a clamorous success. The extremely beautiful two-movement 58 C had a milder reception. The *London* Sonata no. 62 in E♭ came out after a certain delay despite the exclusive rights supposedly given to Therese Jansen Bartolozzi. The two other *London* sonatas, 60 C and 61 D, were not made available for printing for a long time.[25] When Breitkopf and Härtel issued the famous *Oeuvres Complettes* in 1800–1806 (not a true complete edition by our standards), they included thirty-four sonatas by Haydn. This collection became the basic source of commercial editions for more than a century.

4. *Formation and Revision of Sonata Subgenres and Types*

For a better understanding of the trends and changes in Haydn's style, we will now take an overall view of the sonatas that he wrote in the course of three decades. In the case of Haydn's music, more than that of many other composers, the understanding of any individual work, whether a modest or an extraordinary one, whether for analysis or interpretation, is much enhanced by widening one's perspective to include related works. Haydn seldom wrote isolated instrumental works, "individual" in style and endeavor. He usually thought in terms of a set of pieces, in part because of the normal publication practice of his time of releasing works in groups of three or six, but, more important, because his musical invention, from the late 1760s on, seems to have unfolded spontaneously in chains of works. Whenever, after a hiatus, Haydn decided to resume the composition of quartets, symphonies, or sonatas, he seemed to be flooded by a number of new ideas, which he worked out gradually over a series of pieces. For instance, if he devised a new concept for an opening movement, his first realization of this novelty was usually complemented by a slow movement or finale written in one

slightly corrected or revised version of his old catalog number was available. The discovery of such variants under the same plate number usually is the result of the comparison of existing copies collated during the preparation of a scholarly edition.

25. For details, see Landon, *HCW,* 3:440–43.

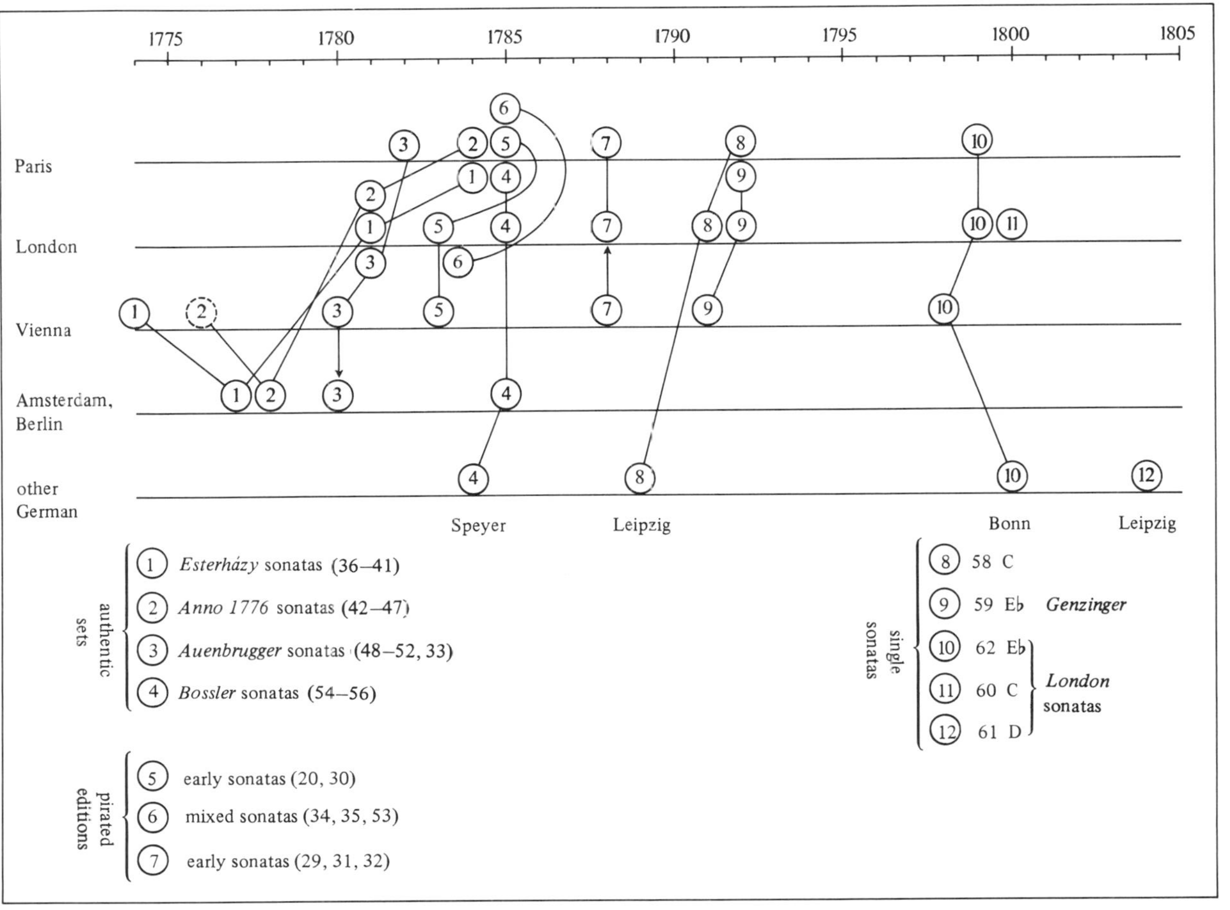

FIGURE 10 First publication of Haydn sonatas in European cities.

of his well-established older models. Next, he would write two or three more realizations of the new concept for the opening movement, changing it, making it more impressive or more polished. After he had made considerable progress in one compositional issue, he had more creative energy available for working on new ideas for other movements in less complex forms.[26] Little by little, a new "opus style" was born. Most of the compositions making up a set of six were individual enough but had a great many common features. Thus, the artistic novelty of an opus manifested itself not so much in the individual movements as in the composite of the variants of the same type. Most of his sets of works included a few movements or even whole works that, for the sake of completeness or else owing to pressures of time, represented an earlier style or type.[27]

The "novelty" of the new concept that set off a creative chain reaction was not necessarily an abstract idea of a style. Haydn usually did not notate short "memo sketches"[28] for use in some future, as yet undecided work (in contrast, e.g., to Beethoven's practice). And in contrast to Mozart, Haydn did not routinely begin to draft a piece in full score and later, when inspiration died down or when an organic development of the piece became impossible, leave it as a fragment.[29] I believe that, before Haydn began to collect his musical ideas and develop them to the point that he could write a compositional draft, he already had a clear idea of the style of the piece. One of his initial decisions was the purpose of a composition, that is, whether it was meant for professional performers or for dilettantes, whether it would be a difficult piece or an attractive but easier one.

The classification of many individual artworks, our task at hand, has the natural disadvantage that for the sake of brevity we use terms that necessarily simplify the extreme complexity of individual cases into types based on common features. As long as the inventor of these labels, and the reader, remembers that a classification is simply an abbreviation and not a condensed analysis, there should be no serious misunderstanding. Almost two decades ago now, my awareness of a need for a consensus of terminology led me to introduce names for the

26. For details and examples, see my "Opus-Planung und Neuerung bei Haydn."

27. To take some examples from Haydn's string quartets, op. 20 A I–III, op. 33 D I–III, G II, B♭ II–III, all represent more conservative styles.

28. I do not agree with the definition of a sketch in Feder's basic survey "Bemerkungen zu Haydn Skizzen." Another classification can be found in Hollace Schafer's "'A wisely ordered *Phantasie'*: Joseph Haydn's Creative Process from the Sketches and Drafts for Instrumental Music" (Ph.D. diss., Brandeis University, 1987).

29. Autograph fragments of piano-sonata movements by Mozart, based on the sixth edition of Köchel, are K. 372a (ninety-one measures), K. 569a (nineteen measures), K. 590a–d (eight, fifteen, thirty-three, 178 measures), and a *Sonatensatz in C,* KV[6] deest (twenty-five measures, *Neue Mozart Ausgabe* IX/25/2, 173). Incomplete piano-concerto movements are K. 452c (ten measures), K. 459a (thirty-seven measures), K. 488 a–d (ten, twenty-three, twenty, eleven measures), K. 491a (three measures), K. 502a (nineteen measures), and K. 537a–b (twenty-one, six measures). Mozart scholars assume that the majority of these fragments were intended as movements of sonatas and concertos that were completed with other movements.

sonata types by Haydn.[30] Many of these names are rooted in eighteenth-century terminology.[31]

The titles that Haydn himself used were traditional and simple, revealing practically nothing particular about the type. For more than two decades, *Divertimento* was an almost all-purpose inscription. Several mature keyboard sonatas were called *Divertimento,* just as the String Quartets opp. 9, 17, and 20, composed between 1769 and 1772, were called *Divertimento* or *Divertimento a quattro.* Among the keyboard sonatas, the change in title from *Divertimento* to *Sonata* in the existing autographs that have titles does not follow a strict chronological pattern. 29 E♭, composed in 1776, and the 1774 draft of 44 F are called *Divertimento.* The 1771 draft of 33 c is already titled *Sonata,* however, and the now incomplete autograph of nos. 36–38 and 41, written in 1773, has the title *Sei Sonate.* Naturally, 59 E♭ from 1790 and 62 E♭ from 1794 are called *Sonata.* The customary term on good copies from the mid-1770s on is *Sonata.* Haydn's published editions, starting with the 1774 set, invariably used the word *Sonata,* without additional modifiers such as C. P. E. Bach sometimes used. This applies in all languages—French, Italian, English, or German. Only the two late sonatas written for Therese Jansen were printed with the fashionable title *A Grand Sonata* (60 C [1800]) or *Grande Sonate* (62 E♭ [1798]).

Despite the reticence of their titles, Haydn's solo keyboard sonatas show striking diversity in type and style. The branching out and individualization of types is stronger and more significant than, for example, in his string quartet oeuvre. The variety of types, on the one hand, and the stylistic determination of an "opus" set, on the other hand, is undoubtedly greater in Haydn's piano sonatas than in Mozart's. Perhaps only the keyboard compositions of C. P. E. Bach—Haydn's ideal in his younger days—exhibit an even greater variety of types.

The survey given in figure 11 is an attempt to delineate the crystallization of types and the general trends in Haydn's solo sonatas. Seven main types may be distinguished, accounting for twenty-five sonatas. Ten more sonatas may be called prototypes, intertypes, or mixed types. Part III of this book is dedicated mainly to a detailed examination of sonata subgenres, types of movements, and their variants. At this point, I will do no more than characterize the main types briefly.

In the "workshop" sonatas, written between 1765 and 1772, Haydn worked out a three-movement and a two-movement basic type. Both types are

30. At the International Haydn Conference in Washington, D.C., in 1975, at a roundtable discussion entitled "Haydn and Mozart," I presented a table of the piano-sonata types (not printed in *Haydn Studies,* 415–16) similar to fig. 11 below and to the table in my article "Stilfragen" on p. 149. I use the same terminology in my essay that accompanies the recording *Haydn: The Complete Keyboard Solo Music* (Hungaroton, 1975–76).

31. See Newman, *The Sonata in the Classic Era,* 43–58.

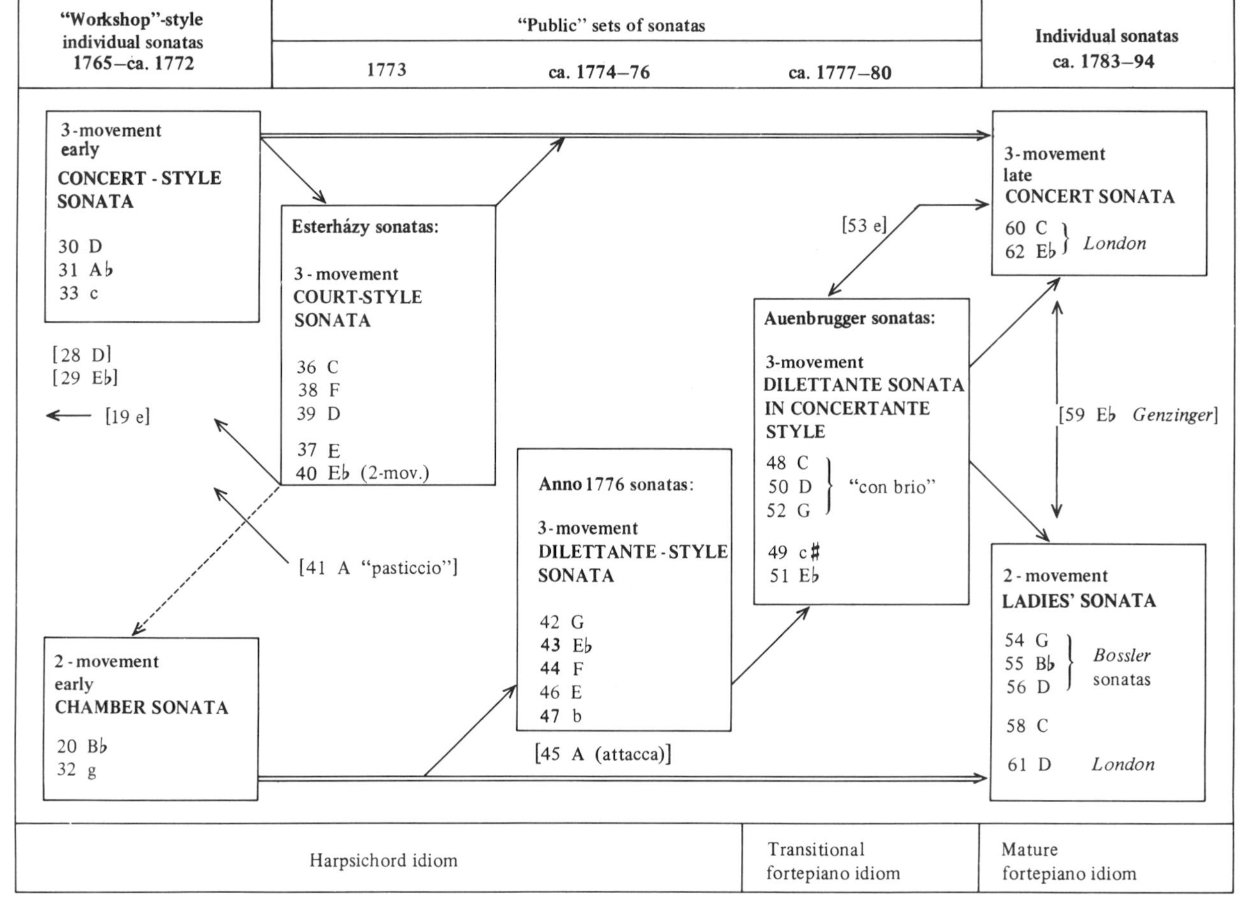

FIGURE 11 Crystallization of types and the general trends in Haydn's mature solo sonatas.

difficult to perform now, as they were when they were composed. The workshop sonatas are unusual pieces, influenced by C. P. E. Bach, and in a sense not really suitable for either of the categories of performer at that time. They were too personal, eccentric, and difficult for the dilettante but not enticing enough for the virtuoso harpsichordist, who generally played his own compositions.[32] In spite of the high critical estimation in which these works are now held and their advocacy by outstanding pianists on both historic and modern instruments, they are far from staples in the modern concert repertoire. The rich and diverse musical material in these movements demands not a performance stressing "Classical" unity but rather one displaying healthy exaggeration, with strong contrasts and grand-style rhetoric, that is, a boldly "Romantic" interpretation.

Our first main type, the early three-movement *concert-style sonata,*[33] is a forerunner of the late grand sonatas. The works in this group were suitable for performance by professional keyboard players. Most of the movements are cast in complex sonata-form structures built on numerous attractive themes and motives. The first movement is a Moderato or Allegro moderato in common time; the second is a $\frac{3}{4}$ Andante or Adagio; the third movement is very fast, Presto, Allegro assai, Allegro di molto, or a really quick Allegro. The characteristic feature of a true concert-style sonata is a long toccata-like or fantasia-like insertion in the opening movement (30 D, 31 A♭, 33 c) and sometimes a cadenza to be improvised before the end of a slow movement (30 D, 31 A♭). The prototype among the earlier sonatas was 29 E♭. The first movements of 37 E, 41 A, and 46 E, written later, refer back to this type.

The second main type, the two-movement *chamber sonata* (*im Kammerstil*) is more lyrical. Its style is akin to a noble branch of the *empfindsamer Stil* of the age. The flexible progression of musical motives, rich in sentiment and marked by sudden pauses, depends on the performer's eloquence and elevated

32. H. C. Robbins Landon's idea that "Haydn seems to have composed most of these sonatas for pupils" (*HCW,* 2:336) lacks convincing support. Landon quotes a contemporary criticism that might have led Haydn to feel that he could usefully change his piano idiom: "*Herr Hayden,* a famous and worthy composer in another genre, has also written various items for the clavier, but this instrument does not seem to suit him as well as the other which he uses in the most fiery and *galant* symphonies" (Hiller, in *Wöchentliche Nachrichten* [1768], cited in *HCW,* 2:337).

33. A. Peter Brown (*Keyboard,* 235) thinks that my titles of types "are misleading from a historical viewpoint: such terms as 'chamber' and 'concert' are questionable, because none of the works in the two groups can be confirmed as having a background in either the court chamber or the public concert. Instead, these keyboard sonatas appear in the main as *Hausmusik,* even if they were used in the residences of the aristocracy and perhaps even occasionally in a concert-like environment." He adds that, with the possible exception of the "grand" sonatas, "all the sonatas . . . were in the best sense 'dilettante' and 'Damen' sonatas." This seems to be an oversimplification. In my interpretation, a "concert" in the 1760s and through the 1780s is not exclusively a public concert in a large hall or theater. Rather, it is a performance by a professional—who is not only a master of his instrument but can add, embellish, and improvise in the proper style, making the event a "concert"—in the court chamber or bourgeois salon, and in the presence of guests. In this respect, the Haydn sonatas called *concert* or *court style* were indeed not written or meant for the keyboard-playing dilettante.

taste for its effect instead of the vitality and glitter of the concert-style sonatas. The main movement is in duple time, while the second movement moves in $\frac{3}{4}$ meter stylized from the minuet. By and large, the fastest notes in the small-note figures in the two movements go at the same speed. In the two examples of this type, 20 B♭ and 32 g, the balance between the two movements is masterful. 28 D, a two-movement composition of which a complete second movement and a fragment of the first has survived, does not fit into the character of a Haydn chamber sonata.

The third main type, the *court-style sonata,* was realized in a set of sonatas written in 1773, dedicated to and printed for Prince Esterházy. These three-movement sonatas of moderate length were more attractive than any keyboard works Haydn had previously written. With lively contrasts in tempo and the fast motion of the fingers, they give a virtuoso impression without making severe demands on the player's technique. The opening sonata-form movement, in $\frac{2}{4}$ or $\frac{3}{4}$, has a simpler thematic composite than the earlier types. The finale is a Presto in sonata form or else with ternary contours. The middle movements are in a new style, true Adagios. The $\frac{3}{4}$ Adagio of 36 C is the most mature version; the slow movements of 38 F and 39 D (and 34 D as well) are in minor and project a Baroque or archaic flavor. The idea of proceeding *attacca* from the slow movement to the finale first appears in 34 D and 39 D. The clearest representatives of the court-style sonata are 36 C, 38 F, and 39 D. 37 E and 34 D branch off from the type; they conclude with Tempo di Menuet movements in double variation form. The last sonatas of the set, 40 E♭ and 41 A, partake of the special glamour of the court-style sonatas, but their opening movements clearly refer to earlier types.

The next cycle of six sonatas, the fourth main type, was cataloged by Haydn as the *Anno 1776* sonatas. They were clearly meant for the Viennese *Liebhaber* and represent the most characteristic set of *dilettante-style sonatas.* This was a new venture on Haydn's part. He would seem to be testing the preferences and limits of those keyboard players whose sphere of performance was their own homes, who played harpsichord, clavichord, or fortepiano for their own pleasure or that of their friends. The three-movement sonatas in dilettante style were a simplified type. They contained hardly any true Adagios in sonata form since the performance of such movements would require a more polished style and a better knowledge of embellishments than the intended performers of these sonatas would be likely to have. In four of the *Anno 1776* sonatas, minuets take the place of the slow movement, as is the case in Haydn's very early divertimento sonatas. In the two sonatas in which the second movement is not a minuet, 44 F and 45 A, the finales are Tempo di Menuet variation forms. For the rest, the finales are Presto movements, in $\frac{2}{4}$. The finales of 42 G, 43 E♭, and 46 E are in an unusual strophic variation form; that of 47 b, the most difficult sonata of the set, is in sonata form. The $\frac{2}{4}$ Allegro con brio opening movement of 42 G suggests a new direction, but this suggestion is picked up only by the $\frac{2}{4}$ Allegro of 45 A. The other first movements return to Haydn's preferred Moderato type, although with a somewhat simplified and compressed thematic structure, especially in 46 E and 47 b. The first movement of 44 F shows unusual and experimental features. 43 E♭ contains the only triple-time first movement of this set.

The *Auenbrugger* sonatas, six three-movement sonatas collected and published in 1780,[34] formed Haydn's second authorized printed set. They constitute the fifth main type, *dilettante sonatas in concertante style,* and can be understood as a revision of the concept of the fourth type, dilettante-style sonatas. By this time, Haydn had become better acquainted with some talented Viennese amateur musicians. The Auenbrugger sisters, Katharina and Marianne, demonstrated a remarkably high standard of performance. Haydn wrote to Artaria on 25 February 1780, "The approval of the Desmoiselles von Auenbrugger is most important to me, for their way of playing and genuine insight into music equal those of the greatest masters" (*CCLN,* 25).[35] Haydn recognized the importance of musicians such as these for forming or educating the taste of a broad Viennese audience, not only for keyboard music, but for other genres as well. Composing for these special amateurs, Haydn increased the technical demands of the pieces and created quick movements that, although requiring practice, make a very lively impression. (The first movements of 48 C and 50 D have proved their pedagogical usefulness to such an extent that some professional performers now, unfortunately, avoid these sonatas.) Haydn introduced new types of slow movements in this opus. The middle movements of 48 C and 50 D tend toward a light, captivating style, while those of 51 E♭ and 52 G, the latter with a written-out cadenza, demand a more cultivated style and taste. The finale of 52 G is in sonata form, but most of the finales are either quick rondos or minuets. In general, there is a great variety of styles in this opus, and each sonata shows notable individual features. An interesting change from the usual fast–slow–fast pattern of movements is the Moderato–Allegro con brio–Moderato tempo sequence of 49 c♯.

The importance to Haydn of a favorable response to his published work is

34. The actual dates of composition of the Sonatas nos. 48–52 has been much debated (see the Catalog of the Sonatas, p. 353). In the *New Grove Haydn* "Work-List," Feder suggests ca. 1770–75 for 49 c♯ and 51 E♭. H. C. Robbins Landon states that 51 E♭ "sounds like a work of the 1760s" (*HCW,* 2:584). These judgments neglect two circumstances. First, it was Haydn's habit to mix new types of movements with well-established, already successful ones, some of which referred back to Baroque-like styles. Second, a work as strong as the C♯ Minor Sonata, no. 49, would hardly have failed to be published in 1774 or 1776 if it had been composed by then. The belated publication of the C Minor Sonata does not provide a counterargument. It has a strange, experimental opening movement, but its second and third movements do not go beyond what was normal for the time. The second movement of 49 c♯, on the other hand, has a form typical for the late 1770s only. (Brown, *Keyboard,* 121, proposed the "mid-1770s" for 49 c♯ and 51 E♭, the "late 1770s to 1780" for 48 C, 50 D, and 52 G.)

35. In the *Jahrbuch . . . 1796,* Schönfeld gave the following description: "Zois, Freyinn von, née von Auenbrucker [*sic*] was some time ago one of the first female artists on the Fortepiano, an instrument she played not only fluently but also with good taste" (*Facsimile-Nachdruck der Ausgabe Wien 1796,* ed. Otto Biba [Munich and Salzburg, 1976], 68).

shown in his *Avertissement* to this set of sonatas and his comment on it in a letter dated 25 February 1780 to Artaria:

> Incidentally, I consider it necessary, in order to forestall the criticism of any witlings, to print on the reverse side of the title page the following sentence, here underlined:
>
> *Avertissement*
>
> Among these 6 Sonatas there are two single movements in which the same subject occurs through several bars: the author has done this intentionally, to show different methods of treatment.
>
> For of course I could have chosen a hundred other ideas instead of this one; but so that the whole *opus* will not be exposed to blame on account of this one intentional detail (which the critics and especially my enemies might interpret wrongly), I think that this *avertissement* or something like it must be appended, otherwise the sale might be hindered thereby.[36]

Haydn was acutely aware of what his audience expected and how far he could lead them beyond their expectations.

The sonatas of the last decade gravitate toward two types. First (the sixth main type in our survey) is the late successor of the two-movement chamber sonatas. Perhaps arbitrarily, I call this type Haydn's *ladies' sonata* (*Damensonate*). In the mid-eighteenth century, a keyboard instrument was thought to be more suitable for a lady, and gentleman amateurs tended to play violin, cello, or flute. This image became even stronger in relation to the subtler and more impressive fortepiano. In 1770, C. P. E. Bach published a set of sonatas "à l'usage des Dames," or *Damensonaten*. Haydn's *Damensonaten* were ladies' sonatas in a more special and concrete way. He composed these works for and dedicated them to specific music-making ladies, and the pieces may have contained delicate personal messages. The prototype is the *Bossler* sonata set, nos. 54–56, composed in 1784 and dedicated to Princess Maria Hermenegild. These sonatas are still abstract in a way that is quite appropriate to the special social situation. The C Major Sonata, no. 58, bears no dedication, although its first movement clearly proceeded to refine the type. After Haydn became acquainted with Marianne von Genzinger, the noblewoman who was the model and inspiration for at least one of his works, the type was manifest and concrete. The Adagio of the *Genzinger* Sonata, no. 59, is probably the clearest "portrait" piece Haydn ever wrote.[37] It is

36. *CCLN*, 25.

37. The authentic edition of the *Genzinger* Sonata was—had to be—dedicated to Prince Esterházy's housekeeper (later Johann Tost's wife), "Mademoiselle Nanette" (Maria Anna Gerlischek [Jerlischek]). However, as Haydn wrote on 20 June 1790 to Mrs. Genzinger, it "was written especially for your Grace." He continues, "This Sonata was destined for Your Grace a year ago, and only the Adagio is quite new, and I especially recommend this movement to your attention, for it contains many things which I shall analyze for Your Grace when the time comes; it is rather difficult but full of feeling" (ibid., 105).

certainly possible that the F Minor Variations of 1793, which might have been intended as the first movement of a planned sonata, was a response to the death of Frau von Genzinger on 26 January 1793.[38]

The sonatas of this sixth main type are not easy or superficial salon pieces. They give expression to "feminine," capricious, refined feelings—one of the great innovations of Haydn's music. The double variation form, with one theme in major and the other in minor, replaces the sonata form as an opening movement in 54 G, 56 D, and 58 C. When the first movement is in sonata form, the primary affect is caprice, as in 55 B♭, or a kind of lyricism far removed from sophisticated motivic elaboration, as in 61 D. The second movements, unlike those of the early two-movement chamber sonatas, are fast, brilliant, capricious, technically difficult, and sometimes written in a surprising form, as, for example, 56 D. The *Genzinger* Sonata, in three movements, is a special, intertype case. The second and third movements gravitate toward the ladies'-sonata concept, but the opening Allegro movement is more like that of a concert-style sonata.

Contemporary with the ladies' sonatas are the two sonatas of our seventh main type, the *concert sonata* or *grand sonate*.[39] These were composed expressly for and dedicated to Therese Jansen Bartolozzi. Perhaps more important than this lady's individual performing style for his formulation of this new type was Haydn's own experience with the English fortepiano, to which I attribute a free style in part writing, the use of a variable number of voices, and several impressive pianistic effects new to Haydn. The opening Allegros of 60 C and 62 E♭ are considerably more brilliant than any Haydn had previously composed. In the E major Adagio of 62 E♭, Haydn invented a concert-style slow movement. Moreover, he produced virtuoso finales equally successfully in scherzo or sonata forms.

For a fuller understanding of the sonatas that Haydn wrote during his last decade of work in this genre, let us survey here the piano trios that he composed during approximately the same period. Haydn wrote twenty-nine accompanied sonatas between 1784 and 1796. Eighteen of these were assembled in authorized publications, six sets of three trios each. One of these sets, Hob. XVI: 11–13 (E♭, e, c), was published by Artaria without a dedication. The rest were dedicated to women. The set XV: 6–8 (F, D, B♭), published by Artaria in Vienna in 1787, is dedicated to Countess Marianne Witzay (Viczay), née Grassalkovich, the granddaughter of Prince Nikolaus Esterházy.[40] The set XV: 18–20 (A, g, B♭), published by Longman and Broderip in London in 1794, is dedicated to Princess Maria

38. Possible impetuses for the composition of the F Minor Variations were the death of Marianne von Genzinger and the personality and pianistic style of Mozart's pupil Barbara von Ployer, for whom the dedication was originally intended (see Landon, *HCW*, 3:437–39).

39. 53 e (ca. 1780–82) stands nearer to the style of the *Auenbrugger* sonatas than to the late concert-style sonatas.

40. In a letter of 26 November 1785, Haydn urged the publication by Artaria because he was going to visit the countess at her father's manor in Nagylózs.

Theresa, née Hohenfeld, the widow of Prince Paul Anton Esterházy, who died on 22 January 1794. The set XV:21–23 (C, E♭, d), published by Preston in London in 1795, is dedicated to Princess Maria Esterházy, née Liechtenstein, to whom the *Bossler* sonatas were also dedicated. The set XV:24–26 (D, G, f♯), published by Longman and Broderip in London in 1795, is dedicated to Madame Schroeter.[41] The set XV:27–29 (C, E, E♭), published by Longman and Broderip in London in 1797, is dedicated to Therese Jansen Bartolozzi, to whom the *London* concert sonatas were also dedicated.

The pianist in these trios has a shared role in shaping the style of the performance, a role that is challenging and difficult. In a sense, all the trios belong to the category *concert style* because of their technical and musical difficulties. The Bartolozzi set is in an emphatically professional style. The Schroeter set is also in an attractive concert-like style, but it could also be performed by a well-prepared nonprofessional. The two sets dedicated to the Esterházy ladies are less homogeneous. Both sets begin with decorative movements in a pleasant *sonata facile* manner (XV:18 A I, 21 C I–II), but both sets also include truly difficult pieces (XV:19 g, 23 d). Many passages in these works, if well executed, would naturally garner praise for the performer, notably the *Solo con mano sinistra* passage in the Andante of XV:20 B♭. The Grassalkovich set, next to the *Bossler* sonatas in chronology, has the nearest connections with solo-sonata types. It has the appearance of a careful combination of the *Auenbrugger*-sonata and ladies'-sonata concepts. The result, however, is not a hybrid style but a new approach. The urgent requests from his publishers in London for trios and the favorable reception these works enjoyed in Vienna steered Haydn toward the composition of accompanied keyboard sonatas rather than solo ones. Or, to be more precise, Haydn, responding to the fashion of the time, used the accompanied sonata for his more public utterances and on special occasions turned to the solo-keyboard works as a labor of love for his more personal musical thoughts.

5. *Meter and Tempo in Multimovement Works*

Composers of genius differ considerably with regard to how much they may change the rhythm and tempo of a theme between its inception and its final, printed form. For example, there are cases in Beethoven's work in which a theme's notation was diminished or augmented, its meter changed from 𝄴 to 𝄵, or vice versa, or the tempo marking changed considerably through sketches, drafts, and fair copies. Haydn was a composer of a different type. As mentioned, we believe that he began to notate a piece only after its genre, style, and character had been

41. She was the widow of Johann Samuel Schroeter (d. 1788), a German composer who settled in London. She must have been a close friend of Haydn's while he stayed in London, as her letters, copied by Haydn, suggest.

determined, either in his head or at the keyboard. An investigation of drafts and fair copies written by Haydn shows exceptionally few examples of changes of time signature, tempo, or the scale of rhythmic notation. (When Haydn changed the shade of a tempo indication, as in the case of 33 c,[42] we may assume that in the course of a decade his understanding of the tempo had changed slightly or that he took a new aspect of performance practice into consideration.)

In Haydn's work, the choice of meter and tempo was a well-thought-out decision, one that determined the basic style of a movement in many respects. Moreover, the meter and tempo of the first movement also influenced the choice of meter and tempo in succeeding movements. Whether he finds it a virtue or a weakness, a performer does well to be aware of the orderly, disciplined, and logical nature of Haydn's compositional world. Statistics and comparisons give us a clearer view of this world, helping us recognize changes in style and distinguish between special cases and typical ones. Comparisons of Haydn's solo sonatas with one another, with his trios, and with the solo sonatas of Mozart all provide useful and relevant information.

Haydn's choice of meters was neither rich nor surprising. The ninety-nine movements of his mature sonatas (from *WUE* 19 e on) make use of a total of six meters. The fifty-four movements of Mozart's eighteen mature sonatas use the very same selection.[43] In the following chart, we are comparing the number of movements by Haydn using a given meter with the percentage of movements by Mozart, giving a 1 : 1 ratio, for example, ninety-nine movements by Haydn compared with 100 percent of the movements by Mozart:

Symbol[44]	Signature	Haydn (no.)	Mozart (%)
◫	¢	5	8
□	4/4	21	26
▯	2/4	23	20
○̄	3/4	42	31
○	3/8	2	6
∞	6/8	6	9

Let us now consider the succession of meters in two-movement and three-movement sonatas (see table 8). Since minuet movements are the most common

42. The draft of the first movement, written in 1771, had the inscription *Moderato* (see n. 11, chap. 7), while in the authorized edition, printed in 1780, the tempo indication is *Allegro moderato*.

43. In the sonatas of C. P. E. Bach, we find movements in $\frac{9}{8}$ and $\frac{12}{8}$, meters neglected in Mozart's and Haydn's sonatas.

44. In the following pages, I will be using three square and three round symbols to express graphically the six basic time signatures that Haydn used in his mature sonatas. One further symbol, ⊙, will be used to distinguish minuet movements from other $\frac{3}{4}$ movements (○).

TABLE 8 THE SUCCESSION OF METERS IN TWO- AND THREE-MOVEMENT SONATAS

	Meters	Sonatas
1.	◫▯	55 B♭
2.	◫○	61 D
3.	□○	32 g
4.	□⊙	28 D, 40 E♭
5.	▯○	20 B♭
6.	○▯	56 D, 58 C
7.	∞□	54 G
8.	◫◫○	48 C
9.	◫⊙▯	35 A♭
10.	□□⊙	44 F
11.	□▯⊙	49 c♯
12.	□○▯	30 D, 31 A♭, 46 E, 50 D, 62 E♭
13.	□○○	29 E♭, 33 c, 60 C
14.	□⊙▯	41 A, 47 b
15.	□∘⊙	37 E
16.	□∞⊙	51 E♭
17.	▯○⊙	34 D, 45 A
18.	▯○∘	36 C
19.	▯○∞	52 G
20.	▯⊙▯	42 G
21.	▯∞▯	38 F
22.	○□○	39 D
23.	○○⊙	59 E♭
24.	○⊙▯	43 E♭
25.	∞▯⊙	19 e
26.	∞○▯	53 e

Note: ◫ = ¢, □ = $\frac{4}{4}$, ▯ = $\frac{2}{4}$, ○ = $\frac{3}{4}$, ∘ = $\frac{3}{8}$, ∞ = $\frac{6}{8}$.

type in Haydn's sonata oeuvre, with their own special rhythmic style, it is useful to distinguish $\frac{3}{4}$ minuet movements, with the symbol ⊙, from other $\frac{3}{4}$ movements, with the symbol ○. Altogether, there are twenty-six meter combinations among Haydn's thirty-six mature sonatas. For this survey, I have followed a systematic order rather than one that is chronological or style oriented. The most frequent combinations for the three-movement sonatas are $\frac{4}{4}$–$\frac{3}{4}$–$\frac{2}{4}$, used five times;[45] $\frac{4}{4}$–$\frac{3}{4}$–$\frac{3}{4}$, used three times; and $\frac{4}{4}$–minuet–$\frac{2}{4}$ and $\frac{2}{4}$–$\frac{3}{4}$–minuet, both used twice. In the two-movement sonatas, the combinations $\frac{4}{4}$–minuet and $\frac{3}{4}$–$\frac{2}{4}$ are both used twice. Note that there is hardly any sonata without a triple-time movement and

45. This combination of duple and triple time with diminishing measures—i.e., four, three, and two quarters per bar—strikes us as natural. Note that the reverse order, $\frac{2}{4}$–$\frac{3}{4}$–$\frac{4}{4}$, does not occur in Haydn's sonatas.

TABLE 9 TEMPOS AND METERS IN HAYDN'S MATURE PIANO SONATAS

		1765–72	1773–76	1780–94	
1. Prestissimo	1	—	—	∞	
2. Presto	15	▯	▯▯▯▯▯▯▯○ ∘	▯▯□○∞	
3. Vivace molto	1	—	—	▯	
4. Vivace assai	1	—	—	▯	
5. Allegro molto	1	—	—	○	62.9% = $\frac{2}{4}$
6. Allegro di molto	2	○	—	▯	
7. Allegro assai	1	▯	—	—	
8. Allegro con brio	5	—	▯	▯▯□⎅	
(27)					
9. Presto ma non troppo	1	—	—	▯	No typical relation
10. Allegro	12	▯○	▯▯▯○	○○○□□⎅	
(13)					
11. Allegro moderato	7	▯□	□□□○	□	
12. Allegretto	2	○	○	—	50.0% = $\frac{4}{4}$
13. Allegretto innocente	1	—	—	∞	
(10)					
14. Moderato	12	□□□□□○	□□□ ▯ ⎅	□	Without the minuets: 75.0% = $\frac{4}{4}$
15. Menuet	7	○	○○○○○	○	
16. Tempo di Menuet	7	○	○○○○○	○	
(26)					
17. Andante	4	○○	∞	⎅	
18. Andante con moto	1	○	—	—	71.4% = $\frac{3}{4}$
19. Andante con espressione	2	—	—	○○	
(7)					
20. Adagio	14	○∞	○○○□□∞	○○○○⎅∞	
21. Adagio e cantabile	1	—	—	○	
22. Largo e sostenuto	1	—	—	○	62.5% = $\frac{3}{4}$
(16)					
(99)		(21)	(41)	(37)	

that the only sonata consisting of three movements in triple time is the immensely rich and variegated *Genzinger* Sonata.

Let us now bring tempo markings into consideration. Table 9 surveys the sonatas organized in terms of tempo markings, gathered in six classes of speed and in three approximately equal periods of years.[46] The meters are once again

46. For this survey, and in contrast to my practice in other parts of this book, I have begun the last chronological period not in 1784 but in 1780, the year of the publication of the *Auenbrugger* set, because of the decisive changes in Haydn's notation of rhythm and tempo at this time (see pp. 218–19).

indicated by symbols. I have separated tempo indications that are similar but not identical.[47] The twenty-two tempo markings are arranged in order of decreasing speed, with the understanding that the relation of the speeds of menuet and tempo di menuet is equivocal.[48] The modifications of allegretto, andante, and adagio, which suggest a difference in character rather than speed, follow the unmodified terms. The distribution of the tempo indications into six classes of speed is to a certain extent arbitrary, but nevertheless useful.

We may make a few observations on the basis of this survey. In Haydn's music, certain tempos and meters have an elective affinity. The broadest meter, $\frac{4}{4}$ time, is the typical companion of allegro moderato or moderato tempos. This combination of meter and tempo provides a frame for those movements that are the most sophisticated and rhythmically differentiated, involving many unpredictable events, movements that require great freedom and creativity on the part of the performer. For slower or faster than moderate tempos, Haydn preferred shorter measures. Andante and Adagio movements are most often in triple time; 77 percent of the Allegros are in $\frac{3}{4}$ or $\frac{2}{4}$ time, and $\frac{2}{4}$ is favored for faster tempos.

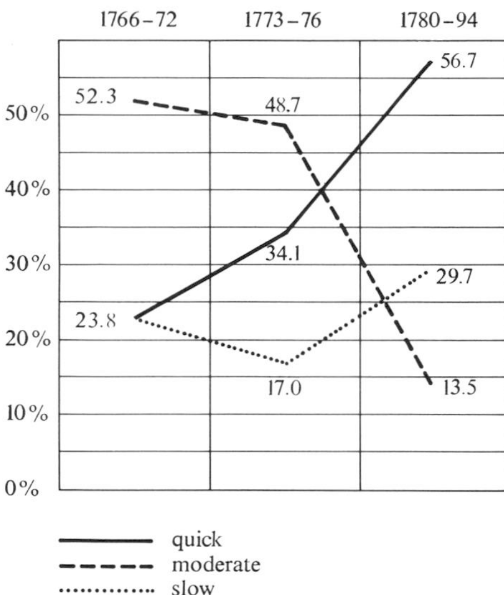

FIGURE 12 The proportion of quick, moderate, and slow tempos in sonata movements in the three main chronological periods.

47. *Allegro molto* and *Allegro di molto* may have had different meanings for Haydn. He used both indications in the late sonatas 55 B♭ and 60 C. However, Haydn did not see the proofs of these sonatas when they were published, and the tempo indications, thus, may not be authentic. *Presto ma non troppo,* which appears in 50 D III with the modifier *innocentemente,* might be grouped with tempos 1–8 as well as with tempo 10.

48. See the discussion on p. 316.

An examination of the tempos chosen over the course of three decades reveals that for his later works Haydn gravitated toward the extremes of the range of tempos. Figure 12 shows in graph form that, in the "workshop" sonatas, moderate tempos prevailed. Slow movements became less frequent in the period of the dilettante sonata sets. Finally, among the last fourteen sonatas, rapid tempos preponderate.

Table 10 compares the meters and tempos in Haydn's piano sonatas with those in Mozart's. Although there are certainly common features in the twenty-two tempos used by Haydn and the eighteen used by Mozart, individual profiles, probably reflecting differences in temperament rather than background, clearly emerge. Mozart explores a wide range of shades of andante tempos—andante grazioso, andante cantabile, andante amoroso. The proportion of slow movements by Haydn is less, and he prefers tempos that are adagio or slower. Mozart prefers moderately fast allegros that leave room for lyricism; Haydn is comfortable with tempos in a faster range. In figure 13, these differences in preference are shown in the form of a graph.

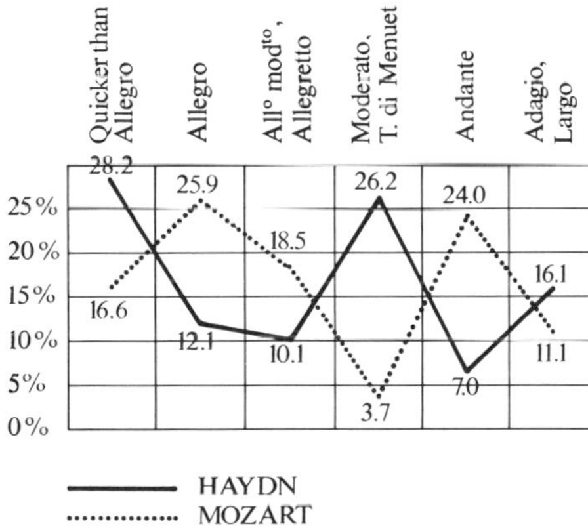

FIGURE 13 The ratio of tempos in the sonata movements by Haydn and Mozart.

Table 11, comparing the tempos in Haydn's solo sonatas and piano trios,[49] is also illuminating. There is a striking increase in the use of many shades of adagio and andante as well as of lyric allegros and allegrettos in the later keyboard genre. In Haydn's trios, perhaps because the genre was less experimental, the varieties of tempos are closer to those used by Mozart.

49. I use Hob. XV:2, 5–32, in this survey.

TABLE 10 A COMPARISON OF THE TEMPOS AND METERS IN HAYDN'S AND MOZART'S SONATAS

Haydn				Mozart		
	∞	1	1. Prestissimo	—		
	□▯○∘∞	15	2. Presto	3	▯ ∘	
	▯	1	3. Vivace molto	—		
	▯	1	4. Vivace assai	—		
	○	1	5. Allegro molto	—		
	▯○	2	6. Allegro di molto	—		
		—	7. Molto allegro	1	□	
	▯	1	8. Allegro assai	3	□ ○ ∞	
	◫□▯	5	9. Allegro con brio	—		
27.2%		—	10. Allegro con spirito	2	□	16.6%
	▯	1	11. Presto ma non troppo	—		
13.1%	◫□▯○	12	12. Allegro	14	◫□▯○ ∞	25.9%
		—	13. Allegro maestoso	1	□	
	□▯○	7	14. Allegro moderato	1	▯	
	○	2	15. Allegretto	6	◫□▯	
		—	16. All^{tto} grazioso	2	◫ ▯	
10.1%	∞	1	17. All^{tto} innocente	—		18.5%
	◫□▯○	12	18. Moderato	—		
	○	7	19. Menuet (Menuetto)	2	○	
26.2%	○	7	20. Tempo di Menuet	—		3.7%
	◫ ○ ∞	4	21. Andante	6	◫ ○	
	○	1	22. And^{te} con moto	—		
		—	23. And^{te} grazioso	1	∞	
		—	24. And^{te} cantabile	2	○	
		—	25. And^{te} amoroso	1	∘	
	○	2	26. And^{te} con espress.	1	▯	
		—	27. And^{te} cant. con espr.	1	○	
7.0%		—	28. And^{te}, un poco adagio	1	○	24.0%
	◫□ ○ ∞	14	29. Adagio	6	□ ○ ∞	
	○	1	30. Ad^{io} e cantabile	—		
16.1%	○	1	31. Largo e sostenuto	—		11.1%
		(99)		(54)		

TABLE 11 A COMPARISON OF THE TEMPOS IN THE SONATAS AND PIANO TRIOS BY HAYDN

Sonatas				Trios		
	∞	1	1. Prestissimo	—		
		—	2. Presto assai	2	○ ∞	
	□▯○◦∞	15	3. Presto	6	▯○ ∞	
	▯	1	4. Vivace molto	—		
	▯	1	5. Vivace assai	2	▯ ∞	
		—	6. Vivace	4	□▯○	
28.2%	○	1	7. Allegro molto	—		20.5%
	▯○	2	8. Allegro di molto	—		
	▯	1	9. Allegro assai	1	▯	
	⎅□▯	5	10. Allegro con brio	—		
		—	11. Allegro spiritoso	1	○	
(28)	▯	1	12. Presto ma non troppo	—		(16)
12.1%	⎅□▯○	12	13. Allegro	15	□▯○	19.2%
		—	14. Allegro ma dolce	1	○	
	□▯○	7	15. Allegro moderato	10	⎅□▯	
		—	16. Allegro ben moderato	1	○	
10.1%	○	2	17. Allegretto	1	○	19.2%
	∞	1	18. Allegretto innocente	—		
		—	19. Poco allegretto	1	▯	
(10)		—	20. And^{tino} più tosto all^{tto}	1	∞	(15)
	⎅□▯○	12	21. Moderato	—		
26.2%	○	7	22. Menuet	1	○	7.6%
(26)	○	7	23. Tempo di Menuet	5	○	(6)
	⎅ ○ ∞	4	24. Andante	11	▯ ∞	
		—	25. Molto andante	2	□▯	
7.0%	○	1	26. Andante con moto	1	◦	21.7%
		—	27. Andante cantabile	2	▯	
		—	28. Andantino ed innocente	1	∞	
(7)	○	2	29. Andante con espressione	—		(17)
	⎅□ ○ ∞	14	30. Adagio	3	▯○ ∞	
		—	31. Adagio non tanto	1	○	
		—	32. Adagio ma non troppo	2	○	
16.1%		—	33. Poco adagio	2	□ ○	11.5%
		—	34. Adagio pastorale	⟨1⟩	⟨∞⟩	
		—	35. Adagio cantabile	1	○	
	○	1	36. Adagio e cantabile	—		
(16)	○	1	37. Largo e sostenuto	—		(9)
(99)			22 variants	26 variants		(78)

A characteristic contrast in dramaturgy in a general sense appears when we compare the tempo-character combinations in Haydn's sonatas with those in Mozart's, even if we examine only the opening and final movements. Table 12 shows that Haydn's first movements are typically in a moderate tempo, Mozart's typically in a fast tempo. For final movements, Haydn prefers either fast movements or minuet-style movements. Mozart prefers allegretto movements in common time, especially in his full maturity.

TABLE 12

	Haydn (36 sonatas)		Mozart (18 sonatas)
Opening movement:			
Quick	13 (36)	≪	14 (78)
Moderate	20 (56)	≫	2 (11)
Slow	3 (8)	~	2 (11)
Finale:			
Quick	22 (67)	>	9 (50)
Moderate	12* (33)	<	8† (44)
Slow	—	<	1‡ (6)

Note: Numbers in parentheses are percentages.
~, similar ratio; >, more than; <, less than; ≫, much more; ≪, much less.
* Only $\frac{3}{4}$ with Haydn.
† $\frac{2}{4}$, $\frac{4}{4}$, **C** with Mozart.
‡ Slow variations with quick end (K. 284).

The final stage of our examination of meters and tempos in Haydn's sonatas is to look once again at the sonatas as multimovement works. Table 13 is a graphic representation of the chronological developments of the basic sonata types formed by various tempo-character combinations. Adding "coloration" to the time-signature symbols (solid black = fast, striped = moderate, white = slow) allows the symbol to depict tempo as well as meter.

The characteristic contrast of the chamber-style two-movement and the concert-style three-movement basic type of the "workshop" sonatas is obvious. A new formation (41 A, 47 b) seems to be a combination of these two types. Two other forms, one with a moderato and the other with an allegro opening, are outlined in the middle period, which is extremely rich in variants. And preparatory forms lead to the two main types of the late period, of which one belongs to the Classical structures of the time, whereas the other is specifically Haydnesque.

TABLE 13 TEMPO-CHARACTER COMBINATIONS IN THREE PERIODS OF THE MATURE HAYDN SONATAS

3-Movement Sonatas		2-Movement Sonatas	
1766–72			
(13 e *archetype*)		32 g	2-mov. type
29 E♭, 33 c	3-mov. type	28 D	2-mov. type
30 D, 31 A♭	3-mov. type	20 B♭	2-mov. type
1773–76			
(35 A♭ *nonauth.?*)		40 E♭	2-mov. type
41 A, 47b	new types with variants and transitory forms		
46 E	new types with variants and transitory forms		
44 F	new types with variants and transitory forms		
37 E	new types with variants and transitory forms		
38 F	new types with variants and transitory forms		
43 E♭	new types with variants and transitory forms		
39 D	new types with variants and transitory forms		
34 D, 45 A	new types with variants and transitory forms		
36 C	new types with variants and transitory forms		
42 G	new types with variants and transitory forms		
1780–94			
51 E♭		56 D, 58 C	new 2-mov. type
49 c♯		54 G	new 2-mov. type
48 C	preparatory forms	61 D	
52 G	preparatory forms	55 B♭	
53 e	preparatory forms		
59 E♭	classical type		
50 D, 62 E♭	classical type		
60 C	classical type		

■ = 4/4 etc. in fast tempo
▤ = 4/4 etc. in moderate tempo
□ = 4/4 etc. in slow tempo
⊙ = Menuet, Tempo di Menuet, etc.

nonauth. = nonauthentic

6. *Forms of Movements and Their Combinations*

It has already been indicated that there is a direct interconnection between the character of the types (subgenres) of Haydn's sonatas and the forms of the individual movements that make up a multimovement structure. The presence of certain forms per se is not significant. Haydn wrote hardly any instrumental work without one or more of the movements in sonata form. The inclusion of some forms, or the unusual position of others in the cycle, might, however, add considerably to the style of the sonata.

At this point we must traverse a well-worn battlefield of musicology and analysis, the matter of terminology for forms and structures. My background exempts me from strict allegiance to the terminologies of any of the established schools of style analysis—American, British, or German. None of these terminologies is specific enough to describe the basic forms that Haydn developed in his sonatas over a period of time. Nor am I interested in developing a new theory of form applicable to music of other chronological periods or even to other composers of Haydn's time. This book is intended as a special investigation of Haydn's keyboard sonatas, for which we need a sufficiently specific terminology.[50]

The following list contains twelve basic forms and eight additional combination forms:

Basic forms

1. Sonata form ("allegro form" or "first-movement form")
2. Binary sonata form
3. Andante form ("sonata form without development section" or "sonatina form")
4. Scherzo form
5. Rondo
6. Sonata rondo
7. Minuet (Menuet-Trio-Menuet)
8. Ternary form (A B A)
9. Theme and variations
10. Strophic variations (irregular)
11. Double variations ("alternating strophic variations")
12. Transitional or open forms

Combinations

13. Minuet sonata form (without trio)
14. Minuet binary sonata form (without trio)
15. Minuet theme and variations

50. A terminology of instrumental forms based entirely on eighteenth-century vocabulary might lead to new vistas in the analysis of Haydn's music (see Elaine Sisman's "Small and Expanded Forms"). For our purposes here, however, this terminology would not be sufficiently specific or differentiated. For example, Koch's terminology (discussed by Sisman) was developed after studying the music of Haydn and his contemporaries. It is an analytic by-product of the music and as such, of course, could not influence its composition. The limitations of depending solely on eighteenth-century terms is shown in Wolfgang Budday's *Grundlagen musikalischer Formen in der Wiener Klassik*.

16. Minuet strophic variations
17. Minuet alternating variations
18. Rondo variations
19. *Liedform* ternary variations (varied *Liedform* with trio episode)
20. A B A′ (or A A′ A) ternary variations

1. *Sonata form* is a form in three sections, with a repeat sign articulating the end of the exposition. In Haydn's time, this was called an *allegro* (form) or *the first allegro* because the opening movement of a symphony or some other multimovement form, in an allegro or related tempo, generally adopted this structure. In this book, *sonata allegro* or *main sonata movement* will be used as alternative terms for this same form. Some slow movements in sonata form proper also belong in this category.

2. *Binary sonata form* is articulated with a repeat sign after the first section. The second section starts with the primary theme in the second key. There is no double return, that is, no recapitulation of the first theme in the tonic.[51]

3. *Andante form* is sometimes called *sonata form without development section.*[52] It differs from the binary sonata form in two significant features. First, there is no double bar line articulation and hence no repetition of the exposition. Second, the development section is replaced by a short retransition to the full recapitulation with the first theme in the tonic.

4. *Scherzo form*[53] differs considerably from regular sonata form, resem-

51. This is sometimes called *Scarlatti sonata form.*

52. The terms *Andanteform* and *Adagioform,* of Austro-German origin, were introduced in the theoretical works of Schoenberg, Webern, and their students. Their use of these terms was neither consistent nor unanimous. Schoenberg preferred *Andanteform* (see his *Fundamentals of Musical Composition* [London, 1967]). His pupil Erwin Ratz used *Adagioform* in *Einführung in die musikalische Formenlehre* (Vienna, 1951), while Anton Webern, in his letters and analyses, used both. Only the two-part andante (or adagio) form corresponds to the structure we are dealing with; a three-part andante (or adagio) form means simply a ternary form. *Sonatina form* is yet another well-established term for this structure. I have decided to use *andante form* for three reasons. First, the term *sonata form without development* suggests absence or imperfection. But these movements are fully developed and regular forms. Similarly, to call a mature and fully developed slow movement a *sonatina form* seems inappropriate. Second, this form is used by Haydn most often for movements that do indeed have *Andante* or *Adagio* tempo markings. Finally, these slow movements are related to first allegro movements primarily in that the themes introduced in a secondary key will be recapitulated in the tonic. The proportion of time spent presenting themes compared to the time spent in modulations, transitions, elaborations, and other developmental techniques is quite different in allegro or andante sonata forms.

53. The term *scherzo form* also originates in the analysis of the Schoenberg school. According to Schoenberg (*Fundamentals,* 150–51), scherzos "differ from smaller ternary forms and the minuet in that the middle section is more modulatory and more thematic. In some cases, there is a special type of *modulatory contrasting middle section* which approaches the elaboration (*Durchführung*) of the Sonata Allegro." Neither Schoenberg nor other theorists associated with him acknowledged that the pioneer of the full-movement scherzo form (without trio) was Haydn in his sonatas.

bling instead the form of a scherzo without a trio. The first section, up to the double bar line, is relatively short and is followed by a disproportionately long second section. The first section normally has one theme or rather a homogeneous motivic-rhythmic motion that does not modulate but ends on V of I before the double bar. In Haydn's sonatas, the scherzo form is typically used as a "surprise form."

5. *Rondo* is used in this book for structures that can be diagrammed A B A C A. In the mature and authentic sonatas by Haydn, excepting 35 A♭ III, this form always involves some degree of variation in the later A sections.

6. *Sonata rondo form*—typically A B (dominant) A C A B′ (tonic) A—does not occur among Haydn's sonatas. The single authentic movement titled *Rondo,* 58 C II, is a borderline case that could be called a monothematic sonata rondo.

7. *Minuet* indicates the traditional Menuet-Trio-Menuet three-part form. In one sonata, 51 E♭, it is called *Finale.*

8. *Ternary form* (A B A) is a structure in three sections; in German terminology, this form is called *dreiteiliger Liedform* (three-part song form). The first part is by no means a sonata-form exposition, nor is the second part a development section. The second section contains new thematic material. In Haydn's sonata output, ternary form appears only in combinations (see forms 19–20).

9. *Theme and variations* signifies a set of variations in which the sections are called *theme, variation 1, variation 2,* etc. and are separated from one another by double bar lines. There are no through-composed or irregular sections in this form. In contrast to Mozart, Haydn rarely used this form when composing for keyboard solo.

10. *Irregular strophic variations*[54] is a special structure used in the presto finales of 42 G, 43 E♭, and 46 E. It may be diagrammed A A^1 A^2 A^{minor} $A^{3/recap.}$, with certain irregularities. This form is not a simple theme and variations, for its sections are not labeled *variation 1, variation 2,* etc. It is not rondo variations either, for it has no secondary material in contrasting keys. Nor is it alternating variations, with a regular alternation of major and minor sections.

11. *Double variations* or *alternating strophic variations*[55] is a variation set alternating a major theme and a minor theme, or vice versa. In Haydn's sonata output, this form first appears in minuet-finale structures (34 D, 37 E); later, it is used for fast and slow movements alike. In his late sonatas, this form occasionally substitutes for a sonata-form first movement (54 G, 56 D, 58 C). It is the only formal type to do so. The two themes are often, but not necessarily, related. The number of variations is small, most typically I II I^1 II^1 I^2, sometimes extended to

54. In the Hungarian edition of this book, I called this simply *variation form.*

55. See Elaine Sisman's "Haydn's Hybrid Variations."

II^2 I^3.[56] In the late sonatas, the periodic return of both themes is not obligatory; hybrid forms appear, such as I I^1 II I^2 in 56 D or an even more liberal version in 58 C.

12. *Open (transitional) form* is a sui generis structure found in 45 A. It serves as a link between the opening and closing movements. In this Adagio, there is no return to the opening material or to the first key.

The following combination forms (13–20) are worth considering as individual structures. In this way, we can specify the rich variety of forms connected with the minuet or minuet-like movements. We can also see the infiltration of C. P. E. Bach's *mit veränderten Reprisen* technique into several different structures used by Haydn.

13. *Minuet sonata form* contains a relatively long Menuet section with clear ternary sonata-form contours.

14. *Minuet binary sonata form* (see form 2).

15. *Minuet theme and variations* is used only once in Haydn's keyboard sonatas, in the third movement of 45 A. The theme is marked Tempo di Menuet and is followed by six variations.

16. *Minuet strophic variations* or *hybrid variations* is a combination form involving a varied reprise after the Trio. The third movement of 44 F, for example, can be diagrammed M T M^1 $M^{2/\text{recap.}}$; in M^2, there is a recapitulation of M, but with a new variation of each section instead of a repeat. The third movement of 59 E♭ is an even more novel and complex form.

17. *Minuet alternating variations* are found in the last movements, marked Tempo di Menuet, of 34 D and 37 E. The structure may be diagrammed I II I^1 II^1 I^2. A less regular example is the second movement of 32 g.

18. *Rondo variations* arise from a modification of the A B A C A rondo form (see form 5), in which the returning A sections are varied. Typically, the B section is in the parallel minor, and the C section is in another related key. Examples of this form are the third movements of 30 D and 50 D.

19. *Liedform ternary variations* can be diagrammed A B A^1 on the large scale, in which A is a *Liedform*. Their characteristic feature is the use of varied reprises on the phrase level within each large section. For example, in the second movement of 59 E♭, the first A section may be diagrammed a a^1 b+a^2 b^1+a^3. The return of the A section brings further variations—a^4 b^2+a^5.

20. *Ternary variations* (A B A^1 or A A^1 A) is a structure used in slow movements such as 62 E♭ II as well as in fast finales such as in 54 G and 55 B♭. Sometimes the proportions are irregular, such as A A^1 A^{coda}, as in 39 D III.

Table 14 surveys the forms found in the thirty-six mature sonatas. The two-

56. As in the F Minor Variations, Hob. XVII:6. The form of the first movement of the String Quartet in F Minor, op. 55/2, is I II I^1 II^1 I^2 II^2.

TABLE 14 FORMS FOUND IN THE THIRTY-SIX MATURE SONATAS

3-Movement Sonatas				2-Movement Sonatas			Form Preferences
	I	II	III		I	II	
19 e	sonata	sonata	minuet-sonata/2	20 B♭	sonata	minuet-sonata	
29 E♭	sonata	sonata	sonata	28 D	sonata	minuet	85.7% sonata form
30 D	sonata	sonata/2	rondo var.	32 g	sonata	minuet-var.	
31 A♭	sonata	sonata/2	sonata				
33 c	sonata	sonata	sonata				
34 D	sonata	sonata	minuet-2/var.				73.9% sonata form
(35 A♭	sonata	minuet	rondo)				
⁄36 C	sonata	sonata	sonata	40 E♭	sonata	minuet-sonata	13% variation forms
37 E	sonata	sonata	minuet-2/var.				
38 F	sonata	sonata/2	sonata				
39 D	sonata	sonata*†	ternary AAA var.				
∖41 A	sonata	minuet	scherzo sonata*				
⁄42 G	sonata	minuet	strophic var.				50% sonata form
43 E♭	sonata	minuet	strophic var.				
44 F	sonata	sonata/2	minuet-str. var.				27% variation forms
45 A	sonata*†	(trans.)†	minuet-th. & var.				
46 E	sonata	sonata*†	strophic var.				
∖47 b	sonata	minuet	sonata				

movement and three-movement sonatas appear in separate columns. The percentage of times certain forms are used is not, in itself, surprising. Comparison with the forms found in Mozart's sonatas (see table 15) shows characteristic differences between the composers. Haydn prefers minuets and variation forms, while Mozart prefers rondos and ternary forms. One can also study how Haydn's preferences for

TABLE 14 CONTINUED

3-Movement Sonatas				2-Movement Sonatas			Form Preferences
	I	*II*	*III*		*I*	*II*	
48 C	sonata	sonata/2	rondo				60% sonata form
49 c♯	sonata	2/var.	minuet				
50 D	sonata	sonata/2†	rondo var.				
51 E♭	sonata	sonata†	minuet				
52 G	rondo var.	sonata	sonata				
53 e	sonata	sonata	2/var.	54 G	2/var.	ternary ABA var.	54.5% sonata form
59 E♭	sonata	ternary var.	minuet-str. var.	55 B♭	sonata	ternary ABA var.	
60 C	sonata	sonata/2	scherzo sonata	56 D	2/var.*	scherzo sonata	40.9% variation forms
62 E♭	sonata	ternary ABA var.	sonata	58 C	2/var.*	sonata rondo	
				61 D	sonata*	scherzo sonata	

Note: Sonata/2 – binary sonata form or andante form; 2/var. = double variations; str. = strophic; th. = theme.

**Attacca.*

† Irregular variant.

certain forms changed over the course of time. In the "workshop" sonatas, all of which are serious works, there is no exception to the rule that at most one movement is not in sonata form. As Haydn approached his ideal of "public" sonatas for the dilettante, he wrote fewer sonata-form movements and more minuet combination forms and variation forms. The culmination of this ideal is the *Anno 1776* set. Later, his interest in forms incorporating variation elements increased. He may have come to consider such hybrids as the ideal form for solo-sonata movements.[57] We may note that the piano trios written during the same time period as the last sonatas show different preferences. In addition to thirty-six sonata-form structures (46 percent), there are eighteen simple or varied ternary forms (23 percent), seven rondos (of which five are regular), and relatively few minuets.

Sonata form is not only the most frequently used and distinguished structure in Haydn's sonata oeuvre but also the most variegated. Thus, a major part

57. In 54 G, neither of the two movements is in sonata form. 56 D uses a combination sonata-scherzo form, 58 C a sonata rondo, and 61 D a quite unusual sonata-form opening.

TABLE 15 COMPARISON OF FORMS USED BY HAYDN AND MOZART

	Haydn, Solo Piano Sonatas			Mozart, Solo Piano Sonatas	
Sonata forms	63%	51 11	Sonata allegro Binary sonata or andante form	29 4	61%
Rondo forms	6%	2 1 3	Rondo Sonata rondo Rondo variations	9 2 —	20%
Minuet movements	14%	8 3 3	Minuet (with trio) Minuet sonata form or minuet binary sonata form Minuet strophic variations	2 — —	4%
Ternary forms	5%	— 5	ABA ternary form Ternary variations (*Liedform* with trio; ABA′; AA′A)	5 1	11%
Variation forms	11%	— 1 3 5 2	Theme & variations Minuet theme & variations (Irregular) strophic variations Double variations Minuet double variations	2 — — — —	4%
Other	1%	1	Transitory (open) form	—	—
		(99)		(54)	

of the rest of this book will be dedicated to a study of it. Another family of forms is extremely characteristic and deserves a closer look here, a group of hybrid forms including unusual rondos, rondo variations, irregular variations, and combinations with minuet forms. We will survey these forms along two lines. The systematic classification aims at grouping the movements, as we did in the previous catalog of forms. Next, we will examine how Haydn manipulated these forms over the course of time, adapting them to different functions, different tempos, and different positions in the multimovement work.

The keyboard sonata, and later the piano trio, was a hotbed of combination forms and of hybrids.[58] In symphonies and string quartets,[59] hybrid forms are

58. I am indebted to József Ujfalussy's pioneering study, available only in Hungarian, "Egy különös formacsoport Haydn zongoraműveiben."

59. See table i of Elaine Sisman's "Haydn's Hybrid Variations."

used almost exclusively in the slow or final movements of the four-movement work.[60] Since Haydn's keyboard sonatas had a looser overall structure, with two or three movements and with minuets replacing either slow or final movements, they were ideal compositions in which to experiment with hybrid forms. The evolution of Haydn's hybrid forms took place basically and primarily in his keyboard music and was then transferred to other instrumental genres.

A number of forms that were stable and well-established components of wind or string divertimentos, symphonies, and baryton trios were transformed when they were incorporated into solo keyboard pieces. For example, the Menuet-Trio-Menuet form was traditionally played with exact repetitions in ensemble pieces. But it was not idiomatic in a keyboard sonata because the harpsichord player would have preferred nicely varied returns, embellished sections, variations for his fingers and soul—and perhaps he could not improvise all this. The minuet finale of 28 D was still an orthodox minuet with regard to form, although remarkable in other musical aspects. In 20 B♭ and 32 g, written soon after, Haydn devised more flexible minuet-related structures. The finale of 20 B♭ is a minuet-sonata form with a slightly varied return. The second movement of 32 g is a fascinating hybrid structure with minuet-like themes and a form that can be diagrammed A B A^1 b^1, b^1 being a coda-like section considerably shorter than B. This movement, combining ternary elements (Menuet [minor]–Trio [tonic major]–Menuet) with the phenomenon of varied return, has the additional interesting feature that sections A and B have motivically related material.

In figure 14, I outline my hypothesis regarding the development of structural ideas in several of Haydn's hybrid forms. The circled numbers direct the reader to the following observations.

1. The Allegro assai $\frac{2}{4}$ rondo-variation form (A B A^1 C A^2 A^3) that is the finale of 30 D (1767) is not related to Haydn's experiments with the minuet. More likely, it is a reflection of his study of C. P. E. Bach's music.

2. The A A^1 a structure of the finale of 39 D (the lowercase letter represents a fragmentary return of A), without major-minor contrast, was a bold experiment in 1773.

3. The archetype of the double-variation form first appears as a Tempo di Menuet finale around 1772–73. I II I^1 II^1 $I^{r/2}$ is a representation of its form.[61]

4. The next appearance of double variations is as a fast movement in $\frac{2}{4}$ time with unusual interpolations or revised phrase structure.[62]

60. There are two borderline cases, the opening movements of the String Quartets in D and E♭ of op. 76. Both start as a theme and variations but arrive at a considerably extended, through-composed coda variation that creates unusual proportions, giving the impression of hybrid forms.

61. The superscript *r*/2 stands for reprise variation. This includes, in a written form, the recapitulation of both halves of the original theme as well as the varied repeats, in this case, indeed, the second variation.

62. For the phrase structure of 53 e III, see p. 328–30.

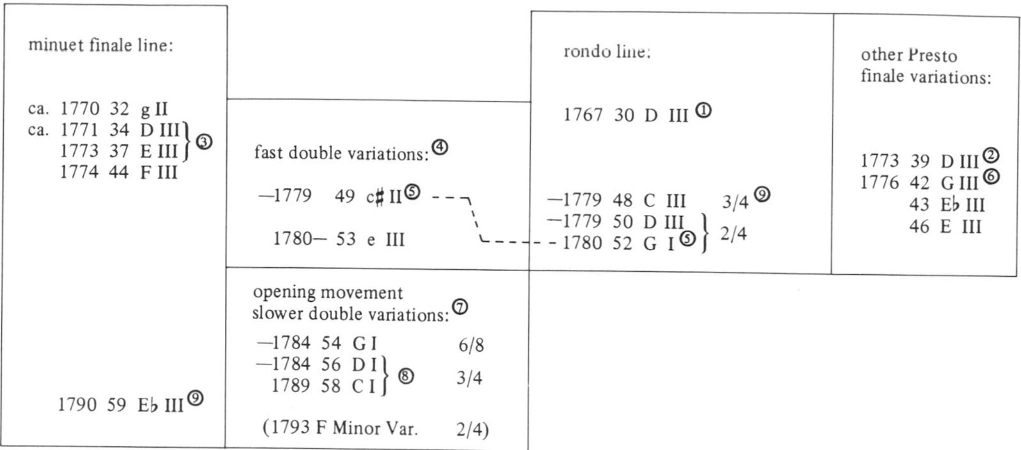

FIGURE 14 The development of structural ideas in several of Haydn's hybrid forms. (Circled numbers direct the reader to numbered observations in the text. A dash before or after a date refers to usage up to or following that date.)

5. The double-variation form and the rondo-variation form practically merged when Haydn rewrote the second movement of 49 c♯ as the opening movement of 52 G. From a structural point of view, the only change he made was to replace the II^1 section with a new theme in the submediant. With this change, the section we would have heard as II in a I II I^1 II^1 I^2 form becomes B in an A B A C A form.[63]

6. It would be pointless to derive the A A^1 A^2 A^{minor} $A^{r/3}$ structure[64] of the three fast finales of 1776 from either the rondo variations or the double variations. Chronologically isolated, as a substitute for the earlier sonata-form Presto finales, these are highly idiomatic finales in the dilettante genre based on contradanse thematics (42 G III).

7. The double variations in moderately slow tempo that serve as the first movements of 54 G, 56 D, and 58 C all have a seriousness of purpose that allows them to replace the sonata form as an opening movement. The phrase structures of these movements—and to this august group we may add the F Minor Variations—are far removed from the 8 + 8 and 8 + 8 symmetry of the earlier double-variation form, such as occurs in the third movement of 34 D. Instead, we find highly differentiated phrase structures: 8 + 16 and 6 + 6 in 54 G, 8 + 12 and

63. Only the first part of this "pseudo second theme" in the minor mode is repeated; the second part, like the couplet in a rondo, remains open, on the dominant. A similar relation exists in 37 E III, which is an irregular variant of 34 D III. The minor second theme still has a regular form in 34 D with repetition of both parts, whereas it has an a a b open form in 37 E.

64. In 42 G and 43 E♭, the third variation starts as a return of the theme, and only the second phrase is turned into a *minore* variation.

8 + 10 in 56 D, 10 + 16 (= 7 + 9) and 29 (= 5 + 5 + 5 + 5 + 9) in 58 C, and 12 + 17 and 10 + 10 in the F Minor Variations.

8. The opening movements of 56 D and 58 C, both in triple meter and with a tempo indication of *Andante con espressione,* are such irregular double-variation forms that other analyses of their forms are also possible. In 56 D, the minor theme occurs only once. This minor statement could be thought of as a Trio or as a minor variant of the theme with an irregular phrase structure. In 58 C, the fragmentary returns of both themes create the unusual scheme I II I^1 ii^1 i^2 (in A♭!) i^3.

9. The startling form of the finale of the *Genzinger* Sonata is foreshadowed by the finale of the popular sonata 48 C. The earlier finale is marked *Allegro,* the latter *Tempo di Minuet,* but they both have minuet-like themes. Their structures may be diagrammed as A a^x + a B (minore) A (48 C III) and A B b + a A (minore) A′ (59 E♭ III).

We have seen (as outlined in table 14 above) that in Haydn's sonatas many different forms are organized and brought together in a number of different ways. The one relatively fixed point in this kaleidoscopic variety was the first movement, which, with but a few exceptions, was written in sonata form. Haydn found double-variation form to be a satisfactory substitute for sonata form in the late two-movement sonatas.[65] The irregular opening movement of 52 G, a rondo-

65. In certain chamber music genres as well, a variation-form movement based on a noble theme in a tempo such as andante or allegretto functions as the only substitute for sonata form for an opening movement. Among the string quartets, see op. 9 B♭ and op. 17 E♭ (theme and four variations), op. 54/55 f (double variations), and op. 76 D and E♭ (irregular theme and variations forms with unexpected substantial fugatos at the end). Among the piano trios, there are seven opening movements that are not in sonata form. These include four double variations (XV: 13 c, 19 g, 23 d, 25 G), one theme and variations (7 D), and two ternary variations (29 E♭, 31 e♭). The 125 baryton trios, written at the same time as the "workshop" sonatas, around 1765–71, were not intended for publication. With the exception of a few divertimentos, the baryton trios were in three movements. There was considerable variety in cyclic plan:

a)	moderato	minuet	fast	(36)
b)	slow	fast	minuet	(35)
c)	slow	minuet	fast	(25)
d)	fast	minuet	fast	(10)
e)	fast	slow	minuet	(4)

Twelve of the baryton trios have variation-form opening movements. One is in $\frac{4}{4}$ time with the tempo marking *più tosto Adagio.* Of the remaining eleven, all in $\frac{2}{4}$ time, there are five marked *Andante,* two marked *Allegretto,* and one each marked *Poco Andante, Poco Adagio, Un poco Adagio,* and *Adagio.* In six of the movements the theme is followed by four variations, in seven by three variations; in two there are three variations and five variations, respectively, and in one six variations. These opening variation movements seem more closely related to those of the opp. 9 and 17 string quartets than to the variation forms in the keyboard sonatas.

variation form, seemed to be so unorthodox, even to Haydn, that he thought it necessary to accompany its publication with an *Avertissement* that, most likely, was a belated rationalization to cover an inspiration of the moment.[66]

There are two main types of two-movement sonatas, each characterized by its finale. One type has a minuet-like, relaxed, even *galant* ending; the other has a fast-tempo ending featuring humor and surprise. For all their variety of combinations of movements, the three-movement sonatas can be grouped into a few main types as well. A strikingly irregular combination standing out from the general type of an opus or period often indicates a sonata that is extraordinary in many ways (see, e.g., 47 b, with its impressive finale, or the bold *attacca* form of 45 A, only superficially reminiscent of C. P. E. Bach's *attacca* cyclic structures). It would seem that Haydn thought in terms of a hierarchy of forms, ranging from less sophisticated, easier forms through more intellectually and technically demanding ones, and this conception helped him in molding sonatas for a given purpose or audience. Gradations among the dilettante-style sonatas were probably best determined by the arrangement of forms. In the late sonatas, he made a careful distinction between sonatas intended for a Viennese audience and those intended for London: chiseled, refined, chamber-style forms versus those rich in effects and surprises. Sonata no. 60 in C, with a Viennese Adagio set between the pillars of London-style movements, is a unique hybrid.

7. *Haydn's Choice of Keys*

Strange ideas circulate among musicians about the alleged "character" or even the "color" of individual major and minor keys (or triads) in tonal music. Superficially known old and new theories, the remembrance of hundreds of items of the Classical repertory, an upgrading of absolute pitch,[67] and a great many other factors contribute to our sense that we recognize different keys. In recent years, performance on instruments pitched lower than A = 440, or in temperaments other than equal temperament, has undermined the self-confidence of many musicians with absolute pitch. At the same time, the effect of the temperament of a keyboard instrument on our perception of the diversity of the characters of keys has become more obvious.

66. It is more than probable that the fifth sonata of the *Auenbrugger* set, 52 G, was written in great haste; that seems to be the reason why Haydn could not compose a decent opening sonata-form movement. With his letter of 31 January 1780, Haydn sent the sixth sonata of the set, 33 c, because the fifth was not yet finished. 52 G was mailed on 8 February, but on 25 February, after reading the proofs of all six sonatas, Haydn decided to ask the publisher to print the famous *Avertissement* (see p. 178).

67. Among practicing musicians, there is seldom a clear distinction between "genuine absolute pitch," "pseudo–absolute pitch," and "quasi–absolute pitch."

The subject of pitch and temperament has generated a good deal of scholarly writing in the past few decades.[68] A study of pitch and temperament in Haydn's music is inhibited by a paucity of relevant evidence such as could be supplied by his organs with original pitch and temperament, woodwind or brass instruments used by members of his orchestra, and *Acta musicalia* bills in the Esterházy archives going beyond the repair of instruments or buying of new strings. Directions to string players in some of Haydn's autograph scores, such as *sapienti pauca, the Same Tone, l'istesso tuono,* and *das leere A,*[69] indicate his concern for clean intonation. These directions are unique in Viennese Classical music and may be interpreted as signs of Haydn's demands for "just" intonation in unstable tonal situations. He was probably not satisfied with equal temperament and was especially sensitive about the leading tone.

We cannot state with certainty which tunings Haydn preferred or practiced. No doubt Haydn had his own opinion about the nature and character of keys.[70] He probably worked with a tuning system that was irregular, that is, one that was well in tune up to four or even five sharps or flats but that had characteristically "tense" tonic triads, that is, triads with a lot of beats, as, for instance, E♭ major. It is also likely that the tuning Haydn used for keyboard instruments produced triads that were not absolutely identical to those produced by a well-in-tune string quartet, even in the basic keys.

Table 16 surveys the keys of Haydn's mature keyboard sonatas (thirty-six), piano trios (twenty-nine), and string quartets (fifty-eight) as well as the keys that Mozart chose for his eighteen piano sonatas. It shows characteristic differences in the key preferences of Haydn and Mozart. We also find that in these three genres Haydn shows general preferences as well as genre-oriented main keys.[71] The keys C, D, F, and B♭ account for approximately three-fourths of Mozart's sonatas. Haydn shows a striking inclination toward E♭ in all genres. This is complemented by a preference for D major for piano sonatas and C major for string

68. Good starting points are the articles on "Pitch" and "Temperament" by Mark Lindley in *The New Grove Dictionary of Musical Instruments,* ed. Stanley Sadie (London, 1984).

69. See my "A Bold Enharmonic Modulatory Model in Joseph Haydn's String Quartets," in *Studies in Eighteenth-Century Music* (London, 1970), 370–81; and my commentaries to the facsimile edition of the autograph in *Joseph Haydn: String Quartet in G 1799* (Budapest and New York, 1972).

70. Certainly, Haydn knew the opera-seria traditions whereby certain keys were considered appropriate for certain dramatic situations or for the expression of certain sentiments. Starting in the 1770s, Haydn was deeply involved with opera, both as a conductor and as a composer. Nevertheless, we do not find in Haydn's instrumental music the kind of operatic references and even self-quotations that we find in the instrumental works of Mozart.

71. Haydn's symphonies have not been included in this survey. The capabilities of the wind instruments of the time placed certain restrictions on the keys that Haydn felt free to choose. The capabilities of the *ripienist* string players also had to be taken into account. Occasionally, Haydn selected a remote key for a symphony, e.g., F♯ minor for the *Farewell* Symphony. In general, however, the factors determining Haydn's choice of keys for symphonies—or baryton trios—were not the same as those for keyboard sonatas, trios, or string quartets.

TABLE 16 KEY PREFERENCES

I Mozart sonatas
II Haydn sonatas
III Haydn trios
IV Haydn quartets

I	II	III	IV			IV	III	II	I
works in major						works in minor			
	2	1	2	E	c♯			1	
1	2	2	3	A	f♯	1	1		
3	7	3	7	D	b	2		1	
1	3	4	7	G	e		1	2	
4	4	2	8	C	a				1
3	2	3	4	F	d	4	1		
3	2	2	7	B♭	g	2	1	1	
1	6	5	8	E♭	c	1	1	1	1
	2	1		A♭	f	2			
					—				
					e♭		1		

quartets.[72] In the smaller group of works in minor, Haydn's avoidance of A minor, in all genres, is noteworthy.[73]

It seems likely that Haydn chose certain keys because of their strong individual flavor and other keys for just the opposite reason, that is, because they were essentially neutral. C major and D major were neutral enough keys on the keyboard to allow him to experiment with novel and original compositional ideas. Each of the first two authorized sets of printed sonatas, the *Esterházy* and *Auenbrugger* sonatas, begins with a sonata in a distinctly new style in C major, nos. 36 and 48. If our dating is correct, each of the late C major sonatas represents Haydn's first response to a new instrument. 58 C was composed on and for Haydn's own new Schanz; 60 C was written after Haydn became acquainted with the English fortepianos.[74] Each of the mature D major sonatas introduced impor-

72. Haydn did not use A♭ major for the outer movements of any string quartets, but he did consider it an appropriate key for the slow movement of quartets in E♭ major.

73. The inclusion of the seven lost sonatas would have changed the statistical picture to some extent. There are two in A and one each in B (!), C, B♭, e, and d. We do not know, however, which of these sonatas belong to the period of the mature sonatas.

74. The first movement of 58 C may have been the first solo piano movement that Haydn wrote at his Schanz fortepiano. Haydn acquired this instrument in late October 1788. In a letter of 10 January 1789, Breitkopf asked Haydn to send him a new sonata; Haydn responded with 58 C in April

tant new types of movements. 30 D introduced the true concert-style opening movement and the rondo-variation form; 34 D contains the first minuet in variation form; 39 D opens with the first exciting sonata-allegro form in $\frac{3}{4}$; 56 D presents an Andante con espressione variation movement; 61 D, the most unorthodox of the sonatas, dissolves the opening sonata-form structure. The sonatas in E♭ are significant synthetic works—some, such as 40 E♭ and 51 E♭, referring to the finest of traditional types and some, such as 59 E♭ and 62 E♭, summarizing the most valuable experiences after a short period of experimentation.

It is frequently true that sonatas in the same key—there are three in G and two each in E, A, F, B♭,[75] and e—are quite different from one another in character and style. Another factor that influenced Haydn's choice of key was the sonata's inclusion in a published collection, that is, an opus. The majority of his mature sonatas were thought of as constituents of a set of six or of three works. Haydn never put two works in the same key in one set. Table 17 gives the keys of the thirty-six mature sonatas, organizing them to show the distribution of keys in sets of sonatas and to distinguish between the typical and the complementary keys in a set. In addition to his three favorite keys—E♭, D, and C—Haydn considered E, F, A, and G suitable for sonatas in sets.

Haydn undoubtedly did not think of an opus of sonatas as a performing unit, although it might not seem unusual to hear them performed so today.[76] Nevertheless, the order of works in a set clearly shows thought and planning on the composer's part. It was yet another aspect of Haydn's interest in and concern for the public reception of his works.[77] Sometimes, the order in which a group of works was published reflects the order in which they were composed. The 1773 *Esterházy* set (nos. 36–41), printed as it was numbered and written out in the autograph fair copy, probably represents the succession of composition rather than an arbitrary sequence. On the other hand, we cannot reconstruct the intended order of the *Anno 1776* sonatas, if, indeed, there was one.[78] The order in

1789. The order of composition of the three *London* sonatas is open to question. Only 62 E♭ (1794) has survived in a dated autograph. Oliver Strunk's classic study "Notes on a Haydn Autograph" suggested the sequence 62 E♭, 61 D, 60 C. Feder's suggested dating is E♭ (1794), C (ca. 1794–95), D (ca. 1794–95?). Brown (*Keyboard*, 123) proposed D (1791–96), E♭ (1794), C I, III (16 May–15 August 1795). If, as I believe, Haydn's habit of initiating styles in C major and consolidating them in E♭ major holds true, the most likely order of composition would be C, D, E♭. The most eager and daring exploitation of the new London fortepiano is seen in the opening movement of the C Major Sonata, with detailed dynamics, *open Pedal* places, and, in its finale, a range beyond f^3. The middle movement of this sonata is an Adagio written in Vienna in an earlier fortepiano style. The E♭ Sonata shows a considerably more settled handling of the new instrument. Its range did not rule out performance on the shorter keyboards of the Continental fortepianos. Furthermore, this sonata contains a true concert-style Adagio.

75. A♭ major is not included in this list because 35 A♭ is probably not an authentic work.

76. Recordings of whole sets of sonatas have accustomed listeners to such performances.

77. See my "Opus-Planung und Neuerung bei Haydn."

78. See Christa Landon's remarks in *Kritische Anmerkungen*, 58.

TABLE 17 THE KEYS OF THE THIRTY-SIX MATURE SONATAS

	OPUS KEYS													
	basic keys in set composition							complementary opus keys			other keys			
workshop sonatas	E♭	D D D	—	—	—	—	—	B♭	—	—	e	A♭ (A♭)*	g	c†
1773 (sets)	E♭	D	C	E	F	A	—	—	—	—	—	—	—	—
1776 (sets)	E♭	—	—	E	F	A	G	—	b	—	—	—	—	—
1780 (sets)	E♭	D	C	—	—	—	G	—	—	c♯	—	—	—	—
1784 (sets)	—	D	—	—	—	—	G	B♭	—	—	—	—	—	—
late sonatas	E♭ E♭	D	C C	—	—	—	—	—	—	—	e	—	—	—
	the three main keys													

* 35 A♭.

† Later added to the 1780 set.

which they are usually printed today, that is, nos. 42–47, is the order of the first edition, brought out by Hummel without Haydn's consent.

The *Auenbrugger* set, the one opus in which the published order is definitely not the same as the order in which the sonatas were written, shows a number of remarkable features (ex. 88). Haydn used a *Gradus* arrangement, with an easy, dilettante-style sonata, 48 C, at the beginning of the set and the C Minor Sonata, which Haydn described in a letter to Artaria dated 31 January 1780 as "die längste und schwerste," at the end.[79] The special key order—C, c♯, D, E♭, G, c—with a chromatic segment followed by a third-related group, shows a unique "opus tonality."[80] The tempo indications are in an alternating sequence: the first, third, and fifth sonatas open Allegro con brio, while the second begins Moderato, the fourth Allegro moderato, and the sixth Moderato.[81]

79. Haydn, *Briefe,* 89.

80. The only key order comparable to this but less accentuated as an "opus tonality" in D is Haydn's two-volume organization of the String Quartets op. 76: G-*d*-C; B♭-*D*-E♭.

81. Similar organization of alternating opening tempo characters can be found in the Artaria edition, *revue et corrigée,* of the printed parts to op. 20: vol. 1, E♭-A-f (Moderato–Allegro di molto–Moderato); vol. 2, D-C-g (Allegro di molto–Moderato–Allegro con spirito).

Ex. 88. *Auenbrugger* sonatas: opus organization. *a,* With Allegro con brio first movements. *b,* With Moderato, Allegro moderato first movements.

Example 89 examines the relation between the keys of first and middle movements. The works surveyed are sixteen three-movement sonatas by Mozart, twenty-two three-movement sonatas by Haydn, sixteen three-movement piano trios by Haydn, and forty-six four-movement string quartets by Haydn. For the sake of easy and schematic comparison, the first movements of these works are all transposed to C major or A minor. Mozart's choice for the second movement of a work in major is normally the subdominant or the dominant. The two exceptions are K. 331, with a minuet middle movement in the tonic, and K. 280, with a siciliano middle movement in the tonic minor. Haydn writes the middle movement in the subdominant about half the time in his string quartets in major and a third of the time in his piano sonatas in major; curiously, in his piano trios he writes the middle movement in the subdominant only once. The tonic minor is a favored key in the Baroque-style slow movements of the earlier sonatas as well as in the mature piano trios. Haydn also uses third-related keys, particularly in the late trios and quartets. In each of the genres, Haydn experiments with a remote key written in enharmonic notation. The *London* Sonata no. 62 in E♭ has an Adagio movement in E (an enharmonic equivalent of the Neapolitan); the piano trio XV:14 A♭ has a slow movement in E, and XV:29 E♭ has a slow movement in B; the String Quartet in E♭ of op. 76 has a slow fantasia in B (enharmonic equivalents of ♭VI). The Adagio of 45 A is a transitional movement with no fixed tonic. In minor works, the tonic major, parallel major, and subdominant are all favored keys.

It is surprising how many of Haydn's mature piano sonatas keep the same tonic for all the movements; twenty-one of thirty-six sonatas belong to this tonally economical group. Nine of the two-movement sonatas have both movements in the same key. The three-movement sonatas with a major-minor-major alternation of movements—34 D, 37 E, 38 F, 39 D, 46 E, and 50 D—all have archaic-style slow movements. 47 b has as its middle movement a minuet in B with a trio in b; its overall key plan can be diagrammed minor-major-minor-major-minor. The slow movements in the subdominant, dominant, or submediant keys exhibit particularly attractive keyboard writing, sometimes in concertante style. Sonatas nos. 29, 30, 31, and 33; the two opus-opening C-major works, nos. 36 and 48; and the late three-movement sonatas, 59 E♭ and 60 C—all are good examples of this phenomenon.

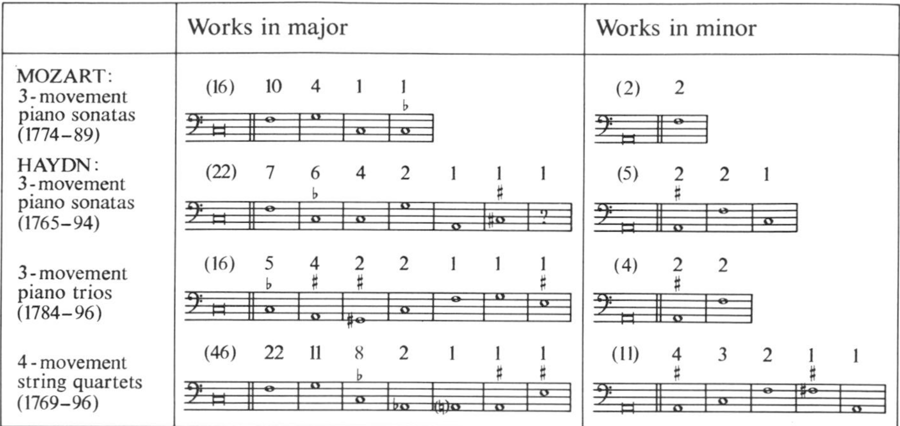

	Works in major	Works in minor
MOZART: 3-movement piano sonatas (1774–89)	(16) 10 4 1 1 ♭	(2) 2
HAYDN: 3-movement piano sonatas (1765–94)	(22) 7 6 ♭ 4 2 1 1 ♯ 1	(5) 2 ♯ 2 1
3-movement piano trios (1784–96)	(16) 5 ♭ 4 ♯ 2 ♯ 2 1 1 1 ♯	(4) 2 ♯ 2
4-movement string quartets (1769–96)	(46) 22 11 8 ♭ 2 1 1 ♯ 1 ♯	(11) 4 ♯ 3 2 1 ♯ 1

Ex. 89. Key of the middle movements (first movements transposed to C major and A minor, respectively).

Haydn's use of the same tonic for all the movements of a sonata might suggest a more archaic taste in key relations between movements than that of Mozart or other contemporaries. A better interpretation might be that Haydn liked a strong cohesion in the overall key structure. It might even be suggested that this strong cohesion provided a counterbalance for the inner structure of the movements that, owing to the great variety of rhythmic vocabulary, textures, and thematic material, was extremely dynamic.

This, however, belongs to the study of Haydn's language and style as developed in the individual movements.

PART III

STRUCTURES *and* STYLES

Eleven

Originality *and* Personal Language: The Options *of* Analytic Methods

In Haydn's time, originality—the ability to surprise and delight an audience—on the one hand, and a mastery of the compositional conventions and expectations, on the other, were equally appreciated. Originality is a relative phenomenon. Original compared to what? one may ask. Where does originality end and eccentricity begin? How did the composer himself view his carefully contrived originalities? He would of course assume that the listener, and naturally the performer, was familiar with the common musical language of his time. Within that framework, the listener and performer would recognize the individual style of a favorite composer and appreciate new ideas, themes, and characters, in short, the surprises of a piece.

The writings of musicians and critics of Haydn's time seem to distinguish clearly between the common style, the personal style of the composer, and novelties within that composer's style. They show that Haydn's original manner and his surprising novelties were highly appreciated. The following selection of quotations is, of course, just a sampling, but it does not give a distorted view:

> *Herr* Joseph Haydn, the darling of our nation, whose gentle character puts its stamp on every piece. His movements have beauty, order, clarity, a fine and noble expression which will be felt sooner than the listener is prepared for it. . . . The art of writing the outer parts in parallel octaves is his invention, and one cannot deny that this is attractive, even if it appears rarely and in a Haydnish fashion.[1]

1. "On the Viennese Taste in Music," *Wiener Diarium,* 18 October 1766, translated in Landon, *HCW,* 2:130.

> The famous *Herr Kapellmeister* Haydn achieved a thorough success with the oratorio entitled "The Return of Tobias" . . . and displayed his well-known skills once again to their best advantage. Expression, nature and art were so finely woven in his work that the listener must perforce love the one and admire the other.[2]

> When we speak of Joseph Haydn, we think of one of our greatest men; the pride of our age. Always rich and inexhaustible; forever new and surprising, forever noble and great, even when he seems to be laughing.[3]

> It is not wonderful that to souls capable of being touched by music, HAYDN should be an object of homage, and even of idolatry; for like our own SHAKSPEARE [*sic*] he moves and governs the passions at his will.—His *new Grand overture* was pronounced by every scientific ear to be a most wonderful composition; but the first movement in particular rises in grandeur of subject, and in the rich variety of *air* and passion, beyond even his own productions.[4]

> I had the great pleasure of hearing your new *quartetti* (*opera* 76) well performed before I went out of town, and never received more pleasure from instrumental music: they are full of invention, fire, good taste, and new effects, and seem the production, not of a sublime genius who has written so much and so well already, but of one of highly-cultivated talents, who had expended none of his fire before.[5]

> I was never a fast writer, and always composed with deliberation and industry. Such works, however, are made to last, and this is at once revealed to the connoisseur by the score. When Cherubini looked through several of my manuscripts, he always hit on the places that deserve respect.[6]

> I could, as head of an orchestra, make experiments, observe what enhanced an effect and what weakened it, thus improving, adding to, cutting away, and running risks. I was set apart from the world, there was nobody in my vicinity to confuse and annoy me in my course, and so I had to be original.[7]

Today, a musician seeking a full understanding of a work by Haydn may choose between approaches that emphasize either what is unique or what is typical in a work. Even masterworks of music, from Bach cantatas to Beethoven symphonies, are not safe from a kind of study that narrows one's view and calls one type of procedure proper and other types irregular, strange, subtle, or compli-

2. *K. K. priv. Realzeitung der Wissenschaften,* no. 14 (Vienna, 1775), translated in ibid., 215.

3. E. L. Gerber, *Historisch-Biographisches Lexicon der Tonkünstler,* pt. 1 (Leipzig, 1790), translated in ibid., 750.

4. *London Morning Chronicle,* 12 March 1791, quoted in ibid., 3:49.

5. Charles Burney to Haydn, 19 August 1799.

6. Haydn as recorded by Griesinger, translated in Gotwals, *Haydn,* 61–62.

7. Haydn as recorded by Griesinger, translated in ibid., 17.

cated. Most theoretical studies of the music of an earlier time aim at learning the general grammatical rules—rules that may be valid even beyond that historical context. A hypothetical, abstract norm is constructed, and a sample piece is sought to illustrate the theory. How would Haydn's music fare in such a course of study? In learning the Classical form of a main theme, for example, a theme by Haydn might be chosen showing the regular form of a period or sentence. But is this type significant in Haydn's style? Is it typical? Does it represent a higher level of evolution? Does it replace some other thematic structure, and if so, what sort? Was it one of Haydn's more original themes or a more stereotyped one? What are the most typical themes by Haydn for a given time or genre? Textbooks in form or analysis are not likely to deal with such questions, which are nevertheless well worth raising and answering.[8]

Two currents of musical scholarship, the study of the musical vernacular by historians and structural analysis by theorists, have provided only limited stimulus for a full understanding of Haydn's piano sonatas. By studying the works of lesser masters as well as of greater composers, historians can provide detailed and accurate information about the general musical style, the vernacular, with its geographic boundaries and historic layers, in different genres. On the basis of this, one might hope, the unique profile of a great composer or a great composition might be understood in a more accurate way. The other approach, that of structural analysis, concentrates on individual works. The composition by itself is full and authentic; the life history of the composer and his musical experiences in general are considered marginal or merely anecdotal. In the given work, however, even the tiniest event in pitch and duration (or any parameter that the analyst has decided is crucial) becomes an indispensable component of a unique masterwork.

Of course, both the historical approach and the analytic approach are useful in the study of Haydn's sonatas. Individual features can be isolated only if the general vocabulary, grammar, and rhetoric of a style are understood. And detailed analysis of many layers of a structure is needed to discern the fabric of a great and novel piece. Nevertheless, either approach is capable of distortion. Instead of explicating the truly common rules (reflexes), most studies of the musical vernacular have confined themselves to superficial catalogs of thematic similarities—without using elementary methods of frequency investigation or statistical analysis at all. Detailed structural analysis, Schenkerian[9] or otherwise, has at-

8. Charles Rosen's distinguished *The Classical Style* caused a great stir when it appeared, in part because it avoided a textbook orientation and concentrated, instead, on great individual compositions.

9. I have not yet seen many significant analyses of Haydn's works using Heinrich Schenker's approach, either in the true "first-generation" style or in the current American Schenkerian method. One worthwhile exception is Roger Kamien's "Aspects of Motivic Elaboration in the Opening Movement of Haydn's Piano Sonata in C♯ Minor." I find Eugene Narmour's criticisms in *Beyond Schenkerism: The Need for Alternatives in Musical Criticism* (Chicago, 1977) entirely valid. Schenker himself, it should be noted, made some significant analyses of works by Haydn. See his analyses of

tracted many acute thinkers. It has some of the same appeal as the physical sciences: the procedure can be repeated and controlled and the results abstracted. A full and definitive exposure of the secrets of a masterwork seems tantalizingly attainable. But a work can easily be buried under piles of irrelevant observations serving the demonstration of an analytic method rather than the understanding of the work itself. Analysis is useful and necessary, but no analysis is equal to the work itself. Nor does any performance—in a way the most complex and synthesized analysis of a work—give a definitive, full understanding of a work. For this one is grateful, for the work offers its challenge anew to each analysis and performance. It must be admitted that Haydn's piano sonatas have not been overwhelmed by a rich variety of great analytic essays.[10]

I felt it necessary, however, to state my point of view before presenting the basis of my analytic approach. Because of the nature of Haydn's piano sonata genre, my preference is for a chronology- and genre-oriented analysis. Detailed analysis of individual movements is both necessary and rewarding, but it is not my intention to provide a roadmap for such analyses. I hope, instead, that what follows will be a guide revealing interconnections and trends. I believe that a clear understanding of the background and motivation of the composition of a new group of works can improve the interpretation of individual pieces.

The examination of the sonata genres can lead to a deeper understanding of Haydn's intentions. If we can abstract a type from related works, by means of similarities in form, tempo, meter, basic rhythmic vocabulary, and texture, we can reconstruct several of the parameters about which Haydn made decisions prior to composition. I have mentioned earlier that, before beginning to improvise at the keyboard, Haydn already had a clear idea about the material he was shaping; he had already decided the genre, the type of movement, and probably the time signature and rhythmic framework. When his biographer Griesinger remarked on the clearly written picture of his scores, Haydn replied, "This is because I do not write until I am sure of the thing." He also stated that he always composed at the keyboard: "I sit down, begin to improvise, sad or happy according to my mood, serious or trifling. Once I seize upon the idea, my whole endeavor is to develop and sustain it in keeping with the rules of art."[11] In his maturity, Haydn did not compose quickly, at least compared to some of his contem-

the first movement of 32 g in "Organic Structure in Sonata Form" and of the development of the first movement of 59 E♭ in *Five Graphic Music Analyses*. See also his "Haydn: Sonate Es Dur" and "Haydn: Sonate C Dur."

10. Donald Francis Tovey's essay on 62 E♭ deserves special attention. See his *Studies in Musical Analysis: Supplementary Volume: Chamber Music*, 7th ed. (Oxford, 1972), 93–105. Hermann Abert's two classic studies, "Joseph Haydns Klavierwerke" and "Joseph Haydns Klaviersonaten," and William Newman's chapter on Haydn (*The Sonata in the Classic Era*, 457–77) are still worth reading. I also find very much of interest in Peter Brown's "The Structure of the Exposition in Haydn's Keyboard Sonatas."

11. Griesinger, 61.

poraries. In London, he spent one month on a symphony; in his late years, he spent three months on a mass.[12]

In the first phase of composition, while Haydn improvised at the keyboard, there must have been only a few practical decisions to be made about the function, type, and style of a movement. Self-taught, using Fux's *Gradus ad Parnassum,* Haydn would have had no rules to guide him in the unfolding of an instrumental form. The codification of "rules" of first-movement form lay in the future; indeed, these rules would be drawn up by Koch's generation partly through the study of Haydn's music. However, his concept of a "first Allegro" might have included a ternary framework, with a repetition of the two sections, and certain procedures regarding modulation. Of course, Haydn had a mental stock of practiced patterns of his own. Whether these patterns were better or worse, more conventional or more novel, than those put forward in later theoretical studies is beside the point here. But how these patterns work compared with one another can best be judged by an analytic survey of the types and by distinguishing between main types and variants. Likewise, the originality of the best pieces can be most clearly understood by studying them in the context of their particular type.

12. See ibid., 62.

Section 1: The First Movement

Twelve

SURVEY *and* CLASSIFICATION

EVEN IN HAYDN'S EARLIEST divertimento or partita sonatas (printed in *WUE*, vol. 1a), the opening movements are in sonata form.[1] This was a trademark of works composed in Vienna in the 1750s and 1760s. From around 1765, when he began writing the mature piano sonatas on which we will be focusing, Haydn was already a master of this form in which he could express himself so eloquently. Only a few of Haydn's thirty-six mature sonatas have opening movements that are not in sonata form. 19 e is an archaic form;[2] the first movement of 28 D, which exists only in the form of a thematic incipit and the last part of the music, cannot be discussed in detail; and 52 G, 54 G, 56 D, and 58 C begin with variation forms. This gives us thirty sonata-form opening movements to examine. Widening our investigation to include second and third movements, we gain thirty-one more sonata or sonata-like forms—sixteen slow and one fast second movements, twelve fast and two minuet-like third movements. However, these will be considered separately from the opening sonata forms because of their different function and simpler structure.

The opening-movement sonata forms can be easily classified in terms of tempo and meter. Leaving out 35 A♭, which is probably not by Haydn, and 61 D, whose time signature may be **C** or **¢** and whose form, lacking a double bar at the end of the exposition, is unusual, four main types can be discerned. These types

1. The pasticcio version of 5 G, beginning with a ternary-form movement that is in fact the finale of 4 G, and 7 D, with a Theme and variations opening movement, are not authentic works. The first movement of 12 A is in an unusual tempo, Andante, but it is in sonata form.

2. Feder suggests that the Adagio movement with which 19 e begins might have been the second movement of a sonata whose first movement is now lost—perhaps *WUE* 25, of which we have only the incipit. For a counterargument, see n. 1, chap. 10.

fall into clear chronological groups and give us a first means of interpreting the evolution of Haydn's style (see fig. 15).[3]

The *first main type* is in fact a whole family of related types, composed in three periods—1766–72, 1773, and 1776–80. These movements have in common $\frac{4}{4}$ meter and *Moderato* or *Allegro moderato* tempo markings. In and through them, Haydn created new-style, extended first movements similar to the opening Moderatos in many of the first mature string quartets, opp. 9, 17, and 20. Until about 1771, Haydn might not have had an alternative to this type in the sonata genre.[4] The longest and most differentiated movements of his piano sonatas were written in the first period. From 1773 to 1780, the $\frac{4}{4}$ Moderato type remained an important alternative to the newly fashionable faster first movements. Several of these conservative-style works, such as 41 A and 40 E♭ in the *Esterházy* set and 47 b in the *Anno 1776* set, were well above the standard of their opus neighbors. By around 1780 (1781 for the quartets), Haydn seems to have exhausted this type, in part because he had revised his notation. Up to about 1780, Haydn had used a rich rhythmic vocabulary in his Moderato and Allegro moderato opening sonata forms, as is shown in example 90.[5] Missing from this vocabulary are eighth-note triplets.

C (All°) Mod^to

Ex. 90. The rhythmic vocabulary in Haydn's Moderato and Allegro moderato opening sonata forms.

Such a rich rhythmic vocabulary leads to a highly differentiated style with finely worked surface rhythms and a good balance between the main stresses in a measure and the small rhythmic motion in between. Playing these movements—in solo and chamber music alike—requires of the performer a combination of noble ease, freedom, and creativity. As long as Haydn himself was the performer—or supervised the performance through teaching or coaching—the notation was completely adequate. When his music was distributed to a larger public, including diligent dilettantes or even professionals accustomed to a different style, a "short bar" notation ($\frac{2}{4}$ instead of $\frac{4}{4}$) or the augmented notation of rhythms in $\frac{4}{4}$ or ¢ had the advantage of being easier to read, easier to feel the beat.

3. The three dates in parentheses in fig. 15 are suggestions rather than established dates; see the Catalog of the Sonatas, p. 353.

4. The rediscovery of one or more of the lost sonatas, such as *WUE* 23 B in C or 26 C in $\frac{3}{4}$, might considerably change our finding that there was no fast opening movement as an alternative to the Moderatos.

5. Regarding the performance of different dotted formulas, e.g., and , in the same movement, see pp. 88ff.

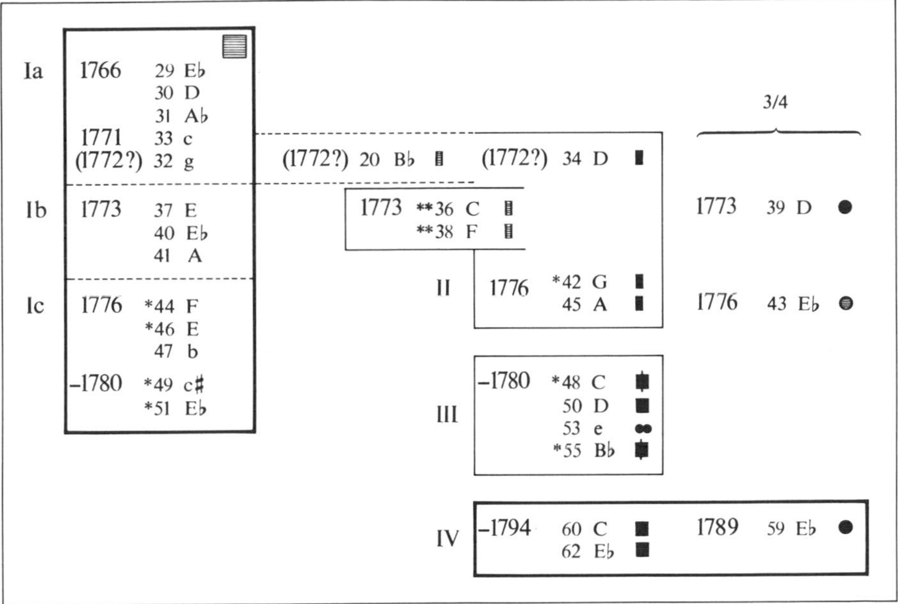

FIGURE 15 Four main types of opening sonata forms—a chronological survey. (* Equally long exposition and recapitulation. ** No tempo indication in the manuscript.)

The style of this simpler notation could to some extent exclude greater freedom, variety, and eloquence in performance. But the composer could hope that his works would be better understood and realized, even by performers with a different musical background. Thus, Haydn, who may well have encountered such performances in the 1770s in Vienna, made certain changes in his notational style beginning around 1780 with the editions printed by Artaria, over which he exerted a certain control. The rhythms can be symbolized as in example 91.

a	C All° mod^to	
b	C All°	
c	₵ All° con brio	
d	₵ (All°) Mod^to	

Ex. 91. *a,* Haydn's second moderato type. *b,* Mozart allegro.* *c,* Haydn's *alla breve* con brio. *d,* Haydn's *alla breve* march.* (* Isidor Saslav introduced the terms Haydn's "*alla breve* march" and Mozart "**C** " or "Classical sonata-allegro" in his "Tempos in the String Quartets of Joseph Haydn" [Ph.D. diss., Indiana University, 1969]. See his summarizing study "The *alla breve* 'March': Its Evolution and Meaning in Haydn's String Quartets," in *Haydn Studies,* 308–14.)

The *second main type* of opening sonata movement took shape only gradually. Around 1771–73, Haydn, seeking some new concept, composed two sonata-form opening movements in $\frac{2}{4}$. By reducing the number of triplet and dotted figures in 34 D I, he produced a new and economical Allegro rhythm. Owing to the thirty-second-note motion, the tempo of this Allegro is not as fast as those written from 1776 on. 20 B♭ I, marked *Allegro moderato,* maintains the Moderato rhythmic vocabulary but, perhaps in part because of the more "compact" $\frac{2}{4}$ meter, omits the more adventurous deviations. In this way, we arrive at a compact style with a little "marching" force in the movement. 36 C and 38 F, composed in 1773, have no tempo indications in Haydn's autograph, but 36 C is marked *Allegro* in the Kurzböck print. The characteristic "rhythmic code" of these movements is quite limited. At a next stage Haydn did well to notate such themes in larger note values with faster tempo indications (see ex. 92).[6]

Ex. 92.

Another feature of the *Anno 1776* set, which we will discuss later, has to do with the relative size of the exposition and recapitulation. For the first time in the mature piano sonatas, we find extensive sonata-form movements in which the exposition and recapitulation are equal in length (see the asterisked sonatas in fig. 15 above). Since the process and functions of the two sections are considerably different, this equality of size was not the result of mere mechanical repetition.

The opening movements of 39 D and 43 E♭ show that there are real differences between $\frac{4}{4}$ and $\frac{3}{4}$ sonata-form movements composed at the same time and for the same set. The tempo of the triple-meter movement is faster. The sixteenth-note triplets in the Allegro moderato of 43 E♭ are only sporadic, while the sixteenth notes in the Allegro of 39 D are almost as fast and brilliant as the thirty-seconds in the opening movement of 38 F in $\frac{2}{4}$.

In the *third main type,* with considerable diversity of tempo and meter (¢, $\frac{4}{4}$, $\frac{6}{8}$; Allegro con brio, Presto), the change to the new scale of rhythmic notation is almost complete. The models for this type were probably 48 C I and 55 B♭ I, two attractive and powerful opening movements with stormy left-hand motion. The restricted rhythmic style of 50 D I, suggestive of a harpsichord idiom, is

6. The tempo indication of 45 A I is *Allegro,* probably because of the dotted sixteenth notes.

atypical for Haydn. The $\frac{6}{8}$ Presto of 53 e may be a borderline case as far as the type is concerned, but it is an important piece.

The *fourth main type,* the rhythmic motion of which is most similar to that of Mozart's piano works in the 1780s, is represented by only three of Haydn's sonatas. All three are in concert style, but they have different and individual rhythmic vocabularies. Indeed, although all three have the same tempo indication, *Allegro,* they benefit by being played at different speeds, as shown in example 93.

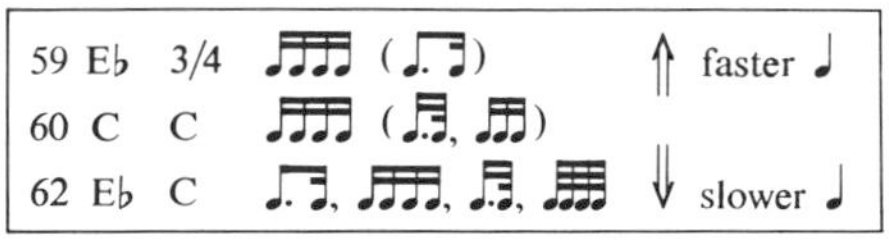

59 E♭	3/4		⇑ faster ♩
60 C	C		
62 E♭	C		⇓ slower ♩

Ex. 93.

The opening sonata-form movements in the piano trios composed from 1784 on show a greater diversity of types. This is not surprising since these eighteen movements vary considerably in style and degree of technical difficulty. A survey of the "rhythmic codes" (see ex. 94) shows that there are two common types among both the virtuoso Allegros and the more comfortably paced Allegro moderatos, but with several individual variants.

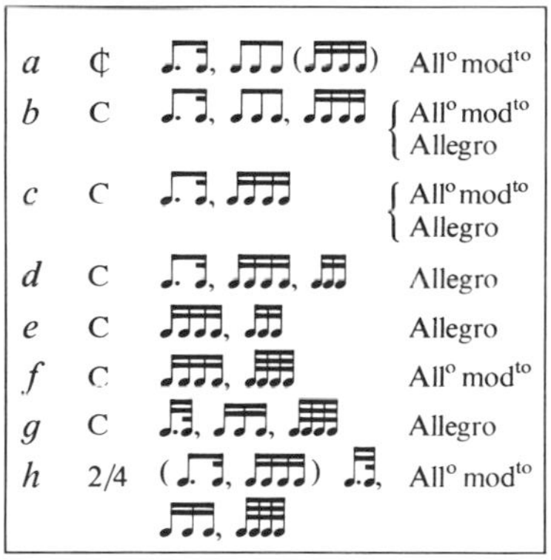

a	¢		All° mod^to
b	C		All° mod^to / Allegro
c	C		All° mod^to / Allegro
d	C		Allegro
e	C		Allegro
f	C		All° mod^to
g	C		Allegro
h	2/4		All° mod^to

Ex. 94. Rhythmic "codes" of Haydn's piano trios (Hob. XV).* *a,* 18 A, 11 E♭. *b,* 10 E♭; 15 G, 24 D. *c,* 8 B♭, 12 e, 30 E♭; 16 D. *d,* 26 f♯, 27 C. *e,* 20 B♭. *f,* 28 E. *g,* 17 F.** *h,* 14 A♭, 22 E♭.† (* See the *JHW* edition of the trios or the urtext edition published by Doblinger, edited by H. C. Robbins Landon, for the original tempo markings of the trios. They are often distorted in other editions. ** The autograph of Hob. XV:17 F is missing; the tempo marking *Allegro* comes from an early printed edition. The rhythmic concept and vocabulary suggest to me, rather, a tempo of Allegro moderato. † The first movement of XV:22 E♭ includes the rhythmic formulas in parentheses. This is one of the most mature of the opening movements of the trios, with highly differentiated surface rhythm.)

Thirteen

Grammar, Syntax, *and* Analytic Terminology

HAYDN SCHOLARSHIP of the past decades has brought more clearly into focus Haydn's distinctive treatment of the Viennese Classical forms and procedures.[1] At the same time it has become evident that, for analytic discussions of Haydn's works, much of the standard terminology is inadequate or inappropriate. For example, explanations of sonata form in terms of first or main theme and second theme (*Hauptsatz, Seitensatz*) are misleading in the case of Haydn, whose second theme is frequently a variation of the first.[2] An approach that concentrates on the key structure of a form rather than on thematic content may be more useful. The move away from the tonic and the establishment of the second key, the length of the sections and the means by which they are articulated, the strategy of the cadences—all are important aspects of Haydn's treatment of sonata form and all as much a part of his personal style as his thematic manipulation.

A look at a brief, early sonata by Haydn will show some of the deficiencies of analysis in terms of themes and keys alone. The opening movement of the divertimento sonata 9 D, in $\frac{4}{4}$ in Moderato character, is brief but fully characteristic of Haydn. Can a textbook description of the thematic content of this nineteen-measure-long exposition grasp its individuality? There is a seven-

1. The seminal work concerning Haydn's individual style with regard to sonata form was Jens Peter Larsen's "Sonatenform-Probleme."

2. Koch's description of the thematic content of the exposition of the first movement of a symphony is well worth reading. He points out that, in contrast to other movements, in the first section of the initial Allegro, "(1) the melodic ideas are likely to be more extended at their first appearance than in other pieces, and, especially, (2) that these melodic ideas usually relate to each other and stream forth more compellingly than in the sections of other pieces—that is, they are so drawn together that their cadences are less perceptible" (*Versuch einer Anleitung zur Komposition,* vol. 3 [Leipzig, 1793], quoted in Newman, *The Sonata in the Classic Era,* 33).

measure main theme that arrives at a full cadence; after a caesura, a six-measure transitional passage leads to a new theme in the dominant in measure 14, with its own rhythmic profile. It is not clear if this new theme is the second theme or the closing theme. Some would call this a "sonatina-form exposition," but it would be neither a relevant nor a helpful term.

A description concentrating on key structure is similar through measure 7. Measures 1–7 are in the home key, confirmed with a tonic cadence; measures 8–10 modulate to the dominant, which is confirmed in the following measures. Nine measures are clearly in the tonic, nine in the dominant, and one (m. 10) effects the transition; the modulation is made through V of V.

These two descriptions of even this embryonic exposition leave several important questions unanswered. (1) What is the thematic content of measure 11, the significant moment when the second key is confirmed? Is it neutral figuration, a transitory motive, a new theme, or a development of previous material? (2) Why is the first theme asymmetrical, that is, seven measures long (see ex. 95)? (3) Why is the second group, from measure 14, also asymmetrical in a sense, and what is the purpose of the shift of primary and secondary accents in this theme?

Ex. 95. Seven-measure main theme of 9 D I.

It will not do to say that this is merely a short and immature piece written by a young composer searching for his own style in a transitional period in the history of music. In fact, this movement has a masterfully controlled form, with true Haydnesque ideas expressed in a kind of *sonata facile* character. The primary theme extends itself naturally through seven measures. This is achieved by expanding a four-measure nucleus.[3] Measures 1–3 and 7 could be played in succession if one's goal were but a simply regular theme. Instead, Haydn elaborates. Measure 4 is a repetition of measure 3, measure 6 is a slightly varied repetition of measure 5; measure 7 contains a condensed, diminished variant of measures 5 and 6.

Symmetrical and *asymmetrical, regular* and *irregular, extended* and *condensed*—these terms must be used with sensitivity to their connotations and an awareness of their historical appropriateness. From about 1775–80, phrase structures built in multiples of two or four measures were already standard; investigating and evaluating "irregularities" of phrases written at that time has some justification. But around 1760 in Vienna or Eisenstadt, a seven-measure phrase such as begins 9 D was setting the standards, not defying established ones.

Let us examine the parameter of rhythm, both thematic rhythm or composite rhythm of the treble and bass and harmonic rhythm. Most of the thematic rhythmic formulas of the movement are presented in the opening theme (see ex. 96*a–d*). The acceleration of the harmonic rhythm with chords changing once, twice, four times, and eight times per measure has a sophisticated directionality

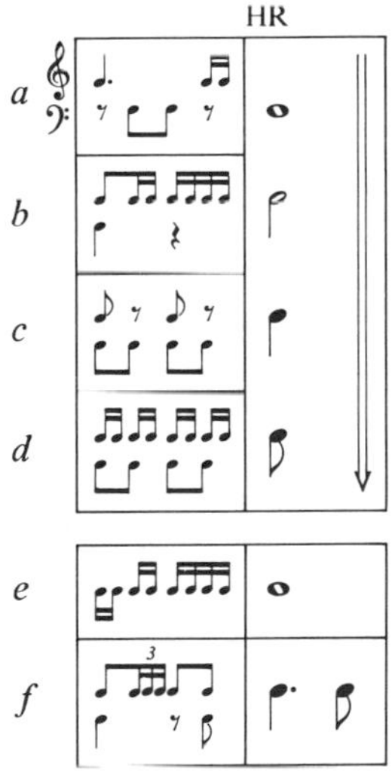

HR

a

b

c

d

e

f

Ex. 96. Thematic and harmonic rhythm of 9 D I.

3. This hypothetical four-measure phrase is acceptable, from the motivic point of view, only if one supposes that mm. 5–6 forecast the contents of m. 7.

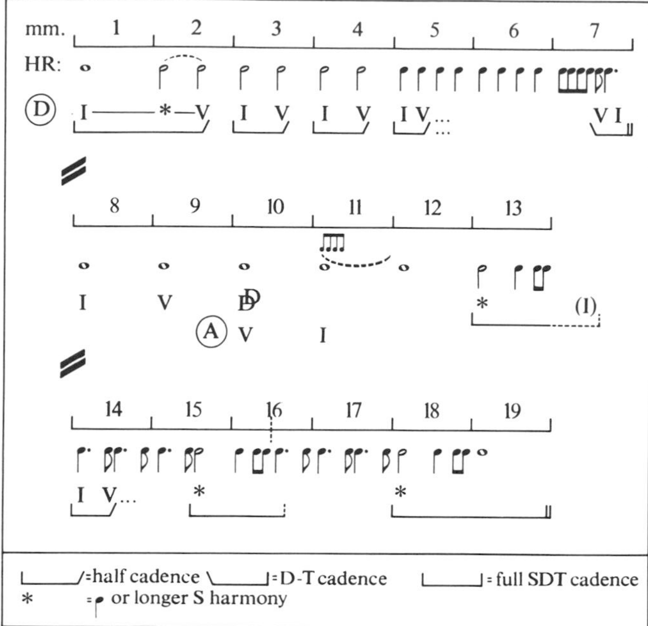

FIGURE 16 Harmonic rhythm in the exposition of 9 D I.

leading to the cadence (see fig. 16). The differentiation of the harmonic rhythm alone reflects the thematic function of the sections during the exposition: presentation, or articulation, or transition, or elaboration.

A close look at the thematic rhythm reveals certain subtle connections. Note that, when the new key is established in measure 11, the cadential rhythm of the first theme (m. 7) reappears. The rhythm of the bridge passage (m. 8; see ex. 96*e*) is related to the inner "transition" of the first theme (m. 3; see ex. 96*b*). Also, the cadence in measure 13 brings together the head motive of measure 1 and the inner cadential formula of the first theme (end of mm. 5 and 6).

The other theme, with triplet and sextuplet rhythms, has a true half-measure pulsation (see ex. 97). This is true of many closing themes of expositions in $\frac{4}{4}$ time in Haydn's mature sonatas. Going further into the movement, it is worth noting that the sixteen-measure development fully corresponds, on a miniature scale, to the pattern of the development section with counterexposition (Koch's first main type), a pattern that Haydn used frequently in his mature sonata-form works (see pp. 282–83).

Ex. 97. Thematic–rhythmic connections in 9 D I.

This discussion of just a few features of a brief movement points up the need for a simple terminology with easily recognizable abbreviations and symbols for a comparative analysis of types. I have found Jan LaRue's symbols,[4] with a few modifications, most useful. The letters and symbols I will be using in the rest of this book, primarily in dealing with sonata-form structures, are summarized in table 18 (see next page). To demonstrate their use in describing the thematic working out of a rich form with many thematic and motivic interactions, I give below a diagram of the first movement of 59 E♭, the *Genzinger* Sonata:

Exp.:	P	T	Pa^1 + 1S$^{(Pb)}$	2S$^{(Pb)}$	1K	2K	
(mm.)	(1–12)	(13–24)	(25–28–41)	(42–52)	(53–59)	(60–64)	
Dev.:	(2K)	Pa^1 + (1S + 2S)		(1K) + (1K + Pa)			
(mm.)	(65–80)	(81–84–107)		(108–126–131)			
							Coda
Recap.:	P	T	1S	2S	1K	2K	(2K + T)
(mm.)	(132–143)	(144–157)	(158–171)	(172–178)	(179–185)	(186–190)	(191–218)

4. Jan LaRue, *Guidelines for Style Analysis.*

TABLE 18 ANALYTIC SYMBOLS AND ABBREVIATIONS

Exp.	Exposition
Dev.	Development section
Rec., recap.	Recapitulation
	Basic symbols
P	Primary subject, primary theme (= first group, first theme, opening theme)
T	Transition (= bridge passage), transitional theme, motive
S	Secondary subject(s), secondary theme(s) (= second group)
K	Closing group, theme(s), motives
k	Closing motive of any theme
(I) (II)	First, second (etc.) fantasia-, toccata-like inserts in the Exp. or Dev.
X	New theme in the Dev.
	Combined symbols
1K, 2K	First, second etc. (e.g., closing) theme
Pa, Pb, Pk	Fragments or sections of a theme (e.g., first, second, closing motives of the P)
P, P^1, P^2	Theme and its characteristically changed, rephrased form(s)
P, P^v, P^w or P^{1v}, P^{2v}	Theme and its embellished, varied form(s)
I^r, $I^{r/3}$	In double variations: reprise or reprise and (by repetition of segments) third variation of the first (variation) theme
$T^{(P)}$, $T^{(Pa)}$	Theme using elements of a previous theme (e.g., T with characteristics of the P)
(P)	Theme significantly changed, developed
[S]	Instead of a firm thematic formation (e.g., of a S): loose motivic, rhythmic etc. texture functioning as a theme

Fourteen

Exposition Strategies

IT IS NOT ALTOGETHER EASY to categorize the types of construction found in Haydn's sonata-form first movements because of the richness of his strategies, not to mention the innumerable variations of detail. In the final analysis, however, we can understand every exposition as follows: the specific musical material of the main theme suggests its own most adequate continuation. To this extent, an abstract classification of procedures is simply irrelevant. If, on the other hand, we were to appeal to the compositional rules found in treatises of Haydn's time, we would run the risk of producing a mere list of plans and principles. Perhaps this would have been appropriate in pedagogical contexts during the eighteenth century, but it is hardly sufficient for modern interpretations of Haydn's style. Even though distinctions among various plans and strategies in Haydn's expositions are necessarily arbitrary (and even though they interact in complex ways during the act of composition), for practical reasons it will be helpful to classify them here.[1]

It will be worthwhile to examine the exposition structure of Haydn's sonata-form first movements on three different levels:

1. *Tonal plan*

    a) How does Haydn leave the tonic, and how does he approach the new key of the second group?

    b) At what point is the new key firmly established?

    c) Do we also encounter digressions to other keys or tonally unstable sections?

1. Another classification, which came out after the original edition of this book, is Michelle Fillion's "Sonata-Exposition Procedures in Haydn's Keyboard Sonatas."

d) What kinds of cadences articulate the sections of the exposition, and how are they distributed?

2. *Thematic material*

a) How long is the P section? What proportion of the exposition does it occupy?

b) What other themes—T? S? K?—appear? What are their functions? Do we find fantasia-like or toccata-like passages? Does this new material form independent thematic structures or loosely organized motivic groups?

c) What is the relation of the later material to P? Does the movement exhibit "monothematic" tendencies?

3. *Rhythm, texture, and idiomatic instrumental writing*

a) What is the rhythmic "vocabulary"? Do we find rhythmically homogeneous phrases or longer paragraphs? What kinds of continuity and contrast do they exhibit?

b) What distinctions exist regarding texture and number of voices? What sorts of idiomatic instrumental styles occur? How are these related to the thematic material?

The forms on these three levels—tonal, thematic, textural—will by no means necessarily be congruent in a given exposition. From a synthesis of them, however, the formal contour of an exposition emerges, whether it comprises two, three, or even four sections.

Some of these issues (e.g., 1*a*, 1*d*, 2*a*, 2*c*, 3*a*) can be addressed analytically only after scrutiny of the main theme. But others (What proportions do we find? What statistical patterns do these data suggest?) can be summarized immediately.

Establishment of the key of the second group. This key is always the dominant if the tonic is major, the relative major if the tonic is minor. In seventeen of the twenty-eight movements (fourteen in major, three in minor), the new key serves as a vehicle for a new theme (S) and appears following a clear division by a rest. In six additional movements, the arrival in this key is clearly articulated, despite the absence of a caesura.

1. In the main type of modulation, characteristic in all periods from the earliest mature sonatas to the last ones, the end of the modulating passage (T) arrives on V of V; S begins in V (*a*) with caesura: nos. 20, 31, 32, 40, 43, 44, 47–49, 59; (*b*) without caesura: nos. 29, 38, 45, 46, 62.

2. A subsidiary type, exhibiting a simpler connection between the two main sections, first appears in the less highly differentiated sonatas from 1773 on. At the end of P (or T), we find a half cadence on V, followed directly by the beginning of S in V (*a*) with caesura: nos. 34, 36, 39, 50, 51, 60; (*b*) without caesura: no. 42.

Both these types were typical in Haydn's time. In his sonatas, Haydn usually establishes the second key firmly between about one-third and half the way through the exposition (sixteen of twenty-three movements). In two sonatas

(20 B♭ and 49 c♯), the proportion is exactly 1:2; in one (46 E), it is exactly 1:1; in two (40 E♭ and 48 C), the second key appears somewhat later than the middle of the exposition; and in two others (39 D and 36 C), it is established sooner than one-third the way through the exposition. In addition, however, we must note five special cases (nos. 30, 33, 37, 41, and 53) whose tonal plans suggest a characteristic strategy of Haydn's: he postpones all sense of stable establishment of the second key until the closing K area, in the last measures of the exposition. Although the "potential" new key may be touched on quite early (e.g., in m. 9 in 33 c or in m. 9 in 37 E), Haydn either soon visits the dominant minor (30 D I, 19, 22; 41 A I, 10–11) or moves in this sudden dominant merely as a temporary guest (53 e I, 14–15). Hence, one cannot speak of a true second group in these expositions, only of hypothetical S (dominant) formations of fantasia- or capriccio-like character, interrupted by frequent fermata-like rests.

Tonal deviations in the exposition. In Haydn's expositions in major keys, the surprising appearance of the minor dominant often plays a significant role; his contemporaries seldom used this procedure to such good effect. Haydn might have been inspired by C. P. E. Bach (e.g., m. 14 of 20 B♭ seems to point to Bach), but his use of the effect is highly characteristic. The minor dominant nearly always comes as a surprise and creates a dramatic or often decidedly pathetic impression. It is especially telling when the major dominant has already been prepared as a new key area, only to slip, if momentarily, into the minor (see ex. 98).[2]

Ex. 98. Minor dominant deviations. *a,* 41 A I, 10–12. *b,* 30 D I, 21–23. (D^min.^ = Dominant minor.)

2. In this respect, the exposition of the *Farewell* Symphony, no. 45, is the most adventuresome. It modulates from F♯ minor toward A major but, as a surprise, arrives at A minor instead. Next, as

Another kind of tonal darkening of the exposition occurs later in the S area. Usually, it is only an echo in minor (50 D I, 29; 33 c I, 17–19) or a momentary cadential darkening, a contrast to the major-key brightness of the K area (31 A♭ I, 31; 51 E♭ I, 16). On some occasions, there is a thematic statement in minor in the S group (36 C I, 36 = 3S; 55 B♭ I, 25, and 62 E♭ I, 29 = 2S). The tonal instability of the "toccatas" between the returns of P head motives is also characterized by a liberal use of minor keys (39 D I, 24, 40). Two opening movements contain a strong turn toward ♭VI of V in the exposition (38 F I, 29; 39 D I, 42),[3] one of Haydn's favorite harmonic devices. A surprising use of a foreign key, one that gives an archaic, Baroque flavor, occurs in 40 E♭ I, 12–14 (ex. 99*a*). Here, after P cadences in the tonic, what appears to be a counterstatement in the relative minor turns into a bridge passage leading to the dominant. Probably the most interesting tonally unstable area in an exposition, extending for several measures, appears in 60 C I, 37–41 (ex. 99*b*). Indeed, the strong effect of the unstable tonality allows us to perceive this passage as "quasi thematic" in the environment of tonally simple motivic and contrapuntal elaborations of the first theme.

Ex. 99. *a*, 40 E♭ I, 12–14. *b*, 60 C I, 37–41.

The number of themes and their disposition in the exposition. For a general study of the distribution of themes in the exposition, we will have to make certain simplifications and in some sonatas not debate whether a certain phrase still be-

another surprise, the exposition ends in C♯ minor. In the development section, tonal peregrinations continue. The first theme appears in A major, a modulation reaches V of B minor, but the trio-like episode is in D major instead of B minor. In the recapitulation, the first theme is restated in the tonic. Then the dominant, C♯ major, is darkened into C♯ minor, and the first theme reappears, this time in B minor, before the movement concludes in F♯ minor.

3. In 62 E♭ I, 38, the mysterious G-G♭ piano passage, followed by the forte I$^6_4$ in the dominant, is a highly original variant of this conventional ♭VI of V turn.

longs to P or rather to T, S, or K. If we set such debates aside for the moment, the following observations can be made.

The first part of the exposition, until the establishment of the second key, either is a separate and independent paragraph entirely in the tonic (P) or is built up from a P and a T. In the former case, the P is usually connected to the S area by a cadence on the dominant, which is then taken to be the new key. When both a P and a T precede the S, they may exist as two blocks, separated by a rest or caesura (P ‖ T); or P and T may be clearly separated harmonically but integrated by a continuous texture and rhythm (P, T); or the sections may be elided so that the end of P is the beginning of T (P + T):

[P], 7 works	30 D, 36 C, 37 E, 39 D, 41 A, 42 G, 49 c♯
[P] [T], 10 works	32 g, 33 c, 34 D, 43 E♭, 44 F, 45 A,* 46 E, 47 b,* 50 D, 55 B♭ (*T derives from Pa)
[P, T], 6 works	20 B♭, 31 A♭, 38 F, 48 C, 59 E♭, 62 E♭ (T derives from Pb)
[P + T], 5 works[4]	29 E♭, 40 E♭, 51 E♭, 53 e, 60 C

In the twenty-four expositions in which the S and K areas can be clearly distinguished, the S area usually consists of only one theme, although there are sometimes two or three. In some sonatas, it could be more accurate to speak of "motivic formation" or "secondary area" than of a second theme or themes. In 20 B♭, 39 D, 40 E♭, and 53 e, to be discussed later, there is no clear distinction between S and K:

[1S], 12 works	29 E♭, 31 A♭, 38 F, 42 G, 43 E♭, 44 F, 45 A, 47 b, 48 C, 49 c♯, 50 D, 51 E♭
[1–2S], 5 works[5]	32 g, 34 D, 46 E, 55 B♭, 59 E♭
[1–3S], 2 works	36 C, 62 E♭ (in each 1S = P^1), 60 C
[[S]], 4 works	30 D, 33 c, 37 E, 41 A

There are simpler and more complex K areas. Perhaps the simplest is one built on the repetition of K that may be extended by an additional closing measure. The most common type contains two different short closing themes, occasionally with an additional codetta measure:

[KK(k)], 8 works	29 E♭, 31 A♭, 34 D, 36 C, 46 E, 50 D, 51 E♭, 55 B♭
[1–2K(k)], 10 works	33 c, 38 F, 42 G, 43 E♭, 44 F, 47 b, 48 C, 49 c♯, 59 E♭, 62 E♭ (1K = P^2)[6]

4. Note the frequency of sonatas in E♭ in this group.

5. Measures 13–16 and 17–21 of 46 E are different realizations of the same basic material.

6. As an experiment, one may combine the most frequently occurring types of P, S, and K areas to produce a supposedly "typical" Haydn sonata exposition. However, a [P] [T] [1S + 1–2K(k)] combination, although not entirely a chimera, can be found in only three, not very characteristic sonata expositions—43 E♭, 44 F, and 47 b.

1–3K, 2 works   45 A, 60 C
[K], 4 works   These contain highly individual formations:
30 D: 9½-measure-long K chain, Kaa′ Kbb′ Kkk^v + k;
32 g: Kab* $b^v b^w$ + modulation in two bars, altogether 10 measures (*Ka = T);
37 E: 3 + 2 measures "sentence"-form K;
41 A: K theme of coda character for 3 measures

In the exposition of four opening movements, any distinction between S and K themes would be forced and artificial. A short description of their motivic content, their specific proportions, and their cadences follows.

The exposition of 20 B♭ is irregular, articulated as 12 + 1 + 26 measures; after the P area and T, there is a rest of almost one full measure. There follows a coherent motivic chain: ccc+k (mm. 14–17), $dd^1d^2d^1$(c)+k (mm. 17–28), $e^1e^2e^1e^2$+k (mm. 29–35), d^3d^4+k (mm. 36–39).

39 D has a three-part exposition, articulated by the repeated statements of the beginning of the first theme: (14 + 20 + 17 measures) + cadences. These three parts can be described as Pa^1a^2b; Pa^3 and a "fantasia" (S area); and Pa^4 and the continuation of the fantasia + K + Codetta (K area). The monothematic tendencies in this exposition will be dealt with later.

40 E♭ has an unusual exposition, the formal contours of which are partly dissolved in a fantasia-style growth and partly reaffirmed by means of subtle motivic connections. The P block, which is itself in two distinct portions, cadences in measure 12 on the tonic.[7] After a quarter rest and a statement of the head motive of P in C minor, there is a modulation to the dominant of B♭ (mm. 12–14; see ex. 99). The remaining fourteen measures are richly articulated with cadences (V of B♭ in m. 21, deceptive cadence on vi of B♭ in m. 25). The new themes (in mm. 22 and 25) are expansions of the second and first motives of S (m. 15), but the rhythm of the first S motive itself is derived from measure 6, and the scale figuration in measures 17–19 is familiar from measure 11.[8]

53 e has a dramatically shaped exposition that can hardly be described adequately with traditional terminology. Should the theme that starts after the fermatas in measures 30 and 36 be called 1K or S? Depending on the choice of label, is measure 42 2K or a coda? On the basis of rhythmic texture—thematic material in eighth notes, motivic material in sixteenths—one can divide the exposition into four distinct parts:

first ♪ theme + first 𝅘𝅥𝅯 area (= P + T);
second ♪ theme + second 𝅘𝅥𝅯 area (= K, K + Codetta).

7. Measures 8–12 are a kind of *faux* transition. They occupy the place of a T area, but no modulation takes place.

8. The motivic coherence of P, T, and S is particularly striking in the shortened recapitulation (mm. 57ff.).

It would be useful at this point to survey Haydn's monothematic expositions, asking how frequently they occur and how important they are in the general picture. First, however, one must distinguish between motivic references and monothematic structures proper. Motivic reference is a standard feature of Classical style and by no means special to Haydn. According to the eighteenth-century ideal of unity and diversity (*Einheit und Mannigfaltigkeit*), a longer movement based on several themes was in good taste only if the themes presented later in the movement had an original character while still manifesting a connection to the earlier themes through motivic or rhythmic references. Such references, especially rhythmic ones, are common in Haydn's sonatas (see, e.g., 29 E♭,[9] 34 D, 55 B♭). In 32 g, it is exactly this principle that organizes the growth, development, and variation of the thematic material.

The small group of true monothematic expositions among Haydn's sonatas begins with the opening movement of 39 D, written in 1773. In such expositions, the role of S or S and K, or at least of 1S and 1K, is taken over by a return of P, sometimes in a varied form. (*Monothematic* is not a completely accurate description of such movements, for the passage work and the cadential motives of S and K are often quite individual and characteristic.)

The sonatas in this group all differ from one another and deserve to be considered individually. At the same time, each one can be regarded as an experimental and improved form of an already existing structure, and they can be considered collectively as a chain of structural variants. This process, the shaping of a "corrected form" of a structure, is a familiar compositional technique of Haydn's.[10] All in all, one can outline three models:

1. The second theme is an adapted form of the first theme:

P . . . ‖ P^1 . . . K	49 c♯ (–1780)
	51 E♭ (–1780)
P . . . ‖ P^1P^2 . . . K	60 C (1794)

2. Three variants of the first theme articulate the exposition, as if ritornelli:

P ‖ P^1 + (I) P^2 + (II) + K	39 D (–1773)
P, T; P^1 + 1–2S; P^2 + K	62 E♭ (–1794)

3. Fragments of the first theme, either motivically or rhythmically, are present in almost every section of the exposition:

P, $T^{(P)}$ ‖ $1S^{(P)}$, $2S^{(P)}$, $1K^{(P)}$, 2K	59 E♭ (–1789)

9. A special feature of the exposition of 29 E♭ is that K (mm. 27–30) is an elaborated form of a motive from the T area (mm. 14–16).

10. See my "The London Revision of Haydn's Instrumental Style."

The number of voices and their typical textural combinations in the exposition. It is rare to find a mature first-movement sonata-form exposition in Haydn's keyboard work in which the number of voices is rigidly the same from the beginning to the end or even within the various thematic areas. This kind of textural economy was common, however, in the sonatas that Haydn composed in the second half of the 1760s. Two-voice texture predominates in the expositions of 29 E♭ and 30 D and three-voice writing in 31 A♭. This feature occasionally recurs in later years, in dilettante-style works such as 42 G, in which a consistent two-voice texture extends from the P to the K, or in expositions with toccata-like inserts, such as 39 D. In the majority of the mature sonatas, important articulations of the form are emphasized by a change in the number of voices. 20 B♭ shows a markedly orderly and regular alternation of voice parts—measures 1–8, P = 3 voices; measures 9–12, T = 2 voices; measures 14–28 = three voices; measures 29–39 = two voices.[11] It is more typical, however, to find a first theme with a fixed number of voices, a transition of rhapsodic texture, and an S-K area again with a strict number of voices (see, e.g., 32 g and 33 c). The next stage of development in textures, brought about by Haydn's search for an idiomatic and attractive harpsichord style, leads to looser construction with regard to the number of voices. The use of multivoice chords, which produces a strong accent on the harpsichord (see pp. 129–31), was recalled by Haydn even when he was composing for the fortepiano—as in 55 B♭. These chords have a real thematic significance in some first themes, as in 37 E and 44 F, and in second themes, as in 34 D and 47 b. The apparent evolution toward textural freedom was not without its recollections of earlier periods.[12] After Haydn became acquainted with the Viennese fortepiano and experimented with a bold use of free-textural style in the first movement of 58 C, he resumed composing in a strict number of voices, with a few multivoiced chords for accents, as in the first movement of 59 E♭, composed in 1789. After becoming acquainted with the English fortepianos, he returned to a predominantly free-textural style of writing, his most advanced keyboard style. But even in the expositions of his two late concert sonatas, which are so rich in bursts of multivoiced chords, there are long thematic sections that strictly maintain two- or three-voice writing.[13]

11. In mm. 36–37, the texture thickens momentarily in two chords. In the recapitulation, this textural enrichment is fully realized (mm. 110–16), probably owing to the different compass.

12. This evolution can be depicted in the following stages: (1) fixed two- or three-voice writing (at the end of the 1760s, as in 29 E♭, 31 A♭); (2) changes in texture used to articulate sections of the form (at the beginning of the 1770s, as in 20 B♭, 33 c); (3) a more flexible texture with occasional "accented chords" (in the middle of the 1770s, as in 44 F, 47 b); and (4) mature style of textures with varying number of voices (*London* sonatas 60 C, 62 E♭).

13. 60 C I, 1–6, 8–22, 30–41, 44–52; 62 E♭ I, 4–8, 11–13, 27–32, 36, 41–42.

 *Fifteen*

THE PRIMARY THEME

Each musical composition, be it a real melody composed for words or merely an instrumental melody, has to have a distinct character of its own and awake distinct emotions in the listener's soul. . . . In a piece of music the principal sentence [Hauptsatz][1] *is a period* [Periode][2] *which bears within itself the expression of the melody*[3] *and its whole substance. It is stated not only at the beginning of a work but is often repeated in the course of the piece in various keys* [in verschiedenen Tönen] *and with various changes. The principal sentence is generally called the theme* [Thema].[4]

—Sulzer, *Allgemeine Theorie der schönen Künste*[5]

WELL-TRAINED MUSICIANS of the eighteenth century, be they composers, performers, or theorists, believed that in the very first measures of a composition what we may call a "bridge of communication" (they would not have used such a fashionable term) had to be erected between the work and the listener. Thus, the task of the first musical sentence was manifold—it introduced the general character or mood, which, on the basis of previous musical experience, evoked

1. In spite of the many possible meanings of the stem word *satz*, in German musical terminology the word *Hauptsatz* still involves the original meaning "sentence."

2. In German grammar, *Periode* means a complex sentence.

3. The terms *Melodie* and *Gesang* were used in eighteenth-century German treatises to denote the leading voice of the composition and, indirectly, to refer to the development of the piece.

4. "Der Hauptsatz wird insgemein das Thema genannt." In this sentence, there is a distinction made between the term *principal sentence* (*Hauptsatz*), which expresses the grammatical view of musical forms, and the term *theme* (*Thema*), which is the fundamental starting material for the musical development of the movement.

5. A rich collection of the original German texts is in Fred Ritzel, *Die Entwicklung der "Sonatenform" im musiktheoretischen Schrifttum des 18. und 19. Jahrhunderts*, 3d ed. (Wiesbaden, 1974). The major monograph in this field in English is Leonard Ratner's *Classic Music;* see also his important earlier studies "Harmonic Aspects of Classical Form," *Journal of the American Musicological Society* 2 (1949): 159–68, and "Eighteenth-Century Theories of Musical Period Structure," *Musical Quarterly* 42 (1956): 439–54.

certain emotions in the listener; it announced the originality and individual style of the composer; and, finally, it clarified the musical genre and type of the piece. Such a first statement can be rightly compared to the grammatical and literary terms *sentence, main clause,* and *period.*

Unfortunately, these terms cannot now be used in their original senses without the danger of confusion. German terminology has still preserved the more abstract meaning of *Satz* in *Hauptsatz* and *Seitensatz* (principal and secondary theme). According to Koch, "The sentence is any single part of the composition that has an independent meaning."[6] Traditional German analytic vocabulary makes the distinction between sentence and period (*Satz* and *Periode*). According to Koch, the structure of the shortest possible *Hauptperiode* is a four-measure *Absatz* (first phrase) and a four-measure *Schlussatz* (closing phrase).[7] Later German terminology changed these terms to *Vordersatz* (antecedent) and *Nachsatz* (consequent). Arnold Schoenberg gives a useful exposition and interpretation of the traditional terminology in *Fundamentals of Musical Composition.* He notes that "the distinction between the sentence and the period lies in the treatment of the second phrase, and in the continuation after it." The beginning of the sentence contains a statement and an immediate repetition, while in the antecedent of a period "the first phrase is not repeated immediately, but united with more remote (contrasting) motive-forms." The completion of the sentence is "a kind of development, comparable in some respect to the technique of 'liquidation,'" while in the period the consequent is "a modified repetition of the antecedent."[8] Schoenberg quotes examples from Haydn's piano sonatas for sentence structure (42 G II, Trio; 42 G III; 45 A III; 43 E♭ I; 34 D I; 55 B♭ I; 53 e II; 33 c I; four of these are main themes of opening movements). He believes that real period-structure main themes were rare in the works of the Viennese Classical composers and quotes only works in other genres by Haydn.

I have decided to be eclectic in my choice of terminology, referring to eighteenth-century treatises or modern analytic ideas as they prove useful. The value of a chronological study of Haydn's themes is clear. Haydn composed solo keyboard sonatas for most of his career. First, the inexperienced young composer simply imitated local styles. In his first mature sonatas, he developed a highly individual style. Around 1780, he further developed this personal style to pro-

6. Heinrich Christoph Koch, *Musikalisches Lexikon* (Frankfurt a.M., 1802; facs. reprint, Hildesheim, 1969), col. 1290.

7. If periods are expanded into a complex principal period, then, according to Koch, the longest *Hauptperiode* equals the exposition of the sonata form (see Elaine Sisman's "Small and Expanded Forms").

8. Arnold Schoenberg, *Fundamentals of Musical Composition,* ed. Gerald Strang and Leonard Stein (London, 1967), 21, 25, 58, 29; see also 20–22, 25–31, 58–59. The distinction is also briefly discussed in Edward T. Cone, *Musical Form and Musical Performance* (New York, 1968), 29, 43.

duce one that soon set a standard for the age, a standard imitated by many contemporaries. A consideration of the opening themes of Haydn's sonatas in chronological order, beginning with the fundamental types of sonatas composed in the second half of the 1760s, allows us to gain some insight into Haydn's thinking and development.

1. *The Main Types of Opening Themes in Sonatas*

A detailed description of motivic content is not necessary for a comparative survey of the forms of primary themes (P; see fig. 17). It suffices to symbolize the thematic material. "AA" stands for phrases of similar content or phrases that at least have a motivically similar beginning. "AB" stands for strongly contrasting phrases or thematic sections. It is important to mark the cadences of phrases to show Haydn's "punctuation" in the opening theme. Haydn occasionally uses an open–closed pattern ("-, -."), but more frequently he uses a pattern of two closures of differing intensities ("-. -.") or else a closed–open pattern ("-. -,"). Also significant is the length, in measures, of the phrases within a theme because it is possible to compare the real length of the themes and the proportions of phrases. (In order to know the actual number of beats and the actual sizes and proportions of phrases, it is necessary to make a distinction between short measures and long measures, using small-size numbers for measures of $\frac{2}{4}$, $\frac{6}{8}$, etc. and large-size numbers for measures of $\frac{4}{4}$ or $\frac{3}{4}$.) Even at this point, furthermore, it is necessary to note if P arrives at the establishment of the second key (marked // in the figure) or if there is an elision or phrase overlap with the last bar of P being simultaneously the first bar of T. Elision is relatively rare in the first themes of Haydn's sonatas and indicates a special relation between P and T.

Figure 17 classifies twenty-eight opening themes, giving some fundamental insights about chronological and stylistic trends regarding the symmetrical model, with AA content, and the asymmetrical model, with strong thematic contrast. The symmetrical model begins to take shape around 1771 and seems especially favored by Haydn in the decade when he was writing sonatas in sets. The simple symmetry of his early works[9] has by this point transformed itself into a highly organized, sophisticated symmetry. The three prototypes—20 B♭, 32 g, and 33 c—are similar in that, in each, the two phrases are the same length and

9. In the eleven unquestionably authentic early sonatas, the most common form of opening theme is 4 + 4 measures (A.A,), seen in 6 C, 13 G, and 16 D. There are two examples of 4 + 4 A.B,—1 G and 3 F. The extended second phrase, seen in 11 B♭ (4 + 6 A.B.) and 15 E (4 + 8 A.A,), does not yet mean true asymmetry. In addition to the seven-measure main theme in 9 D, which we have already analyzed, there is a Baroque-like irregular theme in 4 G (7 + 5 A.A,) and a three-phrase theme, which prepares the way for the later asymmetrical archetype, in 14 C (4 + 4 + 4 A.B.B^{v}.).

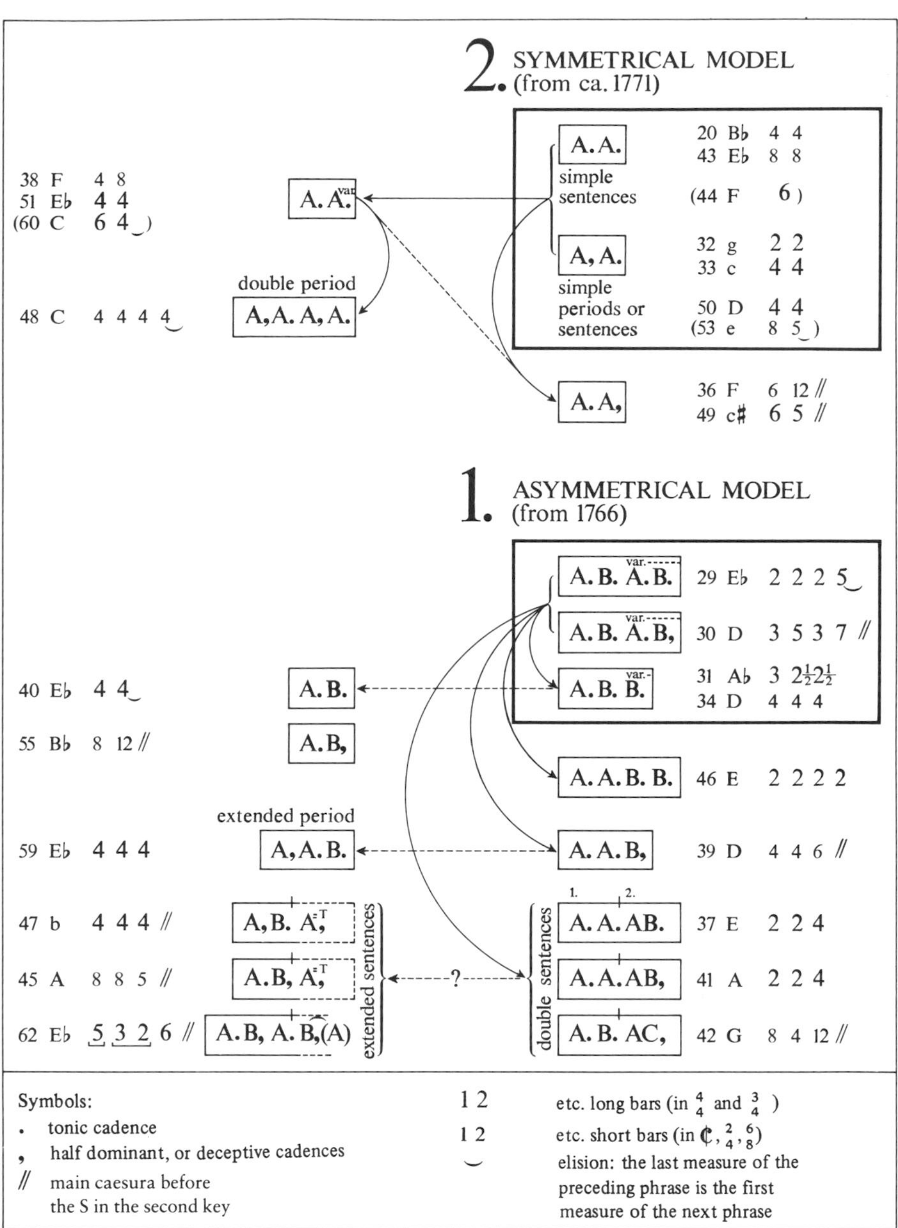

FIGURE 17 The two basic forms of primary themes.

have identical motivic content, at least at the beginnings of the phrases. The absolute lengths of the phrases may be different (8 = 4 ≠ 8), and there are two kinds of cadential structures (A.A.[10] and A,A.). The motivic content is different too. According to Schoenberg's terminology, we would have to call the G minor opening theme a period and the one in C minor a sentence. The more complex organization and the increase in length suggest that the C minor theme is more developed: G minor A(ab), A(ac) = 2,2 measures; C minor A(abbbk^1), A(aaack^2) = 2 + 2, 2 + 2 measures. These prototypes are later developed not only in regular but also in irregular structures. In 48 C there is a double period, in 53 e a period of asymmetrical phrase length, and in 38 F and 60 C similarly asymmetrical sentences. The word *irregular* is, of course, in no way meant to be pejorative. Many times, Haydn gradually developed already established forms into more individual, more original, more irregular formations.

The asymmetric model is earlier and richer in variants. Perhaps it is more characteristic of Haydn; at least it occurs somewhat more frequently. The archetype, first seen in 29 E♭ (1766) and 30 D (1767), is a sentence consisting of a dotted-rhythm A section and a cantabile B section, with varied repetition, all punctuated by tonic cadences.[11] The two sentences, and even the two phrases within the sentence, tend toward asymmetrical proportions. This A B A^v B^v structure appears condensed in the A B B^v structure of the opening theme of 31 A♭, written somewhat later, in which the division of eight measures is entirely asymmetrical. In about 1773, symmetrical phrase lengths begin to outnumber asymmetrical ones (34 D), and various P structures appear with weaker contrasts—double sentences, simple sentences, or, occasionally, extended simple sentences. Some of the three- and four-phrase themes beginning with AA may also be related to the symmetrical types; very individual themes, such as the A,A.B. extended period in the *Genzinger* Sonata, cannot be classified mechanically into either group.

2. *Character, Expression, Originality*

Many writers in the Baroque era, from Descartes to Mattheson and Quantz, discussed the power of music to evoke or alter feelings in the listener. These ideas

10. Note, however, that in the theme of 20 B♭ (mm. 4 and 8, respectively) a phenomenon similar to the contrast of half close and full close takes place in the melody:

11. 30 D, without a real T area, arrives at a half cadence.

were amplified in the nineteenth century to suggest that certain stereotyped musical figures communicated specific information.[12] Of course, Haydn was not a Baroque composer. His musical language and his theoretical and aesthetic assumptions cannot be explained by the doctrine of affections. Nevertheless, in his time certain rhythms and motives could be grouped to suggest general thematic characters. Specifically, unambiguous characters of opening themes, as, for example, in a dotted, march-like character, could serve as a signal for the listener. The presentation of a theme in an already well-known character needed to be amplified by new formulations, new expressions, and the striking presence of the composer's originality.

Thus, it is useful to group opening themes of sonatas according to characteristic types. The following survey groups the sonatas according to those types; it is not chronological. Let us begin with the most frequent type—themes with dotted rhythms and their variants.

Dotted rhythm with contrasting cantabile. This type first appears in sonatas written toward the end of the 1760s, sonatas with opening movements in a moderato tempo. Its purest formulation is found in 29 E♭ and 30 D. (The contrasting cantabile in 31 A♭ and, to a certain extent, in 33 c can be derived from the same type.) The essential feature of the type is the contrast of an assertively instrumental figure with a lyrical, vocal-style melody. Two different rhythmic patterns characterize the contrasting motives (see ex. 100).

Ex. 100. *a,* 29 E♭. *b,* 30 D.

In 30 D, the potentials of the contrast of instrumental and vocal ideas are expanded with superb richness—an application of C. P. E. Bach's principle of *veränderte Reprise.* The faster dotted rhythm of the opening measures is later dissolved into gentle triplets, while the slow dotted rhythm and large leaps of the contrasting theme are filled in with coloratura scales (see ex. 101).

12. For a critical view of *Affektenlehre,* see George J. Buelow, "Rhetoric and Music," in *The New Grove,* vol. 6.

Ex. 101. 30 D.

The originality of 29 E♭ (see ex. 102) lies in the playfulness of the motivic organization. Nearly every tiny fragment of P is derived from the interval of a third (a), announced in the first two notes of the piece. The third can be filled in with a dotted motive (b) or a fluttering rhythmic embellishment (c), it can be inverted and presented in a more melodic style (d) and the left hand can present the same motive in imitation or in parallel thirds.

Ex. 102. 29 E♭.

Dotted "monochrome" rhythm. The second type is used frequently in dilettante-style sonatas in a simpler, more lyrical vein. In this type, the whole theme, sometimes the whole movement, is built on an economical set of rhythmic patterns well suited to one another in size and shade—what I call *monochrome* rhythm. Dotted rhythms always play a significant role in these themes, sometimes supplemented by ♫♩ and ♬♬. After 1780, Haydn alters his notational practice, as we have mentioned before, writing these themes in augmented rhythm, frequently as sonatas with ₵ meter and with faster tempo indications.

Individuality in this monochrome type is often the result of emphasis on a certain performance technique or manner (see ex. 103). 20 B♭ emphasizes turns, 36 C short trills, 38 F staccato eighth notes, 48 C sharp staccatos and short appoggiaturas, and 55 B♭ quasi overdotted passages notated with rests and tied notes. Perhaps the two most striking themes, 20 B♭ and 48 C, are as unlike one another as could be. In 20 B♭, composed around 1771, Haydn complements the neat and strong cadences of the first phrase with the exquisite ornamental fluency of the cadence of the second phrase (see ex. 104). The performer may emphasize this by balancing strict rhythms with rubato playing.

Ex. 103. *a,* 20 B♭. *b,* 36 C. *c,* 38 F. *d,* 48 C. *e,* 55 B♭.

Ex. 104. 20 B♭.

The opening movement of 48 C, composed a decade later, can be impressively played by any performer who simply reads the rhythm accurately, for certain subtleties are composed right in. The right-hand theme is completely symmetric and strongly articulated within itself, but the sudden changes in the left-hand motion in the closing bars of the phrases (mm. 8 and 16) elide the phrases, welding the articulation and building up a longer textural surface in which rhythm is perceived as being central.

Themes in dotted rhythms with overdotted motives. Our third type of opening theme is found most frequently in the more elaborate movements in a moderato tempo. Its most characteristic rhythmic feature is the coexistence in the theme of dotted motives on different rhythmic levels, first slow dotted formulas with the smallest written note a 𝅘𝅥𝅯, followed by dotted formulas in which the smallest written note is a 𝅘𝅥𝅰, giving the appearance of rhythmic diminution. This notation reflects a Baroque convention: musicians in Haydn's time certainly performed the dotted figures as shown in example 105.

Ex. 105. *a,* 16 D. *b,* 28 D (fragment).

The opening themes of 31 A♭, 40 E♭, and 51 E♭, sonatas all in rather conservative styles, vigorously make use of contrasting levels of dotted rhythm— ♪.𝅘𝅥𝅯, ♪.𝅘𝅥𝅰, and also ♩ ♪.𝅘𝅥𝅯 in 31 A♭ (see ex. 106). As was explained in the first part of this book (pp. 87–89), these places should be played so that the shorter note of a dotted pair is adjusted to be no longer than the shortest note in the passage, here a 𝅘𝅥𝅰. That is, the slower dotted motives need to be double dotted. In these themes, the slower dotted pair is presented first; thus, there is always a sense of diminution as the passage proceeds, whether or not the performer double dots. The opening theme of 33 c is another type. Here, the three rhythmic terraces constitute one of the basic features of the theme.

Complex dotted-rhythm themes. Three further, very original opening themes, 41 A, 45 A, and 62 E♭, make use of dotted rhythms but are distinct from the types of themes already discussed. The characteristic feature of these themes is their very wide compass, going beyond the one- to two-octave range of the themes mentioned above. In addition, the texture of the themes of 41 A and 62 E♭ is unusual owing to the strong linear and contrapuntal elaboration. The left and right hands have almost equal roles in presenting the motivic material. 45 A is unusual in its marshaling of three different varieties of march-like dotted rhythms—the brilliant (ex. 107*a*), the conventional (ex. 107*b*), and the Scarlatti-like version (ex. 107*c*) that, at the same time, would almost fit into Schumann's *Kinderszenen.*

a Allegro moderato

b Moderato

c Allegro moderato

d (Allegro) Moderato

Ex. 106. *a,* 31 A♭. *b,* 40 E♭. *c,* 51 E♭. *d,* 33 c.

Ex. 107. 45 A.

The sophisticated organization of the other two themes deserves a closer view of their motivic content. Examples 108 and 109 present my analysis of their phrase structure and motivic content. The A major theme (ex. 108) could have been an ideal for the 1770s, while the E♭ major theme is a masterpiece of mature Classical style, foreshadowing Beethoven. Even a twentieth-century serial composer would find that there is no "free note" in the A major theme. The energy-accumulating first micro-move (a[1]) starts a chain reaction. Conventional motivic elaboration such as fragmentation, variation, imitation, and contrary motion can be discovered in the theme along with a variety of less conventional but very Haydnesque techniques such as diminution and extension in rhythm and the contrast of different octave ranges and of dense and transparent textures.

The organization of the E♭ major theme (ex. 109) is also remarkable; it is fascinating to see how the small ornamental scale fragment of the first measure (x) obtains motivic meaning in measure 3, then serves as a transition between measures in measure 5, finally becoming a strong closing gesture in measure 10, rushing downward through the full compass of everything presented thus far. The middle voice of the opening chords, e♭-d♭-c, is the source of the melodic line in measures 6–7. The fragmentation of the first two measures of the theme, combined with rhythmic diminution and compression in measures 4–5, is ingenious. Probably the cleverest idea is the use of the material of measure 6 for a transition, starting in measure 10, written in a kind of invertible counterpoint. Yet the most original feature of this theme, adumbrating Beethoven's fully developed piano style, is textural—the rich variation and structural use of the different registers of the piano as well as changes in the number of voices. For example, compare measures 1 and 9, 2 and 3, or note the grand passage that sweeps away the chords in measures 9–10.

Closed-form themes. When Haydn composed two sonatas in minor keys, around 1771, he seems to have been searching for a new type of opening theme, one different from the works in major. (The same procedure can be observed in the quartets and symphonies written at about the same time.) The main themes of 32 g and 33 c have a kind of "abstract" instrumental character. Not only are they symmetrical, but they have a rigorous organization of texture and motivic elaboration as well. It would be easy to transcribe these openings for string trio, given their strict three-voice texture and the high level of rhythmic cohesion between the melody and accompanying voices. The first two phrases of the G minor opening theme are, to borrow a term from another musical realm, *isorhythmic,*[13] a feature also found in 34 D, written some years later, in an idiomatic keyboard style with a much more playful character. The C minor theme has its divertimento-style analogue in 46 E (see ex. 110).

13. *Isorhythm,* the repetition of a rhythmic pattern throughout a voice part, is a term used both by writers on medieval music and by ethnomusicologists. Béla Bartók called melodies in which the rhythm of all the phrases of a four-line stanza is the same *isorhythmic.*

Ex. 108. Motivic organization of the opening theme of the A Major Sonata, no. 41.

Ex. 109. Motivic organization of the opening theme of the E♭ Major (*London*) Sonata, no. 62.

Ex. 110. *a,* 32 g. *b,* 34 D. *c,* 46 E.

The C minor theme, which appears to have made a deep impression on Brahms—or so several of his themes would suggest—deserves closer investigation (see ex. 111). The harmonic background of the opening motives unambiguously establishes C minor. The micro-organization of the first eight measures is almost inexhaustibly rich in organic references and details. The transformations of the head motive (1–2) are unusually varied and present a real challenge for the performer. As is shown in example 111*b*, there are variations with anacrusis (3, 4, 5), syncopation ("per arsin et thesin") in diminished rhythm (11–12), doubly diminished dotted rhythm (9, 10), and dotted rhythm in normal diminution (13). All three appearances of the scale that descends from a♭^{2} to b^1 lead to the cadence with different rhythmic patterns (I, II, and III in ex. 111*b*). The second section of the theme starts an octave lower than the first, a procedure also seen in 36 C and 46 E.[14] Haydn makes an ingenious transition to the original octave, arriving at the peak note of the theme at the end of measure 6 by means of an ascending natural minor scale.[15]

14. In 40 E♭, the second part of the theme is restated an octave higher.

15. Late eighteenth-century theory considered the minor scale without any specific name to be what we call melodic minor, i.e., a scale that ascending has a minor third degree but major sixth and seventh degrees and descending is the same as the natural minor scale. When Mozart notated the

Ex. 111. 33 c.

This highly sophisticated profile of metric and rhythmic accents in the opening theme is a true test for our understanding of Haydn's rhetoric. Riemann would have interpreted this theme as a half-measure anacrusis, placing the real metric accents on the third quarters of the bars. Many musicians would stress the first beat in such an opening measure. But in the second measure the voice leading into the cadence requires the primary accent to fall on the third beat. The third and fourth measures also have a stronger stress on the third beat. In measures 5–7, the accented changes of rhythm, motive, and texture at the beginning of each measure throw the stress onto the first beat. In measure 8, beats 1 and 3 are equally accented.

Measure	1 2 3 4 5 6 7 8
Accented beat in the measure	1 - - 3 - 3 - 3 1 - 1 - 1 - 1 3

Idiomatic keyboard themes. In contrast to the many cantabile opening themes that start out with a melodic line, a few sonatas, mostly in a moderato tempo, begin with some striking instrumental effect. In those sonatas that begin with silence-breaking broken chords or tutti-style head motives, one gets the impression that Haydn wished to transfer to the harpsichord the concept of a full orchestra versus quiet strings as in his symphonies. After a few less skillful attempts,[16] there is a perfectly formed theme in 15 E, among the last of the early divertimento sonatas. Another main theme of this type is that of 37 E (Haydn may have retained the key consciously or unconsciously) from the *Esterházy* series, written in 1773 (see ex. 112).

---

minor scale for his student Thomas Attwood, he wrote A-B-C-D-E-F♯-G♯-A A-G-F-E-D-C-B-A (see *Attwood Studies*, ed. Daniel Heartz et al., Neue Mozart-Ausgabe, x/30/1).

16. See the main themes of 2 C and 3 F.

Ex. 112. *a,* 15 E. *b,* 37 E.

The six-measure opening theme of 44 F, sketched in 1774, is more manifestly symphonic (see ex. 113). The combination of a many-voiced opening chord, insistently repeated tonic bass note (a theme that would lie comfortably on strings or woodwinds), and the string-and-timpani rhythm in measures 1 and 4 is exceptional in the idiom of Haydn's solo keyboard sonatas.

Ex. 113. 44 F.

There is reason to believe that the two opening themes in minor written around 1776–80, 47 b and 49 c♯, also had symphonic inspiration.[17] The rhythm of the B minor theme in the right hand may refer to the unison beginning of the Symphony no. 46 in B Major or the Symphony no. 44 in E Minor. The unison opening theme of 49 c♯, the only unison first theme among Haydn's mature keyboard sonatas, is evidently a more advanced version of the same type. One more

17. The close ties between these two themes and their Haydnesque character, beyond the strong similarity between the motives with the repeated dominant note right after the head motive, are thrown into relief when we compare them with the opening of Mozart's Sonata in A Minor, K. 310, composed at about the same time, 1778. Mozart's theme has a much denser but more idiomatic fortepiano texture, with forceful left-hand chords.

strong similarity between the two themes is the singing, repeated dominant note in the second measure, right after the head motive (see ex. 114).

Ex. 114. *a,* 47 b. *b,* 49 c♯.

Another special case, again in minor, is the opening theme of 53 e. Instead of being characterized by contrasts, exquisite detail, and noble style, the opening theme is simple and full of pathos, strongly foreshadowing Beethoven. The ostinato rhythm and the continuous alternation of groups of staccato and legato notes build up a long arch and accumulate an energy not typical of Haydn's sonatas. This energy is released with dramatic force in measure 14, where a change in dynamics and right-hand rhythm sweeps in the new key, G major.[18]

We should not neglect a group of opening themes with less strikingly marked but still very attractive and playful instrumental effects. 50 D and possibly 42 G suggest external influences; they are in part reminiscent of Scarlatti. The

18. Another unusual feature of this opening theme is its harmonic rhythm. In spite of alterations in mm. 6–8, mm. 1–8 form a single arch traveling from the tonic, via the strongly accentuated subdominant (m. 4), to the dominant. In general, the harmonic rhythm of the opening themes in Haydn's sonatas is simpler and more tonic centered. Some first themes—e.g., 44 F I, 1–6—rest on an almost purely tonic plane, but most typical are themes based on the progressions I-V-I-IV-I (31 A♭) or I-IV-I-V-I (34 D and 41 A). The abundance of subdominant chords in 50 D or submediant chords and chords built on ♯IV in 40 E♭ and 46 E gives these opening themes a Baroque flavor. The inclusion of the Neapolitan sixth chords in the cadence is characteristic of themes in minor keys, as in 33 c and 49 c♯. Naturally, quite a number of opening themes use the chord progression I-IV-V-I. However, the assertion by Riemann and his followers that the subdominant function is as important as the tonic and dominant function in the Classical style is certainly not borne out in Haydn's sonatas. Such a "regular" new-style theme is the still rather timid I-IV-V-I-IV+V-I progression in mm. 1–6 of 36 C. See also the themes of 45 A or 51 E♭; in the latter, the harmonies revolve around the tonic center. The opening themes of Haydn's keyboard sonatas seldom contain real harmonic surprises. This contrasts with some of his string quartets written in the 1780s and 1790s, such as op. 50 D, which starts off the tonic, op. 33 B♭, which starts on a secondary degree, or op. 33 b, whose theme fluctuates ambiguously between two keys.

ingenious opening of 60 C also belongs in this group. The cryptic, bare-bones opening seems to adumbrate Beethoven's trick of first presenting a very simple, abstract *Urform,* with a more idiomatically instrumental version following, as in the finale of the *Eroica* Symphony, but one need not push this comparison very far. Haydn's idea is extremely sophisticated, and the material is potentially explosive. In the first six measures, the whole progression gets thicker and more urgent, punctuated by the staccato notes. Starting in measure 7 as the strongest possible contrast to this abstract thematic phrase, he immediately states the theme in its full flesh-and-blood form (see ex. 115).

Ex. 115. 60 C.

Opening themes in triple meter. Sonata-allegro forms in $\frac{3}{4}$ that are not stylized or accelerated minuets are relatively rare in Haydn's music; hence, the opening themes of such movements are of particular interest. The three mature movements in $\frac{3}{4}$—39 D, 43 E♭, and 59 E♭—present extremely coherent, vigorous, and disciplined thematic ideas. The set of rhythmic patterns is considerably simpler than in similar themes in duple meter. The opening theme of 43 E♭, from the

Anno 1776 set, still has some connections with related types in $\frac{4}{4}$, connections such as the left hand starting with a rest, thus emphasizing the melody in the right hand, the right-hand figuration in measures 10–11, and the sequences of one-measure-long motives in measures 12–15. The opening theme of 39 D, however, is a genuinely original conception. Rippling down from a graceful ornament, it is a relaxed and poetic harpsichord-type cantilena with loose metric and harmonic contours, which contrast with the following toccata-like sections in sixteenth-note motion. The nearly exact correspondence of the A.A.B, form of this first theme to the A,A.B. form of the opening theme of 59 E♭ cannot be accidental.

The opening theme of 59 E♭, the *Genzinger* Sonata, is one of the most perfect and characteristic themes of Haydn's keyboard music and as such deserves close scrutiny. The intriguing element here concerns the rhythmic organization of the motives that make up the theme. Motive *a* (see ex. 116) establishes the key, meter, and tempo with its relatively static rhythm (two ♪ upbeat to four ♪ beat). Motive *b,* in contrast, has a more kinetic rhythmic pattern (three ♪ upbeat to three ♪ beat) that swings up to a subdominant harmony with an appoggiatura above it and descends to a half cadence on an incomplete dominant seventh. These two motives form an organic, contrasting pair. Note, however, that motive *c,* which initiates the bridge passage, whirls along with a one ♪ to five ♪ rhythm. At the end of the T passage, in measures 20–22, there is a return to the rhythm of motive b, with its ***fz*** accent shifted to the upbeat, that slows the passage down to the fermata before the secondary theme.

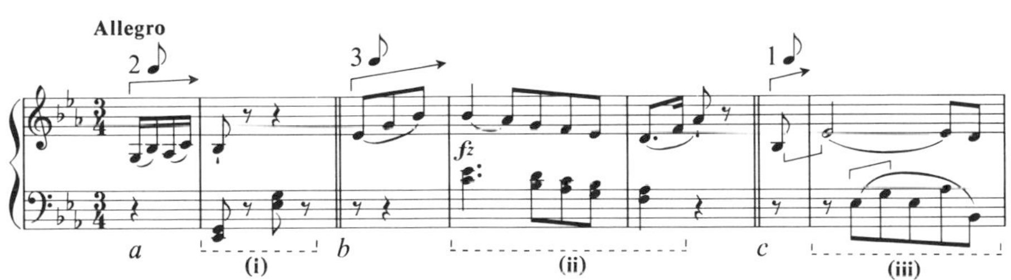

Ex. 116. Rhythmic organization of the three motives (*a–c*) in the opening theme of the *Genzinger* Sonata, 59 E♭, with rhythmic bass (i), synchronous bass (ii), and bass emphasizing the right-hand melody (iii).

Is it misleading to define the A,A.B. form of the twelve-measure opening theme as an extended period? Is it an irregular, overrefined variant of the classic A,A. period? Or is the concept of period counterproductive in analyzing this theme? These twelve measures sound like a perfectly natural statement of a theme (see ex. 117). The cadence of the antecedent phrase in measure 4 raises expectations on several levels, expectations that the cadence of the consequent phrase in measure 8 satisfies only in part. Since the tonic chord is in the first inversion, the melody ends on a weak beat after ascending to the fifth and in a sense starts on a weakened first beat because of the ornament; this cadence accumulates tensions that require some further resolution. As in a bar form, the third phrase provides the final resolution. The motivic content of measures 9–12 is organic but condensed (instead of a a b b there is an a b k k composite), and the cadence is as strong as one could desire in an opening theme. The bar form is also emphasized by the range covered by the two hands. The third phrase is simultaneously an opening up of the ambitus and a summary, an expansion to a higher tessitura and an emphatic statement of E♭ in four different octaves.

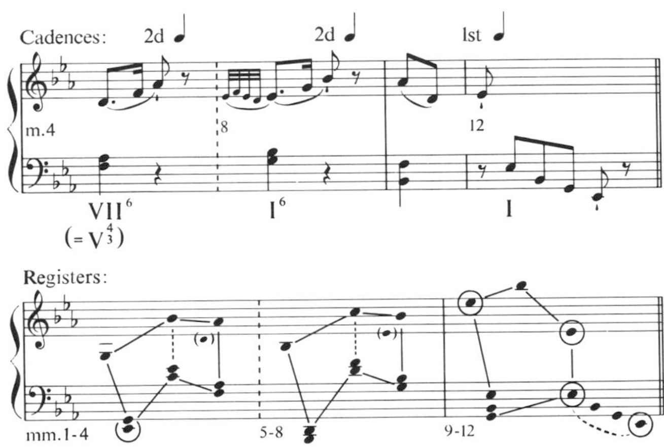

Ex. 117. 59 E♭.

This opening theme differs from the block-like main themes of some earlier sonatas primarily in its potential for continuation. In 33 c, the extremely rich but strict eight-measure theme gives no hint as to how it will continue. What and how long will the transitional theme be? In 59 E♭, it is quite natural that the twelve-measure primary theme be followed by a twelve-measure T section that contains P elements and makes a bridge to the secondary theme area, also based on P. The opening theme determines its continuation.

3. *Idiomatic Primary Themes in the Piano Trios*

In order to arrive at a deeper understanding of the idiom of Haydn's keyboard sonatas and to illustrate some differences between the genres, let us look at a few primary themes of first movements of some mature trios, composed from 1784 on. In his trios, Haydn avoids opening themes that abound in details and are richly articulated with rests and changes of texture. Instead, the trio themes show an easy and natural coordination of the instruments producing an effective chamber-music style characterized by "a brilliance and a massivity."[19] The texture of the trio themes is simpler and more continuous. The emphasis in the thematic contours lies in motivic elaboration. Motives are often welded into larger arches supported by continuous motion in the left hand of the keyboard part. A comparison of the opening themes of the Trio in F, Hob. XV:6, and the Sonata no. 44 in F provides a good illustration of differences in thematic construction in the two genres. The sonata (see ex. 113) was composed ten years earlier than the trio.[20] When Haydn remolded its primary theme, he produced an opening that is less orchestral and less colorful, despite the use of three instruments instead of one. On the other hand, the structure has a new sweeping force (see ex. 118). The right hand has not even a quarter note's worth of rest for thirteen measures, and the first break in the texture comes only after twenty-five measures.

Ex. 118. XV:6 F.

The lighter trios, including the flute trios, favor short opening themes, with the structure A.A. or A,A., that join up with the transitional material without a strong demarcation. A few of these trios contain P structures and rhythmic styles reminiscent of certain solo keyboard sonatas, for example, XV:30 E♭, but they are not the majority. Compositional techniques that Haydn considered particularly appropriate to and effective for trios include the curtain-raiser chord, as in XV:18 A, 24 D, and 29 E♭; the curtain-raiser chord built into the theme, as in XV:8 B♭; and using a slow introduction to foreshadow motivic material that will be taken up in the subsequent fast movement, as in the Adagio pastorale and the Vivace assai of XV:21 C.

The most idiomatic opening themes of the piano trios combine quiet and cohesion of detail with assertive, long melodic arches in vigorous concertante style. The wide range of expression and atmosphere that Haydn explores can be illustrated, on the one hand, by the explosive piano texture ranging widely over the keyboard in XV:20 B♭ and, on the other, by the softly hummed melody that evokes the effect of a string quartet in XV:24 D (see ex. 119).

19. Rosen, *Classical Style,* 358.

20. Similarly, the opening theme of 45 A was probably the source for the beginning of the Trio in D Major, Hob. XV:16. In this case, the sonata was composed thirteen or fourteen years before the trio, and there are differences in meter and notation.

Ex. 119. *a,* XV:20 B♭. *b,* XV:24 D.

Among the trios that Haydn composed after his visits to London, there are two with extremely ingenious and idiomatic opening themes (see ex. 120). The linear design of XV:27 C is brought out in the chiseled arpeggios, which are marked staccato, in the strings, and in the contrary motion of the voice parts, which converge, cross, and rebound. The characteristic sound of the opening of XV:28 E results from the simultaneous playing of smoothly connected and detached lines. The melody in the right hand of the piano, marked with slurs and with the direction *tenute,*[21] must be played very smoothly. The violin doubles this melody, but pizzicato. The cello also plays pizzicato, reinforcing the detached line of the left hand of the piano part. The middle voice in the piano part, played mostly by the right-hand thumb, is a carefully notated imitation of strings playing pizzicato.

Ex. 120. *a,* XV:27 C. *b,* XV:28 E.

It is clear that, if keyboard sonatas allow a maximum of individuality in performance and string quartets demand disciplined ensemble performance, the last piano trios stand somewhere between these extremes. The pianist in a trio is chief among equals. He has a freer reign than the first violinist in a quartet to direct actively, passionately, and personally the progress of the music. He is, however, less free than the performer of a solo sonata.

As a final intergenre comparison, let us return to 62 E♭ and examine its opening theme alongside that of two other late works in E♭—a London piano trio, XV:22, composed about 1794–95, and the String Quartet op. 64, composed in 1790 with a London public in mind (see ex. 121).

The quartet theme, kept at a soft dynamic level, radiates magnetic tension.

21. The recent *JHW* urtext should be preferred to the older Doblinger urtext edition by H. C. Robbins Landon.

Ex. 121. *a*, XV:22 E♭. *b*, Op. 64, E♭.

The four-measure phrases project a self-assured tranquillity that is paradoxically heightened by the expressive rests. The rhythmic structure is simple, with accelerated motion (i.e., two halves slurred, four quarters slurred, a pair of two-quarter-note slurs, a pair of ♩.♪ slurs, and a staccato quarter) in both the antecedent and the consequent phrases. The piano trio begins with a pair of contrasting phrases; the spaciousness and dignity of the arpeggiated chords in the first four measures are set against the restless and exuberant motion in the next four measures. Rhythmic changes are reinforced by changes in dynamics. The phrases have a quiet symmetry, and there are no strong changes in texture between the antecedent and the consequent phrases or between the opening theme and the bridge passage. The pianist has the major responsibility for unfolding the beauties of this theme but for the sake of the ensemble cannot take too many agogic liberties. The uniqueness of the theme of 62 E♭ is emphasized by a comparison with these two other works. It is passionate, capricious music, full of pathos, punctuated by rests, pushed into extremes of *piano* and *forte,* involving a precise rendition of certain rhythms as well as great freedom and creativity, all in all demanding a highly individual interpretation from the performer.

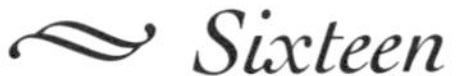 *Sixteen*

Continuation: Secondary Group, Closing Group, *and* Fantasia-Like Insertions

After the statement of the primary group, personal reflexes and individual procedures are more strongly asserted. In the continuation of the exposition we cannot expect the kind of originality manifested, in Haydn's mature style, in every opening theme. Nor can we expect here the complexity of material and form embodied in even a simple primary subject. If we had an instrument capable of measuring the density of musical information in proportion to time, we would find that in Haydn's expositions it is exceptional to find areas as rich in information as the primary group. By *information* I mean any kind of data or musical stimulus that can be grasped intellectually or emotionally. A bit of information may be a new element or one that reminds us of something already known. A familiar element can behave according to our expectations, or it can surprise us.

It therefore seems natural, after our close inspection of first themes, to analyze the continuation of the exposition, primarily in order to see common compositional procedures in structure and reflexes characteristic of the composer in parallel situations. In searching for the best analytic methods for this, the interests of the musicologist and the performer might lead in different directions. For example, the musicologist interested in Haydn's *Personalstil* might find little of interest in routine methods; he might not be intrigued by how a piece in C major gropes about and finds the dominant and strengthens it with cadences. One of the main tasks of the performer, on the other hand, is to relive the search, the attainment and establishment of the new key in its unparalleled dramatic force, and to convey this experience to listeners. Fortunately, for the most important questions, the interests of the analyst, historian, and performer are linked. Is the primary theme followed by contrasting material or by an organic continuation?

What outstandingly beautiful or original contrasting sections are there in the exposition? What is the relation between the primary group and the rest of the material? What motivic, rhythmic, textural, and emotional references are there in the exposition that demand the conscious attention of the performer?

1. *Transition*

Not every sonata exposition contains an independent transition, a bridge passage. We have already noted that, in about one-quarter of the expositions, the primary group cadences on the dominant, making possible an immediate statement of the secondary theme or a substituting fantasia-like insertion in the second key (see fig. 17 above). In the other sonatas, there are two basic types of transition—one that makes a strong contrast with the primary group and one that forms an organic continuation.

Contrasting transition is the more archaic type in Haydn's sonatas. In the "workshop" sonatas of 1766–71, which had long, elaborated, closed P blocks, Haydn built his transitions from new motivic material and, more important, new textures and basically different rhythmic material. In some instances, in order to achieve interest in the continuation Haydn even started the transition in a foreign key. Examples of this type are in 20 B♭, 31 A♭, 33 c, and 44 F; 34 D and 43 E♭ can also be grouped here. In major-mode sonatas, Haydn often increases the impact of T novelties in such a way that the first phrase of T is presented, mostly unprepared, in the parallel minor—the new key area of the second sequence (see ex. 122).

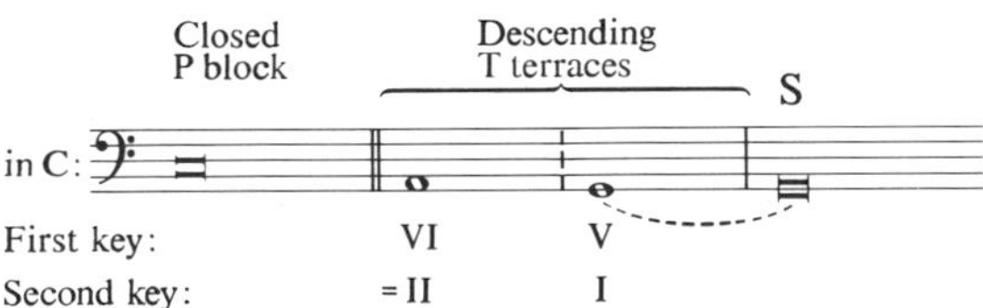

Ex. 122.

Examples of this technique are in 20 B♭, 31 A♭, 43 E♭, and 46 E. The same harmonic procedure appears in other transitions as well, for example, in 29 E♭ I, 15; 40 E♭ I, 12; and 62 E♭ I, 10–11.[1] In 33 c, the contrast in rhythm and texture is most effective. Note the attractive contrasts in rhythm (overcrowded ornaments vs. even sixteenth-note passages), dynamics (in addition to ***f*** and ***p***

1. It is noteworthy how strong a pull C minor had for Haydn when he composed sonatas in E♭.

phrases, a ***p-f-p-f*** shift of accents in m. 14), and texture (after the strict three-voice texture of P, a dialogue of four-voice and one-voice textures). The harmonic plan here is a pair of ascending sequences, a statement in A♭ followed by a statement in B♭. Although arriving quickly at the dominant of E♭ by this procedure, Haydn avoids any clear-cut cadence in the new key until the closing area (see ex. 123).

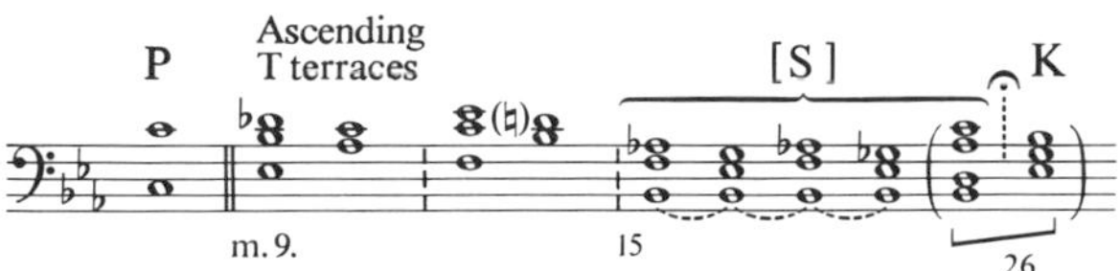

Ex. 123. Harmonic plan of the transition in 33 c.

The *organic transition* makes a first tentative appearance in 32 g at about the same time and with the same type of strict P blocks as the contrasting transition. The primary theme of 32 g, a closed four-measure block, is stated in strict three-voice texture; the transition, beginning in measure 6, contrasts in rhythm, texture, and key. Measure 5, built on motives from P, mediates between P and T (see ex. 124).[2]

Ex. 124. Organic transition in 32 g.

A new style of organic continuation is to be found in the popular 48 C. In this movement, the various themes are organically derived, step by step, from P. Essential to these themes are three rhythmic elements—a dotted rhythm on the second and fourth beats, repeated staccato quarter notes, and eighth-note triplets, normally in the accompaniment but occasionally replacing the dotted figure as a pickup. The two main melodic motives, Pa and Pb, are indicated in example 125.

2. 38 F follows a similar pattern. In 39 D and 45 A, one may argue as to what to call the pivot point—mm. 15 and 17, respectively. But whether we decide that S = P or that the last phrase of P = T, the key to the continuation is the restatement of the head motive of P.

Ex. 125. 48 C.

The transitional sections in the expositions of 55 B♭, 60 C, and 62 E♭ have similarly organic continuations. The rhythmically organic transition of 59 E♭ has already been mentioned in relation to its first theme (see ex. 116 above). We find an organic treatment of the rhythm in the exposition of 51 E♭ as well.[3]

2. *Second Theme Area*

The concept of a contrasting, "lyrical" second theme, a cornerstone of some textbook explanations of sonata form, is not one derived from the study of Haydn's works. Contrasting second themes are found more frequently in Mozart's works and still more frequently during Beethoven's time. In the last third of the eighteenth century, however, a contrasting second subject was certainly neither a requisite nor an ideal. Koch suggests that the cantabile sentence (*cantabler Satz*)

3. An interesting case of a sonata not fitting into either of the two main T types is 53 e. Here, the alternation, in stark contrast, of blocks of thematic material in eighth notes and blocks of motivic elaboration in sixteenth notes takes precedence over other sonata procedures.

should not be in utter contrast to the primary theme but should rather present a specific variation reminiscent of it. In 1777, Carl Ludwig Junker stated, "Each secondary subject [*Nebenthemata*] is a consequence of the original ruling passion of the work and so is related to it. Otherwise the whole piece will be incoherent, and the fundamental emotion will remain hidden."[4]

If we do not want to replace one incorrect concept with a new and equally fallacious one, we must be conscious of this point: in Haydn's sonata-form expositions, the secondary group is the most diverse and varied section possible. One lyric theme, more than one secondary theme, a secondary group formed from the primary group, contrasting secondary themes, and a second thematic group without a clear-cut thematic formation are all found in his keyboard sonatas.

The real *cantabler Satz,* a melodic theme contrasting with the main theme, is a type present throughout Haydn's sonata oeuvre. In this type, the melody in the right hand is supported by a steady rhythmic accompaniment in the left hand that supplies energy and ensures cohesion between phrases of several measures. In 29 E♭, a harpsichord sonata, the contrasting theme has the same sweeping force as the contrasting theme of 55 B♭, written in the fortepiano style of the 1780s (see ex. 126). For that matter, both secondary subjects of 59 E♭ are also supported by Alberti basses.

Ex. 126. *a,* 29 E♭. *b,* 55 B♭.

Contrasting themes built on arpeggios, completed with either an ascending sequence or a melodic closing phrase, are characteristic of the 1770s. In this respect, 32 g and 44 F are close relatives (see ex. 127).

4. Carl Ludwig Junker, *Tonkunst* (Bern, 1777), quoted in Ritzel, *Entwicklung,* 92.

Ex. 127. *a,* 32 g. *b,* 44 F.

The short-motive contrasting theme also appears early in Haydn's sonatas. In 30 D, after an impressive primary-theme block, we find the prototype of a secondary theme built up of one-measure motives, alternating between tonic and dominant over a pedal point. In 33 c, the short-motive secondary subject is more melodic in character (see ex. 128). In other works, such as 47 b (m. 17), the motoric rhythm is the focus of the theme.

Ex. 128. *a,* 30 D. *b,* 33 c.

The short-motive contrasting subject can be seen in its most mature form in 62 E♭. Here, the source motive is juxtaposed with its diminished form, confronting *forte* with *piano* and minor with major (see ex. 129).

Ex. 129. 62 E♭.

Often, a short-motive contrasting theme will have some motivic connection with the primary theme. The first important example of this among the mature sonatas is in 31 A♭. The secondary theme is related to both the primary theme and the transition through the rhythm of sixteenth-note triplets (cf. mm. 4, 10, 13–14, and 18). The secondary theme contrasts strongly with the primary theme, however, in its texture and its regular alternation of tonics and dominants. Motivic references are easily recognizable in 40 E♭, where measure 15 is related to measure 6 and measure 22 (i.e., 2S) derives from measure 15. In other works, these references are less obvious, as in 34 D, in which measure 31 (i.e., 2S) derives from measure 18, or in 38 F, in which measure 21 (1S) refers back to measure 13 (T). Even the potpourri of themes in the exposition of 45 A is united by motivic references, as, for example, when 1S evolves from the extension of P (see ex. 130).

Ex. 130. 45 A.

Finally, let us consider a few modest contrasting themes from the *esserczizi*-type sonatas such as 42 G and 50 D. These themes purposely minimize the contrast in an exposition. More or less regular, sometimes even rigorously symmetric, they establish and confirm the already reached second key.

Before investigating the expositions with monothematic aspirations, let us look at the original and inspired exposition of 41 A, in which fantasia-like sections in the role of a secondary area (mm. 11–24) accumulate more "singing" energy than the song-like themes (see ex. 131).

Ex. 131. 41 A.

The *"varied primary theme" as secondary subject,* or 1S, has no stereotypical model. Similar to the string quartets from op. 33 on, the variant depends on the specific nature of the primary theme. When the melody is kept relatively intact and unchanged, as in 36 C and 51 E♭, the S variant is broken into smaller subphrase units than was the P form of the theme. In 36 C, the four-measure units of P become 2 + 2 units in S; in 51 E♭, the continuous harmonic progression in P is replaced by half-measure articulations in S. Triplet motion, a typical secondary subject rhythm, can contribute to the S-form variant of a primary theme (see ex. 132).

Ex. 132. *a,* 36 C. *b,* 51 E♭.

A particularly fine example of the art of balancing unity and diversity (*Einheit und Mannigfaltigkeit*) can be found in 49 c♯. The beginnings of the primary and secondary themes have many points of contrast—minor versus major, unison versus two-voice counterpoint, staccato versus legato articulation, etc. (see ex. 133). Nevertheless, this sonata shows strong monothematic aspirations. The whole secondary group, measures 12–26, is developed out of material presented in the primary theme. By means of sequences, repetition, and fragmentation, measures 12–16 expand out of motives from measure 1; measures 17–19 are based on measures 2–4, measures 20–23 on measure 5, measures 24–26 on measure 6.

Ex. 133. 49 c♯.

60 C contains a whole S chain formulated from primary-theme material (see ex. 134). Haydn's polyphonic skill is evident in this passage of third species invertible counterpoint. The real subject of the variation process, however, is pianistic articulation and touch. 1S gives a nonlegato presentation of the theme, 2S is a variant with staccato in one hand and legato in the other, and the diminution of measure 31 with new articulation produces 3S.

Ex. 134. 60 C.

The several independent themes—two S and one K—in the exposition of 62 E♭ are introduced by P ritornellos. Since the primary theme is more chordal than melodic–motivic, the variations it undergoes are in the areas of range, density, and position of chords. The two formations known from the P area (see ex. 109 above) are teamed up with two others that announce the S and K areas (see ex. 135).

Ex. 135. 62 E♭.

The secondary-theme area of 59 E♭ is interlarded with thematic material based on the primary theme. The first motive of S is a variant of the beginning of P (Pa[1], m. 25). This is followed by two related melodies based on one of the rhythmic motives from P. Both melodies are supported by a rocking alternation of tonic and dominant harmonies, stated in an Alberti-bass figuration, the second melody weaving above and below the Alberti bass. The effect is similar to two strophes of a poem, or a melody and its variation (see ex. 136).

Ex. 136. 59 E♭.

These tranquil symmetries of the S strophes in the *Genzinger* Sonata are disturbed only at the approaches to the cadences. At the end of 1S (mm. 37–41), an insertion provides an opportunity for pianistic display. The end of 2S is complicated by a dramatic detour, a passage that deserves some further comment. The whole passage starting at measure 50 and extending to the delayed cadence in measures 58–59, with its echoes of "fate knocking at the door," is a single harmonic adventure. Instead of the expected final continuation of B♭, the $a\flat^2$ and the $b\natural^1$ in measure 51 seem to push us toward E♭ major and then C minor, with a deceptive cadence on A♭. The chromatic descent of the lowest voice, a♭-g-g♭-f, returns us to a $^6_4$ cadence in B♭. It is intriguing to note that this type of dramatic detour made an earlier appearance in 49 c♯ and a later one, in a simplified London concert-style variant, in 62 E♭. In all three cases, this "side trip" appears at exactly the same point in the form (see ex. 137).

Ex. 137. *a,* 49 c♯. *b,* 59 E♭. *c,* 62 E♭.

The end of the secondary group was somctimes demarcated in the earlier sonatas by a characteristic slowing down before the closing group. In 33 c, 34 D, and 43 E♭, the end of a fantasia-like section in which the beat seems to dissolve is notated by an *adagio* tempo marking leading to a half cadence marked by a fermata. Among these sonatas, however, only 33 c contains a genuinely peculiar harmonic effect, an unprepared, unresolved dominant ninth chord (see ex. 138).[5]

Ex. 138. 33 c.

3. *Closing Group*

Musical taste in the late eighteenth century expected of the last sentence of the exposition only that it establish the second key by a strong cadence; Haydn's closing material usually does not aspire beyond that. The harmonic content is mainly the alternation of tonic and dominant, occasionally going around a circle of I-IV-V-I two or more times. When the closing group contains altered chords, as in 46 E I, 22, the cadence is reinforced with special care. Repetition of short phrases, occasionally varied, also serves the function of reaching a calming conclusion.

For all this, original ideas are not lacking. Haydn constructs intriguing rhythmic arrangements of various closing motives. In addition to displaying sparkling rhythmic ideas, the closing group of 30 D, for example, establishes a connection between 1K and 3K with the same rhythmic pattern, compressed in diminution. The first part of the closing area of 33 c[6] is built on the basic contrast of short–long and long–short rhythmic patterns; the second part of the closing area uses a five-note descending motive first sparsely (m. 32) and then more densely (m. 34; see ex. 139).

5. The end of the fantasia-like S area in 41 A has no adagio slowing down, but there is a significant ninth chord here too, in m. 24.

6. In spite of the lack of strong tonic closure in m. 31, I consider the K area of 33 c to be mm. 26–37, i.e., the whole *tempo primo* section after the fermata, subdivided as mm. 26–31 and 32–37, and complemented by a genuine codetta motive in m. 37.

Ex. 139. *a,* 30 D. *b,* 33 c.

The isolated coda motives that end the rich flow of musical sentences in the exposition give a fuller sense of Haydn's musical personality. The most beautiful of these may be only a measure or even a half measure long. The most effective ones are the very simple ones, as in 31 A♭, 37 E, and 45 A, or those with a touch of pathos, as in 33 c, 32 g, and 50 D (see ex. 140).

Ex. 140. Coda motives. *a,* 33 c. *b,* 50 D. *c,* 43 E♭. *d,* 32 g. *e,* 31 A♭. *f,* 45 A. *g,* 37 E.

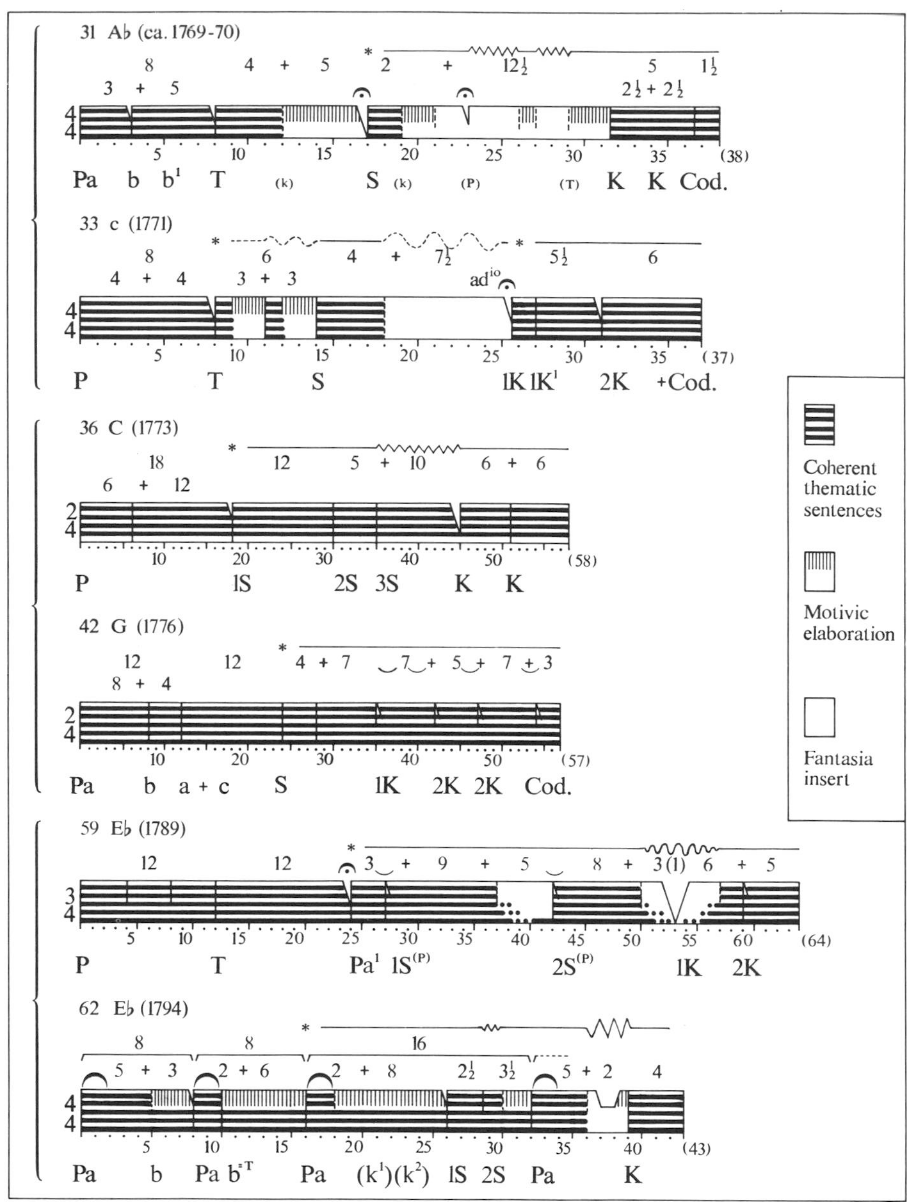

FIGURE 18 The proportion of thematic sections and fantasia-like inserts in the exposition: three main types.

4. *The Proportions of Strict Thematic Sections and Fantasia-Like Insertions in the Exposition*

Thus far, we have not considered one issue significant in the unfolding drama of the exposition and important for its proper interpretation. When is the exposition built from thematic material only and strictly organized into coherent musical sentences, and when do loose, interthematic sections occur?

In general, there is less opportunity for fantasia inserts in sonata movements of specifically dilettante style or in those in a fast $\frac{2}{4}$ meter. Again generally speaking, interthematic, figurative–motivic, texturally loose, and unpredictable sections occur frequently in the $\frac{4}{4}$ Moderato concert-style first movements composed between 1767 and 1776. The dramaturgy of these expositions sets up a basic contrast between the thematic and the interthematic material. Haydn does not commonly use fantasia-like elements in the late, mature sonatas, but when they do occur, they are given strong emphasis and great significance.

In figure 18, I have depicted two examples of each of these three basic types. The diagram differentiates between three kinds of textures—coherent thematic sentences, motivic elaboration, and fantasia inserts. It shows the strongest articulations, sometimes achieved by fermatas or adagio markings, and marks the elision of last and first measures of neighboring themes with a flag-like line, ♪, as in the closing group of 42 G. Here, the number of measures in a phrase suggests asymmetry, but, owing to the elisions, there is an underlying symmetric sentence structure. In addition to labeling the themes, the diagram indicates the establishment of the new key with an asterisk. Occasional tonal deviations or instabilities in the second key area are marked with a wavy line.

Several conclusions can be drawn from these diagrams, some of which are particularly important for performance. Most important, in the early concert-style sonatas, a coherent thematic block should be interpreted as a closed sentence, played in a rhythmically disciplined way; in contrast, the fantasia-like sections should be played more freely. It is also thought provoking to consider the attention that Haydn paid to the proportional placement of important structural points in the movement while at the same time elaborating the small-scale, measure-to-measure progression of the music. In 59 E♭, he presents new material about every twelve measures; all this material is related to the rhythmic pattern of the primary theme. In 62 E♭, the rhythm of the ritornello-like *forte* chords first heard in measure 1 reappears after eight, eight, and then sixteen measures, binding together the asymmetric sentence fragments.

In a few sonata expositions, sections are articulated not primarily through thematic material but rather through dramatic changes of predominant rhythmic patterns or broad textural areas. Figure 19 depicts the structures of three such irregular expositions. They are forms built up on three, four, or five contrasting blocks in the exposition.

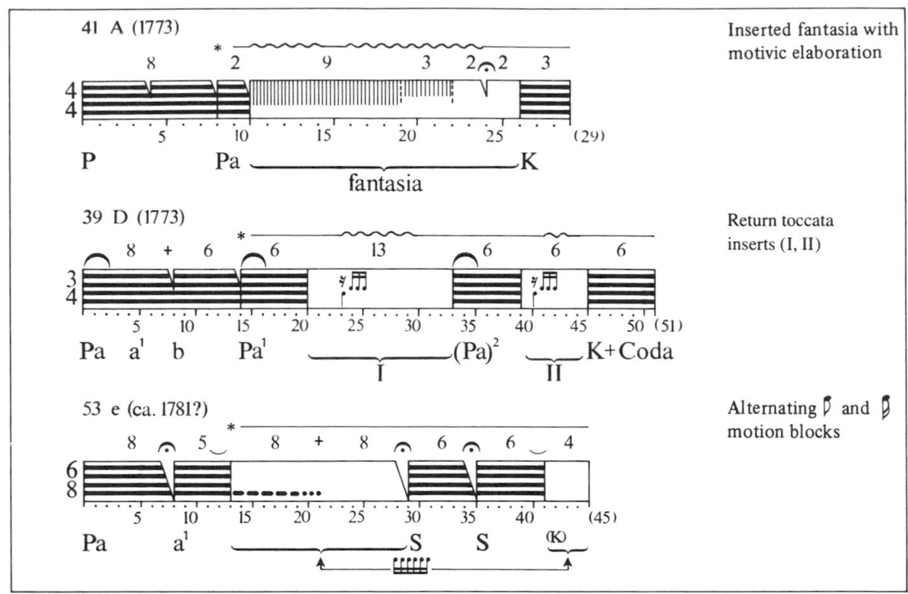

FIGURE 19 Irregular expositions.

Seventeen

STRATEGIES *of the* DEVELOPMENT SECTION

SONATA FORM WAS DESCRIBED in several eighteenth-century books of theory not as a ternary but as a binary form. Eighteenth-century performers considered both sets of repeat signs valid and would have repeated both sections exactly (*a*) or with variations (*b*). If they decided against repeats, they might not have repeated either section (*c*). The most frequent practice today, that of repeating only the first section (*d*), does not seem to have been customary in the eighteenth century:

Customary Eighteenth-Century Patterns of Repeats					Customary Twentieth-Century Pattern of Repeats			
a)	I	I	II	II	*d*)	I	I	II
b)	I	$I^{var.}$	II	$II^{var.}$				
c)	I	II						

The practice of repeating the exposition but not the development and recapitulation, so widespread today, became more usual in the notation at the beginning of the nineteenth century as an alternative to the traditional binary repeat, which was also continued. From a compositional point of view, the repetition of the second section became less viable as the development section became longer and more dramatic—even programmatic, one might say—so that its effect would have been weakened by a repeat. Moreover, the dramatic coda, joined organically to the recapitulation, made it almost impossible to return to the start of the development and state the musical events once more. In Haydn's music, this dramatic charging of the sonata form had not yet taken place.[1] We can happily listen

1. In the 1790s, Haydn gradually altered his concept of sonata form, carefully deciding about the validity of the repeat sign for each composition. The op. 76 string quartets, composed in 1797, con-

TABLE 19 PROPORTIONS IN MODERATO AND ALLEGRO MODERATO OPENING SONATA MOVEMENTS

	Full Length (mm.)	Proportion of the Exposition (%)	Length of the Three Parts		Proportion of the Develop- ment (%)
29 E♭	96	45.8*	4/4	44 :‖: 52 (17 ' 35)	17.7†
30 D	102	41.1	4/4	42 ‖ 60 (26 ' 34)	25.4
31 A♭	112	33.9	4/4	38 ‖ 74 (39 ' 35)	34.8
33 c	100	37	4/4	37 ‖ 63 (31 ' 32)	31
32 g	77	38.9	4/4	30 ‖ 47 (21 ' 26)	27.2
20 B♭	117	33.3	2/4	39 ‖ 78 (35 ' 43)	29.9
37 E	75	32	4/4	24 ‖ 51 (17 ' 34)	22.6
38 F	127	36.2	2/4	46 ‖ 81 (39 ' 42)	30.7
40 E♭	71	38	4/4	27 ‖ 44 (23 ' 21)	32.3
41 A	82	35.3	4/4	29 ‖ 53 (30 ' 23)	36.5‡
43 E♭	155	37.4	3/4	58 ‖ 97 (39 ' 58)	25.1
44 F	90	34.4	4/4	31 ‖ 59 (28 ' 31)	31.1
46 E	65	36.9	4/4	24 ‖ 41 (17 ' 24)	26.1
47 b	70	40	4/4	28 ‖ 42 (19 ' 23)	27.1
49 c♯	97	34	4/4	33 ‖ 64 (31 ' 33)	31.9
51 E♭	76	36.8	4/4	28 ‖ 48 (20 ' 28)	26.3

* Longest proportion of exposition in opening sonata movements.

† Shortest proportion of development in opening sonata movements.

‡ Longest proportion of development in opening sonata movements.

to even the longest and most exciting of his development sections more than once because his dramatic, humorous, pathetic, or capricious surprises do not lose their effect. This is especially true if the performer is willing to engage in some subtle rethinking of the character and intensity of the effects, in addition to some ornamental variations, during the repeat.

The growth of the development section can be measured in terms of the

tain precedents in the first movements for the three different possibilities of repeats. We find there the traditional repeat of the second section (G major), the pattern *1ma volta/2da volta* (C major), which of course excludes the reflex-like notation of the repeat sign, and the omission of the repeat (B♭ major). The first movements of the two last string quartets, op. 77 G and F, composed in 1799, unquestionably omit the repeat of the second section, as one can see from Haydn's autograph. The repeat sign, we should note, is never missing after the exposition section. With regard to the piano sonatas, in 62 E♭ there is no repeat sign for the second section of the first and third movements.

increase of its absolute length and its relative length compared to the other two sections. Although a long development section does not necessarily coincide with the presence of sophisticated developmental techniques, it is still worth comparing the proportion of the sections and then evaluating individual works by checking the music itself. I have separated the Moderato types of first movements, shown in table 19, from the other first-movement sonata forms, shown in table 20. The movements are compared in the tables in proportion to time; that is, the lengths of the horizontal lines reflect slower or faster tempo indications and different meters (including the relatively faster motion of $\frac{3}{4}$).

TABLE 20 PROPORTIONS IN OTHER OPENING SONATA MOVEMENTS

	Full Length (mm.)	Proportion of the Exposition (%)			Length of the Three Parts	Proportion of the Development (%)
34 D	193	35.2	2/4	All°	68 ‖ 125 (48 ǀ 77)	24.8
36 C	149	38.2	2/4	All°	57 ‖ 92 (38 ǀ 54)	25.5
39 D	155	32.9	3/4	All°	51 ‖ 104 (47 ǀ 57)	30.3
42 G	143	39.8	2/4	All° con brio	57 ‖ 86 (29 ǀ 57)	20.2
45 A	162†	37	2/4	All°	60 ‖ 102 (48 ǀ 54)	29.6
48 C	170	39.4	¢	All° con brio	67 ‖ 103 (36 ǀ 67)	21.1
50 D	103	38.8	4/4	All° con brio	40 ‖ 63 (24 ǀ 39)	23.3
53 e	127	35.4	6/8	Presto	45 ‖ 82 (33 ǀ 49)	25.9
55 B♭	151	36.4	¢	All°	55 ‖ 96 (41 ǀ 55)	27.1
59 E♭	218	29.3*	3/4	All°	64 ‖ 154 (67 ǀ 87)	30.7
60 C	150	35.5	4/4	All°	53 ‖ 97 (48 ǀ 49)	32
62 E♭	116	37	4/4	All°	43 ‖ (73)‡ (35 ǀ 38)	30.1
Appendix						
35 A♭ §	148	37.1	¢	Mod[to]	55 ‖ 93 (45 ǀ 48)	30.4
61 D **	111	(38.7)	[¢]	And[te]	43 : 36 · 32	(32.4)

* Shortest proportion of exposition in opening sonata movements.

† *Attacca* ending of recapitulation to a transitional second movement.

‡ The second part without repeat sign.

§ Probably not by Haydn.

** Irregular sonata form without repetition.

We can trace signs of a general evolutionary process and also note features germane to the style of individual sonatas or groups of sonatas. It appears natural that the earliest mature sonata in table 19, 29 E♭, has proportionately the longest exposition and shortest development.[2] As early as 1767–71, in the concert-style workshop sonatas, the exposition, development, and recapitulation divided the sonata into three roughly equal parts. From that time on, the length of the development section indicates the type of sonata. A shorter development means a lighter piece in dilettante style, a longer one a more serious sonata.

In a remarkable group of sonatas, composed between 1778 and 1784, the number of measures in the exposition and recapitulation is equal.[3] Because of the differences in patterns of modulation of these two sections, this equality seems peculiar. In contrast with Mozart, for Haydn mechanical repetition is not to be desired and is almost impossible to realize. This group of movements, with their idiosyncratic symmetry, urges us to make a systematic survey of the relation of lengths of sections, noting how often each type occurs (see fig. 20).

As we might expect with Haydn, the type that occurs most frequently in his sonatas is that in which the exposition is the longest section and the development is the shortest—type A. Perhaps surprisingly, the second most frequent type is one in which the exposition and recapitulation are equal in size, with the development a smaller section—type B. There is at least one authentic example in four further permutations of relative length of sections. Note that there are only two sonatas—type F—in which the development is the longest section and that both these (31 A♭ and 41 A) are genuine early Moderato concert-style sonatas. (It should be noted that both sonatas have huge fantasia-like insertions in their development sections.)

Having surveyed the proportions of sections in Haydn's first movements, we can return to eighteenth-century theory. The theorists usually treated the development section as the first half of the second part of a binary form. Mostly, they studied the tonal scheme of the development rather than methods of thematic development. Koch, however, left an important clue that one can use in classifying Haydn's development sections.

Koch described two main types of development.[4] In the first main type, evidently the more traditional one, the development section begins in the dominant.[5] After a possible brief feint toward the home key, the development arrives at a "soft [i.e., minor] key"—a key built on the mediant, submediant, or supertonic.

2. This sonata form is very unusual. Even early sonatas normally have development sections whose length is longer than 20 percent of the whole movement.

3. Among the early divertimento sonatas, there are two similar fast opening sonata-form movements, however, both with a more or less mechanical repetition of the exposition in the recapitulation: 6 C (21 ‖ 17 + 21) and 16 D (36 ‖ 38 + 36).

4. Koch, *Versuch,* 3:307–11 (translation, pp. 200–201).

5. Koch mentions that the section after the double bar may begin in an unexpected key.

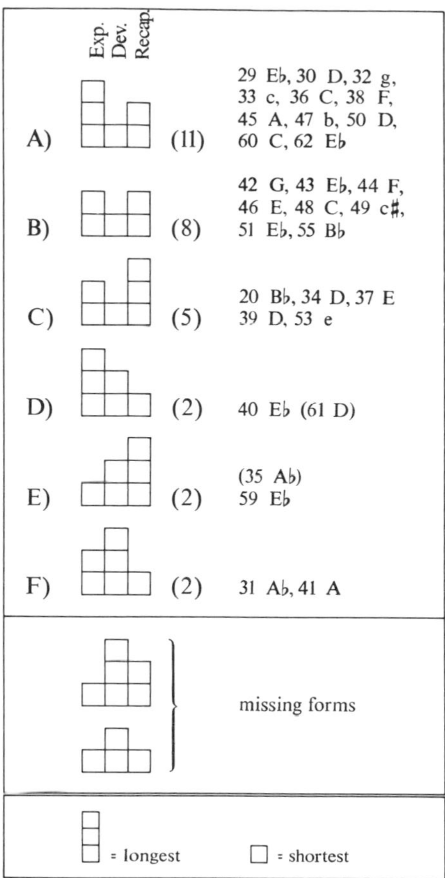

FIGURE 20 The relation between the lengths of the three sections.

One or more of the melodic ideas are expanded or dissected, repeated or stated in sequence in this minor key. Koch's statement clearly refers to the contrasting theme, the *cantabler Satz*. I take Koch's description to mean that, in this type, the first part of the development states primary-theme material in the dominant and occasionally in the tonic. Then it modulates to a minor key, usually the submediant, and reworks in minor other themes of the exposition, excluding the closing material. In Haydn's keyboard sonatas, and in his other instrumental genres as well, this was the most frequent procedure for the development, up until about 1780.[6] Later in this book, I will refer to this type as a development section with *counterexposition*.

Koch's second main type was a novelty at the beginning of the 1780s, one that he believed occurred frequently in the symphonies of Haydn and Dittersdorf.

6. See also Harold Andrews's "The Submediant in Haydn's Development Sections."

It is a development section with predominantly motivic elaboration. He stated that, in movements of this type, a part or only a motive (*Glied*) of the primary theme is repeated in the course of the development, which often modulated to remote keys; the motives were fragmented or transposed (*zergliedert* or *transponiert*).

Of course, these two types mentioned by Koch do not encompass all the types of development sections of Haydn's first-movement sonata forms. Other types can be proposed, from the standpoint of either key structure and modulatory schemes or thematic material.

1. *Modulation*

After a certain amount of tonal instability, most of the development sections of Haydn's keyboard sonatas arrive at a "third key," usually in minor. That is, after the exposition has established a primary and a secondary key, the development launches a third key in which several themes are restated, almost as a counterexposition, and in which, despite some tonal deviations, repeated cadences are established. In sonatas in major, this "third key" is built on a scale degree that played a subordinate role in the exposition; its appearance expands the Classical range of contrasts. Most frequently, the "third key" is vi, the submediant (20 B♭, 29 E♭, 30 D, 31 A♭, 34 D, 36 C, 38 F, 39 D, 41 A, 42 G, 43 E♭, 45 A, 46 E), but sometimes it is IV, the subdominant (37 E, 48 C). In a pair of sonatas in major, two new keys are established in the development—C minor and D minor in 44 F, E♭ major and G minor in 55 B♭. In the development sections of two sonatas in minor, two new keys, the minor subdominant and the minor dominant, are established—E minor and F♯ minor in 47 b and F♯ minor and G♯ minor in 49 c♯.

More daring schemes of modulation are relatively rare in Haydn's keyboard sonatas. Example 141 summarizes the modulation schemes in seven sonatas, of which 33 c and 62 E♭ are the most interesting. A surprising feature of 33 c is how many degrees in the primary and secondary keys, C minor and E♭ major, are given prominence by statements of thematic material or cadences, such as the cadence in G minor in measures 62–65. Also surprising is how many keys are altered to minor or built on altered degrees—B♭ minor, D♭ major, E♭ minor, A♭ minor, and G♭ major. 62 E♭ takes us into even more unexpected tonal realms. Although a progression in which a major submediant leads to a minor or major supertonic (B♭ ‖ G C or G ‖ E A) was not strange, hearing thematic statements in C, E, or A in a work in E♭ certainly was unusual.[7]

7. The restatement of S in E major has special structural significance in that E major is, startlingly, the key of the second movement. Theoretically, these two E majors function differently. In the development section of the first movement, E follows the dominant of C and sounds like a mediant relation. The E major chord that starts the second movement, after the first movement closes in E♭, sounds like a Neapolitan relation; i.e., it sounds like F♭.

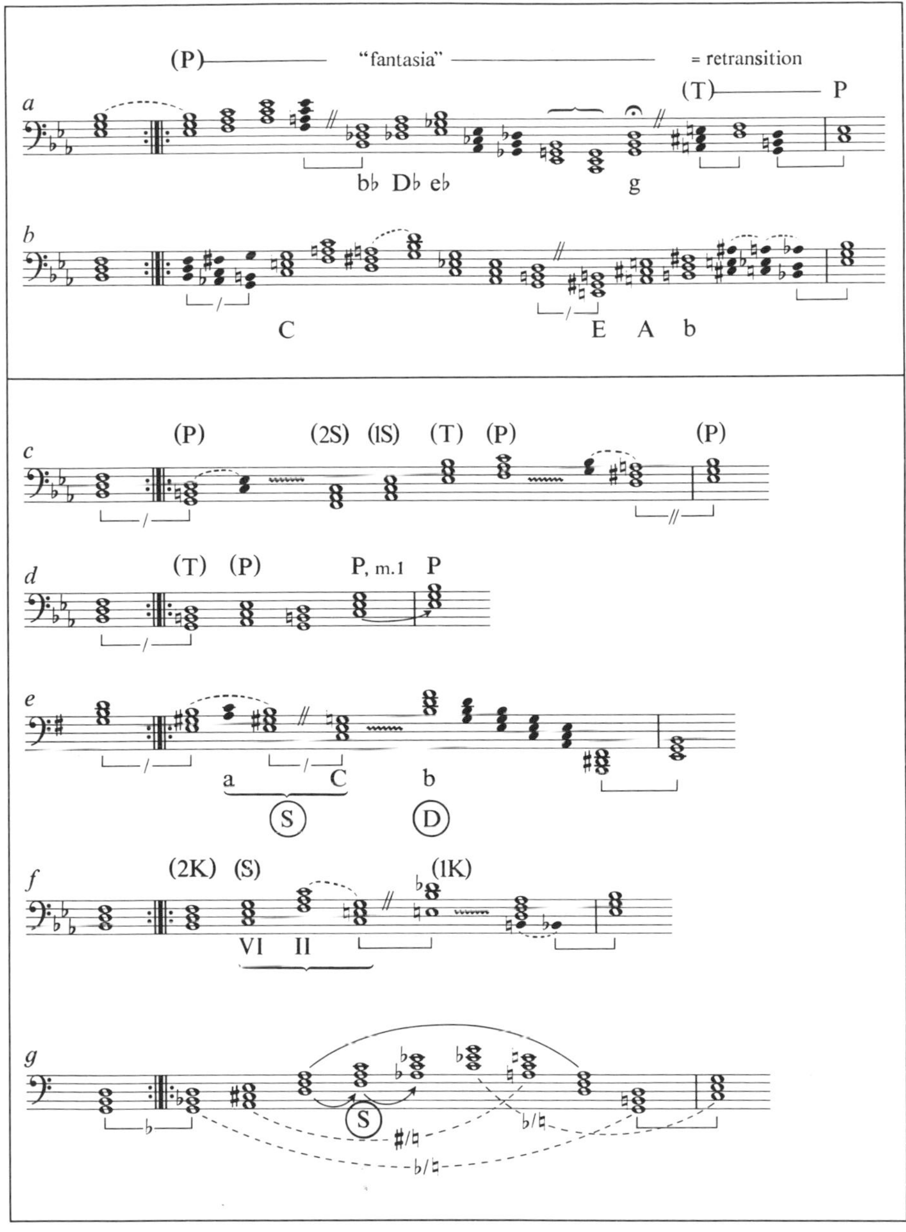

Ex. 141. Modulation in seven development sections. *a,* 33 c (1771). *b,* 62 E♭ (1794). *c,* 40 E♭. *d,* 51 E♭. *e,* 53 e. *f,* 59 E♭. *g,* 60 C. (The circled S and D refer to subdominant and dominant, respectively.)

The other five sonatas considered in example 141 also deserve comment. In 40 E♭, the connection between the development and the recapitulation has a Neapolitan effect. 51 E♭ is noteworthy for its false recapitulation in C minor, 53 e because of its submediant turns and its economy of material, and 59 E♭ for the modulatory elaboration of 1K with its ♫♩ | ♪ rhythm. Finally, 60 C is significant because of the richness of its indirect major–minor relations and use of remote keys.

In connection with this discussion of harmonic surprises in the development section, let us refer to development sections that begin in unexpected keys after the double-bar close of the exposition. These include 29 E♭ (B♭ major ‖: B♭ minor), 34 D (A major ‖: F♯ major), 44 F (C major ‖: C minor), and 55 B♭ (F major ‖: D♭ major). An unexpected, strong cadence in a foreign key, producing a somewhat archaic character, can be found in 33 c (i of G minor before i of C minor), 40 E♭ (V of G minor before I of E♭ major), and 20 B♭ (i of G minor before I of B♭ major). Oddly enough, all three cases involve G minor.

2. *Thematic Content*

With regard to thematic content, one may discern four different types of development section, which I will first define and then illustrate with examples.

Development section with counterexposition (Koch's first main type). In addition to P, there are S and occasionally K or T materials. The "third key" dominates the final portions of the development. Sonatas belonging to this group are 20 B♭,* 34 D, 36 C,* 37 E, 38 F, 40 E♭, 43 E♭,* 45 A,* and 46 E (asterisks mark especially characteristic examples).

P elaboration with fantasia inserts. The fantasia, which in the majority of cases is related to one of the motives in T or K, can be toccata-like in its rhythm and motion. All the sonatas in this group have significant and original development sections. The group includes 30 D, 31 A♭, 32 g, 33 c, 39 D, 41 A, 48 C, and 49 c♯.

Transitional type. This type contains an elaboration of P or P and T. Sometimes the manner of development is a kind of *sonata facile* style, with minimal technical demands. Sonatas in this group include 51 E♭ and 53 e and, in the *facile* subtype, 29 E♭ and 42 G.

Development section focused on motivic elaboration. The stages of evolution of this type of development section are easy to trace. 44 F is built on P elements but also contains new material; 47 b is built on P only. 55 B♭, 59 E♭, and 62 E♭ represent the Classical main type, while 60 C shows strong contrapuntal tendencies.[8] The development sections of 47 b, 59 E♭, and 62 E♭ show extended elaborations of short motives, suggestive of Beethoven.

8. With inversion of right-hand and left-hand motives in the development: 33 c, 41 A (!), 53 e.

3. *A Survey of Selected Examples*

I have chosen a dozen development sections, some typical and some unusual, for graphic representation (see figs. 21 and 22). The length of the line in the diagrams corresponds to the time it takes to play the passage. Counterexpositions, that is, sections of the development in which themes are restated in their original forms, are indicated by thick horizontal lines. Thematic deviations are written above the diagram line, and the plan of modulation is written below.

The early concert-style sonatas are characterized by huge fantasia inserts both in the exposition and in the development. Even if it is motivically related to themes of the exposition, the fantasia constitutes a foreign presence within the movement. Longer fantasia sections, with motor rhythms or left-hand figuration, whether reminiscent of Baroque style or forecasting a Romantic, passionate sound, offer opportunities for virtuoso performance. Compared to the simple but effective development of 31 A♭, with a harpsichord toccata (fig. 21*a*), or the development of 41 A, whose second fantasia insert, with motivic elaboration, is also in harpsichord style (fig. 21*c*), that of 33 c (fig. 21*b*) presents the most significant development section among the solo sonatas of the 1770s. It modulates to a variety of keys and builds up a climax with a crescendo to ***ff***.

The *counterexposition* type of development section can be found from the early, lyrical chamber sonatas on. The expositions of these sonatas are rich in thematic materials. In such simpler examples as 20 B♭ and 43 E♭ (see fig. 22*f, h*), there is a short, modulatory P elaboration that is immediately followed by a restatement of S and K themes in the "third key," here the submediant, giving a different, darker interpretation.

One new type of development, first appearing in sonatas from the second half of the 1770s, is *first-theme centered.* 47 b first breaks up the contrast materials of P (half note with mordent vs. short motives in dotted rhythm), then elaborates, repeats, and reconstructs them (see fig. 21*d*). 48 C has a simpler strategy (see fig. 21*e*). Nearly thirty-two measures of rolling triplet figuration suggest monothematic organization, but at the same time they are the successor of the earlier fantasia inserts.

The *Classical* development section, which became the model for development sections in later textbooks, appears in Haydn's solo sonatas in the middle of the 1770s. Novelty and tradition are both present in the development section of 44 F, symbiotically rather than synthetically, in the aesthetic sense (see fig. 22*j*). The fragmentation of P in measures 32–37 and its elaboration in measures 38–43 seems strikingly modern; the retransition in measures 52–59 is witty. A coherent interpretation of the fantasia fragment and the S area in this context is a genuine challenge for the performer. The two great E♭ major sonatas, on the other hand, present a perfect synthesis. The *Genzinger* Sonata (fig. 22*k*) is more suggestive. Its four-part structural division—modulation, re-exposition, analysis,

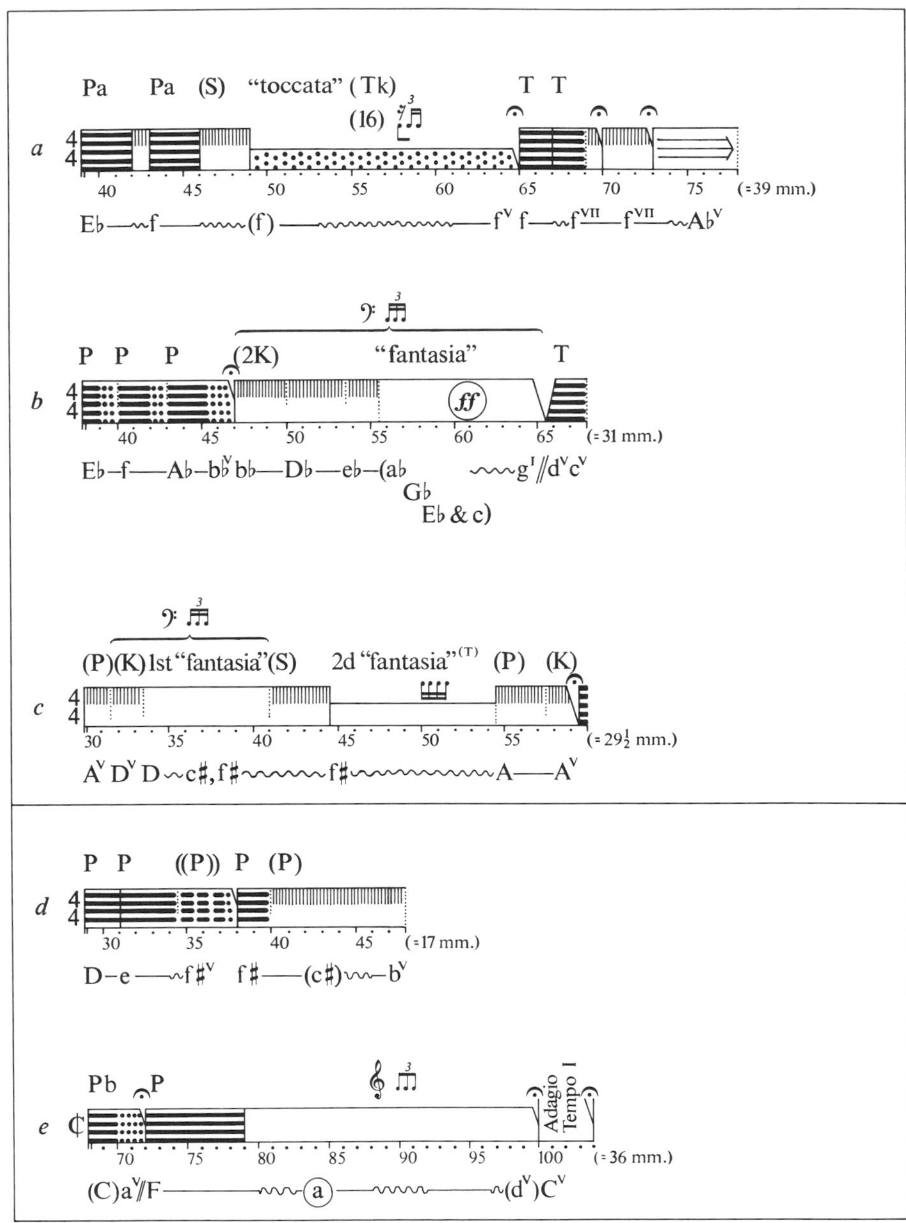

FIGURE 21 Development sections with fantasia inserts (*a–c*) and with P elaboration (*d–e*). *a*, 31 A♭. *b*, 33 c. *c*, 41 A. *d*, 47 b. *e*, 48 C.

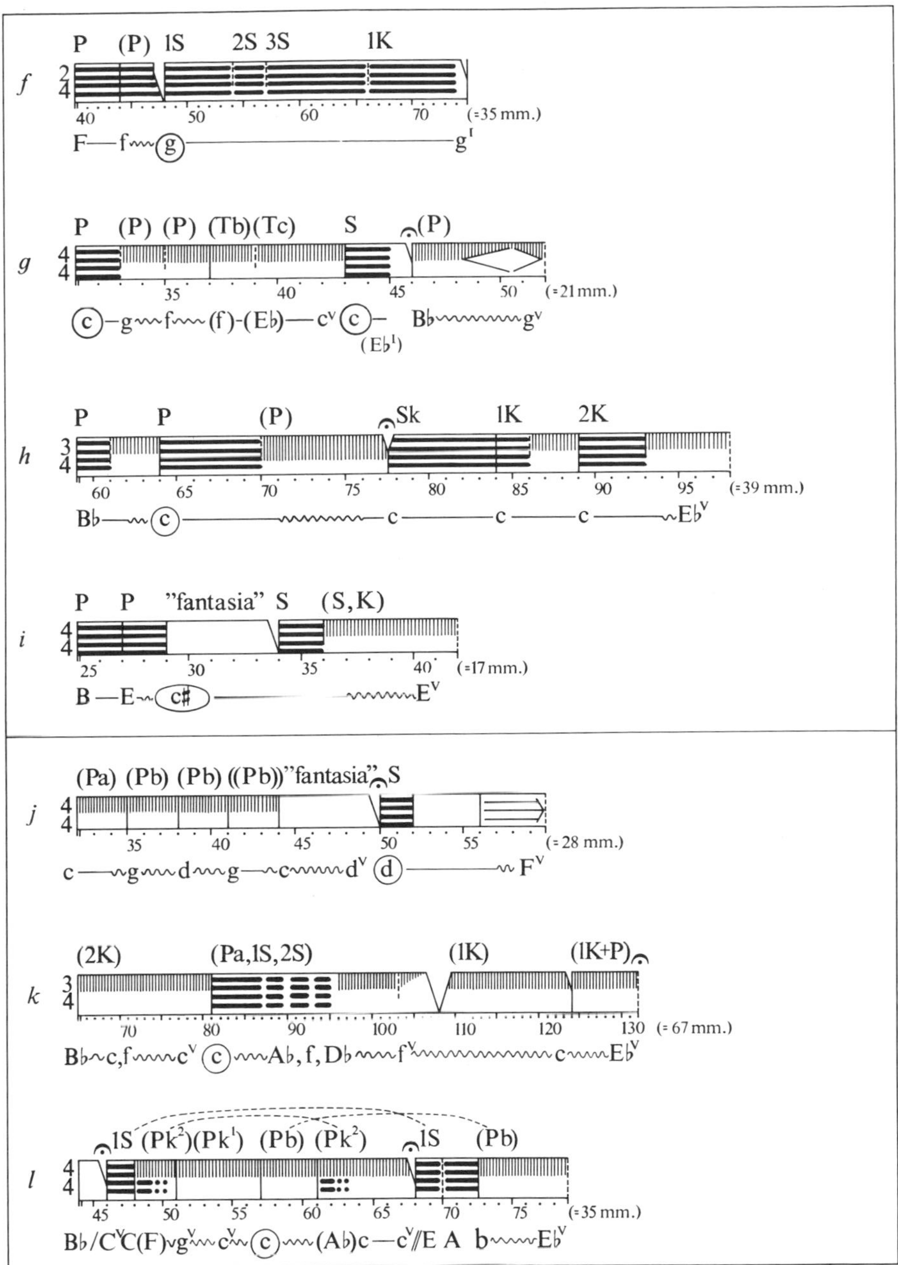

FIGURE 22 Development sections with "counterexposition" (*f–i*) and "Classical"-type development sections (*j–l*). *f*, 20 B♭. *g*, 32 g. *h*, 43 E♭. *i*, 46 E. *j*, 44 F. *k*, 59 E♭. *l*, 62 E♭.

and retransition—became a pattern for many other composers. In this sonata, the homogeneous motion of the large surfaces and the dramatic force of the whole process are perfectly suited to the style of what was presented in the exposition. That is, the pattern of the development is in harmony with the large-scale form. In 62 E♭ (see fig. 22*l*), the reason for the different strategy of the development section can, again, be traced back to the exposition. The head of the opening theme (Pa), which was heard as a ritornello many times in the exposition, is absent from the development section. Instead, 1S, with its sharply dotted rhythm, appears as a block twice, once in C major, then in E major and A major. Two other thematic materials that we hear twice are a virtuoso passage (Pk^2 starting out from F and A♭ major) and the cantabile transition from the first theme (Pb starting out from C minor and B minor). Finally, corresponding to the startling effect in the exposition at measures 37–39, there are two surprise fermatas in the development section over a G major chord, the first of which is followed by a passage in C and the second of which is followed by one in E.

No one would seriously claim that it is precisely in the piano sonatas that Haydn's genius in shaping development sections is most apparent. Indeed, one can hardly disregard the masterly development sections of several of his string quartets or his London symphonies. Nevertheless, the piano sonatas have few rivals with regard to the variety of types and extremes of expression of the development sections. The pianist who plays Haydn's trios as well as his sonatas will realize that, in the late trios, the development sections become even more intriguing in their harmonies and bolder and bolder in their modulations.[9]

9. In two famous development sections, Haydn could write the modulations only in enharmonic notation. In Hob. XV:28 E, there is a deviation into A♭ (= G♯); in XV:26 f♯, the modulation scheme is A ‖ F♯, b, B, c♯, C♯, e♭ (= d♯), E♭, C, e, b vii^7, D V^7, c♯ . . . f♯ vii^7-I. See also Roger E. Chapman, "Modulation in Haydn's Late Piano Trios in the Light of Schoenberg's Theories," in *Haydn Studies,* 471–75.

Eighteen

Recapitulation

Dramaturgy. Haydn's sonata form in general does not have a dramatic sequence of events, a narrative, comparable to the plot of a stage work. It was in the works of Beethoven, his contemporaries, and his successors that great conflicts were raised in the exposition, dramatically analyzed in the development, recalled with a different meaning in the recapitulation, and brought to a conclusion in the coda. The main theme in most of Haydn's instrumental first movements is so complex and suggests so many different possible directions that, instead of further "dramatic" events, the elaboration and variation of the theme and the return to the opening statement fulfill the form. On the few occasions that Haydn seems to want something different, be it simpler, more effective, or more theatrical, he may use a surprise minor mode in the exposition, which will appear brightened in the major mode in the recapitulation,[1] or he may compose a surprise coda.[2]

The restatement of the primary theme in the recapitulation is not a dramatic or victorious moment in Haydn's sonatas. It is, rather, a well-designed, well-prepared, and happy reencounter of the basic idea and principal sentiment of the work. The recapitulation of a solo keyboard sonata by Haydn, in contrast to the recapitulations of some of his string quartets and symphonies, differs from the exposition only as much as is necessary for the tonal coherence and integrity of the work. There will naturally be no call in the recapitulation for strongly contrasting key areas. However, here the player has a free hand in deciding

1. In some of his late quartets in major keys, Haydn begins the sonata-form finale in minor mode to achieve a brightening *maggiore* effect in the major S area of the recapitulation. See, e.g., op. 76 G and C.

2. The most effective of these is the interpolation within the recapitulation of the first movement of the Symphony no. 103, the *Drumroll,* which recalls the slow introduction.

whether or not to include improvised variants in the performance. Keyboard-sonata recapitulations that break new dramatic ground are rare phenomena; they do not necessarily render the work more powerful. It is more important to explore and understand the well-shaped harmonic proportions and the balance realized in the gently varied recapitulation.

Proportions. Our survey of the comparative lengths of expositions, developments, and recapitulations in opening movements (fig. 20 above) showed that in general the recapitulation is shorter than the exposition, although in certain movements the exposition and recapitulation may be equal in length. Numbers of measures alone cannot reveal, however, that the recapitulation is practically always more continuous than the exposition. In the recapitulation, there are fewer strong points of articulation and changes of texture; the thematic material that had led to a strong cadence in the second key is frequently dissolved in continuous motion. Often, events in the recapitulation can be accounted for only if we assume that some kind of "perfect balance" between the exposition and the recapitulation was a key issue for Haydn. If an important thematic passage is left out of the recapitulation, it might be because it has been heard extensively in the development; or Haydn might compose new material for the recapitulation. He constantly plays with the actual or perceived number of measures, to keep his own sense of perfect proportion in order. Haydn's own reflexes governing his sense of form are very effectively revealed in the recapitulation.

Haydn's first maneuver to adjust the proportions of the form is the *transfer of T material to the development.* When the material leading to the second key in the exposition is motivically distinctive or original, its complete abandonment would seem illogical. Instead, Haydn might transfer it to the development, where it either serves as the retransition to the home key (as in 31 A♭, 33 c, and 47 b) or is used for the modulation to the third key (as in 32 g, 38 F, and 40 E♭).

The second maneuver concerns *expositions and recapitulations of equal length.* Of the eight mature sonatas with expositions and recapitulations of equal length, two, 46 E and 55 B♭, have recapitulations that appear rather mechanically repetitive. The other six, 42 G, 43 E♭, 44 F, 48 C, 49 c♯, and 51 E♭, are more interesting, for here Haydn fully reworks the recapitulations, at times restating phrases, but sometimes paraphrasing musical ideas by means of extensions or cuts. Figure 23 presents diagrams of the recapitulations of 44 F, 48 C, and 51 E♭. (I will leave to the reader the adventure of analyzing the recapitulations of 42 G, 43 E♭, and 49 c♯.) In the recapitulation of 44 F, Haydn omits T but adds a remarkable modulatory extension of the head of P. 51 E♭ retains and even extends T but omits the second statement of P, which stood for S in the exposition: without the contrast of tonic and dominant, there is no need for two statements of P. 48 C makes room, by strongly contracting a section, for P to be stated once again, as if it were a closing theme. In each of these movements, the interpolation of one measure toward the very end strengthens the effect of the codetta.

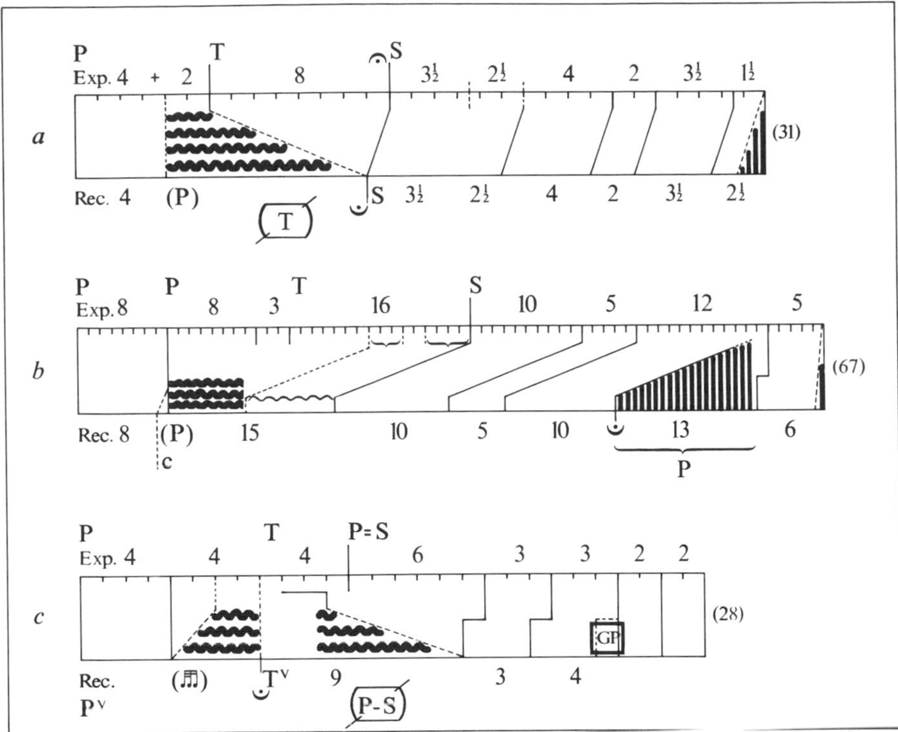

FIGURE 23 Exposition and recapitulation of equal length, thematically rearranged. *a*, 44 F. *b*, 48 C. *c*, 51 E♭.

Revision of the primary theme. In only a few sonatas (34 D, 55 B♭, 59 E♭, and 45 A) is the primary theme restated unchanged in the recapitulation. Primary themes with lengthy sentence structures are usually shortened drastically. In 29 E♭ and 30 D, the phrase structure A B A^1 B^1 becomes A^1 B^1; a complex sentence becomes a simple sentence in 41 A; two sentences are shortened to one in 48 C. A full-period P plus T form is sometimes modified to a half period plus new material evolved from P, as in 43 E♭, 44 F, 50 D, and 51 E♭. There are other kinds of reductions as well: in 38 C, twenty measures are shortened to eleven; in 42 G, twenty-four measures become twenty. The twenty-seven-measure primary area of 62 E♭, comprising P and the consequent Pa return in the dominant, is remodeled into twenty measures in the recapitulation; the A B A / B structure of the theme becomes A B. Haydn employs various stratagems to increase the fluency of his recapitulations, such as changing cadences or entwining textures. Closed A.A.[3] becomes A.A, in 20 B♭; A,A. becomes A,A:cont. in 32 g and 33 c; and A,B. becomes A,B, in 47 b. Several primary themes are restated with embellished or

3. See the abbreviation of cadences in fig. 17.

varied rhythm, in accordance with the idea of *veränderte Reprise*. There are small changes in 36 C, 37 E, and 39 D, an ornamented head motive in 42 G, and new chromatic passages in 46 E. Diminished rhythm resulting from "filling in" of the beats has structural importance in 60 C, where Haydn displays an elaborate chain of varying rhythmic devices stretching throughout the movement. In 37 E, the primary theme is both varied and extended (thirteen measures in the recapitulation against eight measures in the exposition) before arriving at an Adagio. The originality of the changes in the primary theme in three of the sonatas in minor is unprecedented. 33 c is ornamented with a rhetorical caesura that dramatically transforms measures 5–8 of the theme. The passionate reprise of 49 c♯ intertwines variants of the same material in major and minor. Finally, in 53 e, eighteen measures are contracted into five because Haydn decided to close the movement with the passionate primary theme.

Omitted and recomposed passages. Occasionally, Haydn will thoroughly transform the secondary theme or the closing material. A memorable left-hand trill in 38 F I, 105–10, replaces the effect of a digression to the flat submediant. In the recapitulation of 36 C, a longer passage is recomposed. The major and minor motivic complex in measures 29–35 (2S and 3S) is supplanted by a more intense minor coloration in measures 124–37. Even the cadential passage before the closing area changes direction (compare mm. 43–45 with mm. 135–37). Some extensions fundamentally influence the interpretation. One is the lyrical cadence of 32 g, slowing down to *sempre più adagio* (mm. 66–70); another is the beautiful fantasia insert in measures 61–66 of 37 E, which is enlarged from a single measure of the exposition (m. 15). Structurally, the recapitulation of 60 C is the most sophisticated recomposition of all. The recapitulation discards the second-key variants 1S and 2S and introduces the primary-theme variation with the famous ***pp*** open Pedal effect. In all, there are eleven P variants in this movement, an extraordinary amount of character variation and pianistic invention in a sonata form.[4]

Coda. Haydn did not compose any coda in his keyboard sonatas that would challenge the exposition or development in size or dramatic effect—as Beethoven sometimes did. Can we call the final section an independent coda proper when, after it has finished, the whole development can be started again? In Haydn's case, it is never size that determines the originality or significance of an ending. In two relatively early minor-mode sonatas, 32 g and 33 c,[5] Haydn was able to compose—in a mere two measures—a coda with a very strong character, that of a funeral march. Only one opening movement, that of the *Genzinger* Sonata, has a

4. The eleven variants are found in mm. 1, 7, 20, 30, 54, 56, 60, 73, 102, 108, and 120. Some of the variants can be grouped in pairs, such as mm. 20 and 54 or mm. 30 and 56, and some have figurative relations, such as mm. 1 and 102 or mm. 7 and 108.

5. The coda of 33 c, mm. 98–100, is a fourth-power magnification of a half measure in the exposition. Haydn's first-version sketch for the end of the movement (see n. 11, chap. 7) introduced a new

substantial coda of twenty-eight measures. This gentle, capriciously lively, and very effective finish is, not surprisingly, a favorite with pianists. Haydn has saved for these final measures a compositional tour de force. Two motives presented at some distance from one another in the exposition, a T motive in measure 13 and 2K in measure 60, are brought together in the coda. Their rhythms fit into each other; the circle is closed; the musical material has come to an end.

---

six-note motive the rotation of which did not result in $\frac{4}{4}$ bars. The corrected sketch returned to the chromatic passage of the exposition:

Section 2: Other Forms

Nineteen

Sonata Form *and* Scherzo Form *in the* Finale

In this chapter, we will discuss eight finales in sonata form, four finales in scherzo form,[1] one finale in sonata-rondo form, and one fast middle movement in sonata form. There is, of course, a functional difference between sonata forms that open a work and those that close it. This difference is partly expressed in differences in meters and tempos. Haydn's sonata-form first movements are largely in $\frac{4}{4}$ Moderato and have a great variety of rhythmic patterns. The most typical tempo for sonata-form finales is Presto, generally associated with $\frac{2}{4}$ meter (see fig. 24).[2] In performance, of course, some prestos are slower than others or even slower than some allegros. The characteristic "rhythmic code" is a reliable guide (see fig. 25).

The "scherzo $\frac{3}{4}$"-type finales of the *London* sonatas 60 C and 61 D are, regardless of the tempo indications, the fastest of all. The two earlier finales in $\frac{3}{4}$, 29 E♭ and 33 c, are considerably slower; these are accelerated minuet types with a quarter-note pulse.[3] 60 C and 61 D are scherzo types with a dotted-half-note pulse. The Presto movements in $\frac{2}{4}$ can be considered steps in the evolution of a

1. See pp. 194–95. The *JHW* and the *WUE* indicate the repetitions of the finales of 60 C and 61 D differently. *JHW*, perhaps arbitrarily, uses repeat signs in both movements ("entsprechend der wahren Struktur" [*JHW*, 3:ix]). The *WUE*, on the basis of the available sources—the autograph is missing—prints 60 C in full (24 + 24 + 68 + 68 measures) and prints 61 D with one repeat sign (‖: 23 :‖ 62 + 62 measures).

2. Four early sonata-form finales pave the way for the later main type. 6 C, 15 E, and 16 D are in $\frac{2}{4}$ Presto (16 D is, in fact, marked *Presto* in one source and *Allegro* in another); 13 C is in $\frac{3}{8}$ Allegro molto.

3. The tempo of the second movement of 19 e, $\frac{2}{4}$ Allegro, is even slower. This movement contains thirty-second notes in scale passages.

		3/8	6/8	2/4	3/4
Prestissimo	1	–	52 G	–	–
Presto	8	36 C	–	31 A♭ ⟨41 A⟩* 38 F 47 b [58 C]** 62 E♭	⟨61 D⟩*
Allegro di molto Allegro molto Vivace assai	3	–	–	⟨56 D⟩*	29 E♭ ⟨60 C⟩*
Allegro	2	–	–	[19 e]***	33 c

FIGURE 24 Meters and tempos in the finales. (* Scherzo form. ** Sonata rondo. *** Fast middle movement.)

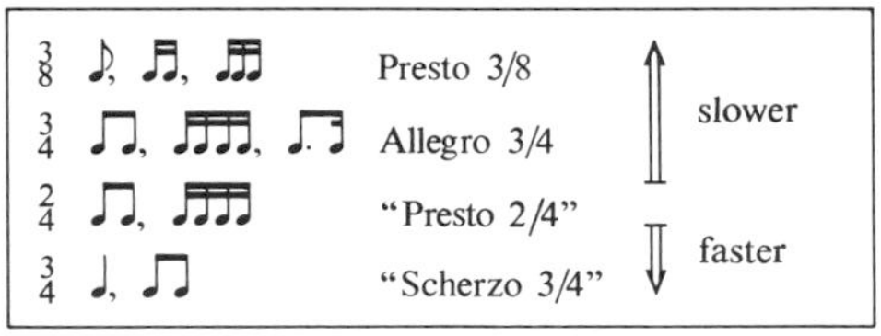

Meter	Rhythms	Code	
3/8		Presto 3/8	↑ slower
3/4		Allegro 3/4	
2/4		"Presto 2/4"	
3/4		"Scherzo 3/4"	↓ faster

FIGURE 25 Rhythmic "codes" of the finales.

specific rhythmic style related to the contredanse,[4] an evolution that can also be traced in the symphonies or string quartets. Features of this contredanse style are an eighth-note upbeat, appoggiaturas in the second and fourth measures, and symmetric simplicity of thematic material. The type appears in an embryonic form in the finale of 31 A♭ and in a developed form in the finale of 38 F. The finale themes of 47 b and 62 E♭, which both begin with a series of repeated notes, bear a clearer imprint of Haydn's musical personality. The characteristic rhythms and accents of the contredanse are retained, but the naive dance-like symmetry of phrases is replaced by a phrase structure full of surprises. 47 b begins with 13 + 5 measures followed by a general pause of two measures. 62 E♭ begins with a pair of eight-measure phrases whose forward progress is twice halted by fermatas; it takes a thundering twelve-measure phrase to get the movement under way (see ex. 142).

With the single exception of the finale of 29 E♭, all the movements we are

4. Heinrich Besseler, "Einflüsse der Contratanzmusik auf Joseph Haydn."

Ex. 142. *a,* 31 A♭. *b,* 38 F. *c,* 47 b. *d,* 62 E♭.

discussing here begin with an upbeat. The upbeat is a quarter note in the scherzo-type movements (see ex. 143). The sonata-rondo second movement of 58 C begins with a half-measure upbeat, like a gavotte (see ex. 144). These movements lack rhythmic patterns involving expressive dotted rhythms and triplets, although strict dotted rhythms are present in the finale of 33 c and ornamental sixteenth-note triplets are found in 36 C.

Ex. 143. *a,* 60 C. *b,* 61 D.

Ex. 144. 58 C.

Since the narrow range of rhythmic patterns is likely to evoke a rather strict performance from the player, Haydn takes special care with the structurally important points of articulation, where the music should relax or come to a sudden stop. His two basic notational means are the fermata and the general pause. The finales of 47 b, 58 C, 60 C, and 62 E♭ contain several grand-style effects and surprises that the player can perform with Beethovenian vigor. Some of the fast sonata-form finales deliberately accumulate surprise effects by means of the asymmetric structure of the main theme. The first example is in 16 D (2; 3. 2; 3,),[5] while the most sophisticated example is in 60 C (5, + 2. 3? + 1 GP 5 + 8). Occasionally, as in 29 E♭, a whole exposition is built up from sections organized in asymmetric contours (11 [= 6 + 5], 8 [= 2 + 3 + 3], 15, 15).

The proportions of the exposition, development, and recapitulation in finale sonata forms are not significantly different from those in first-movement sonata forms. The finale of 62 E♭ is divided into three almost equal sections (102 ‖ 101 + 104). In two sonata-form finales—29 E♭ (49 ‖ 38 + 49) and 52 G (43 ‖ 35 + 43)—the exposition and recapitulation are exactly the same length, with the development section somewhat smaller.[6] The proportions of the scherzo-form finales—60 C: 24 24 68 68 and 61 D: 23 23 62 62—are strikingly different, particularly in their contracted first sections.[7] The proportions of the sections of the second movement of 56 D, a scherzo finale in $\frac{2}{4}$ Vivace assai, are certainly grotesque: 8 8 93 93. These seemingly absurd formal contours are surely against all "rules." Moreover, the opening theme, with its abundance of leading-tone relations, is obscure tonally. This scherzo is a rather broad joke (see ex. 145).

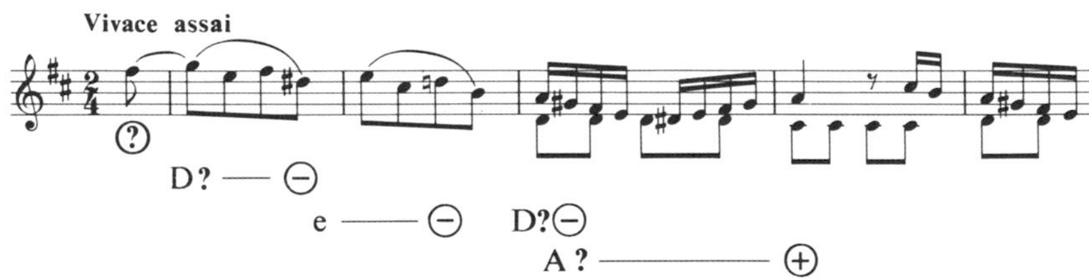

Ex. 145. 56 D.

The main theme resembles a puzzle or a labyrinth game in information theory. It offers various routes to various possible keys, of which only one is fea-

5. The punctuation marks after the number of measures stand for different cadences: period = I; comma = V; semicolon = vi; question mark = unusual harmony, such as a B major chord in a C major theme; GP = general pause.

6. The grotesquely short final movement of 41 A has proportions unlike any first movement (see fig. 20): 8 ‖ 10 + 8. That is, the whole movement is no longer than a rondo theme.

7. The development sections of these movements are just slightly shorter than the expositions, and the recapitulation plus coda is much the longest section; 60 C: 24 ‖ 23 + 45, 61 D: 23 ‖ 22 + 40.

sible. One may ask if this strange wavy line of motives can be considered an opening theme at all in the Classical sense. The eighth-note motive has an unpredictable winding motion, while the sixteenth-note curling motive strengthens any key on which it happens to land. The movement abounds in magnificently prepared half cadences (mm. 25, 60, 82) and has a fine deceptive cadence in measure 45. The first strong, unequivocal, definitive tonic cadence is saved for measure 87, that is, practically the end of the piece (see ex. 146). This finale, a worthy partner to the first movement, is a glorious example of Haydn's inventiveness.

Ex. 146. 56 D.

Twenty

Sonata Forms *in* Slow Tempos

In part II of this book, I mentioned that, in the full maturity of Haydn's style, his most original slow movements had some kind of variation structure, such as double variations or ternary variations. In some sonatas, the minuet replaces the slow movement. However, the majority of the sonatas have slow middle movements in sonata form. There are eighteen such movements in the mature sonatas, to which we may add the precocious slow movements of 11 B♭, 13 G, and 14 C.

We will study the slow movements in major and those in minor separately because the differences between these groups go well beyond mode. The slow sonata forms in major keys show a definite chronological development and a change in type. The course of this development is charted in figure 26. The slow movements in minor show a greater variety of types but tend to look backward rather than forward.

1. *Slow Sonata-Form Movements in Major*

The first type of slow sonata-form movement in major, a $\frac{3}{4}$ Andante, was developed during the period of the workshop sonatas. Although C. P. E. Bach could have seen his own musical reflection in some of the passages and sequences,[1] these movements give the impression of being highly original and significant pieces. One must also add that they are typical harpsichord works, which present a difficult task to the pianist who plays the grand of our days, with its resonance and

1. C. P. E. Bach's influence appears most evident in the slow movement of 33 c, particularly in the main theme, the syncopated cantabile in mm. 14–19, and the sequence closing the exposition in mm. 20 and 22. H. C. Robbins Landon (*HCW*, 2:338) suggests that the slow movement of 30 D cannot be heard without thinking of the "Hamburg" Bach.

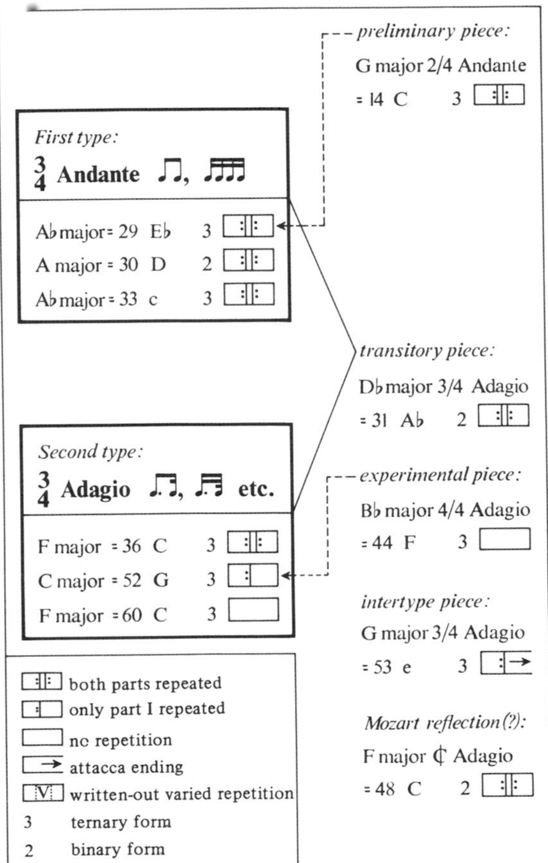

FIGURE 26 Slow sonata-form movements in major. (In the autograph, the slow sonata movement of 30 D is marked *Andante*, but other manuscripts and printed sources have *Adagio* and *Adagio ma non troppo* as tempo indications.)

differences in volume between treble and bass. The A major Andante of 30 D has a definitely experimental character, even on the harpsichord or fortepiano, most obvious in the two-octave leaps in the closing theme (see ex. 147).

Ex. 147. 30 D.

In order to have a clearer idea of the tempo and performing style of these $\frac{3}{4}$ Andante movements, to understand how Haydn might have envisaged their performance, we need to relate them to the movements that precede and follow them. Compared to the concertante-style Moderato first movements, the $\frac{3}{4}$ Andante movements employ a limited set of rhythmic patterns. Sixteenth-note triplet and thirty-second-note passages are exceptional; thematic sections with dotted rhythms are rare. This rhythmic vocabulary is, however, richer than that found in the fast finale movements. The tempo at which certain figures and motives feel natural suggests that the ♩ pulse in the Andante movements can be the same as the ♩ pulse of the Moderato first movements. Even so, the performance of the Andante movements is more fluent, melodic, and coherent than that of the Moderato first movements, which are rich in rhetorical phrases, articulations, changes of texture, and strong cadences.

After the workshop sonatas, Haydn changed the sonata-form slow movement. From the adjustments he made we can infer that he did not consider the earlier type to contrast powerfully enough with the main movement. The uniquely beautiful D♭ major Adagio of 31 A♭ is a great step forward (see ex. 148). To shape a new melodic style, Haydn constructed the parts in a certain abstract way that is reminiscent of the slow movements of his string quartets. Yet he also exploited the character of contemporary keyboard instruments more fully.

Ex. 148. 31 A♭.

The second type is a $\frac{3}{4}$ Adagio that uses an enormous rhythmic vocabulary, including two or three levels of diminution of dotted rhythms, that is, dotted quarter, eighth, and sixteenth.[2] Haydn evolves simple rhythmic variants of

2. This is only a conventional notation in some places; the possibility or necessity of overdotting remains.

themes as well as variants in which the melody is hidden among garlands of ornaments. These slow movements are melodic and rhetorical at the same time; they sing, and they speak. Haydn first composed this new type of Adagio in 1773, placing it in 36 C, the first of the *Esterházy* set, almost as a declaration of a program. It is an equal of the Adagios of the quartets and the symphonies he was writing at that time. The prototype was so perfect that twenty years later, writing for the fortepiano rather than the harpsichord, Haydn could start another Adagio in the same key in fundamentally the same way. Example 149 illustrates both the similarities between the Adagios of 36 C and 60 C and the greater richness of the later work, reflecting Haydn's experiences with other Adagio themes.

Ex. 149. *a*, 36 C. *b*, 60 C. *c*, 52 G. *d*, 44 F.

The finely chiseled style of the Adagio of 60 C (ex. 150) is one of the great originals of Haydn's piano style. How many other composers between Bach and Verdi would have heaped over the simplest cadential formula such a beautiful group of cantabile ornaments?

Ex. 150. 60 C.

The Adagios of 44 F and 53 e are significant contributions to this richly ornamented but still cantabile style. Some themes of the Adagio of 48 C, in *alla breve* time, may remind the listener of Mozart, although Haydn's musical imprint is clear in the ornaments (marked * and ** in ex. 151) and in the formula for ending one phrase and starting another (marked ***). In the late 1770s, when 48 C was composed, Haydn was unlikely to have had any contact with the music of Mozart, who was then in the service of the archbishop of Salzburg, but they both shared in the heritage of the Italian cantabile style.

Ex. 151. 48 C.

The sonata-form principle in the slow movements in major embraces several different patterns, such as binary form and ternary form with double return after a real development,[3] and several ways of dealing with repeats, as is shown in figure 26 above. The first theme does not in itself necessarily determine the growth of the whole movement. It is particularly important, however, in works cast in Andante form, which has no repeat signs and in which the development is primarily a brief retransition to the home key. (In 44 F this section is only five measures long and in 60 C ten measures.) In Haydn's Andante form, the first theme is so heavily ornamented or in so original a piano texture that any repeat—whether exact or varied—would be meaningless. In the slow movements of two earlier concert-style sonatas, 30 D and 31 A♭, Haydn places repeat signs after both the exposition and the recapitulation, leaving to the performer the challenge of devising two improvised cadenzas—perhaps a short *Eingang* first and a longer cadenza when repeated—just before the closing measures of the movement. The Adagio of 52 G, composed in 1780, which has a twelve-measure

3. Double return is the return of the opening theme in the home key at the beginning of the recapitulation. See James Webster, "Sonata Form," in *The New Grove Dictionary of Music and Musicians,* vol. 6.

Ex. 152. Motives (i–iii) used in closing thematic areas. *a,* 31 A♭. *b,* 36 C. *c,* 52 G. *d,* 60 C.

cadenza written out in full (mm. 48–59), has a repeat sign after the exposition only.

Several of the slow movements in major have sonata-form expositions with three or more themes.[4] In these works, the functions of P, T,[5] S, and K can be easily distinguished. The proportions of the Adagio of 60 C, to take one example, are as follows: exposition (8 4 5 6), development (10), and recapitulation (8 6 5 6 + 5). The secondary area is often characterized by homogeneous textures, imitation, sequences, and equal-motion right-hand cantilena; well-shaped thematic formation is not a usual feature. Example 152 shows a group of motives that Haydn used in one form or another in the closing thematic areas of slow movements composed over a period of two decades. We are speaking here not of self-quotation but rather of a reflexive use of formulas within Haydn's individual style.

2. *Slow Sonata-Form Movements in Minor*

It is difficult to classify the slow sonata-form movements in minor because they show a great variety of tempos, meters, opening themes, and procedures for continuation following the opening theme (see fig. 27). The one generalization that we can make about these movements is that they all look back to the past and recompose traditional types in an original way. This ambition for "neo-Baroque stylization" and "Classicism" can be compared to the best of Stravinsky's so-called neo-Classical (or, sometimes, rather neo-Baroque or neo-Romantic) masterpieces, even though Haydn does not go back to very old and outmoded styles. In Vienna of the 1770s, probably owing in part to the current operatic repertoire and the contrapuntal preferences of the emperor's court, many Baroque musical styles and gestures had not yet outlived their usefulness. Sicilianos with sweet melodies and agitating unisons, Italianate slow movements with melodious triplets, Adagios in the embellished, concertante harpsichord style developed in northern Germany, and French overtures all met with the understanding of the audience.

Perhaps the example of Stravinsky can give us a better understanding of Haydn's aspirations. The true poet is able to evoke great emotions and to create original works even when he uses archaic vocabulary and employs the poetic forms of the past. His invention can, perhaps, flow more freely within the framework of a familiar type. Novelty alone is rarely a justification for the survival of a work of art.

The D minor Largo of 50 D is an outstanding keyboard piece in the style of the first section of a French overture. It is unlike any other sonata movement by Haydn and seems to be constructed as a period piece from well-known Baroque formulas. The $\frac{3}{8}$ Andante of 37 E and the Adagio siciliano in F minor of 38 F are

4. The Andante of 30 D presents seven different themes or independent motives.
5. T frequently originates in P.

In early partita sonatas:				
G minor 3/4 Largo	= 11 B♭	2	[ ]	(C. P. E. Bach's influence?)
G minor 4/4 Adagio	= 13 G	2	[ ]	"cantabile ♬ (triplet)"
Special case:				
D minor 3/4 Adagio	= 34 D	3	[:|→	(intermediary to the second type in major)
Stylized or "Classical" Baroque types:				
D minor ¢ Adagio	= 39 D	2	[→]	concertante harpsichord adagio
D minor 3/4 Largo e sostenuto	= 50 D	2	[:|→	"ouverture"-style
E minor 3/8 Andante	= 37 E	3	[:||:]	"cantabile ♬ (triplet)"
E minor 3/4 Allegretto	= 46 E	3	[:|→	three-part invention
E minor 6/8 Adagio	= 19 e I	3	[:|→	♩. ♪♩ siciliano
F minor 6/8 Adagio	= 38 F	2	[:||:]	♩. ♪♩ siciliano
C minor 6/8 Adagio	= 51 E♭	3	[V|→	♩. ♪♩ siciliano

FIGURE 27 Slow sonata-form movements in minor.

attractively melodic and contrast strikingly with some of the more complex slow movements that Haydn composed in the same period. The E minor middle movement of 46 E is such a fascinating example of strict, linear voice leading and contrapuntal elaboration in a keyboard piece that it is worth reminding the reader that Haydn did not, at the time he composed it, know the *Well-Tempered Clavier.* I have included it among the slow movements for lack of better classification, although its tempo is allegretto.

The formal structures of the slow movements in minor are more varied than their counterparts in major. Six of the ten works in our survey end on the dominant, leading directly into the final movement—another Baroque feature. The two least conventional structures are the slow movements of 51 E♭ and 34 D. The form of the Adagio siciliano in C minor—an exposition of thirteen measures, a written-out ornamented repetition of thirteen measures, a short development of six measures, and a recapitulation of thirteen measures—will reappear in the op. 33 string quartets, but in the sonata the recapitulation ends on the dominant. The remarkably beautiful Adagio in D minor of 39 D presents great interpretive challenges for the performer on a modern piano.[6] Its form is most unusual. The total length of the form is thirty-six and a half measures. The first twenty-four measures form the exposition: the first eight-measure phrase a detached, pathetic right-hand theme in D minor with staccato accompaniment; the

6. The staccato accompaniment of the first eight measures suggests a faster tempo than does the continuation, which is rich in thirty-second notes. The difference in time signatures between the autograph (**C**) and the authentic first edition (**¢**) indicates that Haydn may well have hesitated over the correct speed.

next eight-measure phrase an ornamented and developed version of the theme, in F major, above a legato, tenuto accompaniment; the third phrase a second theme and coda in F major. The remaining twelve and a half measures consist of a development of the primary theme and a reprise of the secondary theme. The harmonic plan, with its disjunct tonal terraces, also seems more rooted in the Baroque than in the Classical style (see ex. 153).

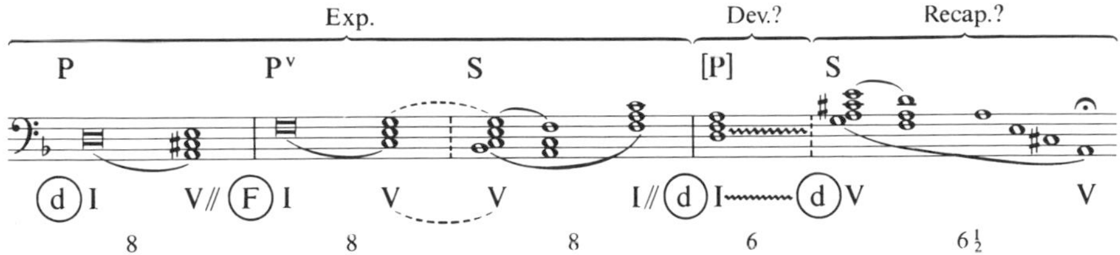

Ex. 153. Form and harmonic structure of 39 D II.

One may speculate about the artistic motivation for these Baroque-style movements, so full of pathos, and wonder to what extent Haydn was reflecting in these movements his experiences with opera or even with spoken drama.[7] Their notation suggests large-scale gestures and a theatrical declamation of the melody (see ex. 154). Works such as these, associated with the noblest *Empfindsamkeit* style of the age, explicitly require audacity in performance, bold gestures, and an inspired interpretation of the music that goes beyond the merely correct deciphering of the rhythm.

Ex. 154. *a,* 34 D. *b,* 51 E♭.

7. Guest theatrical companies appeared at Eszterháza starting in 1768. From 1772 on, Carl Wahr, recognized as a pioneer in the performance of Shakespeare in German, had a contract for his company to appear at Eszterháza each summer. This gave Haydn a special opportunity to become acquainted with masterpieces of dramatic literature. For full particulars, see Mátyás Horányi, *The Magnificence of Esterháza* (Budapest, 1962), 72ff.

Twenty-One

Minuets

Haydn's symphonies and string quartets undoubtedly contain the most illustrious examples of his immensely varied and original output of minuets. The *menuetto serio* type with its dramatic tension, the large minuets with contrast and action on the scale of a sonata form, or the presto minuets approaching the Beethovenian scherzo are in their proper place in four-movement genres. The minuets in the keyboard sonatas cannot rival them. Nevertheless, as we have said before, the solo sonata probably presents the most diversified use of the minuet. The position and function of the minuet within the multimovement work, as well as its structure, show more variation in the keyboard sonata than in other genres. In the mature sonatas, in two and three movements, the minuet appears in seven different positions with regard to the tempos of neighboring movements:[1]

1. Moderato–Minuet	28 D, 40 E♭, [20 B♭, 32 g]
2. Slow–Fast–Minuet	19 e
3. Fast–Slow–Minuet	34 D, 37 E, 45 A, 59 E♭, [48 C]
4. Moderato–Slow–Minuet	44 F, [51 E♭]
5. Moderato–Fast–Minuet	49 c♯
6. Moderato–Minuet–Fast	41 A, 43 E♭, 47 b, (35 A♭)
7. Fast–Minuet–Fast	42 G

What is more, these minuets can be grouped into five different structural types:

1. Minuet-rhythm movements without the title *Menuet* are listed in square brackets; the minuet of 35 A♭, probably not by Haydn, is listed in parentheses.

a. Minuet–Trio–Minuet	28 D, 41 A, 42 G, 43 E♭, 47 b, 49 c♯, [51 E♭], (35 A♭)
b. Only Minuet (= minuet sonata form)	19 e, 40 E♭, [20 B♭]
c. Minuet theme and variations	45 A[2]
d. Double variations on a minuet theme	34 D, 37 E
e. Hybrid variations	44 F, 59 E♭, [32 g, 48 C]

This great diversity of structures is the product of the flexibility of the multimovement form of Haydn's keyboard sonatas. The minuet in the keyboard sonatas, in contrast to string quartets or symphonies, is not obliged to appear as the third movement of the four-movement work—indeed, it is not obliged to appear at all. Haydn can use it, with the freedom of a divertimento or the capriciousness of a soloistic genre, wherever his sense of balance finds it appropriate.[3]

Three kinds of titles for minuet movements, with some variations in spelling, are found in the various primary and secondary sources from the eighteenth century. The regular Menuet–Trio–Menuet form (M–T–M) is marked *Menuet.* (Haydn generally used the French spelling.) Irregular forms, such as types b and e listed above, are called *Tempo di Menuet.* If the minuet is a finale, it is sometimes called *Finale. Tempo di Menuet.* A third group is made up of triple-meter, minuet-related pieces for which the word *Menuet* does not appear at all, only a tempo indication.

Among the mature sonatas, fourteen contain movements entitled *Menuet.*[4] This group can be increased by the inclusion of the following four "disguised" minuets. The third movement of 51 E♭, marked *Finale. Allegro,* has a regular M–T–M form. It is the only minuet in the sonatas with a trio in the subdominant. The second movement of 32 g, marked *Allegretto,* is a hybrid variation with true minuet character. The second movement of 20 B♭, marked *Moderato,* has a distinctly minuet character. There is no trio but instead a 110-measure-long

2. Another solo keyboard piece connected with this group is Hob. XVII:3, a set of twelve variations on a theme in E♭ that originates in the minuet of the String Quartet in E♭, op. 9. Indirectly connected with this group is Hob. XVII:2, a set of variations on a triple-meter theme, clearly of minuet character. This piece exists in two versions, a G major version with twenty variations and an A major version with twelve variations. Also related to this group is Hob. XVII:7, a theme and five variations in D major.

3. With regard to the role of the minuet in the multimovement scheme, three other genres can be considered closely related to the sonata—string trios, duos, and baryton trios. The three-movement form of the string trio, Hob. V, typically includes a Tempo di Menuet finale without trio, ranging from fifty to 164 measures. Menuet finales with trios can also be found. All six authentic duos, Hob. VI, have Tempo di Menuet finales ranging from sixty-four to ninety-six measures. The baryton trios, Hob. XI, also employ a great number of minuet finales, although not in such a varied way as the sonatas. In addition, there are a few Tempo di Menuet finales among Haydn's symphonies written before 1765 (nos. 4, 9, 18, 26, 30). Some of these symphonies are three-movement works.

4. This includes 35 A♭, whose authenticity is debatable. The *JHW* marks the movement *Menuet* and the *WUE Menuetto.*

movement in sonata form.[5] The third movement of 48 C, marked *Finale. Allegro,* with minuet-like thematic material, is a hybrid form combining minuet and rondo. It is obviously the prototype for the *Tempo di Minuet* finale of 59 E♭.

Other finales, in faster tempos but with first themes in minuet character, such as the third movements of 29 E♭ and 33 c, were discussed in the section on finale sonata forms.

If a minuet can replace either a slow movement or a finale, if it can counterbalance a sonata-form opening movement in a two-movement work, it has to be a substantial piece of music with an important message. What is the significance and scope of the minuet movements?

Since the minuets differ substantially in size and in formal structure, from simple minuet forms to complex hybrid forms, let us first investigate the relation between length and complexity of form. The longest minuets are the minuets without trio, in minuet-sonata form. For example, the minuet of 20 B♭ is 110 measures long, that of 19 e sixty-eight measures, and that of 40 E♭ forty-four measures. The shortest minuets, on the other hand, are those that are followed by a set of variations or are part of a double variation form. In 45 A, the minuet theme is 8 + 8 measures, followed by six variations; in 34 D and 37 E, the minuets of 8 + 8 measures are parts of double-variation forms. Table 21 summarizes the structures and numbers of measures of eighteen minuet movements. The number refers to the measures actually performed, including repeats,[6] not just the number of measures printed. The works whose form has not been identified are in the most frequent form, M–T–M. Table 21 suggests that, independent of the average size of the setting determined by the chosen form, even the length reflects the contents and that "significant" works are usually longer pieces than the less significant minuets.

The two longest minuet-trio-minuet movements, 28 D and 42 G, are the proper size for the sonatas in which they are placed.[7] However, they are not richer

5. This would not be unusually long for a sonata-form finale by Haydn with a *Tempo di Menuet* title. See, e.g., the string trios Hob. V:19 (164 measures) and V:12 (109 measures).

6. When a second number appears in parentheses, it gives the total number of measures in the movement including repeats in the *da capo* of the minuet as well.

7. Haydn generally composed longer minuets and trios for his string quartets and symphonies. Listed below, with number of printed measures and total number of measures in performance (in parentheses, including repeats in the *da capo* of the minuet as well), are some of the longest minuet movements in his string quartets and symphonies:

1771	Op. 17 E	50 + 32 = 214 (264)
1772	Op. 20 f	54 + 46 = 254 (308)
ca. 1797	Op. 76 E♭ ("Alternativo"-Trio)	60 + 96 = 276 (336)
1799	Op. 77 G (Presto-minuet)	82 + 100 = 446 (528)
1772	Symphony no. 45 (*Farewell*)	40 + 36 = 192 (232)
1773	Symphony no. 50 in C	56 + 46 = 260 (316)
1794	Symphony no. 101 (*Clock*)	80 + 80 = 400 (480)

TABLE 21 SUMMARY OF MINUET MOVEMENTS

	Measures printed (Performed)	Form		Measures printed (Performed)	Form
45 A	224	Theme and variations	19 e	136	M only
20 B♭	220	Minuet sonata form	32 g	133	Hybrid form
28 D	214 (252)		43 E♭	128 (160)	
42 G	174 (216)		51 E♭	128 (156)	
59 E♭	171	Hybrid form	41 A	108 (128)	
44 F	162	M–T–M^1–M^2	47 b	102 (124)	
34 D	160	Double variations	35 A♭	102 (124)	
48 C	158	Hybrid form	40 E♭	88	M only
49 c♯	141 (172)				
37 E	140	Double variations			

in content or weightier in material than, for example, the minuet of 47 b. Even the proportions and balances within the sonata are not simply a matter of length. The short Tempo di Menuet without trio of 40 E♭ makes a suitable contrast to the vast, eventful Moderato opening movement. The canonic texture of the minuet guarantees that small will not be equated with lightweight.

Since the phrase structure of the minuet has its origins in regular choreographic patterns, any asymmetries or unusual proportions between the sections have special significance. The minuet is ordinarily longer than the trio; in 43 E♭, the thirty-two-measure minuet is in fact twice as long as the sixteen-measure trio. Occasionally, as in 28 D and 41 A, the trio is longer than the minuet, and in one case, 59 E♭, the minuet and quasi trio are equal in length, but this is not a simple M–T–M form. An odd number of measures always means something special, often a written-out ritardando or fermata, as in 44 F (T = 8 + 19), 49 c♯ (M = 8 + 23), and 48 C (first part = 8 + 17). As one might expect, a pair of eight-measure phrases is frequently the fundamental structural unit. In 34 D, both the major and the minor themes of the Tempo di Menuet set of double variations are built on a pair of eight-measure phrases. The same is true of the variation theme of 45 A, the major variation theme of 37 E, the trio in 43 E♭, and the minor-mode section in 48 C.[8] The minuet and trio of 59 E♭ and the trio of 42 G are among the

8. Other balanced pairs of phrases are 10 + 10 in the minuet of 14 A and 12 + 12 in the trios of 41 A and 49 c♯.

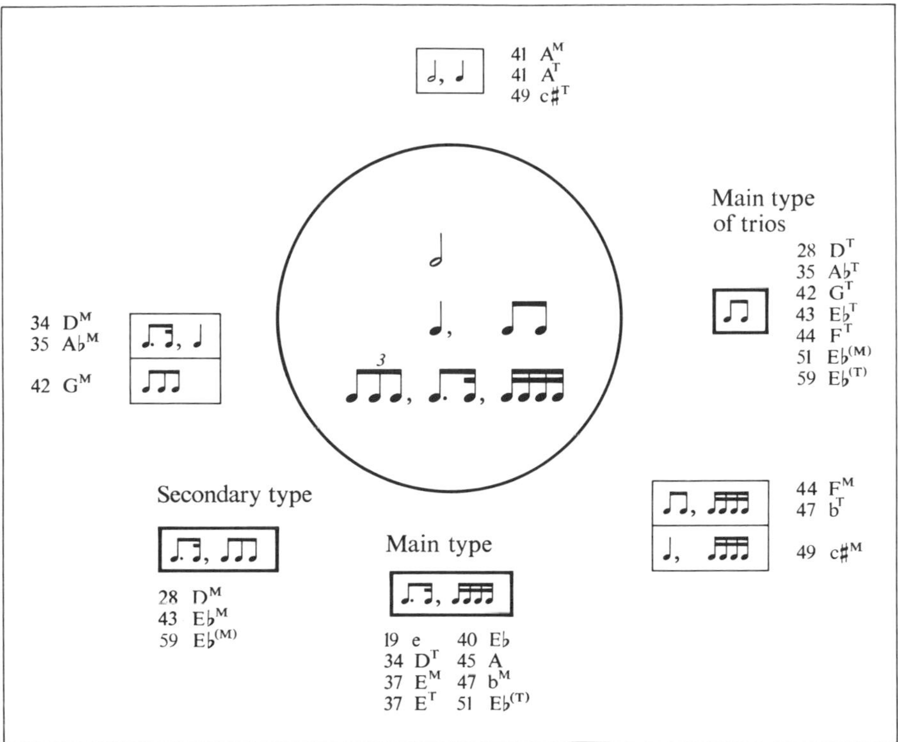

FIGURE 28 A rhythmic classification of the minuets.

very few examples of 8+16-measure phrase structures.[9] Several noble and gentle minuets by Haydn work with a combination of four-measure and six-measure phrases. For example, the phrase pattern of the minuet of 47 b is 4+6 ‖ 6+6 and the trio 4+4 ‖ 6+6, and the pattern of the minor theme of the Allegretto movement of 32 g is 6 ‖ 8+4, 6.

We may also classify Haydn's minuet movements by their characteristic rhythmic codes (see fig. 28). This classification reveals three types—a main minuet type with dotted rhythms and sixteenth-note motion, a secondary *galant* minuet type with dotted rhythms and triplets, and a third type that we find most often in trios. The minuets that contain only dotted rhythms or only triplets tend to be attractive but somewhat lighter in style; true *serio* minuets generally avoid dotted rhythms and triplets.

In addition to the characteristic rhythmic codes, with their strong element of simplification, it is worth looking at the *thematic head rhythm.* Haydn's minuets and trios are almost equally divided between those that begin on the down-

9. In the minuet of 42 G, what might at first look like a simple doubling of the length (14+28) is in fact a rather complex sentence structure (4 4+6 ‖ 4+6 4; 4 2 8).

TABLE 22 RHYTHMIC PATTERNS

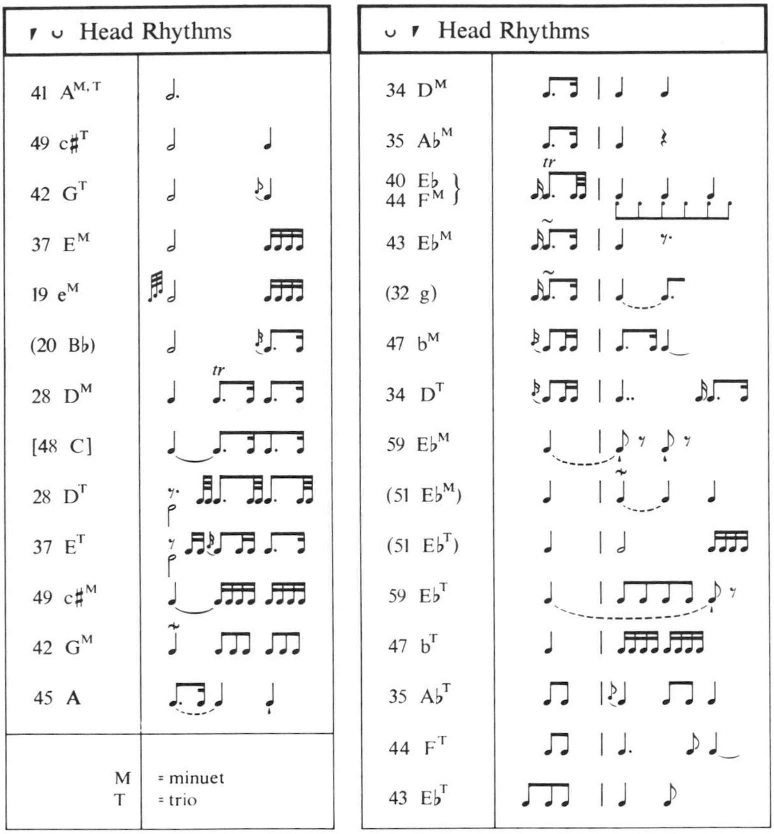

◡ Head Rhythms	
41 A^{M,T}	
49 c♯^{T}	
42 G^{T}	
37 E^{M}	
19 e^{M}	
(20 B♭)	
28 D^{M}	
[48 C]	
28 D^{T}	
37 E^{T}	
49 c♯^{M}	
42 G^{M}	
45 A	
M T	= minuet = trio

◡ Head Rhythms	
34 D^{M}	
35 A♭^{M}	
40 E♭ 44 F^{M}	
43 E♭^{M}	
(32 g)	
47 b^{M}	
34 D^{T}	
59 E♭^{M}	
(51 E♭^{M})	
(51 E♭^{T})	
59 E♭^{T}	
47 b^{T}	
35 A♭^{T}	
44 F^{T}	
43 E♭^{T}	

beat and those that begin on the upbeat.[10] In table 22, the rhythmic patterns are grouped in a systematic order, to some extent going from simpler to more complex. I recommend playing the beginnings of the minuets and trios in the order listed in this table to explore the exquisite details of Haydn's thematic invention and to discover what is reflexive and what is original in the compositions.

The principal contrast in minuet movements is between the largest elements of the structure, that is, between the minuet and the trio, or, in complex and hybrid forms, in the variations. The power and effect of these movements depend on the performer properly enforcing these contrasts. The main parameters producing contrast are key, mode, rhythm, and texture.

Tonal and modal contrast. Contrast between major-mode and minor-mode

10. The basic pattern of head rhythms is the same in the minuet and the trio section of the same movement. Haydn does not begin a minuet on an upbeat and then have its trio begin on a downbeat, or vice versa.

sections is present in almost all minuet movements. Examples of this contrast in its simplest form, minuet in major and trio in minor (M–m–M), are found in 28 D, 42 G, 43 E♭, and 47 b;[11] the converse (m–M–m) is found in 49 c♯. In 34 D and 37 E, the Tempo di Menuet movements alternate major and minor themes and variations. The Allegretto movement of 32 g has a m–M–m–M pattern of contrast. 44 F, 59 E♭, and 48 C all have one contrasting phrase or pair of phrases in minor. Only four minuet movements completely lack sections in a contrasting mode. The minuet and trio of 41 A, borrowed from the Symphony no. 47, is a *canon cancrizans;* the finale of 51 E♭ has a trio in the subdominant; the finale of 45 A is all in major. Finally, the minuet and trio of 35 A♭, a sonata of dubious authenticity, are both in major.

Contrasting rhythm and texture. The contrast between richly varied rhythm (♩.♪, ♪♪♩, ♩♬♬) and simple rhythmic patterns (♩ ♪) or between high and low tessitura (see 47 b) is among the fundamental means for producing a contrast between the minuet and the trio. In addition to these, there are numerous exquisite, organic contrasts of ideas in the minuets. The eighteenth-century ideal of unity and diversity (*Einheit und Mannigfaltigkeit*) can be recognized in the way the minor theme of the finale of 34 D borrows rhythmic elements from the major theme. In 43 E♭, the contrast in rhythm and mode is heightened by the mirror motion of the melody. The minor-mode and major-mode themes in 49 c♯ form organic contrasts down to the smallest details (see ex. 155*a–c*).

Ex. 155. *a,* 34 D. *b,* 43 E♭.

11. Contrast between major and minor is evident throughout 47 b: m (I), M–m–M (II), m (III).

Ex. 155, cont. *c*, 49 c♯.

In 44 F, Haydn seems to use up the possible rhythmic permutations in varied statements of the minuet theme. But he saves for the trio a series of hidden hemiolas (see ex. 156).

Ex. 156. 44 F.

The minuet movements in double-variation form or other hybrid forms have, in addition to the fundamental contrast of major and minor themes, a strategy of rhythmic variation. Since the number of variations in these forms is small, it might be better to speak of *veränderte Reprise,* that is, varied reprise or ornamented embellished return. In 34 D, the variations follow a scheme of rhythmic diminution: the head motive of the theme is in quarters, then in eighths in the first variation, while the second variation unfolds a series of sixteenth notes. In 37 E, the differentiated rhythm of the theme is followed first by simple sixteenth-note motion and then by a chromatic variant in eighth notes (see ex. 157).

Ex. 157. *a,* 34 D. *b,* 37 E.

The essential issue in these variation and hybrid forms concerns the way the open form of a chain of variants is articulated by the strong architectonic effect of the "double return" of the opening theme. 34 D and 37 E, written in close proximity, show Haydn first experimenting with a form, then immediately revising it in another work (see fig. 29).

Major theme
A A B B
(34 D)
a a b b
Minor theme
Var. I
A^1 A^1 B^1 B^1
a^1 a^1 b^1 b^1
Var. 1
Recap. & Var. II
A A^2 B^2 B^2

Major theme
A A B B
(37 E)
a a b
Minor theme
First recap. with written-out var.
A A^1 B B^1
a^x a^x b^x
Recap. with minimal var. by change of voices
Second recap. with written-out var.
A A^2 B B^2

Minuet
A A B+A B+A
(59 E♭)
Rondo theme
Trio
C C D+C D+C c
First couplet
A
Retransition
Short recap. of rondo
Minuet theme in minor
$A^\flat$ $A^\flat$ $(B)^\flat$ $(B)^\flat$
Second couplet
Recap. without repetition with minimal var.
A B $+A^1$ +k
Ritornello

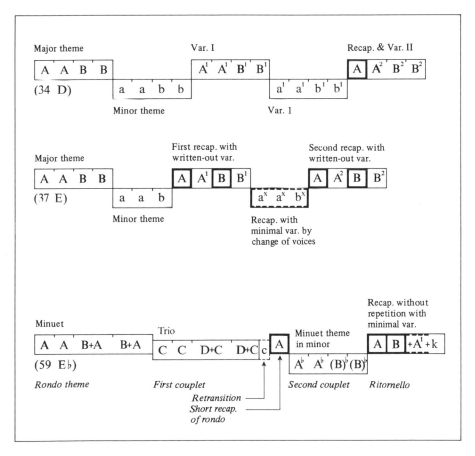

FIGURE 29 Double-return effect in minuet variation and hybrid forms.

In 34 D, the emphasis is on the chain of variations. The return of the first phrase of the theme serves only to announce the approaching end of the movement. In 37 E, the emphasis shifts to the returns of the theme, which then initiate their own variations.[12] The full realization of this form is the finale of 59 E♭, which can be interpreted as an irregular minuet containing variation, recapitulation, and partial recapitulation or else as a rondo. Intriguing as the form is, the most remarkable thing about this movement is the thematic material itself. Slender minuet staccatos, radiant dotted rhythms, triplets flowing like pearls after duplets, are all evoked like visions of memory. Haydn was rightly proud of this piece, meant as a special gift to a dear friend, as we know from his letter dated 20 July 1790.[13]

Finally, let us briefly mention two more fine works that bring together minuet themes and variation procedures, the finale of 45 A and Hob. XVII:3 in E♭, variously titled *Menuetto con variazioni* and *Arietta con 12 variazioni.* Both these works have inspired moments of false recapitulation, that is, points in the chain of variations that start out deceptively as if they were the final return of the theme. In 45 A, this takes place in the second variation; in XVII:3, variations 3, 7, and 11 all begin by quoting the start of the theme.

12. The best example of a pseudo-varied return is found in the third movement of 37 E, mm. 63–75, in which the material of mm. 17–30 recurs with the voice parts exchanged. Haydn might have remembered this movement when he wrote 59 E♭ III (cf. mm. 9–10 and 95–96).

13. Haydn, *Briefe,* 240.

Twenty-Two

Rondos *and* Fast Variation Forms

An important group of fast finales, in addition to those in sonata form or related to minuets, are those based on rondo or on variation principles. The thematic material, the structure, and the style of these movements are very typical of Haydn; all are missing from Mozart's sonatas. These features present a concentrated manifestation of Haydn's musical thought, specifically typical of his keyboard sonatas.

There are twelve works in this group, which omits 48 C III, a hybrid minuet form with rondo elements, and 58 C II, the only sonata rondo, but includes 49 c♯ II and 52 G I. Almost all these movements are delights for the performer. 35 A♭, which may not be by Haydn, can boast an "à la Haydn" rondo as its best movement.

These movements, by and large, have equally fast tempos, although they do not all have the same tempo indications.[1] The slight differences in speed can be compared to the equally justified variations in tempo of first-movement sonata forms marked *Moderato* or *Allegro moderato*. The forms of the movements, on the other hand, are much more varied. The twelve works form five groups.[2]

1. There are, in fact, six different tempo indications. The six movements marked *Presto* are equally fast despite differences in meter (35 A♭, 42 G, 13 E♭, and 46 F are in $\frac{2}{4}$; 39 D is in $\frac{3}{4}$; 54 G is in $\frac{4}{4}$). 50 D marked *Presto ma non troppo,* 53 e marked *Vivace molto,* 55 B♭ marked *Allegro di molto,* and 30 D marked *Allegro assai* are not much slower. The two movements marked *Allegro con brio,* 52 G and especially 49 c♯ because of its dotted thematic material, are just slightly slower.

2. I have adopted some of the terms that Elaine Sisman developed in her study of Haydn's strophic and hybrid variations ("Small and Expanded Forms"). With respect to the piano sonatas, however, I have in some cases found my own terms more useful.

Strophic variations (but not Theme and variations)[3] are found in the third movements of 42 G, 43 E♭, and 46 E. *Double variations*[4] are found in the second movement of 49 c♯ and the third movement of 53 e. *Rondo variations*[5] are found in the third movements of 30 D and 50 D and the first movement of 52 G. The third movement of 35 A♭ is a *rondo*. *A A A ternary variations*[6] forms the finale of 39 D. *A B A forms with varied reprise* are found in the second movements of 54 G and 55 B♭.

The situation is made more complex by the inner development of these structures: each movement is different from the others within the same group. On the other hand, it is simpler because the structures do not exist and develop within Haydn's work at the same time. The typological and chronological relations of the movements are summarized in figure 30. This survey offers insights into the logic of Haydn's experiments and innovations in these movements. The movements marked with an asterisk are especially important in the evolutionary process.

The earliest movement in this group, a true archetype, is the finale of 30 D. Its tempo marking, Allegro assai, was not often used by Haydn at this time. Haydn might have used a C. P. E. Bach sonata as a model[7] for this hybridization of variation and rondo principles, for it is a remarkably assured first attempt. The movement is full of surprises, such as thematic blocks that give no clue as to what will follow and strong episodes that evoke Hungarian or *alla turca* music. The length of each theme and the structure of each sentence are different, as is shown in figure 31. The *innocentemente* finale of 50 D, by comparison, looks like a mild copy.

Another significant step toward the new type is the Presto finale of 42 G. Haydn uses as the subject for variation a contredanse-like theme such as he had used in other finales starting from 1773 on.[8] The structure of the movement is

3. The dividing line between theme and variations and strophic variations is, in my opinion, clear. A theme and variations consists of regular, sharply divided blocks of equal length, articulated by double bar lines; frequently, the variation blocks are formally indicated by giving each a number. Strophic variations are an "irregular" chain in which the cadential structure, or the number of measures in a section, or the key or mode, is variable. Strophic variations is, in short, a more open, more flexible form than theme and variations.

4. Instead of accepting Sisman's terms *alternating variations* or *alternating strophic variations*, I am using the more familiar *double variations*.

5. According to Sisman ("Haydn's Hybrid Variations," 513), the finale of 50 D does not belong to this category.

6. In Sisman's opinion ("New Views"), *ternary variations* comprises strophic variations. However, the ternary contours of an exceptional A A^{v} A content (or rather A A^{v} a, with the shortened reprise that is hardly more than a coda) replacing the usual A B A are so remarkably apparent that we can introduce the term *A A A ternary variations* here.

7. Number 6 of the *Sonaten mit veränderten Reprisen* (1760, H. 140), available in 1767 in Vienna (see Sisman, "Haydn's Hybrid Variations," 512).

8. The finale of 38 F, in sonata form, is Haydn's first use of a contredanse-like theme in the keyboard sonatas (see p. 300).

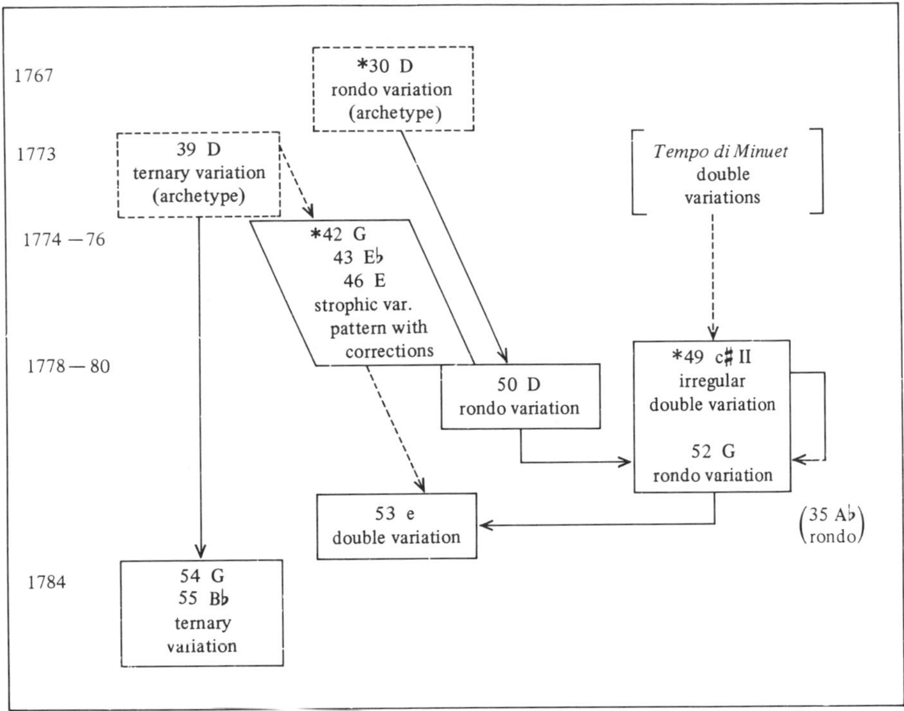

FIGURE 30 Chronology and typology of rondos and fast variation forms. Movements marked with an asterisk are especially important in the evolutionary process.

ingeniously simple, yet rich in surprises (see fig. 31). After the theme and the regular variations are presented ($A\ A^1\ A^2\ldots$; see ex. 158), the first phrase of the theme is brought back, but it immediately darkens into a minor-mode variation ($\ldots A^{3(\flat)}$). This serves as a retransition to a real reprise variation, which is enriched with written-out varied repeats ($A^{r/4}$). The structure of the irregular strophic variations seems to be improved in the finale of another sonata of the set, 43 E♭. Here, the minor variation, $A^{3(\flat)}$, is inserted into a pseudoreprise in major,[9] and an independent fourth variation comes before the true reprise. The finale of 46 E condenses this form (see fig. 31). Its variations are not primarily rhythmic

9. It is a kind of false reprise only because out of the original structure of the A theme—i.e., $a^1\ a^2\ a^3\ a^4$ with phrase lengths 6+6 4+6—it restates only two phrases, a^1 and a^4: a^1 *a^1 a^3 retrans.* $a^1\ a^4$ (the phrases in italic are in minor mode), 6 6+8+8 6 6. We may diagram the original theme (mm. 1–22):

a^1	a^2	‖	a^3	a^4	and the variation	a^1 +	*a^1*	*a^3* +	*retrans.*	a^1	a^4
6	6		4	6		6	*6*	*8*	*8*	6	6

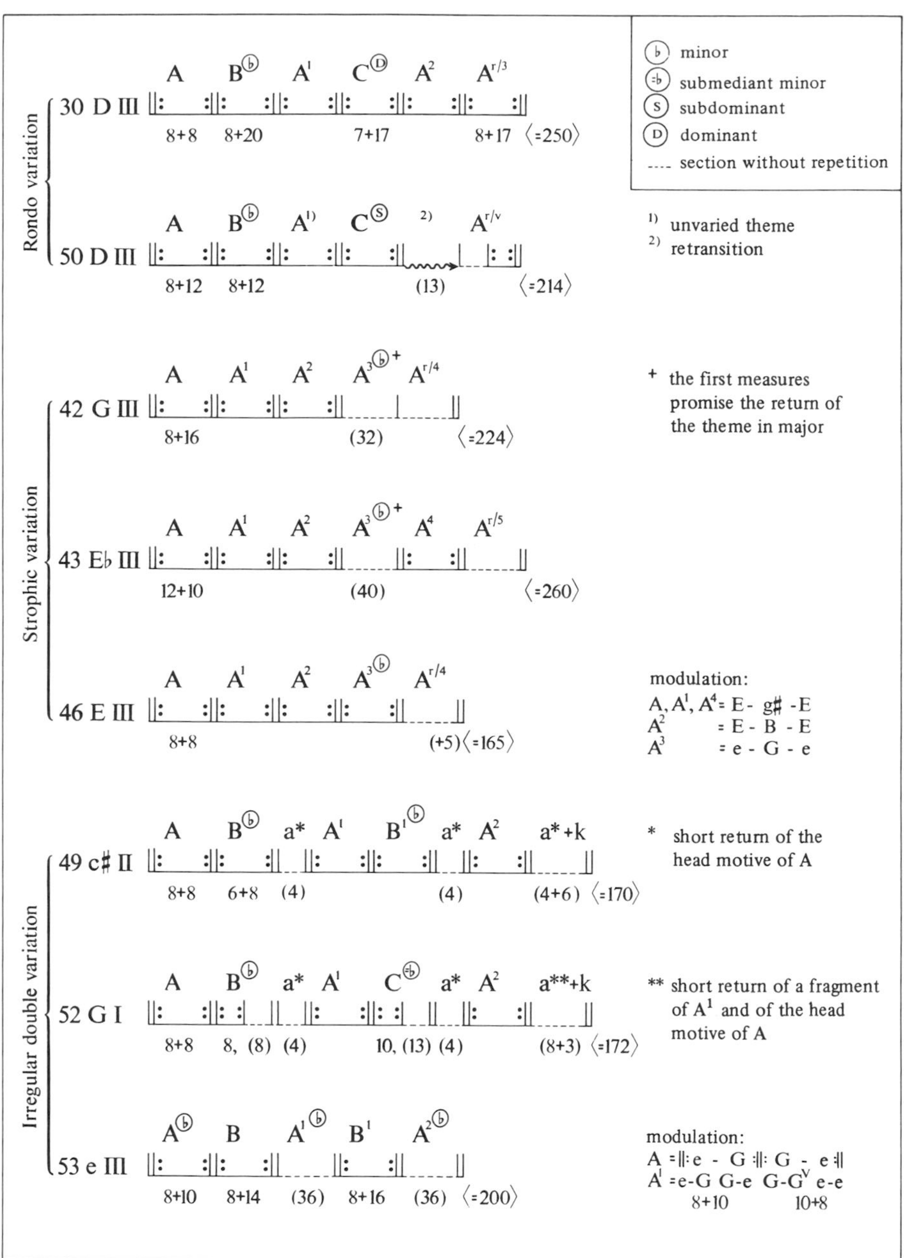

FIGURE 31 Structural evolution of variation forms.

but, rather, show changes in articulation and touch and inventive arrangements of the cadences (see ex. 158).

Ex. 158. *a,* 42 G. *b,* 46 E.

As the third major step forward, the A major Scherzando, Allegro con brio movement of 49 c♯ is also full of structural innovations (see fig. 31). Composed around 1779–80, it is a reworking of the principle of minuet double variations. There is great wit in the idea of recapitulating the first four measures of the theme (a) before every A variation, as if a rondo ritornello were starting. When Haydn reused this theme for the opening movement of 52 G, published in the same opus, an act he defended with a public announcement,[10] he retained the micro-ritornello idea, even though 52 G is in rondo form. The section that was the variation of the minor theme in the Scherzando (mm. 51–64) is replaced in 52 G by new material in the submediant (mm. 53–75), which can be called a second couplet in a rondo form.[11] This pair of movements, often discussed, points up the illusory value of labels and categories for elucidating formal structures. The variations of theme A are characteristically different in the two sister movements: the A major piece is graceful and smooth and leads into a legato variant; the G major form is heavier, more passionate, and the dotted-rhythm patterns are in *all' ungherese* style. Both movements excel in beauty and originality.

The last movement of 53 e,[12] to be played *innocentemente,* continues to

10. See n. 67, chap. 10.

11. Measures 17–32 in G minor and mm. 53–75 in E minor are real couplets because their second halves are not repeated but rather lead back to the rondo theme.

12. This movement is best categorized as a double-variation form, although there are elements of rondo or rondo variation—ritornello, first couplet, varied ritornello, second couplet, ritornello. Haydn explicitly works against the tradition of variations in this movement by insistently using an Alberti-bass accompaniment for the entire movement, excepting the statement of the major theme in mm. 19–40.

play with a structural idea first presented in the finale of 46 E (see fig. 31). In both works, the primary aim of the variations is the ever-changing arrangement of the cadences of the musical sentences. The theme of the E minor finale is made up of an eight-measure phrase, repeated, that moves from E minor to G major and a related ten-measure phrase, repeated, that travels from G major back to E minor ($a^1 + a^2 = 8 + 10$). When the theme returns in measure 41, after a contrasting E major section, Haydn first gives a slightly varied reprise of $a^1 + a^2 = 8 + 10$, without repeats, followed by variants of both phrases in reverse order, that is, $a^2 + a^1 = 10 + 8$, producing the tonal pattern G → G e → e.[13] It is one of the most sparkling among Haydn's humorous and sophisticated tricks.

Finally, we come to a group of fast finales with the simplest shape, ternary form with varied reprise, which Haydn reworked in his own distinctive manner. The two radiantly fresh finales of the *Bossler* sonatas, 54 G and 55 B♭, with minor-mode middle sections and varied reprises, are highly effective works (see ex. 159). Contrapuntal elaboration has a central role in the fiery effect of both movements; both hands are extremely busy playing independent motives, inverted parts, and fast lines in contrary motion. The minor theme of the finale of 55 B♭ is based on the opening major theme. In both finales, the second section of part A begins with an inversion of the head motive, as in some Baroque gigues, but with certain surprises. In the 54 G finale, the first section of A moves from G to D, but the second section begins in B♭; in the 55 B♭ finale, the articulation changes to sorrowful two-note slurs. Inevitably, one senses a certain neo-Baroque style and elegant mannerism.

Ex. 159. *a*, 54 G. *b*, 55 B♭.

The most peculiar and at the same time perhaps the most original of the fast ternary forms is the earliest one, the $\frac{3}{4}$ Presto finale of 39 D, composed in 1773. This striking masterpiece takes all of two and a half minutes to play. The

13. The variation of the major theme (mm. 77–100) is also irregular. Owing to the extension of the fermata (cf. mm. 31–32 with mm. 89–92), the second half is sixteen measures instead of fourteen.

first section, made up of twenty-four measures repeated plus sixteen measures repeated, sounds like a true scherzo. The next section, of the same length and proportions, is a playful variation reminiscent of a chirping *Flötenuhr,* an eighteenth-century mechanical musical instrument. The final section has a truncated reprise followed, after a fermata, by a coda that evokes Beethoven. There is much that seems topsy-turvy in this movement: the second part of the rounded-binary A section is shorter than the first, the second part of this "ternary" form is a variation rather than a contrasting section, and the third part, less than half the size of the first, contains only an eight-measure reprise of the opening phrase plus a twenty-three-measure coda. Can we say that this piece is a whimsical caprice, reminiscent of C. P. E. Bach, not a Classical, mature piece?

Twenty-Three

Slow Variations *and* Double Variations

In the last decade in which Haydn composed piano sonatas, ca. 1783–94, he wrote several novel—indeed, extraordinary—slow movements. With one exception, the second movement of 60 C,[1] Haydn no longer composed slow movements in sonata form. When the slow movement was the second of a three-movement work, Haydn cast it in a ternary form in which variation played an important role. When the slow movement was the first of a two-movement work, he used the double-variation procedure.

In this section, we will forgo a general inquiry into a type in favor of the examination of individual pieces, some of which appear to be among Haydn's most personal compositions. But as we turn from one piece to the next we cannot help but be impressed by the way Haydn's genius continually reworks a concept that even from the outset was created with great care. We will turn our attention to four sets of double variations, the first movements of 54 G, 56 D, and 58 C and the F Minor Variations, Hob. XVII:6,[2] and to the middle movements of 59 E♭, the last Viennese sonata, and 62 E♭, in London style.

We have already discussed Haydn's treatment of the double-variation form in minuets and fast movements and noted the fecundity with which he produced several different types of the same general structure. In about 1783–84, when Haydn first used the slow double variation as the opening movement of a sonata,

1. This movement may have originally been intended as an independent piece.

2. The F Minor Variations might have been composed originally as the first movement of a sonata. The autograph bears the title *Sonata,* and a copy by Elssler, signed by Haydn, is titled *Sonata per il Piano Forte.* However, we have no further movements.

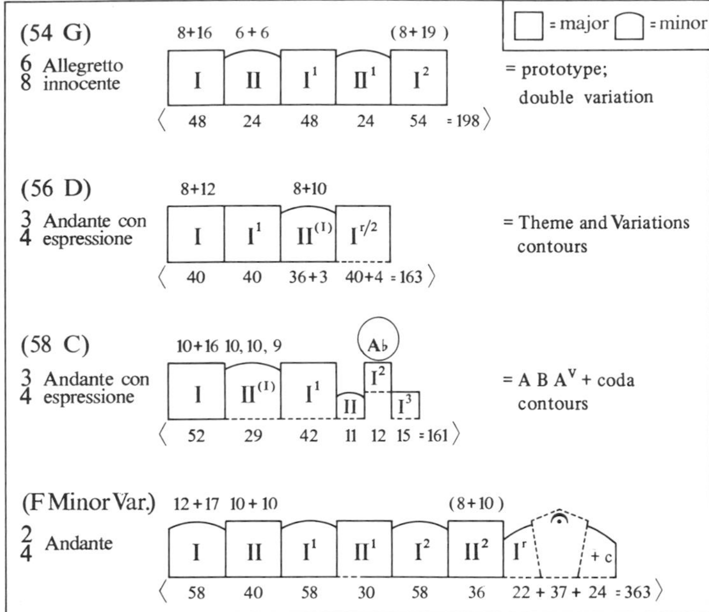

FIGURE 32 Variants of the slow double-variations form.

this same recombinant procedure was repeated (see fig. 32).[3] 54 G, the prototype, is a clearly arranged five-part form. The opening section, almost like a *Lied* in its melodic and harmonic character, is a rare type among Haydn's instrumental themes. Both themes and each variation are supplied with repeat signs, and there is no "recapitulation" in the movement.[4]

The first movements of 56 D and 58 C show Haydn improving on the prototype in several ways. He finds a new character for the theme and a new tempo, composing a $\frac{3}{4}$ Andante con espressione type that is extremely delicate but nevertheless susceptible to further rhythmic diminution and embellishment. Moreover, Haydn no longer feels obliged to keep to a regular pattern of alternation of major and minor thematic sections. In 56 D, he delays the statement of the minor theme and does not compose a variation of it. One could, in fact, consider this movement a theme and variations with one minor variation. In 58 C, he modifies

3. Elaine Sisman ("Haydn's Hybrid Forms," 513) classifies the double-variation-like movements that close with the first theme—among them 54 G I and 58 C I—together with alternative rondo variations. In my opinion, a work that begins I II I^1 II^1 suggests double variations so strongly that an unconventional continuation does not cause us to reinterpret the form as a rondo.

4. The only irregularity is in I^2, which has a three-measure extension (mm. 89–91) before the fermata, producing 8 ‖ 11+8 instead of 8 ‖ 8+8.

the structure again. After measure 98, fragments of the theme are varied, a related key is visited, and the last variation is shortened to almost a coda.[5] These modifications bring the structural contours closer to an A B^{trio} $\text{A}^{\text{var.}}$ ternary form with an especially rich coda. In addition, Haydn seems to be experimenting in these two variation movements with creating the feeling of a real recapitulation. The effect of recapitulation is evoked quite unconventionally in 58 C with the exact repetition of single measures and easily remembered phrases within the varied return.[6]

The F Minor Variations have some points of contact with the variation movements of 54 G, 56 D, and 58 C, such as similarity in range of tempo. However, the $\frac{2}{4}$ meter, the primary position of the minor theme, and the seven-part form all distinguish this work from its predecessors. The enormous fantasia-cadenza, which underwent a later revision,[7] comes as a great surprise. Two other exquisite formal modifications—the lack of repetition of the first phrase of II^1 and the contraction of the first phrase of II^2 from ten measures to eight—are further indications that Haydn's invention with regard to double variations was far from exhausted.

A study of the first themes of those four variation movements gives further indications of Haydn's move away from the typical in favor of more individual and original types. The phrase structures become progressively more asymmetric:

54 G	8 ‖ 8+8
56 D	8 ‖ 4+8
58 C	10 ‖ 7+9
F Minor	12* ‖ 5+12**
	(12* = 6+6 but 12** = 5+7)

The ten-, seven-, and nine-measure phrases of the C major theme are fairly irregular in themselves, and they appear even more unorthodox if we look at their motivic construction. The opening ten measures are not constructed as an extension of an eight-measure phrase but rather group themselves as shown in example 160. The theme evolves from the varied repetition and development of

5. Measures 121–28 are a variation of mm. 18–26, and mm. 129–34 are an extension inserted before the closing measure.

6. The corresponding measures are as follows:

I:	1	2 ...	11	12	13	14	15	16	17 ...	24	25	26
I^1: {	56	57 ...	66		68	69	70	(71)	72 ...		80	81
						(85)	86	(87)	88 ...	95	96	97

7. See n. 50, chap. 4.

Ex. 160. Motivic structure of the first theme of 58 C I.

two- or one-measure motives in a 2 2+1 3+2 structure. Measure 7 has a double melodic function, welding measures 6–7 and 7–8. Simultaneously, the first departure from C major takes place in measure 7. The reduction of the theme given in example 161 shows the striking number of harmonic surprises that Haydn allotted to this extraordinary theme. In just twenty-six measures, the theme touches five keys, some of which are quite unexpected. There is a hint of E minor before we arrive at G major; C minor glides into E♭ major. The tonic-dominant pendulum is ingeniously combined with swift harmonic events, the unforeseeable with a regular cadential idiom.

The first ten measures, shown in example 160, present two compositional features characteristic of all four slow variation movements. One has to do with range and texture and the other with the variation process itself. The rich exploitation of the different ranges of the keyboard combined with the handling of the various textures within the theme is striking in 58 C. The contrast of "male" and "female" vocal registers in measures 1–2 and 3–4, combined first with diminuendo and then with crescendo, presents a musical substance quite unlike a Classical melody based on thematic ideas that are centered on melody, rhythm, and

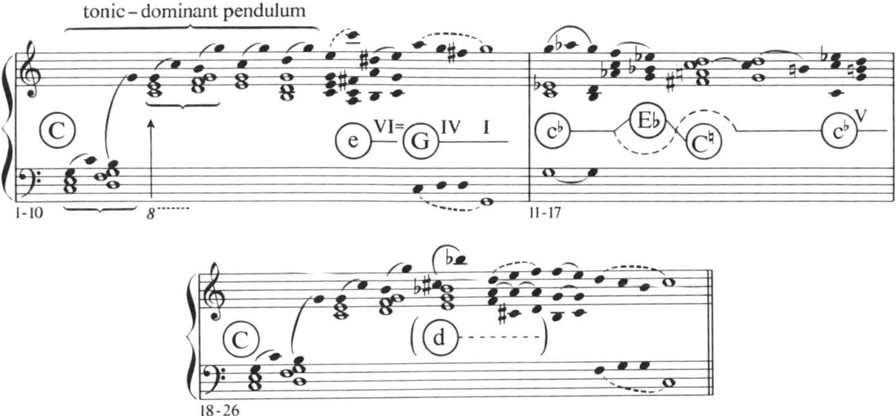

Ex. 161. 58 C I.

harmony. The volume and the quality of tones are taken account of in composition just as much as the density with regard to high or low register, transparent or crowded texture.

The march theme of Haydn's F Minor Variations is a real masterpiece with regard to the exploitation of different registers (see ex. 162). The voices of the left hand and the right hand are constructed according to the rules of double counterpoint; they are interchangeable and can be placed in various registers and at a distance of one or two octaves from each other. In this work, Haydn's dialectics is exceptionally tripolar.[8] In comparison to thesis and antithesis positions, the reprise within the F minor theme seems to be a synthesis since the dotted motive embraces its accompaniment from above as well as from below. The peak point of the theme (*) is the first melodic tone after the repeat sign; the lowest point in register (**) is the last tone of the theme.

8. A subject deserving further explication impossible within the limits of this book is that the variety of Haydn's extremely "dialectical" processes in actual composition can be understood from a bipolar "thesis-antithesis" aspect in which a small-scale contrast—now a "thesis" on the next level—is opposed by an "antithesis" on a higher scale. The "synthesis" of the philosophical dialectical thinking, i.e., the adequate musical sign of this synthesis, is usually absent. This is not surprising when one considers how many elementary musical features on micro- or macro-scale are structures in a bipolar system (examples are opening-closing, imperfect cadence–perfect cadence, symmetry-asymmetry, original form–inversion, upward motion–downward motion, etc.; all these are musical events where the antithesis is explicitly offered after the thesis but there is no place for synthesis). In the dramaturgy of a full movement, there are hundreds of ways to perceive that the achievement of a real, strong synthesis (e.g., in a coda) is not characteristic of Haydn. The tiny tripolar idea of musical dialectics quoted above from the F Minor Variations offers a combinative, higher-scale third (closing) stage only on the level of playful structural ideas and textural patterns.

Ex. 162. F Minor Variations. (* The peak point of the theme. ** The lowest point in register.)

Returning to the theme of 58 C, it is a matter for wonder that this initial material, with its rich vocabulary of rhythmic patterns and melodic embellishments and its complicated process of internal variation, can be subjected to a series of further variations. To a greater or lesser degree, this is true of all four movements we have been discussing. They all have long themes with complex musical material engaged in internal thematic returns. The themes are exposed in a richly embellished form. Further rhythmic diminution and embellishment cannot go far before exceeding eighteenth-century boundaries of good taste. Since these variation forms are based on two lengthy, differentiated themes in contrasting modes, neither figurative nor character variation chains will be distinct. After the exposition of the alternating themes, each new section is experienced primarily as a reprise and only secondarily as a variation. Consequently, C. P. E. Bach's term *veränderte Reprise* might be a more apt description of these movements than any variation form.[9] The technique of variation is based on the performance of the theme with different *Manieren,* to borrow another term that Bach uses.[10] The actual performance of the variation generally gives the global impression of being more homogeneous and simple than the original themes.[11]

9. This view is reinforced by the fact that Haydn does not number the variations in these movements.

10. *Manier* can be translated as "embellishment," but it also implies "manner" and "mannerism."

11. In the F Minor Variations, I^1 investigates syncopation, I^2 explores diminution with continuous thirty-second notes, II^1 is a trill variation, II^2 gives further diminutions, with sixty-fourth notes and thirty-second-note triplets in the melody and sixteenth notes in the accompaniment.

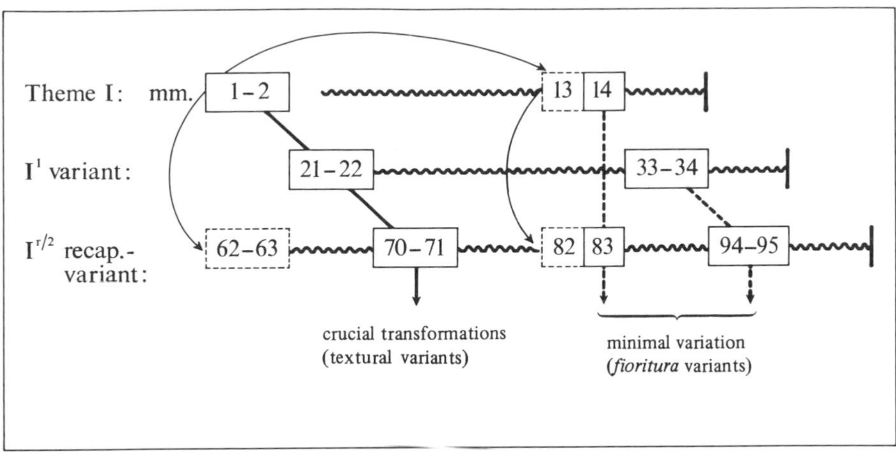

FIGURE 33 Variants of the two opening measures of 56 D.

We have already stated, with regard to sonata-form opening movements, that the main theme, in a key position, contains the most complex musical material of the movement. We can understand, then, how Haydn succeeded in creating a real alternative first-movement form with these unusual double variations based on complex themes. Haydn's followers or imitators might copy his external forms, but the heights of originality and perfection in these movements were inimitably his own, as was the private world of his best sonata-form movements and minuets.

Instead of describing Haydn's variation technique in each individual work, I have chosen one example with general validity, namely, the first two measures of 56 D (ex. 163). The theme itself has an inner reprise. Measures 1–2 reappear in the theme at measures 13–14, appear twice in the first variation, and four times in the reprise variation with varied repetition. Measures 62–63, an exact return signaling the start of the reprise variation, is not indicated in the example; measure 13, an inner reprise variation of the head motive, and measure 82, an inner reprise in the reprise variation, are also exact repetitions. The variants are organized into a logical order. They demonstrate that the two main directions of variation are (1) *fioritura*-like variation of the melody over an unchanged left hand and (2) transformations involving the whole texture. However, the variants do not move in a linear order of increasing complexity; rather, motives in corresponding positions are variants of one another as well (see the arrowed half-circles in fig. 33), again according to the principle of *veränderte Reprise.*

The Adagios of the two last E♭ major sonatas are only a few years apart (1790, 1794), but these years brought a wealth of new musical experiences into Haydn's life. The earlier work was composed in the atmosphere of Eszterháza and Vienna, primarily for his friend Madame Genzinger, who intimately under-

Ex. 163. Variants of the two opening measures of 56 D.

stood and loved Haydn's music. Its audience was the music lovers and fortepianists in the homes of Vienna and other European cities. Haydn composed the later work during his second visit to London. He was by then well acquainted with the concert atmosphere of that city, the art of the virtuosos there, and the capabilities of the English fortepianos. The earlier piece is more intimate and finely chiseled, a classic summary of Haydn's *Personalstil.* The later piece is simpler but very effective. It indicates a new direction in the public performance style of piano playing.[12]

The concert pianist will be fully aware of the many ways—artistic, technical, and instrumental—in which these two Adagios in triple time contrast. The middle movement of 59 E♭, marked *Adagio e cantabile,* is unraveled step by step; the Adagio of 62 E♭ plays with a whole range of surprise effects. The earlier movement is in B♭ major, the later one in E (the enharmonic equivalent of F♭, the Neapolitan of E♭)[13]—a very great contrast indeed. Strict part writing controls the voices of the *Genzinger* Sonata; it is a three-voice texture at the significant points. The London Adagio uses dramatically effective free-style part writing. For example, in measures 1–8, the three-voice texture expands to seven and eight voices and then contracts again; in the recapitulation, measures 34, 39, and 48 call for a fully rhapsodic performance of the arpeggios. The notation of the earlier movement employs a number of conventions that make minute differences possible in performance. The London piece, by comparison, contains extremes of notation. On the one hand, the notation of rhythm, dynamics, stress, and touch is very exact. On the other hand, the grace-note passages allow imaginative interpretation, individual pianistic style, and virtuosity.

The forms of the two movements are also characteristically different. The London Adagio is a concise movement of seventy-two measures, including repetitions (36, 14, 18+4). It achieves dramatic effect with a form of simple outlines: A a A^{v}. The first A section has a form of 8+10 measures, with each subsection repeated. The theme is so detailed that it cannot be varied to any significant extent; hence, the repetition is literal, although the effect might be modified in performance. The *minore* section is derived from the main theme and thus has the effect of a development. After the *minore* section, the first part is recapitulated in a slightly varied form,[14] involving a loosening of the texture and the abundant use of sixteenth-note triplets, followed by a short coda.

The Adagio of the *Genzinger* Sonata is twice as long as that of 62 E♭, and it

12. For further details, see my "The London Revision of Haydn's Instrumental Style."

13. I have mentioned before (see n. 7, chap. 17) that the E major second theme block in the development section of the first movement helps prepare the listener for the surprise key of the second movement.

14. We can find true diminution of the rhythm only at the beginning of m. 36 and in m. 43. Both places refer to figurations from the trio (to mm. 22 and 26, respectively).

sounds even more extensive, leaving the listener with the memory of an expansive, rich movement. The sentences unfold as in a chapter from an eighteenth-century novel—perhaps a description of a meeting or a confession in the manner of the young Goethe. Significant points of orientation in the form are the trio, which is held together by the continuous motion of the passionate accompanimental figure, and the unexpectedly lengthy coda, the thematic material of which is decidedly different from other parts of the movement.[15] These points enrich the lyrical-epic process, which constitutes the essence of the movement, like visions of memory or episodes in a novel that take place in a different time and place.

The motivic elaboration of the opening fifty-six measures and of measures 81–108 allows us to relate this movement to the concept of double variations. Its form states the material in three versions in the A B A^r *Liedform* with varied repetition (mm. 1–56) and in the *Liedform* recapitulation after the trio. To be more exact, each thematic element occurs at least three times, some motives are stated as many as six times, and the first two measures of the movement occur twelve times. The motivic composition is as follows:

A	B	A^r
a b a c	d e	a b a f
2 2 2 2	4 6	2 2 2 4
(8 measures)	(10 measures)	(10 measures)

This is the core of the *Liedform,* which is further expanded by varied repetitions and the recapitulation. Figure 34 shows the points at which motives a, b, c, d, e, and f emerge. It also indicates the number of variations of each motive. Asterisks indicate literal repetitions that have a distinctive function. The exact return of motive a^1 delineates both small- and large-scale structural features. First, on the scale of the sentence, it signals that with measures 1–8 the first period is over and the second period is beginning. Next, on the scale of a whole movement, motive a^1 in measure 81 signals the beginning of the return of part A after the trio in minor. The second kind of literal repetition is more specific. Whenever there is a darkening to B♭ minor (mm. 21, 41, 93), Haydn presents the same minor-mode version of motive e and preserves its exact affect before starting off on the variation process. This has a strong effect, comparable to a repeated vow in confessional prose.

It is instructive to summarize and analyze all the variants of a single motive, assembling a catalog of Haydn's figurations. Example 164 surveys the ten variants of motive a. In performance, the listener can grasp so many different variants

15. It would show a complete misunderstanding of Haydn's music if we hunted for organic, consciously intended references in certain figurations in the coda, such as the farewell motive with dotted rhythm in m. 120, and connected them to the basic material of the movement.

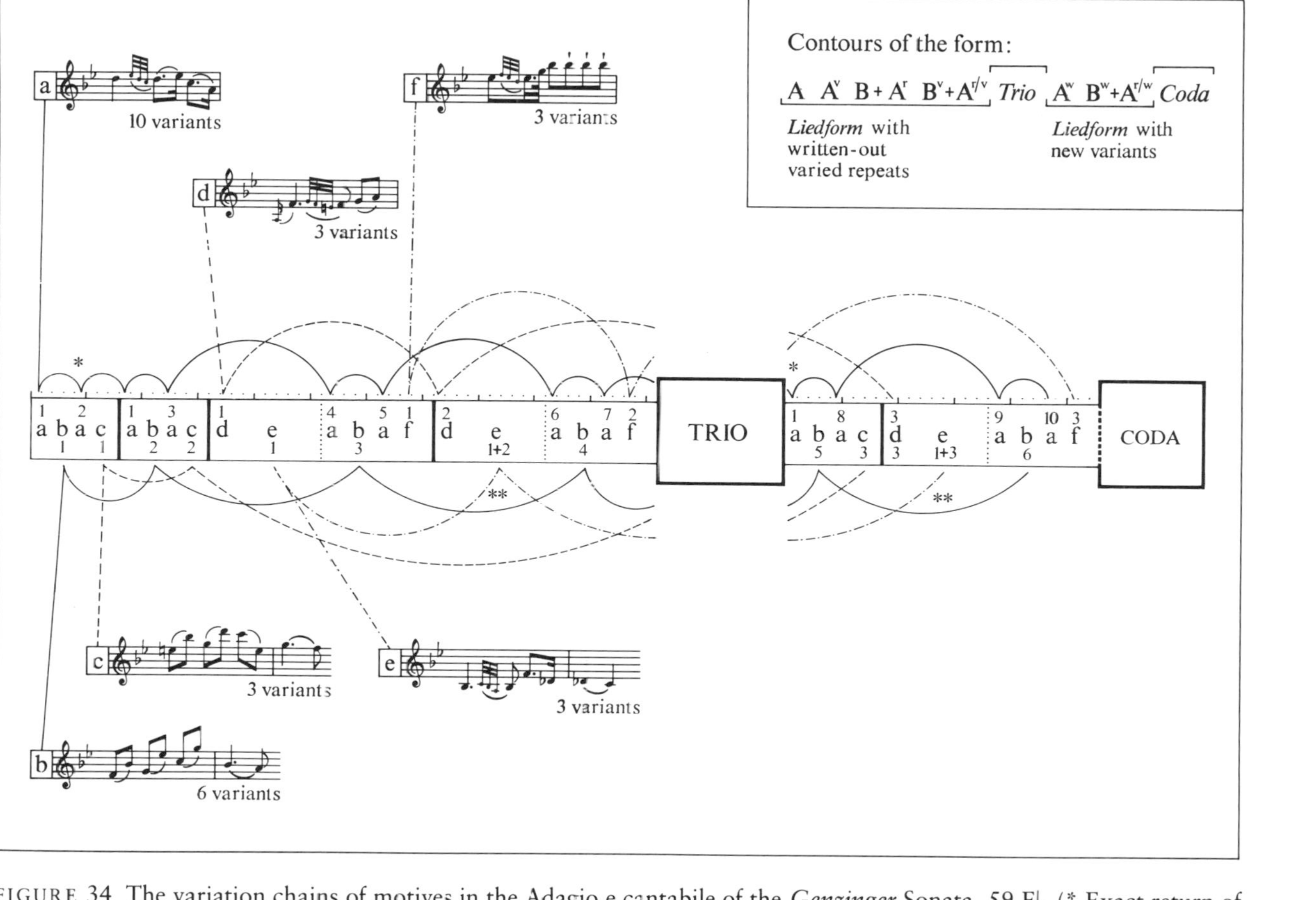

FIGURE 34 The variation chains of motives in the Adagio e cantabile of the *Genzinger* Sonata, 59 E♭. (* Exact return of the head motive. ** Exact return of two measures in B♭ minor.)

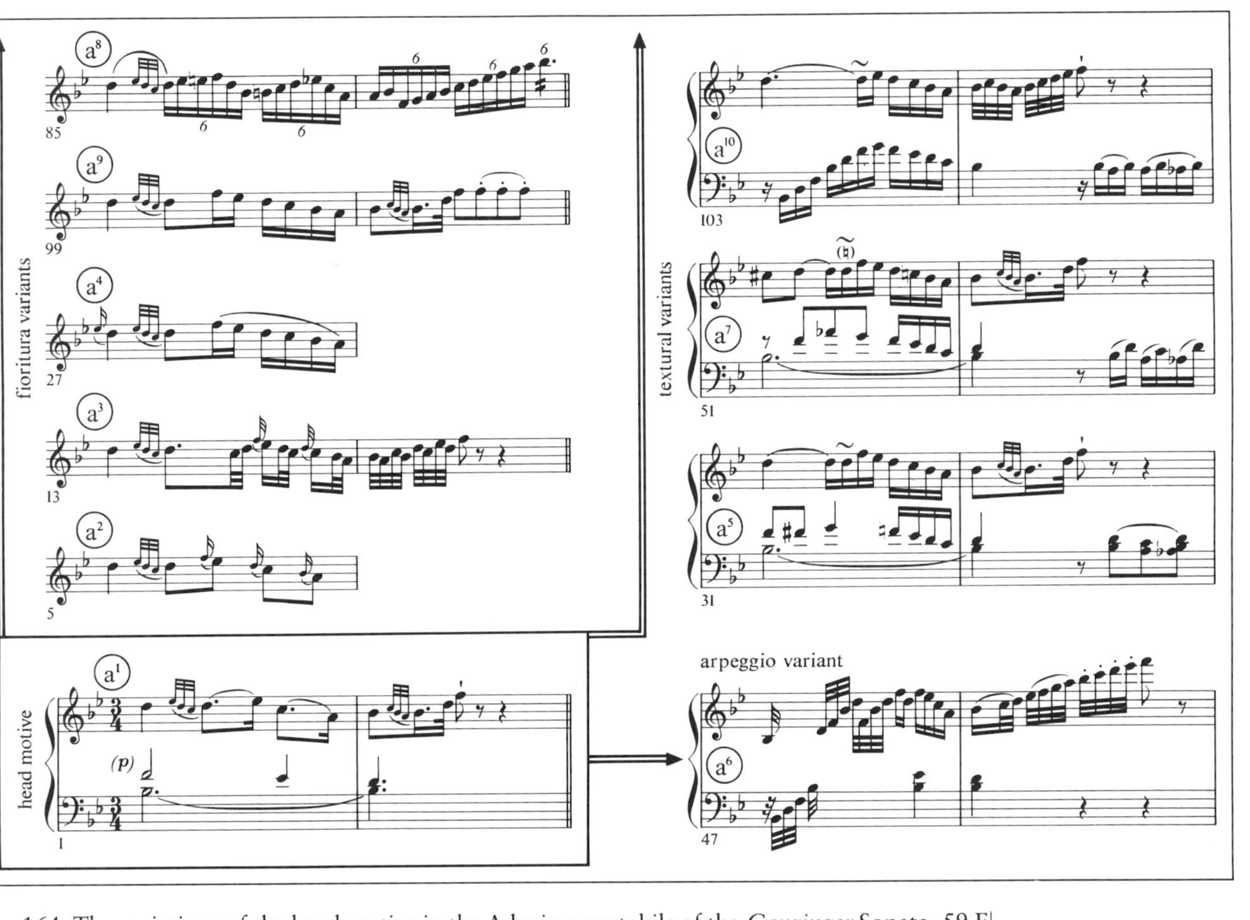

Ex. 164. The variations of the head motive in the Adagio e cantabile of the *Genzinger* Sonata, 59 E♭.

only if the player presents the characteristic feature of each variant by means of differentiation of touch and articulation. The primary goal of the performer must be the individualization of the motives through emphasis on the differences of their details and shades—the cohesion and strict construction of the movement has already been taken care of by the composer.

Twenty-Four

Fantasia *and* Capriccio

HAYDN WROTE TWO significant independent keyboard pieces that are not sets of variations and that would not have formed parts of sonatas.[1] The Capriccio in G Major (Hob. XVII:1, Moderato $\frac{3}{4}$) is 368 measures long, and the Fantasia in C Major (Hob. XVII:4, Presto $\frac{3}{8}$, called *Capriccio* in Haydn's letter to his publisher) is 467 measures long. Both are too long to be part of a two- or three-movement sonata by Haydn. Their independence is established not only by their length but also by their structures and spirit. Both pieces are composed in open, free forms, indicated not only by the lack of repeat signs, representing literal repeats of architectonic value, and the lack of written-out recapitulation but also by the unpredictability that forms the basic characteristic of these works. The listener cannot guess the next step in the key structure or the motivic presentation, although, on the surface, the rhythm and tempo preserve the characteristics of a well-constructed logical form. Wandering is the essence of these two works—wandering from one key to another, always establishing the new key by a statement of all or part of the first theme like a rondo ritornello, and wandering from one style to another, sometimes with several variations in rhythm, figuration, counterpoint, and texture.

The two capriccio forms are divided by two and a half decades, and the differences in style are enormous. The Capriccio in G was composed for harpsichord in 1765,[2] while the Fantasia in C was composed for fortepiano in 1789.

1. The F Minor Variations, by contrast, was probably intended as the opening movement of a two-movement sonata that was never completed (see p. 333).

2. In the preface (pp. vi–vii) to the *Wiener Urtext* of Haydn's *Klavierstücke*, Franz Eibner describes this as a fortepiano piece and suggests its performance as such. Naturally, it can be played well

The Fantasia in C is undoubtedly a more polished piece, but the main difference between these works does not lie in quality, inventiveness, or originality. Rather, the decisive difference is in the themes themselves and in the catalog of variation techniques applied as the piece unfolds. The song-like theme of the Capriccio, with its 5+4 and 5 measure a b a construction and its imitation of rustic "whoops" and fermatas, is taken from an amusing folksong melody, "Acht Sauschneider müssen sein."[3] The theme of the Fantasia, with its 8+8 period construction, is of Haydn's own invention and is more suitable for motivic fragmentation. The contrasting theme, first heard *piano* in measure 70, is derived from measures 5–6 of the first theme.

The large-scale form of the Capriccio in G can be compared to a rondo by C. P. E. Bach; the form of the Fantasia in C appears to be derived from a disintegrated sonata-form structure.[4] The returns of the primary theme in C major in the Fantasia (at mm. 124 and 255 and in the coda) are guides to the form. The tonal adventures of the piece are fascinating, not so much because of the number of different keys arrived at, or even because of the distance of these keys from C major, but mostly because the arrival at certain keys is achieved through an unexpected semitone terrace shift.[5] Also fascinating are the two famous passages (mm. 192 and 302) marked with fermatas, in which the note is meant to be held until the strings stop vibrating. The piece is full of musical humor and surprises, emphasized by the economical framework of an almost monothematic technique. In a letter dated 29 March 1789, Haydn wrote, "In my leisure hours I have completed a new Capriccio."[6]

The form of the G Major Capriccio deserves closer analysis. The theme occurs thirteen times, in different functions—full return, partial return, transitory section formed from the theme, etc.—and in five major and four minor keys. One finds interesting chains of fifths and other key structures by just going around the chosen tonalities (ex. 165 and fig. 35). The articulations caused by

---

and effectively on the fortepiano or on the modern piano, but it was definitely written for the harpsichord, in fact for an instrument with the so-called short-octave keyboard (see p. 27).

3. This Austrian folk tune was also arranged by Mozart in *Gallimathias musicum,* K. 32 (1766). Its comical words describe the number of participants decreasing in each verse, starting with eight ("Acht Sauschneider müssen seyn" ["It takes eight of you if you want to castrate a boar"]) and finishing with one. The text was probably partly responsible for Haydn's choice of a form with many ritornellos. For a full English translation of the text, see Landon, *HCW,* 1:550.

4. If one wanted to describe the C Major Fantasia in sonata-form terms, mm. 1–87, less than one-fifth of the total length, would be the exposition—P area, mm. 1–28; T area (derived from the P head), mm. 29–69; S (contrast? closing?) theme, mm. 70–87. The return of the primary theme in C major in m. 255 can be considered the start of the recapitulation. The secondary theme appears in the tonic starting in m. 305, and the coda starts in m. 324 or m. 356.

5. For example, the dominant of A major is followed by B♭ major (mm. 191–95); a section enharmonically notated C♭ major (written as B major) is followed by C major, theoretically D𝄫 major (mm. 301–4); etc.

6. Haydn, *Briefe,* 240.

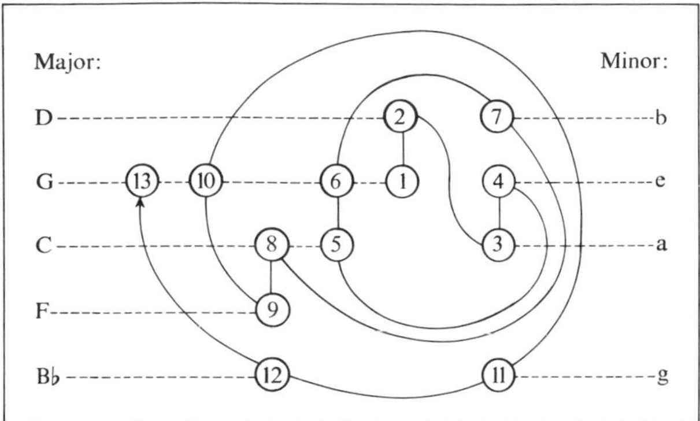

FIGURE 35 Key structure of P returns in the Capriccio in G Major.

the returns of G major reveal remarkable proportions in the form (132 + 132 + . . .). However, the piece is more strongly divided into two parts by the appearance of the triplet accompaniment starting in measure 190. This articulation is independent of the proportions of the key structure.

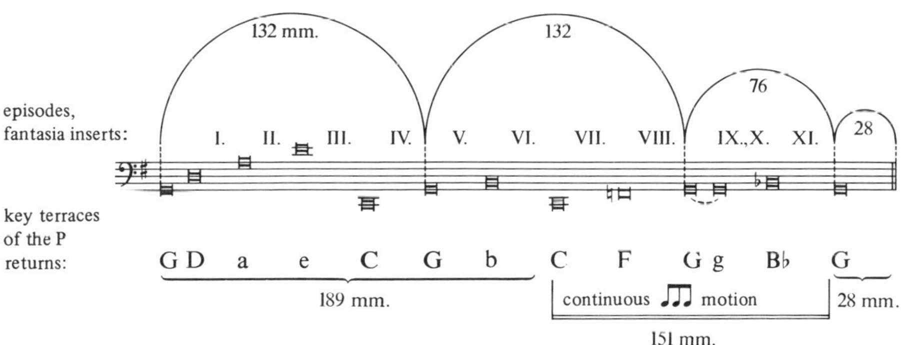

Ex. 165. Form and key structure of the Capriccio in G Major.

The varied returns of the theme (ritornello) sometimes employ contrapuntal techniques (ex. 166*b*, *e*) and sometimes triplet accompaniments (ex. 166*c*, *d*). A characteristic feature is that the theme sometimes appears in the right hand, sometimes in the left. The couplets, the elaborations of the theme, and the fantasia-like insertions[7] that appear between the ritornellos all tend to undergo rhythmic variation. The result is twelve markedly different rhythmic presentations (see fig. 36).

7. A fantasia insert is, above all, a *kleines harmonisches Labyrinth* in mm. 165–89 (VI). Typical couplets are I and II; VII and VIII recall Haydn's development sections (see fig. 36).

I.		VII.	tr
II.		VIII.	l.h.
III.		IX.	
IV.		X.	
V.	l.h.	XI.	
VI.		(coda)	l.h.

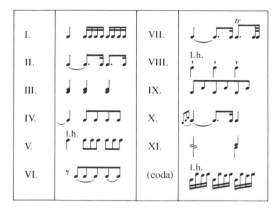

FIGURE 36 Characteristic rhythmic patterns of couplets and fantasia inserts in the Capriccio in G Major.

Ex. 166. Capriccio in G Major.

The Capriccio in G Major of 1765 marks a turning point in Haydn's composition of keyboard music. The early divertimento and partita sonatas, testing grounds for his compositional technique, were behind him. His way forward was partly illuminated by the writings of C. P. E. Bach. Haydn was not a keyboard virtuoso, but had he wanted to continue writing works in the style of the G Major Capriccio, or had he been urged to do so, either by his employer Prince Esterházy or by his public in Vienna, no doubt he could have composed a number of very pleasant and fluent works that would have surpassed those composed by Wagenseil in Vienna.

Fortunately for the genre of the keyboard sonata, this was not the path that Haydn followed. The public pressure that exerted itself on Haydn urged him to compose symphonies, and later quartets, rather than keyboard music.[8] We may also consider ourselves fortunate that Haydn wanted to prove his talent in many different genres—in opera, oratorio, and the mass as well as in instrumental works. Thus, Haydn granted himself six or eight years for inner workshop experimentation with keyboard sonatas. Free from outward demands in this genre, he composed at least half a dozen "workshop" sonatas, the overture to his mature piano music. With these sonatas he began his contribution to the Classical style in this genre. The real topic of this book started there, at these first mature sonatas.

8. Hiller's criticisms that appeared in *Wöchentliche Nachrichten* in 1768 (see Landon, *HCW,* 2: 334) may be taken as typical. The criticism probably refers to such early sonatas as nos. 1–3, 5–6, 8, 12–13, 15 (see 1765, 1766, and 1767 in *The Breitkopf Thematic Catalogue*) and the concertino pieces. After praising Wagenseil and Steffan, Hiller continues, "Herr Hayden, a famous and worthy composer in another genre, has also written various items for the clavier, but this instrument does not seem to suit him as well as the other [instruments] which he uses in the most fiery and *galant* symphonies."

CATALOG *of the* SONATAS: DATA *and* GUIDE

THE SONATAS ARE NUMBERED according to the *Wiener Urtext* edition. Page numbers following the words *Date, Publication, Instrument, Performance practice,* and *Analysis* allow this catalog to be used as an index to Haydn's sonatas. Dates and remarks in square brackets about chronology and authenticity should be understood to be the author's opinion. Letters in parentheses among the references to *Analysis* use the abbreviations and symbols of table 18 (p. 228). References to Brown are taken from table IV-5 ("Proposed Chronology for Solo Sonatas") in his *Keyboard.* "Grove W" is a reference to section W, "Keyboard Sonatas," in the *New Grove Haydn* "Work-List."

Early Divertimento Sonatas

1. G Major Sonata (Hob. XVI:8)

Date. WUE: before 1766; *JHW:* Neun kleine frühe Sonaten no. 3; Grove W.1, 10: before 1760 (?); Brown: ca. 1760. [Probably before 1760, authentic work]: 154–55.
Analysis. 156–57, 239.

2. C Major Sonata (Hob. XVI:7)

Date. WUE: before 1766; *JHW:* Neun kleine frühe Sonaten no. 4; Grove W.1, 9: before 1760 (?); Brown: ca. 1750–55. [Probably before 1760, authentic work]: 154–55.
Analysis. 156–57, 251.

3. F Major Sonata (Hob. XVI:9)

Date. WUE: before 1766; *JHW:* Neun kleine frühe Sonaten no. 4; Grove W.1, 11: before 1760 (?); Brown: ca. 1750–55. [Probably before 1760, authentic work]: 154–55.
Analysis. 156, 158, 239, 251.

4. G Major Sonata (Hob. XVI:G1)

Date. WUE: before 1766; *JHW:* Neun kleine frühe Sonaten no. 6; Grove W.1, 13a before 1760 (?); Brown: ca. 1750–55. [Probably before 1760, authentic work]: 154.
Analysis. 156, 158, 217, 239.

5. G Major Sonata (Hob. XVI:11)

Note. The first movement is identical with 4 G III; this is a potpourri sonata.
Date. *WUE:* before 1766; *JHW:* II and III as nos. 1–2 of Fünf Einzelsätze; Grove W.1, 13b: (?). The Minuet, with another Trio, ca. 1766–67 used in baryton trio Hob. XI:26. [Probably only the minuet is authentic]: 153–54.
Analysis. 217.

6. C Major Sonata (Hob. XVI:10)

Date. *WUE:* before 1766; *JHW:* Neun kleine frühe Sonaten no. 5; Grove W.1, 12: before 1760 (?); Brown: ca. 1750–55. [Probably before 1760, authentic work]: 154–55.
Performance practice. (Turn) 67.
Analysis. 156, 158, 239, 282, 299.

7. D Major Sonata (Hob. XVII:D1)

Date. *WUE:* before 1766; *JHW:* Neun kleine frühe Sonaten no. 7; Grove W.1, 14: (?); Brown: ca. 1750–55. [Probably not authentic]: 154–55, 217.

8. A Major Sonata (Hob. XVI:5)

Date. *WUE:* before 1763 (when registered in the Breitkopf catalog under Haydn's name); *JHW:* Neun kleine frühe Sonaten no. 2; Grove W.1, 2: ca. 1750–55 (?), "doubtful"; Brown: ca. 1750–55. [Not authentic]: 154–55.

9. D Major Sonata (Hob. XVI:4)

Date. *WUE:* before 1766; H. C. R. Landon, *Essays,* 52: around 1765; *JHW:* Neun kleine frühe Sonaten no. 9; Grove W, 4: ca. 1765 (?) ("orig. III apparently lost"); Brown: ca. 1761–62 to ca. 1767. [Probably earlier than 1765; two-movement sonata]: 153–55, 161.
Instrument. 25.
Analysis. 156–158, (I P and Exp.) 223–27, 239.

10. C Major Sonata (Hob. XVI:1)

Date. *WUE:* before 1766; *JHW:* Neun kleine frühe Sonaten no. 1; Grove W.1, 8: 1750–55 (?); Brown: ca. 1750–55. [Probably not authentic]: 154–55.

11. B♭ Major Sonata (Hob. XVI:2)

Date. *WUE:* before 1766; *JHW:* Neun frühe Sonaten no. 7; Grove W.1, 5: before 1760 (?); Brown: ca. 1760. [Probably ca. 1762; see p. 76]: 154–55.
Performance practice. (Trill) 59, (turn) 65, (mordent) 76.
Analysis. 101, 156–58, 305, 312.

12. A Major Sonata (Hob. XVI:12)

Date. *WUE:* before 1766; *JHW:* Neun frühe Sonaten no. 3; Grove W.1, 3: ca. 1750–55 (?) ("? I. doubtful"); Brown: ca. 1750–55. [Weak sources, probably still authentic]: 154–55, 162.
Analysis. 156.

13. G Major Sonata (Hob. XVI:6)
Date. *WUE:* before 1766; *JHW:* Neun frühe Sonaten no. 6; Grove W, 1: before 1760 (?); N.B. I–II–III in autograph, undated; Brown: ca. 1760. [Up to 1760]: 153–54, 161, 163.
Instrument. 25.
Performance practice. 37, (Trill) 59, (turn) 63, (cadenza in III) 81, (rhythm) 93.
Analysis. 156–58, 189, 239, 299, 305, 312.

14. C Major Sonata (Hob. XVI:3)
Date. *WUE:* before 1766; *JHW:* Neun kleine frühe Sonaten no. 8; Grove W, 3: 1765 (?); Brown: ca. 1761–62 to ca. 1767; the first movement, ca. 1766–67, used in baryton trio Hob. XI:37 I. [Probably from the early 1760s]: 153–56, 161.
Instrument. 25.
Performance practice. (Rhythm) 93.
Analysis. 156–58, 239, 305–306.

15. E Major Sonata (Hob. XVI:13)
Date. *WUE:* before 1766; *JHW:* Neun frühe Sonaten no. 4; Grove W.1, 4: before 1760 (?); Brown: ca. 1760. [Probably from the early 1760s]: 154–55, 162.
Performance practice. (Rhythm of turn) 67–69, (dynamics) 129.
Analysis. 156, 158, 251–52, 299.

16. D Major Sonata (Hob. XVI:14)
Date. *WUE:* before 1766; *JHW:* Neun frühe Sonaten no. 5; Grove W, 2: before 1760 (?); Brown (p. 425): ca. 1766–67. [Probably from the early 1760s]: 153–55.
Instrument. 25.
Performance practice. (Overdotting) 88, (harpsichord legato) 116.
Analysis. 156, 158, 239, 245, 282, 299, 302.

17. E♭ Major Sonata (Hob. deest, later XVI:Es2)
Date. *WUE:* before 1766; *JHW:* Neun frühe Sonaten no. 8 ("1. Raigerner Sonate"); Grove W.1, 6: 1755 (?) ("doubtful"); Brown: ca. 1750–55. [Doubtful]: 154–55.

18. E♭ Major Sonata (Hob. deest, later XVI:Es3)
Date. *WUE:* before 1766; *JHW:* Neun frühe Sonaten no. 9 ("2. Raigerner Sonate"); Grove W.1, 7: ca. 1764 (?) ("doubtful"); Brown: ca. 1750–55. [Mariano Romano Kayser's work; the original third movement in *WUE, Kritische Anmerkungen,* 103–5]: 154–55.

Mature Sonatas

"Workshop" sonatas: my suggestion for a collective title for the sonatas written 1766–72: 20 B♭, 28 D, 29 E♭, 30 D, 31 A♭, 32 g, 33 c (on their publication, see pp. 167–68, 171). See also the lost sonatas 21 d, 22 A, 23 B, 24 B♭, 25 e, 26 A: pp. 25, 157, 159–61, 218.

19. E Minor Sonata (Hob. XVI:47 and 47bis)

Date. *WUE:* before 1766; *JHW:* Sieben Sonaten no. 1; Grove W, 12a: 1765 (?) ("earlier and probably orig. version of no. 12b" [= *WUE* 57 F]); Brown: ca. 1765. [Circa 1765; regarding the doubtful version in F, see *WUE* 57]: 159, 162.
Publication. 168.
Performance practice. (Slide) 78, (arpeggio) 98, (embellished performance) 102.
Analysis. (Genre, type) 181–82, 189, 194, (I) 217, 312, (II) 299–300, (III) 315–20.

20. B♭ Major Sonata (Hob. XVI:18)

Date. *WUA:* 1766/67 (?), *WUE:* "probably too early in our chronological list"; *JHW:* Sieben Sonaten no. 6; Grove W, 17: ca. 1771–73; Brown: ca. 1767–68. [Circa 1770–72, probably after 33 c]: 160–61, 163.
Publication. 168, 171.
Instrument. 25, 27–28.
Performance practice. (Appoggiatura) 48–49, (turn) 59, 69, (rhythm of I P) 73–74, (fermata) 83, (dotted rhythm) 87, (embellished performance) 102, (dynamics) 129, 132, (tempo) 148.
Analysis. (Genre, type) 174–76, 182, 189, 194, (I Exp.) 219–20, 230–31, 233–34, 236, (I P) 239–41, 244, (I T) 264, (I Dev.) 280, 283–84, 286–87, 289, (I Rec.) 293, (II) 197, 315–20.

28. D Major Sonata (Hob. XIV:5, later XVI:5a)

Note. Of the first movement, only two measures exist as noted down by Haydn in the *EK*, and the last twenty-one measures in the autograph fragment (in *WUE*, reconstructed by Karl Heinz Füssl and Christa Landon; John McCabe has recorded his own reconstruction).
Date. *WUE:* 1765–66 (?); *JHW:* Sieben Sonaten no. 4 (" . . . das Finale überhaupt nicht erhalten"); Grove W, 15: ca. 1767–70; Brown: ca. 1767–68. [Probably ca. 1768–69 and a genuine two-movement concept]: 160–63, 189.
Publication. 168.
Instrument. 25.
Performance practice. (Overdotting) 88, (embellished performance) 102.
Analysis. (Genre, type) 174, 176, 182, 194, (I P) 217, 245, (II) 158, 195, 315–21.

29. E♭ Major Sonata (Hob. XVI:45)

Date. 1766 (dated autograph); *JHW:* Sieben Sonaten no. 2: 159–63.
Publication. 168, 171.
Instrument. 25–26.
Performance practice. (Original fingering) 42, (appoggiatura) 48, (turn) 59–60, 67, (inconsistent notation) 61, (arpeggio) 98–99, (embellished performance) 102, (notation of I P) 116, (tempo of III) 147.
Analysis. (Genre, type) 173–75, 182, 189, 194, 205, (I Exp.) 219, 230, 233, 235–36, (I P) 240–43, (I T) 264, (I S) 267, (I Dev.) 280, 282–84, 286, (I Rec.) 293, (II) 157, 306, (III) 299–302.

30. D Major Sonata (Hob. XVI:19)

Date. 1767 (dated autograph); *JHW:* Sieben Sonaten no. 3.
Publication. 160–61, 163, 168, 171.

Instrument. 25–26, 28.
Performance practice. (Turn) 60, (inconsistent notation) 61, (slide) 77–78, (cadenza in II) 81–82, (rhythm of triplets) 93, 95, (embellished performance) 102, (staccato in II) 120–21, (accents) 130, (tempo of III) 147.
Analysis. (Genre, type) 174–75, 182, 189, 194, 203, 205, (I Exp.) 219, 231, 233–34, 236, (I P) 240–42, (I S) 268, (I K) 274–75, (I Dev.) 280, 283–84, 286, (I Rec.) 293, (II) 305–6, 309, (III) 193, 197–98, 325–28.

31. A♭ Major Sonata (Hob. XVI:46)
Date. *WUE:* ca. 1767–68 (?); Feder, "Probleme": 1768–71 (?); *JHW:* Sieben Sonaten no. 5; Grove W, 16: ca. 1767–70; Brown: ca. 1767–68. [On stylistic grounds, ca. 1768–69 seems probable]: 160–61.
Publication. 168, 171.
Instrument. 25, 27–28.
Performance practice. 37, (trill) 55, (rhythm of turn) 59, 62–64, (slide) 78, (cadenza in II) 81–82, (fermata in I?) 83, (overdotting in I) 87–88, (embellished performance) 102, (four-part texture) 110, (dynamics) 129.
Analysis. (Genre, type) 174–75, 182, 189, 194, 205, (I Exp.) 219, 230, 232–33, 236, 276, (I P) 240–41, 245–46, 253, (I T) 264, (I S) 269, (I K) 275, (I Dev.) 280, 282–84, 286–88, (I Rec.) 292, (II) 306–7, 309–10, (III) 300–301.

32. G Minor Sonata (Hob. XVI:44)
Date. *WUE:* ca. 1768–70 (?); *JHW:* Sieben Sonaten no. 7; Grove W, 18: ca. 1771–73; Brown: ca. 1770. [Based on the style and form of II, ca. 1771 seems probable]: 160–61.
Publication. 168, 171.
Instrument. (Harpsichord accents) 131.
Performance practice. (Turn) 59–60, 62–63, 71, 73, (fermata) 82, (arpeggio) 98, (embellished performance) 102, (touch of I P) 121, (accents, dynamics) 131, (tempo) 148.
Analysis. (Genre, type) 174–76, 182, 189, 194, (I Exp.) 212, 219, 230, 233–34, 236, (I P) 239–40, 247, 250, (I T) 265, (I S) 267–68, (I K) 275, (I Dev.) 280, 283, 286, 289, (I Rec.) 292–94, (II) 158, 193, 197–98, 315–21.

33. C Minor Sonata (Hob. XVI:20)
Date. 1771 (dated autograph fragment, including sketches); *JHW:* Sieben Sonaten no. 6; Brown: begun 1771, finished by 1780. [Measures 1–46 of I certainly, the rest of the sonata probably, drafted and elaborated in 1771; a revised version published in 1780, including crescendos and other dynamic marks; regarding the problems of the autograph fragment, see n. 11 on p. 132]: 160–61, 163.
Publication. (In 1780 as no. 6 of the *Auenbrugger* sonatas) 11, 13, 168, 171, 200.
Instrument. (Harpsichord?) 25, (clavichord?) 28, (fortepiano?) 23, 26.
Performance practice. 37, (rhythm of appoggiatura) 49–50, (trill) 52, 54, (problems of embellishment) 59, 61–62, (rhythm of mm. 8–9 in I) 59, (slide) 78, (fermata) 83, (dotted rhythm) 86–88, (triplet rhythm) 92–94, (end of III) 98–99, (embellished performance) 102, (voice leading) 108–9, (slurs) 115, (notation of I P) 115–16, (tenuto) 117–18, (slur in mm. 11 and 14 of I) 124, (dynamics) 129, (dynamic marks in the autograph) 131–37, (tempo rubato) 145, (tempo) 181.
Analysis. (Genre, type) 167, 173–75, 181–82, 189, 194, 205, (I Exp.) 219, 231–33, 236, 276, (I P) 283, 240–42, 246–47, 250–51, 253, (I T) 264–65, (I S) 268, 274, (I K) 274–75, (I Dev.) 280, 283–88, (I Rec.) 292–94, (II) 305–6, (III) 299–301.

34. D Major Sonata (Hob. XVI:33)

Date. *WUE:* ca. 1771–73 (?); *JHW:* Drei Sonaten no. 2; Grove W, 38: up to 17 January 1778 (date on a manuscript copy); Brown: mid-1770s. [Based on style and form, ca. 1772–73]: 164.
Publication. (In 1783) 163, 168, 171.
Instrument. 23.
Performance practice. (Problems of embellishment) 61, (turn) 62, (fermata) 83, (dotted rhythm) 86–87, (tempo of I) 220, (tempo of III) 148.
Analysis. (Genre, type) 174, 176, 182, 189, 194, 203, 205, (I Exp.) 219–20, 230, 233, 235–36, (I P) 238, 240–41, 247, 250, 253, (I T) 264, (I S) 269, 274, (I Dev.) 281, 283–84, 286, (I Rec.) 293, (II) 312–13, (III) 192–93, 198, 315–21, 323–24.

35. A♭ Major Sonata (Hob. XVI:43)

Date. *WUE:* ca. 1771–73 (?); *JHW:* Drei Sonaten no. 1; Grove W, 37: up to 26 July 1783 (date of 1st ed.); Brown: mid-1770s. [Although generally accepted as authentic, on the basis of style I think that this sonata is not by Haydn; see pp. 163–64, 168, 171.]
Instrument. 23.
Performance practice. (Fermata) 35, (embellishment) 102, (dynamics) 129, 135, (¢ tempo) 149.
Analysis. (Genre, type) 182, 189, 194, 217, (I Dev.) 281, 283, (II) 315–21, (III) 192, 325–27.

The *Esterházy* sonatas is the collective title of sonatas nos. 36–41 (1773), based on the dedication of the set printed by Kurzböck in Vienna (before February 1774); *JHW:* Sechs Sonaten für Fürst Nikolaus Esterházy; the Italian text of dedication in series 18, vol. 2; and Landon, *HCW,* 2:334. On the manuscript, see p. 163. On their publication, see pp. 167–68, 171. On their genre, see pp. 173–74, 202–3.

36. C Major Sonata (Hob. XVI:21), *Esterházy* Sonata no. 1

Date. 1773 (dated autograph, one folio missing); no. 1 in the incomplete set of the autograph manuscript, the numbering of which seems to be the sequence of composition.
Instrument. (Harpsichord) 24–25, 29, 32.
Performance practice. (Trill) 54–56, (mordent) 59, 74–76, (turn) 62, (dotted rhythm) 86, (passage) 99, (staccato and legato) 119, 123, 126, (slurring) 123, (dynamics) 130, (tempo of I) 219.
Analysis. (Genre, type) 174, 176, 182, 189, 194, 202, 205, (I Exp.) 219–20, 230–33, 276, (I P) 240, 244, 250, 253, (I S) 270, (I Dev.) 281, 283–84, 286, (I Rec.) 294, (II) 306, 308, 310, (III) 300–301.

37. E Major Sonata (Hob. XVI:22), *Esterházy* Sonata no. 2

Date. 1773 (dated autograph).
Instrument. (Harpsichord) 24–25, 28–29, 32.
Performance practice. (Appoggiatura) 48, (trill) 54, (rhythm of turn) 62, 68–69, (triplet rhythm in II) 92–93, (arpeggio) 98, (dynamics) 129.
Analysis. (Genre, type) 174, 176, 182, 189, 194, 205, (I Exp.) 219, 231, 234, 236, (I P) 240, 251–52, (I K) 275, (I Dev.) 280, 283–84, 286, (I Rec.) 294, (II) 311–12, (III) 164, 192–93, 198, 315–20, 323–24.

38. F Major Sonata (Hob. XVI:23), *Esterházy* Sonata no. 3
Date. 1773 (dated autograph, the end of III missing).
Instrument. (Harpsichord) 24–25, 29, 32.
Performance practice. 37, (appoggiatura) 48, (trill) 54, (turn) 62, (slide) 78, (triplet rhythm in II) 92–93, (tenuto) 118, (articulation in III) 126, (tempo) 148.
Analysis. (Genre, type) 174, 176, 182, 189, 194, 205, (I Exp.) 219–20, 230, 232–33, (I P) 240–41, 244, (I T) 265, (I S) 269, (I Dev.) 280, 283–84, 286, (I Rec.) 292, 294, (II) 311–12, (III) 300–301, 326.

39. D Major Sonata (Hob. XVI:24), *Esterházy* Sonata no. 4
Note. This sonata is missing from the fascicle of the autograph manuscript.
Date. 1773; Grove W, 22: 1773 (?).
Instrument. (Harpsichord) 24–25, 29, 32.
Performance practice. (Rhythm of turn) 62–64, (small-note passage) 100, (tenuto) 118, (portato touch) 121, (asynchronous articulation) 125–26, (tempo of I) 220, (tempo of III) 326.
Analysis. (Genre, type) 164, 174, 176, 182, 189, 194, 205, (I Exp.) 219–20, 230–36, 278, (I P) 240, 254–55, (I T) 265, (I Dev.) 281, 283–84, 286, (I Rec.) 294, (II) 312–13, (III) 193, 197–98, 325–27, 330.

40. E♭ Major Sonata (Hob. XVI:25), *Esterházy* Sonata no. 5
Note. This sonata is missing from the fascicle of the autograph manuscript.
Date. 1773; Grove W, 23: 1773 (?).
Instrument. (Harpsichord) 24–25, 29, 32.
Performance practice. (Trill) 55, (rhythm of turn) 62, 68–69, (staccato and portato) 121, (accents) 130.
Analysis. (Genre, type) 174, 176, 182, 189, 194, 203, 218, (I Exp.) 230–34, (I P) 240, 245–46, 250, 253, (I T) 264, (I S) 269, (I Dev.) 280, 283–86, (I Rec.) 292, (II) 158, 315–20.

41. A Major sonata (Hob. XVI:26), *Esterházy* Sonata no. 6
Date. 1773 (dated autograph, II missing; facsimile edition: Henle, 1958, 2d ed., 1982).
Instrument. (Harpsichord) 24–25, 29, 32.
Performance practice. (Rhythm of turn) 61–62, 65–66, 68–69, (triplet rhythm) 93.
Analysis. (Genre, type) 174–76, 182, 188–89, 194, 218, (I Exp.) 219, 231, 233–34, 278, (I P) 240, 245, 247–48, 253, (I S) 269–70, 274, (I Dev.) 280, 282–84, 286–88, (I Rec.) 293, (II = keyboard version of the minuet of symphony no. 47) 315–21, (III) 300, 302.

The *Anno 1776* sonatas is the collective title of sonatas nos. 42–47 (1774–76), based on Haydn's entry in the *EK* and on Viennese copies of these sonatas dated 1776; *JHW* ser. 18, vol. 2: Sechs Sonaten in Abschrift erschienen 1776; Grove W, 25–30: up to 1776. On their publication in the form of copies and in print, see pp. 167–68, 171, 204.

42. G Major Sonata (Hob. XVI:27), *Anno 1776* Sonata no. 1
Date. 1776 [or one to two years earlier]; Brown: "probably late 1760s."
Instrument. (Harpsichord) 25, 29, 32.

Performance practice. (Turn) 62, 68–69, (rhythm of I, 1) 68–70, (tempo of III) 325.
Analysis. (Genre, type) 174, 176, 182, 189, 194, (I Exp.) 219, 230, 233, 236, 276, 278, (I P) 240, 253, (I S) 269, (I Dev.) 281, 283–84, 286, (I Rec.) 292–94, (II) 238, 315–21, (III) 192, 198, 238, 325–29.

43. E♭ Major Sonata (Hob. XVI:28), *Anno 1776* Sonata no. 2
Date. 1776 [or one to two years earlier].
Instrument. (Harpsichord) 25, 32.
Performance practice. (Rhythm of turn) 62–64, 67–69, (fermatas) 83, (dotting) 90, (tempo of I) 148, (tempo of II) 149.
Analysis. (Genre, type) 174, 176–77, 182, 189, 194, (I Exp.) 219–20, 230, 233, (I P) 238, 240, 254, (I S) 264, 274, (I Dev.) 280, 283–84, 286–87, 289, (I Rec.) 292–93, (II) 315–21, (III) 192, 198, 325–28.

44. F Major Sonata (Hob. XVI:29), *Anno 1776* Sonata no. 3
Date. 1774 (dated autograph fragment of the exposition of I) [it is not known when the whole sonata was finished; on the basis of style, this was probably the earliest of the *Anno 1776* set]: 132–33, 163.
Instrument. (Lack of fortepiano dynamics in the autograph fragment) 25, 32.
Performance practice. (Appoggiatura) 48, (trill) 55, (turn) 61–62, (ornamentation of m. 1 in II) 65, (arpeggio) 98, (written-out embellishment) 104, (staccato marks) 120, (staccato and portato) 121, (dynamics) 129, 132–33, (tempo of III) 149.
Analysis. (Genre, type) 173–74, 176–77, 182, 189, 194, (I Exp.) 219, 230, 233, 236, (I P) 240, 252–53, 257, (I T) 264, (I S) 267–68, (I Dev.) 280, 283–84, 286, (I Rec.) 292–93, (II) 306, 308–309, (III) 193, 198, 315–22.

45. A Major Sonata (Hob. XVI:30), *Anno 1776* Sonata no. 4
Date. 1776 [or one to two years earlier].
Instrument. (Harpsichord) 25, 32.
Performance practice. (Rhythm of turn) 62, 69, (double appoggiatura = *Anschlag*) 75, (dotting in II) 90.
Analysis. (Genre, type) 174, 176, 182, 189, 193–94, 200, (I Exp.) 219–20, 230, 233, (I P) 240, 245–46, 253, 257, (I T) 265, (I S) 269, (I K) 275, (I Dev.) 281, 283–84, 286–87, 289, (I Rec.) 293, (III) 193, 238, 315–21, 324.

46. E Major Sonata (Hob. XVI:31), *Anno 1776* Sonata no. 5
Date. 1776 [or one to two years earlier].
Instrument. (Harpsichord) 25, 32.
Performance practice. (Trill) 55, (rhythm of turn) 62, 66, (dynamics) 130, (tempo of III) 325.
Analysis. (Genre, type) 174, 176–77, 182, 189, 194, 205, (I Exp.) 219, 230–31, 233–34, (I P) 240, 247, 250, 253, (I T) 264, (I K) 274, (I Dev.) 280, 283–84, 286, 289, (I Rec.) 292, 294, (II) 205, 312, (III) 192, 198, 325–30.

47. B Minor Sonata (Hob. XVI:32), *Anno 1776* Sonata no. 6
Date. 1776 [or one to two years earlier].
Instrument. (Harpsichord) 25, 32.
Performance practice. (Rhythm of turn) 62, 66, (mordent) 74–75, (accents) 130.

Analysis. (Genre, type) 174, 176–77, 182, 188–89, 194, 205, 218, (I Exp.) 219, 230, 233, 236, (I P) 240, 252–53, (I S) 268, (Dev.) 280, 283–84, 286–88, (I Rec.) 292–93, (II) 315–21, (III) 200, 300–302.

The *Auenbrugger* sonatas is the collective title of sonatas nos. 48–52 and 33 (C minor) published by Artaria in Vienna in 1780, dedicated to Katharina and Marianna Auenbrugger. Opinions about the date of composition of nos. 48–52 vary widely (the comments of H. C. Robbins Landon, Feder, Brown, and others are discussed on p. 177). On publication, see pp. 11, 13, 167–68, 171, 200, 204–5; on instrument, p. 23; and on style, pp. 167, 177, 202.

48. C Major Sonata (Hob. XVI:35), *Auenbrugger* Sonata no. 1
Date. *WUE:* 1777–79 (?); Grove W, 31: up to 31 January 1780 (according to Feder in *JHW,* one of the last of the set). [Probably 1779.]
Instrument. (Fortepiano) 26, (harpsichord style) 133.
Performance practice. (Turn) 62, (pseudo cadenza in I) 82, (triplet rhythm) 93, (dynamics) 133, 136–39, (₵ tempo) 149, (tempo of II) 149.
Analysis. (Genre, type) 164, 174, 177, 182, 189, 195, 202, 204–5, (I Exp.) 219–20, 230–31, 233, (I P) 240–41, 244, (I T) 265–66, (I Dev.) 281, 283–84, 286–88, (I Rec.) 292–93, (II) 306, 309, (III) 198–99, 315–21, 325.

49. C♯ Minor Sonata (Hob. XVI:36), *Auenbrugger* Sonata no. 2
Date. *WUE:* 1777–79 (?); Grove W, 32: 1770–75 (?). [1779 or somewhat earlier.]
Instrument. (Fortepiano) 26, (harpsichord style) 29.
Performance practice. (Rhythm of turn) 62, 68–69, (fermata) 83, (rhythm of closing theme in I) 89, (phrasing or articulation?) 115, (tenuto) 118, (dynamics) 133–34, 136–37, (tempo of II) 326, (tempo of III) 148.
Analysis. (Genre, type) 174, 177, 182, 189, 195, 211, (I Exp.) 219, 230–31, 233, 235, (I P) 240, 252–53, (I S) 270–71, 273, (I Dev.) 280, 283–84, 286, (I Rec.) 292, 294, (II) 198, 325–29, (III) 315–22.

50. D Major Sonata (Hob. XVI:37), *Auenbrugger* Sonata no. 3
Date. *WUE:* 1777–79 (?); Grove W, 33: up to 31 January 1779 (according to Feder in *JHW,* one of the last of the set). [Probably 1779.]
Instrument. (Fortepiano) 26, (harpsichord style) 133.
Performance practice. (Appoggiatura) 41, (trill) 55, (turn) 62, (overdotted performance in II) 88–89, (tenuto) 118, (dynamics) 128, 133–34, 136–38, (tempo of III) 184, 325, (pedal) 138
Analysis. (Genre, type) 174, 177, 182, 184, 189, 195, 205, (I Exp.) 219, 230, 232–33, (I P) 240, 253, (I S) 269, (I K) 275, (I Dev.) 281, 283, (I Rec.) 293, (II) 311–12, (III) 193, 198, 325–28.

51. E♭ Major Sonata (Hob. XVI:38), *Auenbrugger* Sonata no. 4
Date. *WUE:* 1777–79 (?); Grove W, 34: 1770–75 (?). [1779 or earlier.]
Instrument. (Fortepiano) 26, (harpsichord style) 134.
Performance practice. (Written-out *Anschlag*) 75, (fermatas) 83, (overdotting) 88, (portato) 121, (dynamics) 133–34, 136–38, (pedal) 138.

Analysis. (Genre, style) 174, 177, 182, 189, 195, 203, (I Exp.) 219, 230, 232–33, 235, (I P) 240, 245–46, 253, (I T) 266, (I S) 270, (I Dev.) 280, 283, 285–86, (I Rec.) 292–93, (II) 312–13, (III) 192, 315–21.

52. G Major Sonata (Hob. XVI:39), *Auenbrugger* Sonata no. 5
Date. *WUE:* 1780; Grove W, 35: up to 8 February 1780. [See p. 200.]
Instrument. (Fortepiano) 26.
Performance practice. (Trill) 54–55, (rhythm of turn) 64, (written-out *Schneller* in III) 59, 80, (written-out cadenza in II) 82, 103, (overdotting) 87, (rhythm of the theme of II) 41, 90–91, (small-note passage) 99–100, (tenuto) 118, (dynamics) 133, 136, 138, (pedal) 138, (tempo of I) 325.
Analysis. (Genre, type) 174, 177, 182, 189, 195, (I) 198–200, 217, (II) 306, 308–10, (III) 300, 302, 325–27, 329.

53. E Minor Sonata (Hob. XVI:34)
Note. Individual sonata not written for a set.
Date. *WUE:* ca. 1781–82 (?); *JHW:* Drei Sonaten no. 3; Grove W, 39: up to 15 January 1784 (date of the 1st ed.) (according to Feder in *JHW,* ser. 18, vol. 3, ca. 1780); Brown: ca. 1780–83. [II might be an earlier piece; I and III ca. 1782, but not before 1780]: 163.
Publication. (Without Haydn's approval in 1783 in London, together with 35 A♭ and 34 D) 163, 168, 171.
Instrument. 23, 29.
Performance practice. (Fermatas) 83, (dynamics) 128, 133–34, 140–41, (tempo of III) 147.
Analysis. (Genre, style) 174, 179, 182, 189, 195, (I Exp.) 219, 221, 231, 233–34, 278, (I P) 238, 240, 253, (I T) 266, (I Dev.) 281, 283, 285–86, (I Rec.) 294, (II) 306, 309, (III) 198, 325–30.

The *Bossler* sonatas is the collective title of sonatas nos. 54–56 published in 1784 by Bossler in Speyer, dedicated to "Princesse Marie Esterházy née Princesse de Lichtenstein" (Liechtenstein), the wife of Prince Nikolaus II; probably written as a wedding present (the wedding took place 15 September 1783); *JHW,* ser. 18, vol. 3: Drei Sonaten für Prinzessin Marie Esterházy (according to Feder, probably written in 1783; Brown, p. 122 suggests March to midsummer 1784), see pp. 167–68, 171. On instrument (the first Haydn set marked as "pour le Pianoforte"), see pp. 6, 23.

54. G Major Sonata (Hob. XVI:40), *Bossler* Sonata no. 1
Date. *WUE:* ca. 1782–84. [Probably 1783.]
Instrument. (Fortepiano) 23, 26.
Performance practice. (Rhythm of ornaments in I) 77–78, (fermatas in I) 83, (written-out ornaments) 103–4, (dynamics) 128, 136–37, 139–40, (tempo of II) 325, (pedal) 139.
Analysis. (Genre, type) 174, 178–79, 182, 189, 195, (I) 192, 198, 217, 333–35, (II) 193, 325–27, 330.

55. B♭ Major Sonata (Hob. XVI:41), *Bossler* Sonata no. 2
Date. *WUE:* ca. 1782–84. [Probably 1783.]
Instrument. (Fortepiano) 23, 26.

Performance practice. (Turn) 70, (triplet rhythm) 74, 93, (written-out ornaments) 103–104, (dynamics) 134, 140, (¢ tempo) 149, (tempo of II) 147.
Analysis. (Genre, type) 174, 178–79, 182, 184, 189, 195, (I Exp.) 219–20, 232–33, 235–36, (I P) 238, 240, 244, (I T) 266, (I S) 267, (I Dev.) 281, 283, 286, (I Rec.) 292–93, (II) 193, 325–27, 330.

56. D Major Sonata (Hob. XVI:42), *Bossler* Sonata no. 3
Date. WUE: ca. 1782–84. [Probably 1783.]
Instrument. (Fortepiano) 23, 26.
Performance practice. (Original fingering) 42, (turn) 65, (triplet rhythm) 92, (rhythm of mm. 21 and 41 in I) 95, (written-out ornaments) 103–4, (notation of sospiri) 117, (dynamics) 128, 134, 136–40, (pedal) 138, (tempo of II) 147.
Analysis. (Genre, type) 174, 178–79, 182, 189, 195, 203, 333–35, 339–40, (I) 192–93, 198–99, 217, (II) 300, 302–3.

57. F Major Sonata (Hob. XVI:47)
Doubtful compilation; see Sonata no. 19.
Date, publication. 159, 162–63.

58. C Major Sonata (Hob. XVI:48)
Date. WUE: 1789; *JHW:* Zwei Sonaten no. 1; Grove W, 43: before 10 March 1789 (?); commissioned by Breitkopf, 10 January 1789; delivered 5 April 1789. [On the basis of style, it is possible that II was written before 1789.]
Publication. 11, 168–71.
Instrument. (Inspired by Schanz fortepiano?) 23, 26, 29, 202.
Performance practice. (Rhythm of turn in m. 1 of I) 66, (written-out fermata) 83, (end of I) 98–99, (written-out ornaments) 103–4, (notation in C clef) 107, (dynamics) 133, 136–37, 139–40, (tempo rubato) 146.
Analysis. (Genre, type) 174, 178, 182, 189, 195, 202, (I) 192–93, 198–99, 217, 236, 333–37, (II) 192, 300–302, 325.

59. E♭ Major Sonata (Hob. XVI:49), *Genzinger* Sonata
Note. Composta per la Stimatissima Signora Anna de Jerlischeck; according to the autograph title page, however, for Mrs. Genzinger.
Date. 1789 (I, III) and 1790 (II), the date *1:te Juny 790* on the title page of the autograph might be a later addition by Haydn (see the facs. ed. [Graz, 1982] and the "Urtext Edition + Faksimile" [Wien, n.d.]); *WUE:* 1789–90; *JHW:* Zwei Sonaten no. 2; Grove W, 44: 1789–(1 June) 1790.
Publication. (1791 Artaria) 168–71.
Instrument. (. . . *per il Forte-piano* on autograph title page) 25, (inspiration of a Schanz instrument) 13, (fortepiano idiom) 23, 25–26, (harpsichord-style elements) 14, 29.
Performance practice. (Rhythm of trill) 54–55, (rhythm of turns in I–III) 63–64, 71–72, (slide) 78, (fermata) 82, (dotting) 74, 90, (triplet rhythm) 93–94, (passage) 100, (written-out ornaments) 103–4, (clef) 107, (accents) 110, (strict part writing) 109–10, (staccato, legato) 123, (slurring in I) 123, (articulation of the theme of II) 124–25, (asynchronous articulation) 125–26, (opening dynamics in II and III) 128, (dynamics) 133–35, 137, 140, (accent or dynamics) 141–42.

Analysis. (Genre, type) 173–74, 178–79, 182, 189, 195, 203, 205, (I Exp.) 219, 227, 230, 233, 235–36, 276–77, (I P) 240–41, 254–56, (I T) 266, (I S) 267, 272–73, (I Dev.) 212, 281, 283, 285–87, 289, (I Rec.) 293, (I Coda) 294, (II) 193, 333, 339, 341–44, (III) 193, 198–99, 315–21, 323–24.

The *London* sonatas is the collective title of Sonatas nos. 60–62; *JHW,* ser. 18, vol. 3: Drei englische Sonaten. Probably all three, but surely 60 C and 62 E♭ written for Therese Jansen Bartolozzi (Dies: "3 Sonatas for Mrs. Janson"; Griesinger: "Zwey Sonaten für Miss Janson"). 61 D might have been written for Mrs. Schroeter (see Graue, in *Haydn Studies,* 423–24; Feder in *JHW,* ser. 18, vol. 3; and Brown, p. 122). About different interpretations of the sequence of the three sonatas, see p. 203. On publication, see pp. 170–71. On instrument (inspiration of English fortepianos), see p. 23.

60. C Major Sonata (Hob. XVI:50), *London*

Date. WUE: 1794–95 (?); *JHW:* Drei englische Sonaten no. 2; Grove W, 46: ca. 1794–95 ("earlier version of II appeared in 1794": for this version see *WUE,* vol. 3, app.); Brown: (I and III) 16 May to 5 August 1795, (II) early (?) 1794 (1793?). [I and III probably the first sonata movements written in London in 1794 (?)]: 203.
Publication. (1800 London—based on the lost autograph Haydn left in England?) 168–70.
Instrument. (Six-octave English fortepiano) 18, 27–29.
Performance practice. (Appoggiatura) 48–49, (trill) 54–56, (rhythm of turn) 63, (Schneller) 79, (fermata) 83, (rhythm of m. 59 in II) 96, (written-out ornaments) 103, (clef) 107–8, (staccato stroke and dot) 122, (staccato and portato) 119, 122, (dynamics) 128, 133, 136–39, 141, (tempo of III) 147, (*open Pedal* marking) 139–40, (pedal) 138.
Analysis. (Genre, style) 173–74, 179, 182, 184, 189, 195, 202, 205, (I Exp.) 219, 230, 232–36, (I P) 240–41, 254, (I T) 266, (I S) 271, (I Dev.) 281, 283, 285–86, (I Rec.) 294, (II) 200, 306, 308–11, 333, (III) 299–302.

61. D Major Sonata (Hob. XVI:51), *London*

Date. WUE: 1794–95 (?); *JHW:* Drei englische Sonaten no. 3; Grove W, 47: before 1794–95 (?); Brown: 1791–96; (the autograph of "ein Andante und Finale" was left in England). [Probably 1794, after 60 C]: 203.
Publication. (1804 Leipzig) 168.
Instrument. (English fortepiano) 18, 28–29.
Performance practice. (Rhythm of mm. 100–101 of I) 94, (triplet rhythm) 93–94, (dynamics) 133–34, 141, (¢ tempo) 149, (tempo of II) 148.
Analysis. (Genre, type) 174, 179, 182, 189, 195, 217, 219, (I Dev.) 281, 283, (II) 158, 299–300, 302.

62. E♭ Major Sonata (Hob. XVI:52), *London*

Date. 1794: *Sonata composta per la Celebre Signora Teresa de Janson . . . Lond*[ra] *794* (autograph manuscript): 163, 203.
Publication. (1798 Vienna, 1799 London) 11, 168–70.
Instrument. (Broadwood-style fortepiano) 14, 18, 25–26, 28–29.
Performance practice. (Fermata) 82, (rhythm of m. 4 in II) 92, (arpeggio) 97–98, (small-note passage) 99–100, (written-out ornaments) 103, (free-style part writing) 110,

(tenuto) 118, (staccato and portato) 121, (slurring) 123, (dynamics) 128, 134, 136, 139–41, (pedal) 139, (tempo of III) 148, (repetition signs) 280.
Analysis. (Genre, style) 173–74, 179, 182, 189, 195, 203, 205, 212, (I Exp.) 219, 230, 232–33, 235–36, 276–77, (I P) 240, 245, 247, 249, 259, 261, (I T) 264, 266, (I S) 268–69, 272–73, (I Dev.) 280–87, 289–90, (I Rec.) 293, (II) 193, 333, 339, 341, (III) 300–302.

Select Bibliography

For a general bibliography, see A. Peter Brown and James T. Berkenstock, "Joseph Haydn in Literature: A Bibliography," *Haydn-Studien* 3, nos. 3–4 (1974): 173–352; and Horst Walter, "Haydn-Bibliographie, 1793–1983," *Haydn-Studien* 5, no. 4 (1985): 205–306.

Basic Haydniana

Badura-Skoda, Eva, ed. *Joseph Haydn: Bericht über den Internationalen Joseph Haydn Kongress,* Wien, 1982 = Proceedings of the International Joseph Haydn Congress. Munich: Henle, 1986.

Landon, H. C. Robbins. *Haydn: Chronicle and Works.* Vol. 1, *Haydn: The Early Years, 1732–1765.* Vol. 2, *Haydn at Eszterháza, 1766–1790.* Vol. 3, *Haydn in England, 1791–1795.* Vol. 4, *Haydn: The Years of "The Creation," 1796–1800.* Vol. 5, *Haydn: The Late Years, 1801–1809.* Bloomington: Indiana University Press, 1976–80.

Larsen, Jens Peter. *The New Grove Haydn.* Work-List by Georg Feder. Composer Biography Series. New York: Norton, 1983.

Larsen, Jens Peter, Howard Serwer, and James Webster, eds. *Haydn Studies: Proceedings of the International Haydn Conference, Washington, D.C., 1975.* New York: Norton, 1981.

Catalogs, Facsimile Editions, Sources

Bartha, Dénes, ed. *Joseph Haydn: Gesammelte Briefe und Aufzeichnungen.* Kassel: Bärenreiter, 1965.

Brook, Barry S., ed. *The Breitkopf Thematic Catalogue . . . , 1762–1787.* New York: Dover, 1966.

Dies, Albert Christoph. *Biographische Nachrichten von Joseph Haydn.* Vienna, 1810. New German ed. by Horst Seeger. Berlin: Henschel, 1959. (An English translation appears in Gotwals [1968].)

Gotwals, Vernon. *Haydn: Two Contemporary Portraits.* Madison: University of Wisconsin Press, 1968.

Griesinger, Georg August. *Biographische Notizen über Joseph Haydn.* Leipzig, 1810. New German ed. by Franz Grasberger. Vienna: Kaltschmid, 1954. New German ed. by Karl-Heinz Köhler. Leipzig: Reclam, 1975. Reprint of 1810 ed. by Peter Krause. Leipzig: VEB Deutscher Verlag für Musik, 1979. Reprint of 1810 ed. Hildesheim: Gerstenberg, 1981. (An English translation appears in Gotwals [1968].)

Haydn, Joseph. *Klaviersonate A-dur.* Epilogue by Jens Peter Larsen. Munich and Duisburg: Henle, 1958; 2d ed., 1982. (Facsimile of 41 A I and III.)

———. *Klaviersonate in Es-Dur Hob. XVI:49.* Edited by Otto Brusatti. Graz: Akademische Druck- und Verlagsanstalt, 1982. (Facsimile of the *Genzinger* Sonata 59 E♭ with an urtext ed.)

———. *Piano Sonata E Flat Major Hob. XVI:49.* "Urtext + Faksimile" UT 51016. Vienna: Wiener Urtext Edition, n.d.

Hoboken, Anthony van. *Joseph Haydn: Thematisch-bibliographisches Werkverzeichnis.* 3 vols. Mainz: Schott's Söhne, 1957–78.

Landon, H. C. Robbins, ed. *The Collected Correspondence and London Notebooks of Joseph Haydn.* London: Barrie & Rockliff, 1959.

Larsen, Jens Peter. *Three Haydn Catalogues.* Facs. ed. with a survey of Haydn's oeuvre. New York: Pendragon, 1979.

Authenticity, Chronology, Editions

Brown, A. Peter. "Problems of Authenticity in Two Haydn Keyboard Works (Hoboken XVI:47 and XIV:7)." *Journal of the American Musicological Society* 25, no. 1 (1972): 85–97.

———. "Haydn's Keyboard Idiom and the Raigern Sonatas." In *Haydn Studies,* 85–97.

Feder, Georg. "Zur Datierung Haydnscher Werke." In *Anthony van Hoboken: Festschrift zum 75. Geburtstag.* Mainz: Schott's Söhne, 1962.

———. "Probleme einer Neuordnung der Klaviersonaten Haydns." In *Festschrift Friedrich Blume zum 70. Geburtstag,* 92–103. Kassel: Bärenreiter, 1963.

———. "Zwei Haydn zugeschriebene Klaviersonaten." In *Kongressbericht Kassel, 1962,* 181–84. Kassel: Bärenreiter, 1963. (See 17 E♭ and 18 E♭.)

———. "Vorwort." In *Joseph Haydn Werke: Klaviersonaten, XVIII/1–3.* 3 vols. Munich: Henle, 1966–70.

———. "The Source of the Two Disputed Raigern Sonatas." In *Haydn Studies,* 107–11.

———. "Work-List." In *The New Grove Haydn.* Composer Biography Series. New York: Norton, 1983. (The sonatas, pp. 183–87.)

Fruehwald, Scott. "Authenticity Problems in Franz Joseph Haydn's Early Instrumental Works: A Stylistic Investigation." Ph.D. diss., City University of New York, 1984.

Gerlach, Sonja. "Remarks on the Structure and Harmony of the Raigern Sonatas." In *Haydn Studies,* 115–17.

Hatting, Carsten E. "Haydn oder Kayser? Eine Echtheitsfrage." *Musikforschung* 25, no. 2 (1972): 182–87. (See 18 E♭.)

Landon, Christa. "Vorwort." In *Haydn: Sämtliche Klaviersonaten.* 3 vols. Vienna: Universal Edition, 1963.

———. *Kritische Anmerkungen. Haydn: Sämtliche Klaviersonaten.* Vienna: Wiener Urtext Edition, 1982.

Larsen, Jens Peter. "Eine bisher unbeachtete Quelle zu Haydns frühe Klavierwerken." In *Festschrift Joseph Schmidt-Görg zum 60. Geburtstag,* 188–95. Bonn: Beethovenhaus, 1957.

Price, Jane Bostian. "The Chronology of the Early Piano Sonatas of Joseph Haydn: A Comparative Study of Three Editions." In *Haydn Studies,* 133–37.

Radice, Mark A. "Haydn and His Publishers: A Brief Survey of the Composer's Publishing Activities." *Music Review* 44, no. 2 (1983): 87–94.

Steglich, Rudolf. "Eine Klaviersonate Johann Gottfried Schwanbergs (Schwanenbergs) in der Joseph Haydn Gesamtausgabe." *Zeitschrift für Musik* 15, no. 2 (1932): 77–79. (See Hob. XVI:17.)

Strunk, William Oliver. "Notes on a Haydn Autograph." *Musical Quarterly* 20, no. 2 (1934): 192–205. (See 62 E♭ and the question of the sequence of sonatas 60–62.)

Taves, Jeanette. "A Study of Editions of Haydn's Piano Sonata Hob. XVI:52 (ChL. 62) in E-flat Major." In *Haydn Studies,* 142–44.

Webster, James. "External Criteria for Determining the Authenticity of Haydn's Music." In *Haydn Studies,* 75–78.

Winternitz, Emanuel. *Musical Autographs from Monteverdi to Hindemith.* 2 vols. New York: Dover, 1965. (Plates 53–56 are facsimile pages from 62 E♭ and F Minor Variations.)

General Literature on Haydn's Piano Sonatas

Abert, Hermann. "Joseph Haydns Klavierwerke" and "Joseph Haydns Klaviersonaten." *Zeitschrift für Musikwissenschaft* 2, no. 1 (1920): 553–73; 3, nos. 9–10 (1921): 535–52.

Badura-Skoda, Eva. "Haydn, Mozart and Their Contemporaries." In *Keyboard Music,* ed. Denis Matthews, 108–68. Harmondsworth: Penguin, 1972.

Brown, A. Peter. "The Solo and Ensemble Keyboard Sonatas of Joseph Haydn: A Study of Structure and Style." Ph.D. diss., Northwestern University, 1970.

———. *Joseph Haydn's Keyboard Music: Sources and Style.* Bloomington: Indiana University Press, 1986.

Feder, Georg. "Haydn's Piano Trios and Piano Sonatas." In *Haydnfest . . . Washington, 1975,* 19–23. Washington, D.C.: John F. Kennedy Center, 1975.

Landon, H. C. Robbins. "Haydn's Piano Sonatas." In *Essays on the Viennese Classical Style: Gluck, Haydn, Mozart, Beethoven.* London: Barrie & Rockliff, 1970.

Liessem, Franz. "Die Entwicklung der Klaviertechnik in den Sonaten der Wiener Klassiker Haydn, Mozart und Beethoven." Ph.D. diss., Innsbruck, 1956.

Maxwell, Carolyn, ed. *Haydn Solo Piano Literature: A Comprehensive Guide, Annotated and Evaluated with Thematics.* Boulder, Colo.: Maxwell Music Evaluation, 1983.

Mitchell, William J. "The Haydn Sonatas." *Piano Quarterly* 15, no. 58 (1966–67): 9, 20–23.

Newman, William S. *The Sonata in the Classic Era.* Rev. ed. Chapel Hill: University of North Carolina Press, 1972. (Haydn, pp. 452–77.)

———. "Haydn as Ingenious Exploiter of the Keyboard." In *Haydn Bericht,* 43–53.

Parrish, Carl. "Haydn and the Piano." *Journal of the American Musicological Society* 1, no. 3 (1948): 27–34.

Somfai, László. *Joseph Haydn zongoraszonátái.* Budapest: Zeneműkiadó, 1979. (The original edition of this book, in Hungarian.)

———. "Stilfragen der Klaviersonaten von Haydn." *Österreichische Musikzeitschrift* 37, nos. 3–4 (1982): 147–53.

Wackernagel, Bettina von. *Joseph Haydns frühe Klaviersonaten: Ihre Beziehungen zur Klaviermusik um die Mitte des 18. Jahrhunderts.* Tutzing: Schneider, 1975.

Instruments

Adlam, Derek, and William J. Conner. "History of the Piano: England and France to 1800." In *The New Grove Piano,* 19–29. London: Macmillan, 1988.

Badura-Skoda, Eva. "Domenico Scarlatti und das Hammerklavier." *Österreichische Musikzeitschrift* 40, no. 10 (1985): 527. (Contemporary terminology of keyboard instruments in Vienna.)

Belt, Philip R., and Maribel Meisel. "History of the Piano: Germany and Austria, 1750–1800." In *The New Grove Piano,* 13–19. London: Macmillan, 1988.

Biba, Otto. "Die 'Haydn-Instrumente' im Besitz der Gesellschaft der Musikfreunde in Wien—Provenienz und Authentizität." In *Haydn Bericht,* 68–72.

Bilson, Malcolm. "Keyboards." In *The New Grove Handbooks in Music: Performance Practice,* ed. Howard Mayer Brown and Stanley Sadie, 2:223–38. London: Macmillan, 1989.

Dudley, Raymond. "Haydn's Knee Pedal Revealed." *Music Journal* 26, no. 2 (1968): 33.

Eibner, Franz. "Registerpedalisierung bei Haydn und Beethoven." *Österreichische Musikzeitschrift* 20, no. 4 (1965): 190–96. (Errata were published in the next issue.)

Harding, Rosamund E. M. *The Piano-Forte: Its History Traced to the Great Exhibition of 1851.* 2d rev. ed. New York: Da Capo, 1978.

Hollis, Helen Rice. *The Musical Instruments of Joseph Haydn: An Introduction.* Washington, D.C.: Smithsonian Institution Press, 1977.

Kleindienst, Sigrid. "Haydns Clavier-Werke: Kriterien der Instrumentenwahl." In *Haydn Bericht,* 53–63.

Komlós, Katalin, *Fortepianos and Their Music: Germany, Austria, and England, 1760–1800.* Oxford; Clarendon Press, 1995.

Kramer, Richard. "On the Dating of Two Aspects in Beethoven's Notation for Piano." In *Beethoven-Kolloquium, 1977: Dokumentation und Aufführungspraxis,* 160–83. Kassel: Bärenreiter, 1978. (On the "open Pedal" of 60 C I, see pp. 167–69.)

Ripin, Edwin M. "Haydn and the Keyboard Instruments of His Time." In *Haydn Studies,* 302–8.

Schwarz, Vera. "Die Rolle des Cembalos in Österreich nach 1760." In *Der junge Haydn,* 249–58. Graz: Akademische Druck- und Verlangsanstalt, 1972.

Somfai, László. "Regiszter-dinamika Haydn fortepiano kottázásában?" [Did dynamics in Haydn's fortepiano notation indicate registration?]. In *Zenetudományi Dolgozatok, 1978,* 41–50. Budapest: Zenetudományi Intézet, 1979.

Walter, Horst. "Haydns Klaviere." *Haydn-Studien* 2, no. 4 (1970): 256–88.

———. "Das Tasteninstrument beim jungen Haydn." In *Der junge Haydn,* 237–48. Graz: Akademische Druck- und Verlagsanstalt, 1972.

———. "Haydn's Keyboard Instruments." In *Haydn Studies,* 213–16.

Performance Practice and Notation

Aulabaugh, Alan Richard. "An Analytical Study of Performing Problems in the Keyboard Sonatas of F. J. Haydn." Ph.D. diss., University of Iowa, 1958.

Bach, Carl Philipp Emanuel. *Versuch über die wahre Art, das Clavier zu spielen.* Pt. 1. Berlin, 1753; 3d rev. ed. Leipzig, 1787. Pt. 2. Berlin, 1762. Rev. ed. Leipzig, 1797.

Facsimile ed. by Lothar Hoffmann-Erbrecht. Leipzig: VEB Breitkopf & Härtel, 1957. English translation by William J. Mitchell. *Essay on the True Art of Playing Keyboard Instruments.* New York: Norton, 1949.

Badura-Skoda, Paul. "Beiträge zu Haydns Ornamentik." *Musica* 36, no. 5 (1982): 409–18. (Corrections, *Musica* 36, no. 6 [1982]: 575.)

———. "Notes on Performance." In *Haydn: 4 Keyboard Sonatas.* Paris: Leduc, 1982. (13 g, 31 A♭, 33 c, 38 F.)

———. "Playing the Early Piano." *Early Music* 12, no. 4 (November 1984): 477–89.

Bilson, Malcolm. "The Viennese Fortepiano of the Late 18th Century: A Performer's Introduction to the Classical Repertoire." *Early Music* 8, no. 4 (1980): 158–62.

Feder, Georg. "Bemerkungen zu Haydns Skizzen." *Beethoven-Jahrbuch* 9, 1973–77 (1977): 69–86.

Fuller, Richard A. "Andreas Streicher's Notes on the Fortepiano." *Early Music* 12, no. 4 (November 1984): 461–70.

Löhlein, Georg Simon. *Clavier-Schule, oder kurze und gründliche Anweisung zur Melodie und Harmonie.* Leipzig and Züllichau, 1765; 2d enlarged ed., 1773.

Melkus, Eduard. "Die Entwicklung der freien Auszierungen im 18. Jahrhundert." In *Der junge Haydn,* 147–67. Graz: Akademische Druck- und Verlagsanstalt, 1972.

Mobbs, Kenneth. "Stops and Other Special Effects on the Early Piano." *Early Music* 12, no. 4 (November 1984): 471–76.

Mozart, Leopold. *Versuch einer gründlichen Violinschule.* Augsburg, 1756; 3d enlarged ed., 1787. Facsimile of the 3d ed. Leipzig: VEB Deutscher Verlag für Musik, 1966. English translation by Editha Knocker, with a preface by Alfred Einstein. *A Treatise on the Fundamental Principles of Violin Playing.* London: Oxford University Press, 1948.

Neumann, Frederick. *Ornamentation in Baroque and Post-Baroque Music: With Special Emphasis on J. S. Bach.* Princeton, N.J.: Princeton University Press, 1978.

———. "Bemerkungen über Haydns Ornamentik." In *Haydn Bericht,* 35–42.

———. *Ornamentation and Improvisation in Mozart.* Princeton, N.J.: Princeton University Press, 1986.

Newman, William S. "The Pianism of Haydn, Mozart, Beethoven, Schubert . . . Compared." *Piano Quarterly* 27, no. 105 (1979): 14–27, 30.

Pleasants, Virginia. "The Early Piano in Britain (c1760–1800)." *Early Music* 13, no. 1 (February 1985): 39–44.

Quantz, Johann Joachim. *Versuch einer Anweisung die Flöte traversiere zu spielen.* Breslau, 1752. Facsimile of the 3d ed. (Berlin, 1789) by Hans-Peter Schmitz. Kassel: Bärenreiter, 1953. English translation with notes by Edward R. Reilly. *On Playing the Flute.* New York: Free Press, 1966.

Rosenblum, Sandra P. *Performance Practices in Classic Piano Music: Their Principles and Applications.* Bloomington: Indiana University Press, 1988.

Rowland, David. "Early Pianoforte Pedalling." *Early Music* 13, no. 1 (February 1985): 5–17.

Saslav, Isidor. "Tempos in the String Quartets of Joseph Haydn." D.Mus. diss., Indiana University, 1969.

———. "The *alla breve* 'March': Its Evolution and Meaning in Haydn's String Quartets." In *Haydn Studies,* 308–14.

Schenker, Heinrich. *Ein Beitrag zur Ornamentik: Einführung zu Ph. E. Bachs Klavierwerke.* Vienna: Universal Edition, 1904.

Schott, Howard. "From Harpsichord to Pianoforte." *Early Music* 13, no. 1 (February 1985): 28–38.

Schwarz, Vera. "Missverständnisse in der Haydn-Interpretation: Dargestellt an Beispielen aus seiner Klaviermusik." *Österreichische Musikzeitschrift* 31, no. 1 (1976): 25–35.

Somfai, László. "An Introduction to the Study of Haydn's String Quartet Autographs." In *Isham Library Papers,* vol. 3. Cambridge, Mass.: Harvard University Press, 1980.

———. "How to Read and Understand Haydn's Notation in Its Chronologically Changing Concepts." In *Haydn Bericht,* 23–35.

Steglich, Rudolf. "Kadenzen in Haydns Klaviersonaten." *Zeitschrift für Musik* 104, no. 4 (1932): 295–97.

Tolstoy, Christie. "The Identification and Interpretation of Sign Ornaments in Haydn's Instrumental Music." In *Haydn Studies,* 315–23.

Türk, Daniel Gottlob. *Klavierschule.* Leipzig and Halle, 1789. Facsimile ed. by Erwin R. Jacobi. Kassel: Bärenreiter, 1962. English translation with notes by Raymond H. Haggh. *School of Clavier Playing.* Lincoln: University of Nebraska Press, 1982.

Style and Analysis

Andrews, Harold Lee. "Tonality and Structure in the First Movements of Haydn's Solo Keyboard Sonatas." Ph.D. diss., University of North Carolina, 1976.

———. "The Submediant in Haydn's Development Sections." In *Haydn Studies,* 456–71.

Besseler, Heinrich. "Einflüsse der Contratanzmusik auf Joseph Haydn." In *Bericht über die Internationale Konferenz zum Andenken Joseph Haydns, Budapest, 1959,* 25–40. Budapest: Akadémiai Kiadó, 1961.

Brown, A. Peter. "The Structure of the Exposition in Haydn's Keyboard Sonatas. *Music Review* 36, no. 2 (1975): 102–29.

———. "Critical Years for Haydn's Instrumental Music: 1789–90." *Music Quarterly* 62, no. 3 (1976): 374–94.

———. "Joseph Haydn and C. P. E. Bach: The Question of Influence." In *Haydn Studies,* 158–64.

———. "Realization of an Idiomatic Keyboard Style in Sonatas of the 1770s." In *Haydn Studies,* 394–97.

Budday, Wolfgang. *Grundlagen musikalischer Formen in der Wiener Klassik.* Kassel: Bärenreiter, 1983.

Cole, Malcolm. "The Development of the Instrumental Rondo Finale from 1750–1800." Ph.D. diss., Princeton University, 1946.

———. "The Vogue of the Instrumental Rondo in the Late 18th Century." *Journal of the American Musicological Society* 22 (1969): 425–55.

Eibner, Franz. "Die Form des 'Vivace assai' aus der Sonate D-dur Hob. XVI:42." In *Haydn Bericht,* 190–201.

Fillion, Michelle. "Sonata-Exposition Procedures in Haydn's Keyboard Sonatas." In *Haydn Studies,* 475–81.

Graue, Jerald C. "Haydn and the London Pianoforte School." In *Haydn Studies,* 422–31.

Hatting, Carsten E. "Obligater Satz versus Generalbass-Satz: Einige Betrachtungen zur Satzfaktur in Klaviersonaten aus der Mitte des 18. Jahrhunderts, insbesondere zu Haydns Sonaten aus der Zeit vor 1770." In *Festskrift Jens Peter Larsen,* 261–74. Copenhagen: Hansen, 1972.

Henneberg, Gudrun. "Heinrich Christoph Kochs Analysen von Instrumentalwerken Joseph Haydns." *Haydn-Studien* 4, no. 2 (1978): 105–12.

Kamien, Roger. "Aspects of Motivic Elaboration in the Opening Movement of Haydn's Piano Sonata in C♯ Minor." In *Aspects of Schenkerian Theory,* ed. David Beach, 77–93. New Haven, Conn.: Yale University Press, 1983.

Katz, Adele T. *Challenge to Musical Tradition: A New Concept of Tonality.* New York: Knopf, 1945. (Haydn on pp. 99–143.)

Komlós, Katalin. "The Viennese Keyboard Trio in the 1780s: Studies in Texture and Instrumentation." Ph.D. diss., Cornell University, 1986.

Larsen, Jens Peter. "Sonatenform-Probleme." In *Festschrift Friedrich Blume zum 70. Geburtstag,* 221–30. Kassel: Bärenreiter, 1963.

LaRue, Jan. *Guidelines for Style Analysis.* New York: Norton, 1970.

———. "A Haydn Speciality: Multistage Variance." In *Haydn Bericht,* 141–46.

Lowinsky, Edward E. "On Mozart's Rhythm." *Music Quarterly* 62, no. 2 (1956): 162–86.

Mersmann, Hans. "Versuch einer Phänomenologie der Musik." *Zeitschrift für Musikwissenschaft* 5, nos. 4–5 (1923): 226–69. (On 62 E♭, see pp. 255–62.)

Moss, Lawrence K. "Haydn's Sonata Hob. XVI:52 (ChL. 62) in E-Flat Major: An Analysis of the First Movement." In *Haydn Studies,* 496–501.

Neubacher, Jürgen. "'Idee' und 'Ausführung': Zum Kompositionsprozess bei Joseph Haydn." *Archiv für Musikwissenschaft* 41 (1984): 185–207.

Ratner, Leonard G. *Classic Music: Expression, Form, and Style.* New York: Schirmer, 1980.

Reed, Carl H. "Motivic Unity in Selected Keyboard Sonatas and String Quartets of Joseph Haydn." Ph.D. diss., University of Washington, 1966.

Ritzel, Fred. *Die Entwicklung der "Sonatenform" im musiktheoretischen Schrifttum des 18. und 19. Jahrhunderts.* Wiesbaden: Breitkopf & Härtel, 1974.

Rosen, Charles. *The Classical Style: Haydn, Mozart, Beethoven.* New York: Norton, 1971.

———. *Sonata Forms.* New York: Norton, 1980.

Rutmanowitz, Lea. "Haydn's Sonatas Hob. XVI:10 and 26: A Comparison of Compositional Procedures." In *Haydn Bericht,* 154–59.

Schenker, Heinrich. "Haydn: Sonate Es Dur." *Der Tonwille* 1, no. 3 (1922): 3–21. (62 E♭.)

———. "Haydn: Sonate C Dur." *Der Tonwille* 2, no. 4 (1923): 15–18. (60 C.)

———. *Five Graphic Music Analyses.* New York: Dover, 1969. (59 E♭ I on pp. 39–44.)

———. "Organic Structure in Sonata Form." In *Readings in Schenker Analysis and*

Other Approaches, ed. Maury Yeston, 38–53. New Haven, Conn.: Yale University Press, 1977. (32 g.)

Shamgar, Beth. "Rhythmic Interplay in the Retransition of Haydn's Piano Sonatas." *Journal of Musicology* 3, no. 1 (1984): 55–68.

Sisman, Elaine R. "Haydn's Variations." Ph.D. diss., Princeton University, 1978.

———. *Haydn and the Classical Variation.* Cambridge, Mass.: Harvard University Press, 1993.

———. "Haydn's Hybrid Variations." In *Haydn Studies,* 509–15.

———. "Small and Expanded Forms: Koch's Model and Haydn's Music." *Musical Quarterly* 68, no. 4 (1982): 444–75.

Somfai, László. "The London Revision of Haydn's Instrumental Style." *Proceedings of the Royal Musical Association* 100 (1974): 159–74.

———. "Opus-Planung und Neuerung bei Haydn." *Studia musicologica Academiae scientiarum hungaricae* 22 (1980): 87–110.

Tovey, Donald Francis. *Essays in Musical Analysis.* London: Oxford University Press, 1935–44. (62 E♭ in 7:93–105.)

Ujfalussy, József. "Egy különös formacsoport Haydn zongoraműveiben" [A specific group of forms in Haydn's piano work]. In *Zenetudományi Tanulmányok,* vol. 7, pp. 283–93. Budapest: Akadémiai Kiadó, 1960.

Webster, James. "Sonata Form." In *The New Grove Dictionary of Music and Musicians.* London: Macmillan, 1980.

———. "Binary Variants of Sonata Form in Early Haydn Instrumental Music." In *Haydn Bericht,* 127–35.

———. *Haydn's "Farewell" Symphony and the Idea of Classical Style.* Cambridge: Cambridge University Press, 1991.

Westphal, Kurt. "Die Formung in Haydns Sonaten." *Musik* 24, no. 6 (1932): 419–24.

 Index

Pages marked with asterisks include illustrations. For the sonatas, see also the Catalog of the Sonatas, beginning on page 353.

LOCATORS

Ornament

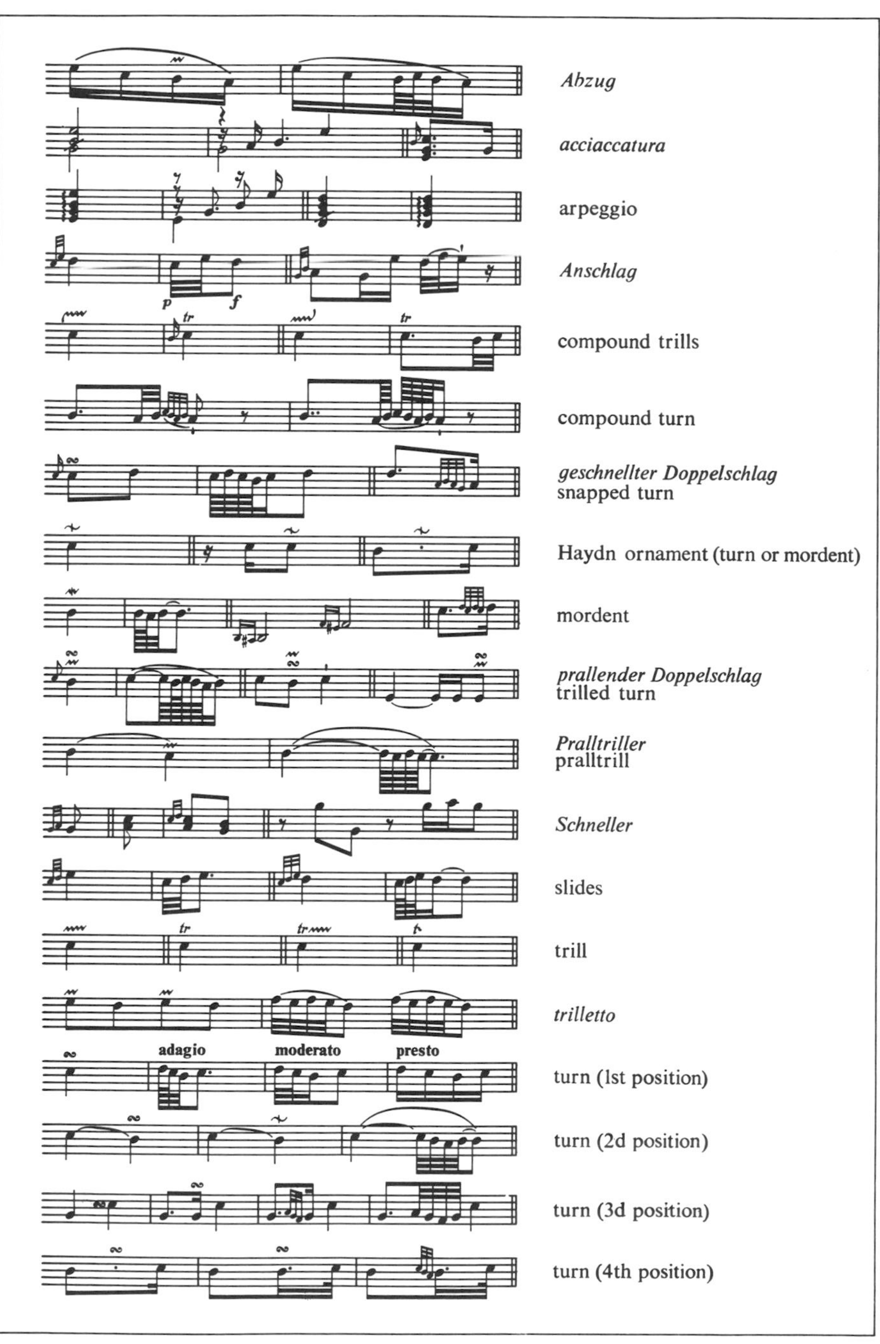

Abzug
acciaccatura
arpeggio
Anschlag
p
f
tr
compound trills
compound turn
geschnellter Doppelschlag
snapped turn
Haydn ornament (turn or mordent)
mordent
prallender Doppelschlag
trilled turn
Pralltriller
pralltrill
Schneller
slides
tr
trill
trilletto
adagio
moderato
presto
turn (1st position)
turn (2d position)
turn (3d position)
turn (4th position)

Locator

No.	Sign	Name	Realization	Reference
1		(a) *Abzug*		Ex. 9
		(b) *Pralltriller*		Ex. 9
		(c) *trilletto*		Ex. 9
		(d) trill	etc.	Table 2
2		trill	etc.	Table 2
3		compound trill = *tr* ;	etc.	Ex. 8
4		compound trill = *tr.*	(etc.)	Ex. 8
5	*tr*			Table 2
6	*tr*			Table 2
7	*t*	trill	etc.	Table 2
8	*tr*			Table 2
9		*prallender Doppelschlag* (trilled turn)		Table 2, notes
10				
11		mordent = ;		Ex. 28
12		Haydn ornament (=turn or mordent)	see 11 and 13	Table 2
13		turn =		Ex. 11
14		*Schneller*		Ex. 31
15		mordent	see 11	Ex. 28
16		slide (2 note)		Ex. 29
17		slide (3 note)		Ex. 29
18		turn	see 13	Table 2
19		*Anschlag*	*p* *f*	Ex. 28
20		*geschnellter Doppelschlag* =		Ex. 14
21		compound turn		Table 2

Thematic

Wiener Urtext, vol. 1a

Early Sonatas

Hob. XVI

1 Allegro 8

2 Allegro moderato 7

3 Allegro 9

4 Allegro G1

(5)* Presto 11

6 Moderato 10

(7)* Tema con Variazioni XVII D1

(8)* Allegro 5

9 4

(10)* Allegro 1

11 Moderato 2

12 Andante 12

13 Allegro 6

14 Allegretto 3

15 Moderato 13

16 Allegro moderato 14

Raigern Sonatas

(17)* Moderato Es2

(18)* Es3

* doubtful

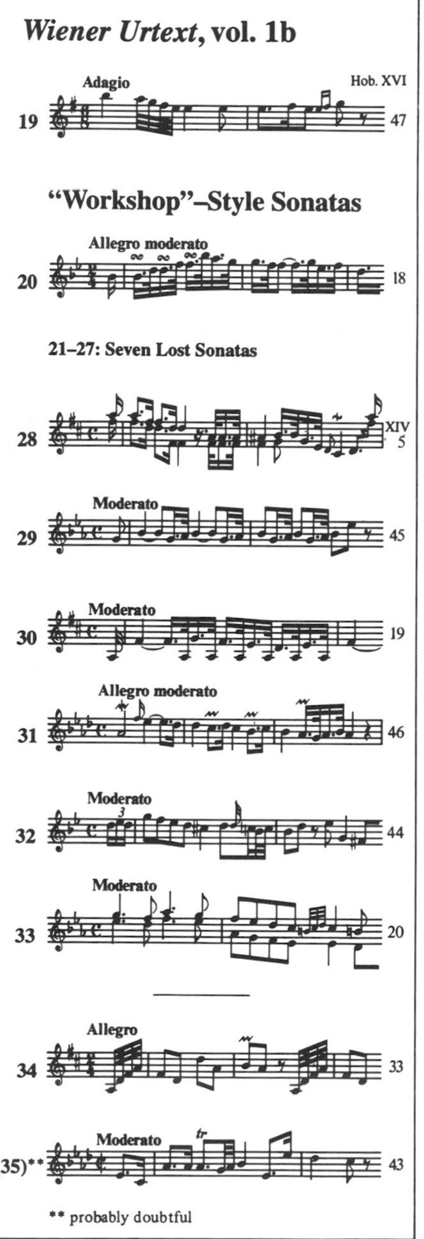

Locator

Wiener Urtext, vol. 2
Esterházy Sonatas
Hob. XVI
36 Allegro 21
37 Allegro moderato 22
38 23
39 Allegro 24
40 Moderato 25
41 Allegro moderato 26
Anno 1776 Sonatas
42 Allegro con brio 27
43 Allegro moderato 28
44 Moderato 29
45 Allegro 30
46 Moderato 31
47 Allegro moderato 32

Auenbrugger Sonatas
Hob. XVI
48 Allegro con brio 35
49 Moderato 36
50 Allegro con brio 37
51 Allegro moderato 38
52 Allegro con brio 39
Wiener Urtext, vol. 3
53 Presto 34
Bossler Sonatas
54 Allegretto e innocente 40
55 Allegro 41
56 Allegro con espressione 42
58 Andante con espressione 48
Genzinger Sonata
59 Allegro 49
London Sonatas
60 Allegro 50
61 Andante 51
62 Allegro 52